BEYOND LEFT & RIGHT:
RADICAL THOUGHT FOR OUR TIMES

Books by RICHARD KOSTELANETZ

AS AUTHOR
The Theatre of Mixed Means

AS CO-AUTHOR AND EDITOR
The New American Arts

AS EDITOR
On Contemporary Literature
Twelve From the Sixties
The Young American Writers
Piccola anthologia della nuova poesia americana
Beyond Left & Right

Beyond
Left
&
Right

Radical Thought for Our Times

Edited and with an Introduction by
RICHARD KOSTELANETZ

WILLIAM MORROW AND COMPANY, INC.

NEW YORK

*This book is dedicated
to its contributors, for
thinking radically
about a better future.*

All the great revolutions in men's lives are made in thought. When a change takes place in man's thought, action follows the direction of the thought as a ship follows the direction of the rudder.
—LEO TOLSTOY

The pace at which various technological, social, political and economic changes are taking place has reduced the relevance of experience as a guide to many public-policy judgments.
—HERMAN KAHN (1967)

Politics offers yesterday's answers to today's questions.
—MARSHALL McLUHAN,
The Medium Is the Massage (1967).

If there is any ideology peculiarly appropriate to the achievement of the transition it is neither capitalism nor socialism but the scientific ideology itself applied to society. An ideology for the great transition must then be a strategy rather than an ideology.
—KENNETH E. BOULDING,
The Meaning of the Twentieth Century (1964).

CONTENTS

VI. EDUCATION

VII. DEFENSE AND DIPLOMACY

VIII. REDESIGNING SOCIETY

PREFACE

Change is the metaphysic of our age, but the fault of so much that passes for "radical thought" in America today is a preoccupation with problems and remedies of industrial malaise and social inequity that concerned the prophets of a century ago; in coping with new realities and radical possibilities, those old ideas belong less in the mind than in the museum. Reformers who find America "resistant to change" offer an implicitly devastating judgment of their own message, rather than an accurate or persuasive analysis of contemporary reality, perhaps because they have been swishing the air with epithets, rather than cutting into the major issues and directions of our time. There is now an urgent need to rethink how we think about radical change, for the final third of the twentieth century will be fundamentally different from the previous sixty-eight years; and largely with new radical ideas beyond the historical "left" as well as the "right," will we construct our guiding faith and common future.

As an anthology of innovative ideas, this book is based in the present, but focused in the future. It concentrates upon the threats and opportunities implicit in new technologies—the primary sources of social change—as well as the basic problems and possibilities that decades ago were either nonexistent or unknown. The tone of this anthology is generally optimistic, not only because pessimism is too facile a posture in these difficult times but also because only if we believe that problems might be solved do we have a hope of alleviating them. The contributors to this book tend to neglect obvious criticisms of their ideas, perhaps because they are less interested in the common wisdom than in the discovery of uncommon possibilities. For that reason, and because many of them are groping through unfamiliar territory, neither their prose nor their thought is as simplistic or as obvious as partisan polemic or political platforms.

Some readers may be surprised and disappointed to find nothing here on Viet Nam or racial justice. These omissions are intentional, stemming in part from the book's primary thesis that radical thought today must concentrate on basic issues, rather than on secondary manifestations. American activity in Viet Nam is essentially a dimension of that larger system of commitments and conventions that constitute our foreign policy. For this reason, the morally estimable position that regards the war's termination as the most important issue we face, is, from a larger perspective, as intellectually parochial as the position that favors its continuance at all costs. Both focus on the small problem, rather than the large; on the current symptom, rather than the long-range trend; on the one issue, instead of the many that haunt us today. The hysterical hawks and the hysterical doves both imply, erroneously, that a single palliative will cure all our ills. As for racial injustice, it will be alleviated by social changes and economic measures that have more to do with general need than racial preference; Black Power, in contrast, promises not a fundamental revolution in man's estate but a changing of the guard. This book presupposes that in America today pernicious discrimination in our society involves more factors than race and that the social ultimate dilemmas confronting both blacks and whites, men and women, WASPS and Catholics, Northerners and Southerners are generally the same; for, as all of us ride this space ship called "Earth" together, pernicious ideas of irreconcilable racial and/or religious and/or geographic differences are false to our common humanity.

Newspaper headlines should not provide the frame for radical discussion; for by nature they are concerned with what happened someplace yesterday. However, the really significant changes—population increase, technological development, intellectual influence, greater affluence, etc.—in our time happen—become visible—not in a day, but a year, if not a decade. For this reason, the medium more appropriate to their report is not the newspaper but the book. In the past few years, I have noticed that certain books I particularly admired, such as Herman Kahn's *On Thermonuclear War* (1960) and Marshall McLuhan's *Understanding Media* (1964), jump far beyond current thinking about the new realities created by the new war machinery and electronic media. If the presupposition of my previous book, *The New American Arts* (1965), was that we should admire true *artistic* innovation as the most appropriate response to an unprecedented historical situation, this volume assumes a related idea—that perhaps the most immediate, though by no means infallible, measure of the relevance of a *social* idea should be its distance not only in content but in form from the pieties of the past. Moreover, since our culture changes with increasing rapidity, relevant thinking will, of necessity, be more open than closed, more exploratory than polemical, more pragmatic than ideological, more committed to social justice than to social order. Indeed, precisely because truly radical thinking is an open-ended process, this anthology should stimulate rather than terminate the discussion; and for that reason, this book ends with a list of other books and essays full of similarly innovative ideas. Furthermore, because the radical ideas of a certain time are liable to become the conservative pieties of the future, I am certain that a comparable book compiled a decade from now would have entirely different contents.

Nearly all the essays included here were published in the sixties; the most conspicuous exceptions, both from R. Buckminster Fuller's *Nine Chains to the Moon* (1938), should indicate why many people consider Fuller one of the greatest visionary minds of our age. The reason most of the authors are American is precisely that the United States, technologically advanced and incomparably affluent, is the first country to step into the unknown future. What happens here now is likely to occur elsewhere in the industrializing world. As the English writer Michael Shanks summed it up, "America's today is our tomorrow."

In doing this book, I discovered a dispersed community of modernists—Boulding's "invisible college"—who needed only a few words to recognize each other. What makes the college invisible is that its members come from a diversity of backgrounds and hold a variety of jobs, for radical ideas for our time come from everywhere, but no one place in particular. Since I doubt if any of the contributors has shaken hands with more than one-third of the others—myself, I have managed to meet about that many—they are not likely to constitute a "radical establishment" with its own vested interests to perpetuate. Indeed, not only do they not necessarily agree with each other, but I suspect that every contributor probably objects to at least two others included here.

My own introduction to *Beyond Left and Right* does not broach a synthesis but explores several generalizations that have informed my thinking and perhaps lend the book coherence, as well as several themes that various contributors subsequently develop. It would be fair, I think, to characterize this essay, as well as the entire book, as a product of coming of intellectual age in the sixties; and this may explain why certain problems that haunt earlier generations of intellectuals are hardly touched upon here. For the selections themselves, let me thank all the authors and/or their publishers for granting me permission to reprint the following essays. Every effort has been made to trace the ownership of all copyrighted material and make full acknowledgment of its use. If any error or omission has occurred, it will be corrected in subsequent editions, provided that notification is submitted to the publisher. I am also grateful to William McPherson and his associates at William Morrow, as well as Julianne Stephenson and Jennifer Seymour, Donald Cohen and Barry Schwartz, John R. Pierce and John Cage, for all kinds of generously extended help. The dedication to the book's contributors hardly measures the admiration I have for them; they are, to my mind, among the most estimable men of our time.

Richard Kostelanetz

New York, New York
14 May, 1968

INTRODUCTION
RADICAL THOUGHT FOR OUR
TIMES

Intrinsic in the new industrial principle, developed more clearly since the War, is the periodic replacement of old forms by new forms.
—R. BUCKMINSTER FULLER, *Nine Chains to the Moon* (1938)

This new age needs a new radical thought, primarily because ideas addressed to an earlier historical time bear meager relevance to the unprecedented problems of the present and the near future, and old "radical" ideas would sooner change a world long gone than confront the puzzles now here. Instead of looking up and behind, truly radical thinking must peer down and ahead; for so much of our common situation today depends upon such wholly new conditions as the Soviet-American détente, the information explosion and computer technology, recently developed nutrients and medicines, transistorized appliances and automation, limited war and nuclear proliferation. The environments before us will be shaped by the impact of present and future technologies, material abundance and greater leisure, and new knowledge about man and his ecology. These forces promise to create a world so unlike anything in the past that its problems demand thinking that is profoundly radical, which is to say integrally related to today's root predicaments and possibilities. By contrast, "radical imagination" in the Marxist, anarchist and even conservative traditions is usually too preoccupied with dilemmas discovered long ago, as well as classic remedies, to recognize what the new realities are and how they have redirected the channels of social change; and despite their invocations of "revolution," the new left of the young, in focusing upon some of our society's most conspicuous sores, devotes more energy to palliatives than to solutions, to protest rather than to prevention, missing the radical jump to a comprehensive vision of what can and will happen in a society that surely will be vastly different from the present. While the necessity for such traditional virtues as common decency, humane consideration and liberal tolerance remains a historical constant, the prerequisite for a relevant radical thought today is a profound sense of our historical uniqueness. Only thinking that transcends the old pieties and categories—that is clearly beyond both "right" and "left"—can discover the new sources of malaise and formulate ideas that will nourish the roots of our future common experience.

The primary reality that a true radical thought must confront is a world which is increasingly molded and changed by technology; for as more cultures undergo industrialization, the whole planet becomes more dependent upon technological development. Indeed, so pervasive is the impact of new machines upon the human environment that technology constitutes a "second nature" which is by now as powerful a shaping force as primary nature. Partly because machines designed for various purposes often complement each other—sometimes the mating of two different machines instantly creates a third distinct machine—and an unprecedented primary technology instigates a "fallout" of new secondary machines, technological advances are so entwined that they drag each other along. This means that today, unlike before, no one set of technological leaps creates as much revolutionary momentum as the process of advance itself. As America is technologically the most advanced of cultures, what happens here, for good or ill, is liable to happen in staggered succession everywhere around the world. Precisely because we are, in Zbigniew Brzezinski's phrase, "the first society to experience the future," America is perhaps the most truly revolutionary elite in the world today.

Indicatively, the pace of technological change perceptibly increases each year—whereas the average time lag, a half-century ago, between a technical discovery and its general use was thirty years, the lag has averaged nine years since World War II and continues progressively to decrease. As Buckminster Fuller perceives, "All the trend curves which we may examine show rates of acceleration which underline the unprecedented nature of changes to come." Moreover, one "generation" of new machines so rapidly supersedes its predecessor that Herman Kahn once conjectured that if the difference between World War I and World War II represents one technological level, then by the late sixties we have survived the hypothetical World Wars III to VI. That is, there have been four complete technological overhauls in twenty-five years. In addition to the changes the new technologies produce by their own impact, industrial revolutions throughout history have always accelerated the speed of human endeavor; for not only do new airplanes transport us rapidly over long distances and electronic media make much communication instantaneous, but thanks to integrated circuits and other advances, the new computers can perform certain tasks one *million* times faster than comparable machines of only a quarter-century ago.

Technology itself instigates the pervasive transformations, regardless of who owns or runs the new machines; for the mere availability of the telephone, the television, the cheap portable radio, the computer and the superbomb created around the world new realities that transcend the influence of differing cultural traditions, as well as the controlling designs of either the machines' inventors and/or their manufacturers and/or their eventual owners. We cannot predict in advance exactly how a major technological jump will transform social, political and psychological relationships, but change they surely will. The power of new technologies is so fundamental and yet autonomous that a particularly crucial machine seems to have more or less the same effect upon both individuals and the environment in every culture that adopts it; and this similarity of effects, this history of shared technological awareness, is probably the greatest ecumenical force in the world today.

The paradox of technology's impact is that for every problem solved a new one is born to be solved; and the more useful and desirable a new technology is, the more disruptive are likely to be its effects, which subsequent technological advances will often alleviate, if not erase. For instance, new medicines and chemicals have so fantastically reduced the death rates in underdeveloped areas that severe increases in human numbers has become a major contemporary problem, which, to extend the paradox, other kinds of technology, the pill and the loop, can successfully combat. Effective "birth control" created the need for better birth control, and even by the middle sixties, both kinds of contraceptives had become so effective that demographers have downgraded their previously high estimates for world population in the year 2000. (These generous figures, one remembers, in turn superseded the rather low estimates for future population that were common in the 1930's.) However, the predicted development of extrauterine child-bearing technologies promises to take so much pain out of giving birth that figures may rapidly jump again. In this example, technology functions as the primary shaping force, producing not only machines that cure eternal ills, but also other new techniques that, in deflecting recent predicaments, exemplify Marshall McLuhan's dictum: "There is no possible protection from technology except by technology." To put it another way, through technology man adapts to his environment, but most major new technologies create a new environment that, for the sake of human adaptation, demands further technology. To cope with mankind's swelling numbers, the near future promises such palliatives as large platforms in the sky for raising crops, more effective systems of climate and birth control, rapid middle-distance transportation that induces population redistribution, the development of both entirely new crops, like wheat-rice-rye hybrids, and delectable artificial substitutes for food, as well as such new technologies for comfortably housing the additional millions as super-skyscrapers, apartment houses raised on stilts, and man-made islands in the lakes and oceans. To the process of technology saving us from technology there seems no end or limit.

In our time, the common intelligence and morality have no more urgent task than concern with new technologies, while education has few greater purposes than inculcating familiarity with the new environments. While one kind of technology created a superbomb, another kind has so successfully reduced the incidence of premature death that unprecedentedly abundant life, rather than needless demise, is the contemporary fact; beneficence, not menace—often beneficence to the point of menace—is technology's truth. The ultimate enemy is not the Machine but a panoply of old ideas that keeps us from using all the new machines available to us as propitiously as we could; and one need not be as complete a technological optimist as Buckminster Fuller to recognize the saving power of new and future machines, as well as appreciate the beneficial impact of technological miniaturization or, in Fuller's word, "ephemeralization." The accelerating process of progressively doing more with less, among other tendencies, has historically increased the amount of energy—"energy slaves," in Fullerese—available to everyone in an industrial society.

Social thinking should recognize the unprecedented opportunities that new technologies create, if only to insure that the common discourses stay intellectually up-to-date; and radical thought must take the entire world as its ultimate frame of concern, if only to recognize that electronic communications have put nearly everywhere on earth in instant aural, if not visual, contact. Moreover, governments must support scientific advance as a principle of public policy; and to curb the detrimental effects of certain current and even anticipated technologies, they should both enact appropriate laws and sponsor technological antidotes. At times, the implications of technology seem thirty years ahead of our thinking and acting, while technology changes at a faster pace than society; so unless government at all levels makes the new technologies a major concern, their laws are liable to fall way behind our lives.

The environment changes so quickly that even the best ideas rapidly become functionally obsolete, yet the major new ideas circuitously penetrate the confusions of current consciousness. The temptation that threatens any social criticism or philosophy today stems from the success of widespread influence, if not reverence, for the popular persuasiveness of an idea often deceives its advocates into believing that it has a relevance more eternal than current fashion. In our era, as never before, every intellectual revolution creates its own conservative class; ideas that were extremely perspicacious two decades ago are more likely than not to be archaic today, and merely reiterating them floods the air with distracting chatter. Wisdom in our time must be more dynamic than static, more metamorphic than metaphoric; for no isolatable principle is as much a cause of social distress in the world today as information lag, which I would broadly define as the discrepancy between what is ultimately known about human and social possibility and the awareness that informs the policies of people who make the crucial decisions in our society.

Forms of information lag include the gap between the general assumptions that stem from new knowledge and the pieties currently informing prevailing actions, as well as the contrast between the problems posed by an unprecedented environment and the preoccupations of the common wisdom. In practice, instead of ferreting out all the information relevant to a contemplated action—all the past, present and speculative solutions, all the pertinent peripheral material—decision-makers often let outrageously archaic assumptions become the sole information shaping their critique, if not their action; and instead of focusing upon the primary cause of a multitude of problems, they often let a secondary dilemma overwhelm their attention. For these reasons, a primary purpose of radical thought must be to discover the hidden sources of distress and to reformulate the strategies of possible change. That is, how we think about our condition— the patterns our analysis takes and the images we hold—can contribute as much to information lag as inadequate data, particularly when the radical shape of a new problem or technology defies our usual cognitive processes. "Organized information is now our major tool resource," writes John McHale. "Social evolution depends upon informational feedback." Knowledge is power in contemporary life; and the more fundamental knowledge an individual, an organization, or a society has in its head(s), the more powerful it is likely to be. Information lag is so urgent a social malaise that the mere dissemination of new data and patterns of understanding, as well as new invention (or reified knowledge), becomes a social act of great importance; for nothing is more reactionary than keeping pertinent intelligence to oneself.

Broad examples of information lag are found in society's lethargy over mobilizing the technology at hand—in the gap between, in Michael Shank's view, "The knowledge of new products, processes and techniques and the successful application of that knowledge." For instance, one especially conspicuous evidence of lag is the number of unwanted babies that are born each year in this age of new contraceptives; and despite scores of unprecedented medicines, millions of people get needlessly ill, largely because unjustified fears about new technologies, both mechanical and chemical, contribute to information lag. In another instance of lag, many people who work in offices recognize that they really do not need to make the arduous trip to the shop every day, because most exchange of information could be done over the home telephone. Here possibility is not translated into action, precisely because convention insists that a worker must occupy an office if he is to be paid for his labor and that face-to-face contact is a necessary ingredient of verbal communication. Furthermore, advances in multi-sensory communication, such as picture-phones, will make commuting less justified, until we acknowledge, in John Pierce's phrases, that we should communicate to work, and travel chiefly for pleasure." It is remarkable how few of us maximally employ all the machines in our everyday environment or discover the full potential of the many machines we own, and how even fewer of us are sufficiently free of social constraints and psychological blocks to acquire and exploit all the technologies ultimately available to us. Although man may never have absolute control over his fate, his panoply of tools at minimum grants power to his conscious desires and intentions. Man, though not perfectable, is adaptable, as well as capable of foresight and the realization of his vision; yet his inertia is the fundamental universal quality that makes information lag possible.

Information-processing technologies, such as the computer, almost by definition serve to diminish lag; for in a culture whose problems and institutions are increasingly complex, "the computer," writes Simon Ramo, "is the foe of disorganization and chaos. Indeed, the computer has arrived just in time." However, not only do we insufficiently use the computers already at hand, but a standard education hardly equips most of us for the future day when a neighborhood computer will be as available as the telephone. "Not knowing how to program," writes John McCarthy, "will be like living in a house full of servants and not speaking their language." Such knowledge bestows and eventually distributes power; for as C. P. Snow warns, "The chap standing next to the machine, who really knows how it makes decisions, and who has the machine under his command, is going to be in an exceedingly influential position."

Even by now, institutional policy-makers could have access to computers whose simulation capacities, allied with the software techniques of systems analysis, would enable them to regard the behavior in time of any organization or activity, even the most multifariously complex, as an integrated unit; and this makes computers an indispensable aid in planning for complex systems. They can fantastically extend and expand the human intellect's capacities for retrieving relevant precedents, remembering a multitude of specifications, processing numerous variables, considering more plentiful combinations, and even envisioning approximate models. Once institutional policy establishes a certain result as desirable, all the available information and hypotheses regarding methods can be fed into a computer which, thanks to its memory store, can then identify the necessary actions and the most propitious sequences for their application. Moreover, in any system of cybernetic control, the relevant information is integrated into a feedback loop, which likewise reduces lag by insuring that the machine gets to consider its output and perhaps adjust itself accordingly, just as the human brain constantly considers the results of its own directives. "Improvements in control," as John von Neumann said, "are really improvements in communicating information within an organization or mechanism." Intellectually, feedback induces a computer's user to think his plan through to its results, in order to formulate an operationally complete system. Economically, computers are largely responsible for the increasing effectiveness of inventory control, which is based upon a feedback process; and this improvement, in turn, provides one major explanation for the absence of economic depressions in the past decade. Informationally, a computer-assisted system promises to grant literally to its user's fingertips and home television screen instant and constant access to the total library of human knowledge. Socially, computers contribute to the increased speed of all kinds of directed communication. "In the future," Simon Ramo continues, "without computer networks none of us would be able to get our paychecks, keep our insurance policies alive, obtain our bank statements, deliver messages, keep track of who owns what, and maintain a semblance of order."

In the larger perspective, information lag describes the discrepancy between the common awareness of a certain truth and institutional behavior. For instance, the image of Soviet-American antagonism, so common a decade ago, no longer provides an adequate guide to political understanding, let alone diplomatic policy.

Similarly, American leaders have barely acknowledged what is obvious to nearly everyone who has studied the situation—that automation and technological ephemeralization replace so much labor that the economic objective of 100 per cent employment must give way to some system of guaranteed annual income. Similarly, if the mammoth computer promises the abolition of privately carried money in favor of instantly debited-credited and universally accessible accounts, the necessity of storing everyone's "ledger" in a single place would create a government monopoly which would render obsolete a private banking system that has scarcely anticipated its own demise. Widespread information lag also lies at the root of the world's failure to solve its poverty; for although mankind, in Fuller's judgment, now possesses the capability of providing 100 per cent of living humanity with all the basic materials of life, only about one-half are now so fortunate. The unprecedented truth is that abundance can be freely distributed with minimal pain to the donor, for it is the nature of a successful productive process to produce even more. If nothing else, therefore, a radical political thought for our time must focus upon closing the innumerable gaps between possibilities and actualities—between our information about what can be done and its actual realization; and in private life as well as public, the capacity to translate advanced knowledge into policies and/or objects is the clearest demonstration of real power in contemporary society.

The enemies of progress are those who hold a vested interest in obsolete forms, for not only do producers and possessors of archaic technologies have an investment in preserving their use, but so do the purveyors of archaic ideas. A large portion of the subsidies that the government donates to American corporations preserves technological antiques, such as the present railroad system, when cars, buses and trucks do the same work more efficiently or when, as in the suburbs, the situation demands newer technologies of rapid transit. The construction business around the world constitutes a reactionary force that preserves all the inefficiencies and superfluous expense of individually designed and fabricated short-life units, instead of manufacturing mass-fabricated and cheaper long-life dwellings with easily replaceable parts. Housing today is so needlessly expensive and inefficient that the necessary reforms will probably come not from within the industry itself but from an outside force—either entirely new organizations or existent enterprises based in industries more firmly tied to technological advance. Finally, perhaps this truth is too obvious, but the greatest vested interest in the world today lies not in property but in ignorance.

The profit motive in contemporary society functions both to increase and decrease lag; the character of the drift depends upon the context. Even though the exploitation of machines is in general more profitable and reliable than the exploitation of people, machines are so expensive an investment that employers are often lethargic about making the necessary, if not inevitable, switch. "This much can be said in round terms," writes the British management consultant Stafford Beer, "what the humans can do, a machine can do, so long as the scientist can find out how the human does or could do it." In another instance, the cost of thorough retooling persuades automobile manufacturers not to make the necessary structural changes that auto safety and and unpolluted air demand and scientific knowledge makes possible; and since they can get away with successfully merchandizing suboptimal products, the automotive industry, notes Donald A. Schon in *Technology and Change*, exhibits "very little utilized research." On the other hand, archaic practices eventually offer only a short-term profit; for if an industry fails to modernize, other kinds of technology are likely to usurp its functions. As commuting railroads succumbed to the automobile and as American steel has recently suffered severe competition from other metals, so the car may soon be succeeded by omnidirectional hovercraft that will fly passengers above the abandoned highways. Finally, it is a contemporary irony that the Cold War probably brings more major research and development, as well as beneficial technological fallout and industrial profits, than all the recent hot ones, which were by implicit agreement fought with submaximal weaponry.

Nonetheless, procedures that reduce lag usually clear the path to industrial success—not only technological development but also the innovative use of new technique—for management, in Jay W. Forrester's definition, "is the process of converting information into action." In Buckminster Fuller's judgment, no isolatable social group has realized as much real revolution in contemporary life as "the approximately 100,000 of the world's industrial complexes—both private corporations and state undertakings." As productive enterprises are primarily responsible for realizing automation, which defines the link of the computer to a cybernated production line, so both private and public groups pioneered the application of scientific method to problems of complex organizations—that area of new technique we now call "operations research" and "systems analysis." Similarly, by rapidly reducing the lag between a new invention or a new idea and its general availability, IBM, DuPont and A.T.&T., as well as the economies of Israel and Japan, have each earned millions; and the process of invention and its manufacture is itself so essential to industrial success that research and development have in the past decade become a major world industry.

Indeed, many of the important new enterprises of recent years have based their escalating rise upon the effective organization of "advanced knowledge," whether for the production of hardware (xerography and computers) or software (inventive programming and systems analysis). One reason that new technologies today are usually developed by young organizations is that older corporations have a vested interest in preserving the technologies upon which they established their success, as well as perhaps the illusion of that machinery's continued, if not eternal, usefulness. As Schon points out, the top officials of a successful establishment generally regard distinct innovation as implicitly challenging the structure of privilege they built upon the organization's current business; therefore, a technological revolution within an industrial enterprise usually accompanies a changing of the guard. Rare is the established institution that is so deeply committed to change that it risks continually altering its operation in favor of recently developed processes and products.

In general, then, the institutions of industrial society that wish to preserve the status quo contribute to information lag, for the needs of the environment invariably outpace a static operation. A similar principle informs today's intellectual life, where not only does the "left" constitute as much of a vested interest as the "right," but so does that interminable century-old argument between them. In the age of electricity, the dichotomy of left-right, itself reflecting the structure of a line of print, has minimal relevance to the metaphysics of positive-negative, which indicatively also informs that mathematical analogue of electricity, the binary number system of the computer. In the short run, a thinker who continues to reiterate his favorite ideas and arguments beyond their immediate relevance can sustain his reputation upon ignorance and charity, yet the intellectual who truly influences us will have insights so fresh and pertinent that they command the common assent. Ideally, then, the identifying marks of an engaged social thinker should be a threefold insistence—to progress beyond earlier positions, to confront problems newly visible, and continually to measure new thoughts against observations and experience; for the contemporary truth is that an idea which diminishes information lag today may contribute to it tomorrow.

A radical thought for our time must recognize that recently developed machinery promises to replace so many laborers at rote tasks and computers to retire so many clerical personnel who work at variable but repetitive jobs that just ahead lies an existence where tertiary occupations, such as education, will employ more people than productive trades. The creation of material excess is so revolutionizing our society that one of the most pressing intellectual needs today is the rejection of ideas rooted in an economy of scarcity for a psychology based upon abundance. This means, first, the end of the competitive view of existence that historically rationalized war—one side survived only at the other's expense—and still informs both capitalism and socialism, which presume, as Ambrose Bierce put it, "that the world's wealth is a fixed quantity, and A. can acquire only by depriving B." In the post-Darwinian universe, the machinery of American society produces wealth far in excess of native need; and precisely because, as Fuller says, "Science continually does more with less every time it scraps old inventions," and technological advance essentially translates potential energy into usable products, as well as reduces labor and costs within the production process itself, the future promises even more abundant wealth and leisure rather than less.

Wealth-creation, as Bernard J. Muller-Thym notes, is the most stunning kind of contemporary magic, whose sources are the exploitation of nature and the organization of knowledge; for the effective deployment of ingenuity and technology can make the most of what already exists. However, if the stuff of nature is more or less circumscribed in quantity, there are no discernible limits to the amount of wealth that can be created by applied knowledge. "This evolution of the brain" Julian Huxley characterizes as "the only inexhaustible, or at least unexhausted, source of human progress." Just as the exploitation of labor is no longer an attractive source of corporate profit, so the coercive creation of jobs should no longer be considered a reasonable solution to unemployment. Therefore, a primary function of enlightened politics should be the distribution of abundance to impoverished areas, both home and abroad; for just as the American government can afford to dispose of surplus foodstuffs, so the giant corporations could literally give away whole markets and even entire foreign divisions and still retain existing levels of assets and profits. Indeed, precisely because the exploitation of nature is not as lucrative as the organization of knowledge, "Imperial adventure or political coercion," writes Kenneth E. Boulding, "is simply an investment with a much lower rate of return than investment in applied science and technological progress at home."

Beyond that, the shift from scarcity to abundance demands that Western society revise the traditional relationship between work and play; for whereas man was once advised to work so that he could earn his play, now the physical and mental effort required for work differs so little from the kinds used in play that the traditional line between them becomes blurred. Just ahead is an economy that simply does not need and cannot accept everyone as a productive laborer; and slightly further beyond is a world so mechanically self-sufficient that only a small percentage of the total population need supervise its functioning. If society formerly ignored and then minimally compensated the unemployed, now we must recognize what Richard E. Farson calls "the right not to work." That is, we must acknowledge that dropping out of the workaday system is just as honorable as staying in, for within the current culture of dropouts are the precursors of life styles destined to become more prevalent in a future world where perhaps 10 per cent of the total population will be "voluntary poor" and where time will have replaced money as the basic form of wealth—payment in leisure will become more desirable than compensation in goods. Such an avant-garde elite, which is to say exponents of manners and modes that others will emulate in increasing numbers, becomes itself a major cause of significant social change.

Right now, the federal government can afford not only to support all the unemployed for as long as they are jobless but also to subsidize the creative, non-lucrative occupations—artists, writers, composers and such—in the same modest manner that it currently supports thousands of graduate students. Precisely because, as Herman Kahn conjectures, "The over-riding problem in the year 2000 will be the question of purpose in a world of leisure," it would be sage public policy to initiate the Guaranteed Annual Wage with people who have demonstrably created self-purpose out of leisure time. Within the next decade, the United States, if not other countries, will probably extend the annual wage to everyone who is not working, whether he wishes to find a job or not, thereby finally abolishing the traditional connection between jobs and income. A Guaranteed Annual Wage will make subminimal wages so unattractive that employers will be induced to replace menial work with machines (such as soon-to-become-available robots), as well as abolish all the demeaning practices of welfare departments; for only through such benevolent procedures can society assume responsibility for the increased unemployment that is among the biproducts of technological advance. Here, as before, technology creates the affluence that permits societies to alleviate, if not solve, the unemployment problems that the new machines create; the poverty that politics alone cannot cure will fall before the spoils of abundance.

Technological advance stems largely from new knowledge, for thought, if not speculation, provides the basic force in the endless revolutions of modern society. "The history of science demonstrates beyond a doubt," writes James B. Conant, "that the really revolutionary and significant advances come not from empiricism but new theories." Intellectuals such as Norbert Wiener, John von Neumann and Claude Shannon provided the theories that made contemporary computers possible; other intellectuals supervised the translation of these ideas into machines. The birth control pill stems from ideas and experiments, as well as an age-old dream; and the theoretical discoveries of quantum physics made several decades ago today inform the development of both transistors and laser technology. Buckminster Fuller's geodesic principles enable builders to enclose a large space at less cost than previous structural conceptions, and Moshe Safdie's Habitat, constructed for Montreal's Expo '67, demonstrates the first radical ideas in two decades for mass-producing an urban dwelling that is considerably cheaper and more humane than the current norm. "The power to initiate—to direct the attention to particular possibilities of action," writes Herbert A. Simon, "is of greatest importance in societies undergoing rapid change," which is to say in practically every society in the world.

Whereas new knowledge in the physical sciences inspires technological development, other kinds of radical thought probe into the mysterious forces shaping both consciousness and social patterns. Since a considerable percentage of significant change is invisible to the naked eye (as well as the daily newspaper), the recognition of implicit tendencies and patterns is a prerequisite for both comprehensive radical thinking and effective social change; and new knowledge often provides the inspiration for necessary reform. For instance, persistent poverty in an affluent culture does not occur suddenly or in one place, but exists everywhere over a period of time; therefore, the pervasiveness of an individual's or a family's problem must be discovered before it can become a public concern. Similarly, recent research into the process of human perception and learning, which revealed the importance of appropriate structure in cognitive processes, has inspired a thorough overhaul of the grade school curriculum, as well as the development of more effective teaching machines; the principles of systems thinking enable analysts to make complex and diversified structures more coherently intelligible; and the discovery of DNA and the genetic code may bring control of previously incurable diseases, as well as more reliable methods of eugenics, if not eventually an individual's biological emancipation from his inheritance. Since the future will be so different from the past, no possibly relevant idea could be so radical that we should not at least consider it; for primarily through changing our minds we can better our lives.

Through intelligence and comprehensive foresight, men gain greater control over themselves and their environment, as well as create the common future before it creates them; and our strongest weaponry for shaping history is *planning*, which should be regarded not as a fixed and systematic ideology but as an attitude that informs decisions—less a body of definite goals than comprehensive techniques for discerning both the manifold possibilities and the various means for realizing desirable ends. Secondary dimensions of planning include, writes Daniel Bell, "the specifications of costs and benefits, the reallocation of burdens, and the probable consequences of different kinds of actions." Successful planning, particularly for long-range social and technological projects, depends not only upon a generalized perspective but on an interdisciplinary familiarity, not only upon experience but on adventurous experiment, not only upon a sure grasp of the actualities of the present but on a keen sense of the likely possibilities in the future. The last, in turn, depends upon shrewd estimates of technological invention and development, which may make today's good plan obsolete tomorrow. Indeed, in speculations about the future lie the most profound guides for planning, as well as politics, in the present, for so much depends upon the successful anticipation of surprise. Because the processes of planning require the consideration of extensive and detailed information, as well as diverse alternatives and complex chain-reactions, the new technologies of knowledge-processing and visualized simulation can provide the planner with his sketching boards. "The great speed of the computer enables us to test the outcome resulting from a variety of changes of initial actions and so to choose the course with the highest pay-off before the march of human events forces us to take some inadequately considered action," writes the research scientist Arthur L. Samuel. "This ability to see into the future, as it were, by simulation on a computer . . . is sure to find application in more and more aspects of our daily lives."

Like much else in radical thought, planning must literally start at home, in our own bodies and immediate environments; for the prime arena for "radical action"—for decisions that will induce a more desirable existence—is our everyday activities. We all must learn to scrutinize our lives more thoroughly and insightfully, to determine what is important and what is not, what gives us pleasure and what pain, what is true necessity and what is excess vanity, and how we can more propitiously employ the tools available to us. As the affairs of life become more complicated and alternatives more plentiful, particularly in cities, personal planning becomes an absolutely essential strategy for coping with diverse commitments; and once we redesign a more appropriate regimen for ourselves, we must then exercise the discipline to hew to our plan. As most of us now use medicines to combat our malfunctioning, so we will soon have access to drugs that induce not just illness-free but optimal behavior, as well as drugs that bestow general immunization against common diseases. The future promises a revolution *within* man himself and the reform of society will parallel and follow changes in ourselves.

Along with developing control over our internal environments, we should redesign all external situations within our reach. After our homes come our cities, our countrysides, our transportation routes; and we are slowly beginning to realize that the planet itself is an environment suitable to a master plan. Moreover, technology promises us the capacity for reliably planning a daily weather more appropriate to an area's habits and needs. Everything in the common environment must be made more humanly efficient before we can afford to consider its possible beauty, even though truly utilitarian structures usually attain their own brand of elegance. The most imaginative planning is bound to be supra-political, if only because, as Herman Kahn judges, "How ill-equipped our government is to perform long-range planning. The most able officials are constantly involved in the meeting of day-to-day crises." Moreover, since we cannot write a *plan* solely out of the present, speculations about the future provide a supplementary guide. In a pluralistic society, the task of anticipatory planning will be willingly assumed by industry, universities, nonprofit organizations and even lone individuals; and because the most persuasive ideas of planners eventually infiltrate the heads of officialdom, governments are likely to function as the levers of design. Here, too, the ultimate power lies in the heads of people with good ideas, for no executive can take a decisive action unless he has some conception of how he should act. In short, every variable dimension of every society must be designed as knowledgeably and comprehensively as possible, preferably upon local initiative within national and international limitations. "Revolution by design and invention," writes Fuller, "is the only revolution tolerable to all men, all societies, and all political systems everywhere." Implicit in this ethic of continual and universal design and redesign is future man's emancipation from the lag of the past.

Technology is primarily responsible for the material abundance that permits American society to tolerate nearly one-third of its population as professional students; and in the society of leisure, no single industry will be as important as education, which also promises to become the dominant interest of both man and his economy. Because future man will need to know more than his predecessor—possess not only more data but more kinds of conceptual approaches—everyone's education will necessarily extend well into his twenties. "Our ability at any moment to accept new knowledge is narrowly delimited by the existing state of knowledge," writes the art historian George Kubler in *The Shape of Time*. "A fixed ratio may mark the two kinds of knowledge: The more we know, the more new knowledge we can accept." Because another by-product of change is new knowledge, certain groups of professionals already must sporadically re-educate themselves every decade, merely to keep up-to-date; for just as nearly half of the products marketed by the chemical industry in 1967 were unknown a decade before, so half of what an engineer knows today will be obsolete in a decade and, experts estimate, half of what he will need to know then is not available today. In the future, all of us will require continual refreshing, merely to acquaint ourselves with the changing environment. "Perhaps," Brzezinski conjectures, "there will even be a constitutional amendment, requiring a President-elect to spend at least a year getting himself educationally up-to-date."

Precisely because education will have no real end greater than itself and grading systems no practical purpose, students will seek their own classes rather than be assigned to them. The strategy of education will of necessity shift from the accumulation of data to the assimilating of intellectual structures, for the measure of true literacy should be not gross facts but diversified understanding. All schools will latch onto the technological revolutions, universally inculcating the languages and logics of computers and other new machines; and they shall exploit such currently available technologies as closed-circuit television, films, video-tape,

and information-retrieval systems in the libraries, as well as conveyor belts to speed everyone around a large campus and computer-assisted "teachers" capable of responding with considerable
subtlety and detail to a student's queries and answers. These last
machines differ considerably from the conventional educational
technologies, from the blackboard to the closed-circuit television,
primarily because they return mass education to the individually
paced situation of the traditional library, where everyone reads
his *own* book at *his* own speed. Nonetheless, computers are no
more likely to retire the good human teacher than his previous
technological competitor, the printed book. "It is quite possible,"
Brzezinski continues, "that a society increasingly geared to learning will be able to absorb more resiliently the expected changes
in social and individual life."

A viable theory of social change must inform any radical
thought with a claim to relevance; for those who wish to change
the world would be wise to discern how the unprecedented environment deflects traditional streams of change, as well as
creates new opportunities. One presupposition of the themes outlined here is that neither formal nor "protest" politics are primary
initiators of significant social change, nor can they possibly be.
The identity of the man who sits in the White House or his party
has less influence upon the major transformations than what
certain individuals and the general populace are thinking as well
as how they are implementing their ideas. Roughly, the fundamental processes of social change today start with dreams (whose
mother may well be necessity); for the desire for something
impossible is the first step toward a vision that can then be realized. "The forecasting of invention is not separate from invention
itself," writes Donald A. Schon. "The principal step is the conceptual one. When you predict the electric car, you have made
the adventure. We are not standing outside the process of change
but participating in it." The inspirations that scientists, in tandem
with technicians, transform into machines in turn create a new
environment, as well as new capabilities for imaginative planning,
all of which, in turn, change the organizations of society; and we
are beginning to suspect that any invention man can imagine
may eventually be realized. Essentially, then, since the organization and application of knowledge is the primary source of social

power, radical thinking is, in the best sense, largely above and beyond politics.

"To ask a politician to lead us," Buckminster Fuller once wrote, "is to ask the tail of the dog to lead the dog," for most talk about "changing the system" fails to recognize that the systems of society are dissolving and re-forming all the time. Indeed, as social changes occur everywhere, all the time, source power in our society is necessarily more pluralistic than monolithic. Since the most important transformations occur outside the influence of politics, which in today's world becomes less an initiating than an adjusting operation, basically providing laws to cope with changes already taking place in society, the government's role can only be more conservative than progressive—it keeps the peace and underwrites the common currency, as well as protects the living space from the excesses and refuses of new machines and preserves continuity with a society's past. The less enlightened a regime is, the more reactionary, laggard or irrelevant are its politics liable to be—the more blocks, for instance, it can place between its citizens and the inevitable future.

The point is that the thrust of history is clearly optimistic, as technology does, can and will make life better for more people, if not eventually everyone; but what stands between us and technology's capabilities is partly politics, which cannot initiate the necessary revolutions but can certainly hinder, if not halt, their taking place. For these reasons, Karl W. Deutsch conjectures that, "It might be more profitable to look upon government somewhat less as a problem of power and somewhat more as a problem of steering." In the new society, democratic government at its best will accomplish what American politics has always done—respond to widespread changes in popular attitudes and mediate among diverse, if not contesting, claims and interests, to insure that the balance of compromise deflects incipient chaos. People skilled, in Fuller's phrase, at these "secondary housekeeping functions" will continue to become the leaders of states.

Certain traditional forms of "radical" thought regard the nationalization of industry as a primary aim; but such a program commits the most common fallacy of presuming that the reform of only one dimension will initiate comprehensive revolutions. In practice, the ownership of giant industries scarcely influences either their function, which is determined by managers, or their relationship with employees. Indicatively, the inequities of industrial society hardly succumb to socialist rule, while certain innovations more prevalent in post-capitalist societies have done more to make laboring work itself obsolete. "To the eternal workingman," writes Eric Hoffer, himself a longshoreman, "management is substantially the same whether it is made up of profit seekers, idealists, technicians, or bureaucrats. The allegiance of the manager is to the task and the results." Therefore, a civil servant who manages an obsolete industrial plant has as much of a vested interest in preserving the illusion of its relevance, as well as in exerting coercive pressure on political officials, as the executives of an automobile enterprise have in preserving structural and mechanical obsolescence. For these reasons, as well as others, new machines, rather than new managers, will be the workers' saviors; for the only final cure for the exploitation of labor will be the eventual abolition of laborious work.

Contrary to Marxist theory, the relationship between a wealth-creating corporation and the general public is so tangled that it is difficult to discover who is profiting from whom. In one important sense, everyone is a beneficiary of A.T.&T., not only because the services provided by telephones are relatively cheap and efficient, the saving in message-passing labor is enormous, and the company pays a huge sum annually in taxes ("Use frequency is predicated," writes Fuller, "on its induced desirability"), but out of its research laboratories have come organized knowledges that initiated information theory as well as the development of transistors—two advances in scientific knowledge that other enterprises as well as Bell turned into social power and disseminated wealth. (Indeed, the transistor has ironically revolutionized the fomenting of revolutions in underdeveloped areas, while Vladimir Zworykin of RCA's laboratories proposes that the telephone system itself, in tandem with a huge computer, could realize the populist ideal of a "voting machine" for a regular, perhaps nightly, referendum on government policies.) Since ideas usually precede action, what industrial managers think—their attitudes to the creativity of the enterprise's intellectuals and the quality of the managers' bureaucratic skills—ultimately have more effect upon that enterprise, if not upon society, than its ownership; and

particularly when a crucial decision requires considerable exper-
tise, the manager's advisor can wield enormous, though perhaps
implicit, power. For these reasons, an ethic and climate conducive
to accumulating intelligence and managing innovation—the translation of invention into policy and/or products—must be essential
ingredients of both research-development programs and a nation's
culture, as well as contemporary radical thought.

The roots of most future transformations lie within history
itself—not in a secular apocalypse but simply through the pervasive impact of such major current historical tendencies as
technological advance and its world-wide dissemination, man's
increasingly comprehensive control over himself and his environment, rising affluence, and the greater influence of various avant-
garde elites, as well as the cumulatively stronger leverage and
broader international scope of *all* these forces for radical change.
For better and worse, the entire world will progressively come to
resemble contemporary America, as much through intentional
emulation of our ways—all former European colonies, for instance,
strive to westernize themselves—as through the inevitable outcome
of certain historical drifts, such as the ecumenical impact of
certain universally pervasive technologies; in more ways than one
we are, to repeat, the world's revolutionary elite.

Another source of change will be the accession to positions of
command throughout American society of a younger generation,
whose attitudes and expectations—collective mind—will seem to
differ considerably from those of their elders. Most of this generation matured in material abundance, experienced interminable
education and found secure employment; they suffered competition only in applying for college and perhaps in graduate school;
relatively few of the potential leaders actually went to war; and
most important, they have as a group the smallest vested interest
in ongoing systems. I would characterize the generation as far
more skeptical than its elders about the efficacy of war, more
enthusiastic about the possibilities of machines, more attuned
to computers, less desperate about accumulating money or conspicuous signs of wealth, more open-minded about ideas, tolerant
of eccentricity, and more committed to the necessity of sweeping
social changes. The character of their common experience has
shaped a sensibility so unlike their elders' that Fuller, for one,

remarks that he prefers to lecture young people because they are less concerned with what they "can get out of the world than how they can make it work." Half of the population in America today is under twenty-seven; by 1972, approximately half of the qualified voters will have been born after 1940. Not only will this generation probably select one of their own as President by 1980, but by that year its members will have assumed commanding positions within corporations, educational institutions and probably even the armed services; moreover, comparable generational jumps will occur in other cultures, perhaps even Soviet Russia. Since bureaucracies generally are conservative until they experience either rapid growth or change in leadership, everything today's young touch will feel their difference.

The traditions shaping the new radical thought are diverse and eccentric; its exponents hardly descend from a common intellectual stream. Peter F. Drucker characterizes himself as a conservative; yet he envisions a radically different future. Zbigniew Brzezinski first became known as a vehement anti-Communist refugee; yet now he regards Communism as less of a threat than out-of-date ideas. Paul Goodman calls himself an anarchist, even though his attitudes toward technology are conservative; and most other advocates of the new thinking would probably classify themselves, for lack of a better term, as enlightened liberals. Behind Fuller's and McLuhan's conception of technology as extending the human organism lies Ralph Waldo Emerson's assertion, "The human body is the magazine of inventions. . . . All the tools and engines on earth are only extensions of its limbs and senses." Indicatively, the role of technology and technicians in social and economic change earned more attention from the American social philosophers Henry Adams and Thorstein Veblen than their European peers, who were more concerned with capital accumulation. Moreover, historical precedents for many of the new ideas lie as much in artistic thought as political philosophy. A pre-1920 Dada manifesto demanded "the introduction of progressive unemployment through comprehensive mechanization of every field of activity," and then proposed "the communal feeding of all," which as any reactionary knows is the first step toward a Guaranteed Annual Wage. In the implications of surrealism we find the idea that the revolution in thinking precedes social transformations; as Louis Aragon once wrote, "I have always placed, and place today, the spirit of revolt far above *any* politics." The artists associated with the Weimar Bauhaus in the early twenties preceded Fuller, Doxiadis and Safdie in proclaiming the fundamental necessity of decent mass housing; and in futurism, the fourth great mixed-means artistic movement of the early twentieth century, we find a precedent for regarding machines as both extensions of human design and the core force in creating the common future. Artistic thought would seem to contain more ingredients of current radical thinking than political philosophy or literary culture, not only because artists invariably presume that mind-change, implicit in the influence of art, precedes social change but also because the avant-garde assumption—what we make and think today will ineluctably differ from what we made or thought a decade ago—has historically had more influence upon artists than writers or political intellectuals; for the latter professions tend to subscribe to the fundamentally conservative bias that regards the present as little different from the past.

The new radical thought is non-ideological, non-utopian and non-systematic; for it offers not final definitions but imaginative suggestions, expanding the mind rather than contracting it. This radical thought represents a style of looking at and thinking about contemporary problems, rather than an itemized program; and it eschews the European fallacy that a single philosophy or group can provide Final Answers for the American truth that valuable ideas come from a diversity of sources. Its advocates believe less in violently imposing change upon history than anticipating and planning transformations within the current trends, to make the world more congenial and equitable for everyone. In contrast to ideology and utopia, whose esthetic presuppositions induce essentially static images of a historical future that instead will be inherently dynamic, a truly viable radical thought must be as open-ended as technological advance itself. It must account for revolution as well as evolution, if not revolution in the shape and causes of evolution.

The nature of wishing makes dreams open-ended, as man is intelligent enough to want better than he has; and there seems no limit to his desires, as well as to his ability to realize his dreams. "The more progress we make," writes Richard E. Farson, "the more we must make." Beyond that, the new radical thought avoids focusing upon one element as the key to historical change, as momentum toward progress stems from a variety of sources, and it endeavors to incorporate new knowledge that makes invisible forces visible and new inventions that make old fantasies feasible. Regarding change, radical thought is more pragmatic than apocalyptic; for revolutionary energy is too deeply embedded in our culture for us to assume that a "big bang" will terminate change with a total solution to history. The pace of innovation, both technical and social, leaps ahead so rapidly and relentlessly that the near future promises not an end to man's time but unending and, if we insist, beneficial change.

I

Man and His Future

Most of the changes in the last thirty-five years that have affected my life and the lives of the people around me have been in part due to technological advances that were unforeseen and in part due to rapid adaptation—almost in spite of our institutions and our government—by the people themselves to things that they wanted. . . . This makes me feel that predicting the future is rather hopeless, but it does bring up one point. If people would stay as flexible as they have been in adapting to things, and if institutions would be a little more flexible and apply fewer brakes upon things, perhaps we would get into the future less painfully. —JOHN R. PIERCE,
Toward the Year 2000 (1968)

AFTER CIVILIZATION, WHAT?

by KENNETH E. BOULDING

W<small>E</small> are living in what I call the second great change in the state of man. The first is the change from pre-civilized to civilized societies. The first five hundred thousand years or so of man's existence on earth were relatively uneventful. Compared with his present condition, he puttered along in an astonishingly stationary state. There may have been changes in language and culture which are not reflected in the artifacts, but if there were, these changes are lost to us. The evidence of the artifacts, however, is conclusive. Whatever changes they were, they were almost unbelievably slow. About ten thousand years ago, we begin to perceive an acceleration in the rate of change. This becomes very noticeable five thousand years ago with the development of the first civilization. The details of this first great change are probably beyond our recovery. However, we do know that it depended on two phenomena: the development of agriculture and the development of exploitation. Agriculture, that is the domestication of crops and livestock and the planting of crops in fields, gave man a secure surplus of food from the food producer. In a hunting and fishing economy it seems to take the food producer all his time to produce enough food for himself and his family. The moment we have agriculture, with its superior productivity of this form of employment of human resources, the food producer can produce more food than he and his family can eat. In some societies in these happy conditions, the food producer has simply relaxed and indulged himself with leisure. As soon, however, as we get politics, that is exploitation, we begin to get cities and civilization. Civilization, it is clear from

"After Civilization, What?" by Kenneth E. Boulding is reprinted from the October 1962 issue of the *Bulletin of the Atomic Scientists*. Copyright 1962 by the Educational Foundation for Nuclear Science.

the origin of the word, is what happens in cities, and the city is dependent (in its early stages, at any rate) on the existence of a food surplus from the food producer and some organization which can take it away from him. With this food surplus, the political organization feeds kings, priests, armies, architects, and builders, and the city comes into being. Political science in its earliest form is the knowledge of how to take the food surplus away from the food producer without giving him very much in return.

Now I argue that we are in the middle of the second great change in the state of man, which is as drastic and as dramatic, and certainly as large as, if not larger than, the change from pre-civilized to civilized society. This I call the change from civilization to post-civilization. It is a strange irony that just at the moment when civilization has almost completed the conquest of pre-civilized societies, post-civilization has been treading heavily upon its heels. The student of civilization may soon find himself in the unfortunate position of the anthropologist who studies pre-civilized societies. Both are like the student of ice on a hot day—the subject matter melts away almost before he can study it.

These great changes can be thought of as a change of gear in the evolutionary process, resulting in progressive acceleration of the rate of evolutionary change. Even before the appearance of man on the earth, we can detect earlier evolutionary gear-shiftings. The formation of life obviously represented one such transition, the movement from the water to the land another, the development of the vertebrates another, and so on. Man himself represents a very large acceleration of the evolutionary process. Whether he evolved from pre-existing forms or landed from a space ship and was not able to get back to where he came from, is immaterial. Once he had arrived on earth, the process of evolution could go on within the confines of the human nervous system at a greatly accelerated rate. The human mind is an enormous mutation-selection process. Instead of mutation-selection process being confined, as it were, to the flesh, it can take place within the image, and hence, very rapid changes are possible. Man seems to have been pretty slow to exploit this potentiality, but one suspects that even with primitive man, the rate of change in the biosphere was much larger than it had been before, because of the appearance of what Teilhard de Chardin calls the noosphere, or sphere of knowledge.

Civilization represents a further acceleration of the rate of change, mainly because one of the main products of civilization is history. With the food surplus from agriculture it became possible to feed specialized scribes. With the development of writing, man did not have to depend on the uncertain memories of the aged for his records, and a great process of accumulation of social knowledge began. The past could now communicate, at least in one direction, with the present, and this enormously increased the range and possibility of enlargements of the contents of the human mind.

Out of civilization, however, comes science, which is a superior way of organizing the evolution of knowledge. We trace the first beginnings of science, of course, almost as far back as the beginning of civilization itself. Beginning about 1650, however, we begin to see the organization of science into a community of knowledge, and this leads again to an enormous acceleration of the rate of change. The world of 1650 is more remote to us than the world of ancient Egypt or Samaria would have been to the man of 1650. Already in the United States and Western Europe, in a smaller degree in Russia and in some other parts of the world, we see the beginnings of post-civilized society—a state of man as different from civilization as civilization is from savagery. What we really mean, therefore, by the anemic term "economic development" is the second great transition in the state of man. It is the movement from civilized to post-civilized society. It is nothing short of a major revolution in the human condition, and it does not represent a mere continuance and development of the old patterns of civilization.

As a dramatic illustration of the magnitude of the change, we can contemplate Indonesia. This is a country which has about the same extent, population and per capita income as the Roman Empire at its height. For all I know it is producing a literature and an art at least comparable to that of the Augustan age. It is, therefore, a very good example of a country of high civilization. Because of this fact, it is one of the poorest countries in the world. It is desperately anxious to break out of its present condition. Jakarta is a city about the size of ancient Rome, though perhaps a little less splendid. All this points up the fact that the Roman Empire was a desperately poor and under-developed society. The Roman cities seem to have been always about three weeks away from starvation, and even at its height it is doubtful whether the Roman Empire ever had less than seventy-five to eighty per cent of its population in agriculture.

Civilization, that is, is a state of society in which techniques are so poor that it takes about eighty per cent of the population to feed the hundred per cent. But we do have about twenty per cent of the people who can be spared from food-producing to build Parthenons and cathedrals, to write literature and poetry, and fight wars. By contrast, in the United States today we are rapidly getting to the point where we can produce all our food with only ten per cent of the population and still have large agricultural surpluses. But for the blessings of agricultural policy, we might soon be able to produce all our food with five per cent of the population. It may even be that agriculture is on its way out altogether and that within another generation or so we will produce our food in a totally different way. Perhaps both fields and cows are merely relics of civilization, the vestiges of a vanishing age. This means, however, that even in our society, which is at a very early stage of post-civilization, we can now spare about ninety per cent of the people to produce bathtubs, automobiles, H-bombs and all the other conveniences of life. Western Europe and Japan are coming along behind the United States very fast. The Russians, likewise, are advancing toward post-civilization, although by a very different road. At the moment their ideology is a handicap to them in some places—especially in agriculture, which still occupies forty-five per cent of the people. And, if the Russians ever discover that super-peasants are a good deal more efficient than collective farms, they may cut away some of the ideology that hangs around their neck and move even more rapidly toward post-civilized society.

I'm not at all sure what post-civilization will look like but it will certainly be a world-wide society. Until very recently, each civilized society was a little island in a sea of barbarism which constantly threatened to overwhelm it. Civilization is haunted by the spectre of decline and fall, though it is note-worthy that in spite of the rise and fall of particular civili-zations, civilization itself expanded steadily in geographical coverage, from its very beginnings. We must face the fact, how-ever, that post-civilized society will be world-wide, if only be-cause of its ease of communication and transportation. I flew last year from Idlewild to Brussels, and on glimpsing the new Brussels Airport out of the corner of my eye, I thought for a moment that we had come back and landed at Idlewild again.

The characteristic institutions of civilization are, as we have seen, first agriculture, then the city, then war, in the sense of clash of organized armed forces, and finally, inequality, the sharp contrast between the rich and the poor, between the city and the country, between the urbane and the rustic. The state is based very fundamentally on violence and exploitation, and the culture tends to be spiritually monolithic.

In post-civilization all these institutions suffer radical change. Agriculture, as we have seen, diminishes until it is a small pro-portion of the society; the city, likewise, in the classical sense, disintegrates. Los Angeles is perhaps the first example of the post-civilization, post-urban agglomeration—under no stretch of the imagination could it be called a city. War, likewise, is an institution in process of disintegration. National defense as a social system has quite fundamentally broken down on a world scale. The ICBM and the nuclear warhead have made the nation-state as militarily obsolete as the city-state, for in no country now can the armed forces preserve an area of internal peace by pushing violence to the outskirts. Poverty and inequality, like-wise, are tending to disappear, at least on their traditional scale. In civilized societies the king or the emperor could live in a Versailles and the peasant in a hovel. In post-civilized society, it is almost impossible for the rich to consume on a scale which is more, let us say, than ten times that of the poor. There is no sense in having more than ten automobiles!

Another profound change in the passage from civilization to post-civilization is the change in the expectation of life. In civilized society, birth and death rates tend to be about forty per thousand and the expectation of life at birth is twenty-five years. In post-civilized society, the expectation of life at birth rises at least to seventy and perhaps beyond. It may be that we are on the edge of a biological revolution, just as dramatic and far-reaching as the discovery of atomic energy and that we may crack the problem of aging and prolong human life much beyond its present span. Whether or not, however, we go forward to Methuselah, the mere increase of the average age of death to seventy is a startling and far-reaching change. It means, for instance, that in an equilibrium population, the birth and death rate cannot be more than about fourteen per thousand. This unquestionably implies some form of conscious control of births. It means also that a much larger proportion of the population will be in later years.

It is perfectly possible to paint an anti-utopia in which a post-civilized society appears as universally vulgar or dull. On the whole, however, I welcome post-civilization and I have really very little affection for civilization. In most pre-civilized societies the fact that the life of man is for the most part nasty, brutish and short, does not prevent the poets and philosophers from sentimentalizing the noble savage. Similarly, we may expect the same kind of sentimentalizing of the noble Romans and civilized survivals like Winston Churchill. On the whole, though, I will not shed any tears over the grave of civilization any more than I will over pre-civilized society. The credit balance of post-civilization is large. It at least gives us a chance of a modest utopia, in which slavery, poverty, exploitation, gross inequality, war and disease—these prime costs of civilization—will fall to the vanishing point.

What we have at the moment is a chance to make a transition to this modest utopia—a chance which is probably unique in the history of this planet. If we fail, the chance will probably not be repeated in this part of the universe. Whatever experiments may be going on elsewhere, the present moment indeed is unique in the whole four billion years of the history of the planet. In my more pessimistic moments, I think the chance is a slim one, and it may be that man will be written off as an unsuccessful experiment. We must look at the traps which lie along the path of the transition, which might prevent us from making it altogether.

The most urgent trap is, of course, the trap of war. War, as

I have suggested, is an institution peculiarly characteristic of civilization. Pre-civilized societies have sporadic feuding and raiding, but they do not generally have permanent organized armed forces, and they do not generally develop conquest and empire; or if they do, they soon pass into a civilized form. An armed force is essentially a mobile city designed to throw things at another mobile or stationary city with presumably evil intent. As far as I know, not more than two or three civilizations have existed without war. The Mayans and the people of Mohenjo-daro seem to have lived for fairly long periods without war, but this was an accident of their monopolistic situation and they unquestionably occupied themselves with other kinds of foolishness. If pre-civilized society, however, cannot afford war, post-civilized society can afford far too much of it, and hence will be forced to get rid of the institution because it is simply inappropriate to the technological age. The breakdown in the world social system of national defense really dates from about 1949, when the United States lost its monopoly of nuclear weapons. A system of national defense is only feasible if each nation is stronger at home than its enemies, so that it can preserve a relatively large area of peace within its critical boundaries. Such a system is only possible, however, if the range of the deadly missile is short and if the armed forces of each nation lose power rapidly as they move away from home. The technological developments of the twentieth century have destroyed these foundations of national defense, and have replaced it with another social system altogether, which is "deterrence."

"Deterrence" is a social system with properties very different from that of national defense, which it replaced. Under national defense, for instance, it is possible to use the armed forces; under "deterrence" is it not—that is, if the deterring forces are ever used, the system will have broken down. We live in a society with a positive possibility of irretrievable disaster—a probability which grows every year. Herman Kahn recently said: "All we are doing is buying time, and we are doing nothing with the time that we buy." The armed forces of the world are caught in a technological process which not only destroys their own function, but threatens all of us. Even if a few of us do crawl out of the fallout shelters, it is by no means clear that we can put the world back together again. Even if the human race could survive one nuclear war, it is very doubtful that it could survive a second; and as the purpose of the first nuclear war would be to set up a political system which would produce the second, unless there is a radical change in attitude towards national defense, the prospects of the human race seem to be dim. Fortunately, "there is still time, brother" and evolution can still go on in the minds of men. The critical question is whether it can go on rapidly enough. The abolition of national defense, which is what we must face, is going to be a painful process, as we have come to rely on it to preserve many of the values which we hold dear. If the task can be perceived, however, by a sufficient number of people, there is at least a chance that we may avoid this trap before it is too late.

Even if we avoid the war trap, we may still fall into the population trap. Population control is an unsolved problem even for the developed areas of the world, which have moved the furthest towards post-civilization. An equilibrium of population in a stable post-civilized society may represent a fairly radical interference with ancient human institutions and freedoms. In a stable post-civilized society, as I have suggested, the birth and death rates must be of the order of fourteen per thousand, and the average number of children per family cannot much exceed two. There are many social institutions which might accomplish this end. So far, however, the only really sure-fire method of controlling population is starvation and misery.

In many parts of the world—indeed, for most of the human race for the moment—the impact on certain post-civilized techniques of civilized society has produced a crisis of growth, which may easily be fatal. In the tropics especially, with DDT and a few simple public-health measures, it is easy to reduce the death rate to nine or ten per thousand while the birth rate stays at forty per thousand. This means an annual increase of population of three per cent *per annum*, almost all of it concentrated in the lower age groups. We see dramatic examples of this phenomenon in places like the West Indies, Ceylon, and Formosa; but thanks to the activity of the World Health Organization, it is taking place rapidly all over the tropical world. Perhaps the most important key to the transition to post-civilization is heavy investment in human resources—that is, in education. The conquest of disease and infant mortality, however, before the corresponding adjustment to the birth rate, produces enormous numbers of children in societies which do not have the resources to educate them—especially as those in the middle-age groups, who after all must do all the work of a society, come from the much smaller population of the pre-DDT era.

Even in the developed countries, population control presents a very serious problem. The United States, for instance, at the moment is increasing in population even more rapidly than India. The time when we thought that the mere increase in income would automatically solve the population problem has gone by. In the United States, and certain other societies, in the early stages of post-civilization, the child has become an object of conspicuous domestic consumption. The consumption patterns of the American spending unit seem to follow a certain *"gestalt"* in which household capital accumulates in a certain order, such as the first car, the first child, the washer and dryer, the second child, the deep freeze, the third child, the second car, the fourth child, and so on. The richer we get, the more children we can afford to have and the more children we do have. We now seem to be able to afford an average of something like four children per family, and as, in a post-civilized society, these four children all survive, the population doubles every generation. A hundred years of this and even the United States is going to find itself uncomfortably crowded. It can be argued, indeed, that from the point of view of the amenities of life we are already well beyond the optimum population.

The third trap on the road to post-civilization is the technological trap. Our present technology is fundamentally suicidal. It is based on the extraction of concentrated deposits of fossil fuels and ores, which in the nature of things are exhaustible. Even at present rates of consumption, they will be exhausted in a time span which is not very long measured against human history and which is infinitesimally small on the geological time scale. If the rest of the world advances to American standards of consumption, these resources will disappear almost overnight. On this view economic development is the process of bringing closer the evil day when everything will be gone—all the oil, the

coal, the ores—and we will have to go back to primitive agriculture and scratching in the woods.

There are indications, however, that suicidal technology is not
absolutely necessary and that a permanent high-level technology
is possible. Beginning in the early part of the twentieth century,
it is possible to detect an anti-entropic movement in technology.
This begins perhaps with the Haber process for the fixation of
nitrogen from the air. A development of similar significance is the
Dow process for the extraction of magnesium from the sea. Both
these processes take the diffuse and concentrate it, instead of
taking the concentrated and diffusing it, as do most processes of
mining and economic production. These anti-entropic processes
foreshadow a technology in which we shall draw all the materials
we need from the virtually inexhaustible reservoirs of the sea
and the air and draw our energy from controlled fusion—either
artificially produced on the earth or from the sun.

This is why I so much resent spending half the world's income
on armaments—because the more we do this, the less chance we
have of making the transition to a stable, high-level society. The
human race is in a precarious position on its planet and it should
act accordingly. It has a chance, never to be repeated, of making
its great transition, and if it fails, at least one good experiment
in intelligence will have gone to waste. I suppose there are similar
experiments of this nature going on in other parts of the universe;
but I must confess to a hopelessly anthropocentric prejudice in
favor of planet earth. It's a nice planet, and I'm in favor of it
and I have no desire to see its principal inhabitant blow it up
or starve it out.

When we look at the nature of possible remedies for our immediate problems, it seems clear that we all are engulfed in a
profound and appallingly dangerous misallocation of our intellectual resources. The misallocation lies in the fact that although
all our major problems are in social systems, we persist in regarding them as if they were essentially problems in physical or
biological systems. We persist in regarding agricultural problems,
for instance, as one of crops, whereas it is clearly fundamentally
a problem of farmers. We persist in regarding the flood-control
problem as a problem of the river and we even turn it over to
army engineers, who treat the river as an enemy. A flood, how-

ever, is no problem at all to a river. It is a perfectly normal part of its way of life. The flood, essentially, is a problem of people and of social institutions, of architecture and zoning. Professor Gilbert White, of the University of Chicago, suggests that after spending over four billion dollars on flood control in this country, we are more in danger of major disasters than we were before. What we really mean by flood control is the substitution of a major disaster every fifty or one hundred years for minor inconveniences every five or ten.

In national defense we have fallen into exactly the same trap. We regard this as a problem in physical systems and in hardware, whereas it is essentially a problem in social systems. Here again, we are building into our societies the eventual certainty of total disaster. In face of the fact that war and peace is the major problem of our age, we are putting practically nothing into peace research; even when we do put money into arms control and disarmament research we spend sixty million dollars for Project Vela, which deals wholly with physical systems, and one hundred and fifty thousand on Project Vulcan, which deals with social systems and with unanswerable questions at that. When we look at biological and medical research, and still more, research into population, the disparity is just as striking. We persist in regarding disease as a biological problem, whereas it is fundamentally a bio-social system. Yet the number of sociologists in our medical schools can be counted almost on the fingers of one hand.

Nevertheless, in spite of the dangers, it is a wonderful age to live in, and I would not wish to be born in any other time. The wonderful and precious thing about the present moment is that there is still time—the Bomb hasn't gone off, the population explosion may be caught, the technological problem can, perhaps, be solved. If the human race is to survive, however, it will have to change more in its ways of thinking in the next twenty-five years than it has done in the last twenty-five thousand. There is hope, however, in the fact that we are very far from having exhausted the capacity of this extraordinary organism that we call man. I once calculated the capacity of the human nervous system in terms of the number of different states it might assume, which is a very rough measure. This comes to two to the ten billionth power, assuming that each of our ten billion neurons is capable of only two states. This is a very large number. It would take you ninety years to write it down at the rate of one digit a second. If you want a standard of comparison, the total number of neutrinos, which are the smallest known particles, which could be packed into the known astronomical universe (this is the largest physical number I could think of) could easily be written down in three minutes. I find it hard to believe, therefore, that the capacity of the human organism has been exhausted.

What we have to do now, however, is to develop almost a new form of learning. We have to learn from rapidly changing systems. Ordinarily we learn from stable systems. It is because the world repeats itself that we catch on to the law of repetition. Learning from changing systems is perhaps another step in the acceleration of evolution that we have to take. I have been haunted by a remark which Norman Meier, the psychologist, made in a seminar a few months ago, when he said that a cat who jumps on a hot stove never jumps on a cold one. This seems precisely to describe the state we may be in today. We have jumped on a lot of hot stoves and now perhaps the cold stove is the only place on which to jump. In the rapidly changing system it is desperately easy to learn things which are no longer true. Perhaps the greatest task of applied social science at the moment is to study the conditions under which we learn from rapidly changing systems. If we can answer this question, there may still be hope for the human race.

THE PHANTOM CAPTAIN

by R. BUCKMINSTER FULLER

W<small>HAT</small> is that, mother?"
"It's a man, darling."
"What's a man?"

Man?

A self-balancing, 28-jointed adapter-base biped; an electro-chemical reduction-plant, integral with segregated stowages of special energy extracts in storage batteries, for subsequent actuation of thousands of hydraulic and pneumatic pumps, with motors attached; 62,000 miles of capillaries; millions of warning signal, railroad and conveyor systems; crushers and cranes (of which the arms are magnificent 23-jointed affairs with self-surfacing and lubricating systems, and a universally distributed telephone system needing no service for 70 years if well managed); the whole, extraordinarily complex mechanism guided with exquisite precision from a turret in which are located telescopic and microscopic self-registering and recording range finders, a spectroscope, *et cetera*, the turret control being closely allied with an air conditioning intake-and-exhaust, and a main fuel intake.

Within the few cubic inches housing the turret mechanisms, there is room, also, for two sound-wave and sound-direction-finder recording diaphragms, a filing and instant reference system, and an expertly devised analytical laboratory large enough not only to contain minute records of every last and continual event of up to 70 years' experience, or more, but to extend, by computation and abstract fabrication, this experience with relative accuracy into all corners of the observed universe. There is, also, a forecasting and tactical plotting department for the reduction of future possibilities and probabilities to generally successful specific choice.

Finally, the whole structure is not only directly and simply mobile on land and in water, but, indirectly and by exquisite precision of complexity, mobile in air, and, even in the intangible, mathematically sensed electrical "world," by means of the extension of the primary integral mechanism to secondary mechanical compositions of its own devising, operable either by a direct mechanical hook-up with the device, or by indirect control through wired or wire-less electrical impulses.

"A man," indeed! Dismissed with the appellation Mr. "Jones"!

Common to all such "human" mechanisms—and without which they are imbecile contraptions—is their guidance by a phantom captain.

This phantom captain has neither weight nor sensorial tangibility, as has often been scientifically proven by careful weighing operations at the moment of abandonment of the ship by the phantom captain, i.e., at the instant of "death." He may be likened to the variant of polarity dominance in our bipolar electric world which, when balanced and unit, vanishes as abstract unity I or O. With the phantom captain's departure, the mechanism becomes inoperative and very quickly disintegrates into basic chemical elements.

This captain has not only an infinite self-identity characteristic but, also, an infinite understanding. He has, furthermore, infinite sympathy with all captains of mechanisms similar to his.

What is this UNDERSTANDING? It consists in an intuitive, non-graphable awareness of perfection, or of unity, or of eternity, or of infinity, or of truth. This awareness of perfection serves as a universal yardstick relative to which any sense experience may be measured, and by virtue of which CONSCIOUS SELECTION may be made.

("This is a better pair of shoes." How does one know? Because it the more closely approximates a "perfect" pair—the "perfect" pair that will *never* hurt, wear out, become dirty, or have weight. "Perfect," though impossible of demonstration, is nonetheless the criterion of selection. "Perfect" is not only a *direction*, but a *time direction*, "perfection" being *never* in "reality" attainable. There is herein to be discerned the meaning of *Never, Never Land*. Children dream truly.)

By the process of conscious selection relative to sense of perfect, the segregation of such phenomena as sounds has developed, followed by the selective recomposition of the segregated sounds into specific sound-continuities, or "words" (sound symbols) provocative of basic understanding in others, adequate for the *moment*. No matter how relatively imperfect the articulation, or the receiver-conception, there is nonetheless some characteristic of "uniformity," though not of "identity," of understanding between sender and receiver. For instance, the word "cow," ("black-white," "daisy" or "bossy" are inconsequential) conveys the concept of a mechanical process which is substantially understood as a composite "cow"—the milk factory. Each phantom captain for himself, however, associates "cow" with the most vividly impressive cow of his particular experience, the speakers a Jersey, the listeners a Guernsey.

This infinite communicating code, based on processes and continuities and not on static fixation identities, enables the phantom captain to signal, via the complicated visual, aural and oral, tactile and olfactory systems of his machine, to captains of other machines, who receive the message through complementary mechanical systems of reception. The success of the transmission depends upon the relative degree of communicated understanding, i.e., upon how "time"-rationalizing vs. statically-reflexing the receiving captain may be.

Curiously, each captain is so impressed by the command of such an elaborate mechanism and one so excellently attuned to operation that it readily yields to his un-self-conscious guidance of its processes and instruments, that he feels himself thrillingly and virtually a part of it. Only when the parts are abused is there awareness of a seemingly separate presence of parts; for instance, when the tongue has been bitten or burned its motions are painful whereas normally it wags merrily, carelessly and unnoted.

Inevitably, the captain's habitual association of his infinite self with his subconsciously subservient mechanisms has inclined him to a dual "presumption": (1) that this mechanism is an ACTUAL (by extension) part of his phantom self, whereas it is purely an electro-chemical combination of inanimate energy molecules that are intrinsically the ship the phantom captain commands, and (2) an attitude of ownership: the mechanism of ordination for his will is "his" permanent "possession," whereas in reality it is only temporarily in his custody. This illusion of "possession" of the mechanism has been further extended, through accustomed relationship, to include "possession" of one's clothes, pencils, house in general, land, friends, wife and children, business, state, nation, world, and, finally, "God"—the last named quite naturally being "pictured" in the exclusively original form of his "own" egotistically important, special mechanistic and chemical process arrangement.

As the "possessor" of all of his extensions, the phantom captain automatically evolves a myriad of illusory necessities for which he assumes a vain, egotistical responsibility. This false-possession and always innocuous myth (which is consumptive of the complete lifetime, from four years onward, of the vast majority of people) stone-blinds the possessor to the simple, delightful truth-trends that are everywhere and at all times about us. For unspoilt children and happily debunked, emancipated grown-ups, these trends make life's courses as evident as a highway through a meadow. Ironically, the non-possession-blinded person's citation of evident trends has always been fearfully hailed as witchcraft, mysticism and quackery by the still mystified, self-be-quackeried majority.

The phantom captain is but mildly shaken in his preoccupation, or possession obsession, by the intermittent necessity of replacement of "his" parts, or by the dissection from, or application to, his mechanism by other phantom-captained mechanisms of such service parts as crude gold inlays inserted in "his" raw fuel crushers, additional lenses or color-filters for "his" range-finders, or an enema bag douching nozzle temporarily passed into "his" clogged canal. The inlay or the douche bag is, temporarily at least, as factually connected to self as a toenail, tooth, hair, or eyeball.

This continual arrogation of "his" mechanisms is closely allied with the captain's habitual assumption that all objects are "seen" at locations outside the phantom captain's mechanism, whereas actually the captain "sees" them inside his turret through his peritelescopic range finders. A long history of mechanical reliability—attested by frequent accurate measurements of the deduced range of, and direction to, an object's external location with the ability to move a crane grappler into an assumed location so that contact with the discovered object is provided, and further attested by the receipt in the turret of affirmative telephone reports, from several of the myriad contact alarms in the crane grappler—seems to justify the captain's habit of thinking "I SEE IT OVER THERE."

The phantom captain's habitual notion not only that he is part of "his" mechanisms but that the mechanisms are himself, is extended still further. He frequently confuses the surface characteristics of other "observed" mechanisms, similar to those he controls, with the identities of the phantom captains controlling them. Forgetting the true, infinite *phantom* character of the other captains, he "logically" evolves two additional illusions: One of these is that the commanded mechanism of the other captain is all that there is to that other phantom captain; the other is that the *surface* is all there is to that mechanism. In other words, he assumes that the tangible surface of the "other" "person" *is* that person's phantom captain, and that this *surface alone* is "reality." (This is the "reality" of the "practical" minded or materialism-dominated personality.) So he customarily interprets the behavior characteristics of the whole of another's mechanism by surface clues only; there has actually developed a language in terms of surface reflexing.

To illustrate: If Mr. and Mrs. Murphy, out for a walk with baby Tim, were to see a plane flying overhead, they might readily exclaim to "darling," "See that aviator!" They might easily be wrong. Planes are being ably controlled by radio without a human pilot on board.

An illuminating rationalization indicates that *captains*—being phantom, abstract, infinite, and bound to other captains by a bond of understanding as proven by their recognition of each other's signals and the meaning thereof by reference to a common direction (toward "perfect")—*are not only all related, but are one and the same captain.* Mathematically, since characteristics of unity exist, they cannot be non-identical.

The phantom captain's *executive officer,* yclept "brain," is a mechanistic device similar to the metal "mike" of the Sperry gyroscope, whose gyroscopic directional-insistence, useful though it is while the captain is absent from the bridge is nonetheless provocative, if unwatched, of habit grooves of motion.

When the complexity of the metal "mike" currently used in aeroplanes and aboard ship in hands-off navigation is compared with that of the "mike" or "brain" of the human phantom-captained mechanism, it is as though one contrasted an Ingersoll watch and a battleship, in the matter of number of parts and precision of operation, except that the human "mike" is as small in relation to the metal "mike" as are the new complex seven-element, glass-lined metal radio tubes "small" in relation to their crude, large three-element forerunners.

The "mike" of the human ship may be "set" by the phantom captain to detect the slightest lack of balance, not only in every one of the ship's external relationships but in all of its interior synchronizing mechanisms. So many settings does "mike" carry, at most times, that he seems ALIVE, and he is so satisfactory to the captain that the latter flies the human ship "hands-off" much of the time. This possibility of hands-off flying encourages the phantom captain to regard the "mikes" of other phantom captains, also, as almost alive—that is, animate rather than animated.

Such a mistaken assumption of surface clues for reality must inevitably lead to a myriad of misunderstanding and erroneous conclusions, into "blind alleys" and "dead end" streets. This is just what happens when (rationalization of an illusion being *ipso facto* impossible and illusion being no further extensible, on the occasion of "death" or the abandonment of a mechanism) those "individuals" whose captains are still at their posts and who are still confusing themselves with the mechanism they are directing, ceremoniously "bury" the abandoned, now disintegrating mechanism under the impression that it is the captain whom they "honor." They might as well bury the can opener that "he" customarily used and which he regarded as "his." Indeed, it would honor the phantom captain more to bury his can opener, since it is a device rationally objectivized by him and is, therefore, more directly creditable to him than the involuntary custody and management of the unit mechanism he had under "his" control. The cans he opened might, also, be honored by burial in dirt.

There are two main types of phantom-captained mechanisms, differing only in their machinery for the reproduction of miniature replicas of themselves (a manufacturing process). The union of these complementary types, or "plants," allows the electro-chemical processing of raw materials into infinitely elaborate, replica structures and instrument ensembles.

There are, of course, innumerable subtypes of the male and female main types, varying widely in external color, size, smell and textural characteristics. In fact, no two are physically identical, although they are miraculously *uniform* from a mechanical, chemical, structural, and process characteristic viewpoint, even to the maintenance of an identical thermal characteristic which, when the machine is in proper running order, is 98.6° F. under most highly diversified exterior environment conditions.

When one of the phantom captains seeks a mechanism of the complementary type to join with his in the manufacture of an improved model replica of their mutual custody mechanisms, he misinterprets his un-self-conscious appraisal of the adequacy of the observed complement to his "own" half-plant as constituting suitable hook-up conditions in the terms of superficial or sen-sorial-surface-satisfactions. The result is often the peculiarly amusing selective sound-wave emission, through the major exit-entrance aperture of the turret, "BEAUTIFUL!"

Phantom captains have fallen into such a careless mythology of surface words and nicknames, to excuse slothfulness in telegraph-ing accurately the observed external phenomena to the turret laboratories, that, although Murphy's phantom captain meant by "beautiful" that he had noted in Julia a mechanism that was highly uniform, i.e., not deformed, and, therefore, so far as he was concerned one that was favorable for plant hook-up, he probably further elaborated inaccurately and meaninglessly, "Julia is the MOST BEAUTIFUL girl in the world!" (The writer does not mean to infer that he does not say "beautiful," and believes that he means it, over and over again.) Murphy also probably would say, "My Julia is a PEARL!" and send her a "rose," the latter being a broken-off portion of another highly intricate, phantom-captained mechanism, but of so relatively wide non-identity with the "Julia" mechanism as to allow of its becoming a "living" sacrifice on the altar of the Julia manufactur-ing-plant worship.

Had Murphy failed at first to convince Julia of favorable con-ditions for plant hook-up, through surface clues observable by her, he would not have ceased his campaign. No, he would have sought to impose on Julia an *illusion* of satisfactory surface clues, by altering his surface conditions—such as adding to the size of his turret with a new "fedora," or subtracting from its size by cutting off part of his hair—just as Julia, were the situation reversed, would have "dressed ship" in velvet "washed down" with attar of roses.

It has been but a step from false adornment and artificial surface extensions of the human body, in the matter of clothing, to shelter; and from shelter to the myriad tools and instruments that were rationally evolved at an earlier time by the phantom captain in the extension of his own mechanism. The tools were born of the necessity to perform a specific function either with greater precision or with greater leverage than could be effected by the integral mechanism of the primary machine,—a tooth-pick, for instance, is better than a fingernail for tooth-picking and is more expeditiously replaceable.

The Murphys are not content, as their "wealth" (mechanical extensions) increases, with simple tooth-picks. Unless completely bereft of "hook-up" potentials, they will probably go in for gold tooth-picks, even gold filagreed tooth-picks, "individualistic" tooth-picks; embroidered roofs and arches; tattooed everythings.

So pleased are human beings by the artifices with which they constantly attain *self*-satisfaction, *despite* bad hook-up conditions, that they experience a constant urge to evolve codes of morals, ethics and laws for the purpose of making permanent the conditions of self-satisfaction that they have attained by artificiality. Out of these morals, ethics, artifices and vanities have been evolved so many "mike" sayings or brainistic words, that, although they are utterly meaningless from the viewpoint of the true phantom captain, they constitute 99% of today's broadcast, printed and person-to-person communication.

The artificial illusion extensions provided by the momentum of the gyroscopic "mike" display a wide range in various races variously located. For instance, when Doctor Jung, able student of psychology, made an extensive visit to Africa for the purpose of carrying on basic psychologic studies, he discovered that the primitive people there demonstrated a most interesting seemingly factual illusion extension from their simple experience memory storage. What had been regarded as purely ghost or demon fabrications, inherited through mythical tradition, proved to be none other than vivid memory concepts. When a leader or a parent died, the people had such simple, clear, visual memory pictures of the deceased that they were able satisfactorily to objectivize him as though still in bodily presence. In other words, they simply reversed our particular civilization's assumption that we SEE objects at a point EXTERNAL to our self-mechanism, although, in fact, the seeing is done, not even in the eye but in the brain or reception end of the nervous system that records the exterior light reflections.

Jung found, also, that African primitives, in common with others throughout the world, have such a simple cosmic problem that they have only two categories of numbers, *viz.*, *"one"* or *"many."* Because they "SEE" either "one" or "many," they have evolved fabulous legendary stories. They recognize that one stranger may be readily matched in physical combat, whereas two or more may be overpowering. So two or three or more strangers are "seen" as hordes, the fear instinct warning the beholder of the risk of being overcome. Combining this "seeing" of either "one" or "many" with the extension of a SEEN factual memory form of a father or leader calls forth the illusion of the close proximity of multitudes of fathers, leaders, demons, *et cetera*.

There is, also, a tracery of the simple number sense limitation in certain old cultures. In Chinese, for example, one carriage is a carriage, many carriages are "noise." The Chinese symbol of "tree" is one tree; "two trees" equals "woods," and "three trees" constitute a "forest"—one, few, many.

Jung had the strange experience of noticing that, while he was endeavoring to understand primitive illusions, his own particular modern civilization's illusion broke down to such an extent that he, too, began to "see" partially in terms of the primitive illusion and partially in his own earlier illusion, with the result that he seemed to himself almost to be crazy, for there was no reliability in any illusion.

In connection with the phantom captain's illusion that the mechanisms of his survival are an intrinsic part of his abstract self, it is to be noted that every physical extension has been a matter of survival adequacy in the phantom captain's command of specific animal and vegetable species. It might almost be said that a new "type" of human animal has developed in the United States and that this type is by way of being an advance demonstration of a world-wide type, inasmuch as the evidences are all in terms of scientific world trends. When a sufficient number of members of a species has become characterized by relatively identical extensions, these extensions may properly be called part and parcel of the "being"-entity of that species.

If we will admit that a section of Julia's hair is just as much Julia's hair after it is cut off as it was when on her head—and it certainly is as much Julia as is the name "Julia," which is a most arbitrary appendage—we must admit, also, that if Julia's cut-off hair were woven into a fabric and worn on her head in the form of a hat, everything in the ensemble would still be "Julia." This would apply equally to any other hat that Julia might don or to the pigment which, for improved hook-up allure, she might apply to her lips and cheeks. Everything that Julia uses in her sometimes by-seeming selection, and again by-inadvertence choice, is "Julia."

The phantom captain of the butterfly has a great variety of mechanical externals for survival, but the apparently different stages of moth-caterpillar-chrysalis-butterfly in no way alter the identity of the phantom captain, which persists as unity throughout. Similarly, at sea, the various ships that Captain "Smith" commands are known to his contemporary skippers simply as "Smith." As Smith's ship, the *Mary*, appears on the horizon they exclaim, "Here comes Smith!" Smith may change commands but the other skippers will continue to say, "Here comes Smith!" whenever they recognize the externals of the ship he happens currently to be commanding.

In the United States passenger automobiles number approximately one per family, and the head of the family is usually the driver thereof. So accelerated are the time-space characteristics of the auto in comparison to the time-space covering ability of the man on legs that every reflex characteristic of the phantom captain of the driver is amplified in direct proportion to the time-space differential between the car's and the unmounted driver's tactical maneuvering ability. People who are not recognized as nervous or physically unbalanced while walking and talking are often seen to be distinctly so in their operation of an automobile. The traffic manners and ethics of people while driving reveal their character as a whole far more readily than would their cultivated mannerisms and behavior while walking.

Holding the full significance of this thought in mind, one can suddenly comprehend, while driving along a heavy traffic artery, that the automobiles seen are extensions of their drivers, just as are the "drivers" hats, coats, shoes and faces; it is the progression of boxes within boxes of childhood play. Accepting this rationalization of man's unity extending into his automobile, it may be said that the average young working American man now weighs better than a ton, since the average automobile weighs 2800 lbs., and that the composite American extensible into his group mechanisms (aeroplane, railroad train, the *Normandie*, and Boulder Dam) is larger by millions of times than any historical animate organism. It is quite possible that Lewis Carroll was writing the poetry of this concept in *Alice Through the Looking-Glass*.

There is another interesting phase of the phantom captain phenomenon. There is to be distinguished in the current era—as differentiated from the early crafts period of individual survival without the aid of mechanical extensions—a set of mechanisms, such as the power dynamo in the city, mutually commanded by phantom captains. When either Julia or Murph' pushes a certain button, the act serves to bring about a mechanical extension of the visual ability of both, although "seeing," let us remember, occurs within the turret and not externally to the mechanism of the phantom captain. This introduces an extraordinary rationalization, namely: Industrial mechanisms so gargantuan as to be without warrant as an extension of any one person are justifiable as extensions of multitudes of persons, proving to mathematical satisfaction that all people, of a species characterized by participation in the use of such mutual extension mechanisms, are one and the same person at the time of such utilization.

This conception of the phantom captain leads to a viewpoint quite the opposite of the "mechanistic" bogey so fearfully heralded and decried in recent years because of an apprehension that the man-created machine will overpower man somewhat as would a Frankenstein monster.

The thrilling inference of the phantom captaincy conception is that it not only precludes the possibility of the operation of extended machinery without the volition of inner man, but that the unit mechanisms are doing for man what politics has consistently failed to accomplish.

Industrial man, being unit, can only be effective in the direction of his own best survival interest.

SCIENCE AND TECHNOLOGY:
A FRAMEWORK FOR SPECULATION

---

by HERMAN KAHN and
ANTHONY J. WIENER

In order to provide a quick impression of science and technology (with an emphasis on technology) in the last third of the twentieth century, we list below one hundred areas in which it is probable that technological innovation will occur in the next thirty-three years.

Each item in the list has the following characteristics:

(1) It is important enough to make, by itself, a significant change in the next thirty-three years. The difference might lie mainly in being spectacular (e.g., transoceanic rocket transportation in twenty or thirty minutes rather than supersonic in two or three hours); in being ubiquitous (e.g., widespread use of paper clothes); in enabling a large number of different things to be done (e.g., super materials);

"Science and Technology: A Framework for Speculation," reprinted with permission of The Macmillan Company from *The Year 2000: A Framework for Speculation on the Next Thirty-Three Years* by Herman Kahn and Anthony J. Wiener. Copyright © 1967 by The Hudson Institute, Inc.

in a general and significant increase in productivity (e.g., cybernation); or simply in being important to specific individuals (e.g., convenient artificial kidneys).

(2) A responsible opinion can be found to argue a great likelihood that the innovation will be achieved before the year 2000—usually long before. (We would probably agree with about 90-95 per cent of these estimates.)

(3) Each warrants the description technological innovation, revolution, or breakthrough. None is simply an obvious minor improvement on what currently exists.

The list is deliberately eclectic and disordered because this communicates a more accurate description of what we know about these future possibilities than the superficial appearance of order and understanding that would be given by a somewhat differently ordered list. Indeed, since serendipities and unexpected synergisms play an important role, reading this eclectic and disordered list is almost a simulation of the process of innovation and diffusion.

We should also note that the one hundred areas are not entirely randomly ordered. Most people would consider the first twenty-five as (largely) unambiguous examples of progress or human benefit. A few would question even these. The first item, for example, lasers and masers, might make possible a particularly effective kind of ballistic missile defense, and thus, some believe, could accelerate the Soviet-American arms race. Or the expansion of tropical agriculture and forestry, as suggested in the eighth item, could mean a geographical shift in economic and military power as well as a dislocation of competitive industries. Indeed nearly all the areas of innovation could involve adjustment difficulties of this kind. Nevertheless there probably would be a consensus among readers that the first twenty-five areas do represent progress—at least for those who are in favor of "progress."

The next twenty-five innovations would clearly have controversial consequences; many would argue that government policy might better restrain or discourage innovation or diffusion here. These twenty-five "controversial areas" raise issues of accelerated nuclear proliferation; of loss of privacy; of excessive governmental and/or private power over individuals; of dangerously vulnerable, deceptive, and degradable overcentralization; of decisions becoming necessary that are too large, complex, important, uncertain, or comprehensive to be left to mere mortals (whether acting privately or publicly, individually or in organizations); of new capabilities that are so inherently dangerous that they are likely to be disastrously abused; of too rapid or cataclysmic change for smooth adjustment, and so on.

The last fifty items are included in part because they are intrinsically interesting and in part to demonstrate that it is fairly easy to produce a long list of items of innovation that entail nontrivial consequences.

One Hundred Technical Innovations Very Likely in the Last Third of the Twentieth Century

1. Multiple applications of lasers and masers for sensing, measuring, communication, cutting, heating, welding, power transmission, illumination, destructive (defensive), and other purposes
2. Extremely high-strength and/or high-temperature structural materials
3. New or improved super-performance fabrics (papers, fibers, and plastics)
4. New or improved materials for equipment and appliances (plastics, glasses, alloys, ceramics, intermetallics, and cermets)
5. New airborne vehicles (ground-effect machines, VTOL and STOL, superhelicopters, giant and/or supersonic jets)
6. Extensive commercial application of shaped-charge explosives
7. More reliable and longer-range weather forecasting
8. Intensive and/or extensive expansion of tropical agriculture and forestry
9. New sources of power for fixed installations (e.g., magnetohydrodynamic, thermionic and thermo-electric, and radioactivity)
10. New sources of power for ground transportation (storage-battery, fuel-cell, propulsion [or support] by electromagnetic fields, jet engine, turbine, and the like)
11. Extensive and intensive world-wide use of high-altitude cameras for mapping, prospecting, census, land use, and geological investigations
12. New methods of water transportation (such as large submarines, flexible and special-purpose "container ships," or more extensive use of large automated single-purpose bulk cargo ships)
13. Major reduction in hereditary and congenital defects

14. Extensive use of cyborg techniques (mechanical aids or sub-stitutes for human organs, senses, limbs, or other components)
15. New techniques for preserving or improving the environment
16. Relatively effective appetite and weight control
17. New techniques and institutions for adult education
18. New and useful plant and animal species
19. Human "hibernation" for short periods (hours or days) for medical purposes
20. Inexpensive design and procurement of "one of a kind" items through use of computerized analysis and automated production
21. Controlled and/or super-effective relaxation and sleep
22. More sophisticated architectural engineering (e.g., geodesic domes, fancy "stressed" shells, pressurized skins, and esoteric materials)
23. New or improved uses of the oceans (mining, extraction of min-erals, controlled "farming," source of energy, and the like)
24. Three-dimensional photography, illustrations, movies, and tele-vision
25. Automated or more mechanized housekeeping and home main-tenance
26. Widespread use of nuclear reactors for power
27. Use of nuclear explosives for excavation and mining, generation of power, creation of high-temperature—high-pressure environ-ments, and/or as a source of neutrons or other radiation
28. General use of automation and cybernation in management and production
29. Extensive and intensive centralization (or automatic intercon-nection) of current and past personal and business information in high-speed data processors
30. Other new and possibly pervasive techniques for surveillance, monitoring, and control of individuals and organizations
31. Some control of weather and/or climate
32. Other (permanent or temporary) changes—or experiments—with the over-all environment (e.g., the "permanent" increase in C-14 and temporary creation of other radioactivity by nu-clear explosions, the increasing generation of CO_2 in the at-mosphere, projects Starfire, West Ford, and Storm Fury)
33. New and more reliable "educational" and propaganda tech-niques for affecting human behavior—public and private
34. Practical use of direct electronic communication with and stim-ulation of the brain
35. Human hibernation for relatively extensive periods (months to years)

36. Cheap and widely available central war weapons and weapons systems
37. New and relatively effective counterinsurgency techniques (and perhaps also insurgency techniques)
38. New techniques for very cheap, convenient, and reliable birth control
39. New, more varied, and more reliable drugs for control of fatigue, relaxation, alertness, mood, personality, perceptions, fantasies, and other psychobiological states
40. Capability to choose the sex of unborn children
41. Improved capability to "change" sex of children and/or adults
42. Other genetic control and/or influence over the "basic constitution" of an individual
43. New techniques and institutions for the education of children
44. General and substantial increase in life expectancy, postponement of aging, and limited rejuvenation
45. Generally acceptable and competitive synthetic foods and beverages (e.g., carbohydrates, fats, proteins, enzymes, vitamins, coffee, tea, cocoa, and alcoholic liquor)
46. "High quality" medical care for underdeveloped areas (e.g., use of medical aides and technicians, referral hospitals, broadspectrum antibiotics, and artificial blood plasma)
47. Design and extensive use of responsive and super-controlled environments for private and public use (for pleasurable, educational, and vocational purposes)
48. Physically "nonharmful" methods of "overindulging"
49. Simple techniques for extensive and "permanent" cosmetological changes (features, "figures," perhaps complexion and even skin color, and even physique)
50. More extensive use of transplantation of human organs
51. Permanent manned satellite and lunar installations—interplanetary travel
52. Application of space life systems or similar techniques to terrestrial installations
53. Permanent inhabited undersea installations and perhaps even colonies
54. Automated grocery and department stores
55. Extensive use of robots and machines "slaved" to humans
56. New uses of underground "tunnels" for private and public transportation and other purposes
57. Automated universal (real time) credit, audit, and banking systems

58. Chemical methods for improving memory and learning
59. Greater use of underground buildings
60. New and improved materials and equipment for buildings and interiors (e.g., variable transmission glass, heating and cooling by thermo-electric effect, and electroluminescent and phosphorescent lighting)
61. Widespread use of cryogenics
62. Improved chemical control of some mental illnesses and some aspects of senility
63. Mechanical and chemical methods for improving human analytical ability more or less directly
64. Inexpensive and rapid techniques for making tunnels and underground cavities in earth and/or rock
65. Major improvements in earth moving and construction equipment generally
66. New techniques for keeping physically fit and/or acquiring physical skills
67. Commercial extraction of oil from shale
68. Recoverable boosters for economic space launching
69. Individual flying platforms
70. Simple inexpensive home video recording and playing
71. Inexpensive high-capacity, world-wide, regional, and local (home and business) communication (perhaps using satellites, lasers, and light pipes)
72. Practical home and business use of "wired" video communication for both telephone and TV (possibly including retrieval of taped material from libraries or other sources) and rapid transmission and reception of facsimiles (possibly including news, library material, commercial announcements, instantaneous mail delivery, other printouts, and so on)
73. Practical large-scale desalinization
74. Pervasive business use of computers for the storage, processing, and retrieval of information
75. Shared-time (public and interconnected?) computers generally available to home and business on a metered basis
76. Other widespread use of computers for intellectual and professional assistance (translation, teaching, literature search, medical diagnosis, traffic control, crime detection, computation, design, analysis, and, to some degree, as intellectual collaborator generally)
77. General availability of inexpensive transuranic and other esoteric elements

78. Space defense systems
79. Inexpensive and reasonably effective ground-based BMD [ballistic missile defense]
80. Very low-cost buildings for home and business use
81. Personal "pagers" (perhaps even two-way pocket phones) and other personal electronic equipment for communication, computing, and data-processing program
82. Direct broadcasts from satellites to home receivers
83. Inexpensive (less than $20), long-lasting, very small battery-operated TV receivers
84. Home computers to "run" the household and communicate with outside world
85. Maintenance-free, long-life electronic and other equipment
86. Home education via video and computerized and programmed learning
87. Stimulated and planned and perhaps programmed dreams
88. Inexpensive (less than 1 cent a page), rapid, high-quality black and white reproduction; followed by color and high-detailed photography reproduction—perhaps for home as well as office use
89. Widespread use of improved fluid amplifiers
90. Conference TV (both closed-circuit and public communication systems)
91. Flexible penology without necessarily using prisons (by use of modern methods of surveillance, monitoring, and control)
92. Common use of (longlived?) individual power source for lights, appliances, and machines
93. Inexpensive world-wide transportation of humans and cargo
94. Inexpensive road-free (and facility-free) transportation
95. New methods for rapid language teaching
96. Extensive genetic control for plants and animals
97. New biological and chemical methods to identify, trace, incapacitate, or annoy people for police and military uses
98. New and possibly very simple methods for lethal biological and chemical warfare
99. Artificial moons and other methods for lighting large areas at night
100. Extensive use of "biological processes" in the extraction and processing of minerals

The following are areas in which technological success by the year 2000 seems substantially less likely (even money bets, give or take a factor of five), but where, if it occurred, it would be quite important, are these:

Some Less Likely but Important Possibilities

1. "True" artificial intelligence
2. Practical use of sustained fusion to produce neutrons and/or energy
3. Artificial growth of new limbs and organs (either in situ or for later transplantation)
4. Room temperature superconductors
5. Major use of rockets for commercial or private transportation (either terrestrial or extraterrestrial)
6. Effective chemical or biological treatment for most mental illnesses
7. Almost complete control of marginal changes in heredity
8. Suspended animation (for years or centuries)
9. Practical materials with nearly "theoretical limit" strength
10. Conversion of mammals (humans?) to fluid breathers
11. Direct input into human memory banks
12. Direct augmentation of human mental capacity by the mechanical or electrical interconnection of the brain with a computer
13. Major rejuvenation and/or significant extension of vigor and life span—say 100 to 150 years
14. Chemical or biological control of character or intelligence
15. Automated highways
16. Extensive use of moving sidewalks for local transportation
17. Substantial manned lunar or planetary installations
18. Electric power available for less than .3 mill per kilowatt hour
19. Verification of some extrasensory phenomena
20. Planetary engineering
21. Modification of the solar system
22. Practical laboratory conception and nurturing of animal (human?) foetuses
23. Production of a drug equivalent to Huxley's soma
24. A technological equivalent of telepathy
25. Some direct control of individual thought processes

We list below ten radical possibilities, some of which hardly make sense. We do not believe that any of them will occur by the year 2000, or perhaps ever. But some of them are discussed today; and such a list does emphasize the fact that some dramatic and radical innovation must be expected. The list may suggest how surprising and exciting (or outrageous) such an event might prove.

Ten Far-Out Possibilities

1. Life expectancy extended to substantially more than 150 years (immortality?)
2. Almost complete genetic control (but still homo sapiens)
3. Major modification of human species (no longer homo sapiens)
4. Antigravity (or practical use of gravity waves)*
5. Interstellar travel
6. Electric power available for less than .03 mill per kilowatt hour
7. Practical and routine use of extrasensory phenomena
8. Laboratory creation of artificial live plants and animals
9. Lifetime immunization against practically all diseases
10. Substantial lunar or planetary bases or colonies

And finally there is the possibility—more far-fetched than popular science fiction would have it, but impossible to exclude—of a discovery of extraterrestrial life; or, much more extreme, of communication with extraterrestrial intelligence.

These lists make only the obvious point that as a result of the long-term trends toward accumulation of scientific and technological knowledge and the institutionalization of change through research, development, innovation, and diffusion, many important new things are likely to happen in the next few decades. It is worth while asking specifically what the consequences of each item—and their synergistic interactions—might be.**

---

* As usually envisaged this would make possible a perpetual motion machine and therefore the creation of energy out of nothing. We do not envisage this as even a far-out possibility, but include antigravity, even though it annoys some physicist friends, as an example of some totally new use of a basic phenomena or the seeming violation of a basic law.

** Implications of technological prospects are discussed further in *The Year 2000*, Chapters II and VIII, and in the essay that follows here.

FAUSTIAN PROGRESS

by ANTHONY J. WIENER

In *The Year 2000*, Herman Kahn and I described a "basic, long-term, multifold trend" that has increasingly characterized Western societies in recent centuries and seems likely to continue for some time. Processes such as economic and technological development, each facilitating the other, have become routinely—one might even say inexorably—cumulative. It is notorious that as a result the rate of change of many aspects of social life has become exponential; nor is it likely that many of the changes that are in process will begin to decelerate during the next thirty-three years.

To speak, to use tools, and to pass on learning; to put energy sources to human use; to gather food, fuel, and clothing for winter; to save, invest, plan, build, and innovate in order to decrease dangers and insecurities and to increase the power to change natural things to suit one's purposes: in sum, to render nature subject to human will—such have been the results, if not the goals, of eons of striving. Success in this sense seems to be at hand. As we approach the beginning of the twenty-first century, our capacities for, and commitment to, economic development and technological control over our environment seem to be increasing without foreseeable limit.

These accomplishments are the results of persistent and concerted effort and intelligence, and on the whole they are occasions for satisfaction. To increase economic development is to increase the availability of at least some of the things that people need

"Faustian Progress," by Anthony J. Wiener. Copyright © 1967 by The Hudson Institute, Inc. Reprinted by permission of the author from the November, 1967, issue of *Natural History*.

The author wishes to acknowledge his debt to Morton A. Kaplan, who collaborated in portions of the work from which this article was drawn. This article is part of a continuing series being prepared at The Hudson Institute.

and want. To develop technologically is to increase the capacity to achieve at least some human purposes that are widespread and legitimate. Clearly it is worthwhile to overcome the deprivations of economic scarcity and the dangers and frustrations of impotence before the forces of nature.

Yet the capacities of our culture and institutions to adapt to so much change in so comparatively short a time may be a major question; the stresses in domestic societies and in the international system may not be managed sufficiently by meliorist policies. Since the underdeveloped countries are even further removed in industrial and social life from these new technologies than we are, the cultural shock of their partial adaptation to the new technologies may prove even greater. The possibility must be faced that man's unremitting, Faustian striving may ultimately remake his natural conditions—environmental, social, and psychobiological—so far as to begin to dehumanize himself or to degrade his political or ecological situation in some costly or even irrevocable manner.

While it is usually desirable to solve old problems even when the solutions themselves give rise to new problems, it has become increasingly clear that our technological and even our economic achievements are mixed blessings. Through progress such threats arise as the accumulation, augmentation, and proliferation of weapons of mass destruction; the loss of privacy and solitude; the increase of governmental and/or private power over individuals; the loss of human scale and perspective and the dehumanization of social life or even of the psychobiological self; the growth of dangerously vulnerable, deceptive, or degradable centralization of administrative or technological systems; the creation of other new capabilities so inherently dangerous as seriously to risk disastrous abuse; and the acceleration of changes that are too rapid or cataclysmic to permit successful adjustment. Perhaps most crucial, choices are posed that are too large, complex, important, uncertain, or comprehensive to be safely left to fallible humans.

One would not wish to arrest the process of technological advancement, perhaps not even slow it down, for it is valuable. There is a widespread response to problems of technology, in which the artifacts themselves become the targets of hostility; surely it would be more useful to criticize human choice, in which technology plays but a passive, instrumental role. Nor do we find plausible the prevalent rhetoric to the effect that technology is about to open gates either to heaven or to hell, that technology now presents man with some simple and decisive choice between immolation and utopias. The latter may sometimes be hard to tell from "brave new worlds"; evils may not be stark and obvious, but subtle, slow acting, uncertain, and well distributed among all the available options.

Our purpose, then, is not to view technological and economic prospects of the next thirty-three years with alarm; to try to arouse a humanistic reaction against the forces of change. We are, on the whole, optimistic, but we wish to call attention to one of the problems that is already becoming discernible and that could —if social responses are not adequate—lead to very bad results. Specifically, we are referring to some ways in which technology might come between man and nature so as to change man's relationship not only with his ecosystem but with himself and his society.

Increasing wealth and leisure and improved technology are unlikely to have the exclusively beneficial results that are often naïvely assumed today. A principal danger in the situation is that a series of decisions can be taken separately for good reasons and yet produce an ultimate condition that—had it been foreseen— no one would have wanted.

Practically all the major technological changes since the beginnings of industrialization have resulted in unforeseen and unwanted consequences that were not taken into account at the beginning of the process. Most obvious has been the "fouling of the nest": the ecological damage done by the accumulation of the waste products—oxides, isotopes, dirt, and junk—of industrial society. Although this is part of the price we have willingly paid for economic progress, too many of the costs of previous pollution and depredation of resources now seem likely to fall on current and future generations.

Another dramatic example is provided by the advances in public health that helped to bring about the population explosion, primarily by dramatically reducing infant mortality in countries with very high birthrates. The ultimate cost of this medical progress in terms of human suffering in much of the underdeveloped world (doomed to remain underdeveloped unless it can reduce population growth) may eventually far exceed the suffering that would have occurred without such progress. Yet people are unwilling to give up medical progress or to refuse it to populations where too many babies are born; indeed, most would judge such action immoral.

It is likely that ways will continue to be developed to prolong human life by means of artificial organs and even, perhaps, through computerized substitutes for damaged (e.g., senile) portions of brains. This raises very starkly several ethical issues, including the possibility of dehumanizing people. While each advance in the capacity to prolong lives is welcomed for good reason, ultimately there is a danger of blurring the difference between human and non-human entities. If this occurs it becomes plausible that a dehumanized view of partly human beings (and, by extension, of all human beings) will be adopted. As humanoid equipment is evolved, maintained, and repaired for various special purposes, it may come to seem appropriate and reasonable to "phase out" this equipment as those purposes change. What begins as an expression of the value of the individual human life could easily become a step toward the treatment of men as objects, manipulatable or even disposable as social purposes dictate.

The possibility of a serious invasion of privacy by the government (or by private individuals) is raised by the rapid progress toward centralized data processing for government, business, and personal record keeping. This is clearly a serious problem, and while some discussion has involved apocalyptic language, we agree that without adequate safeguards some of these warnings may prove justified. Indeed it is possible that such problems will be raised not as a by-product of normal commercial and governmental operations, but because there has been special design and procurement of systems for the surveillance, monitoring, and control of individuals.

It is already possible to monitor conversations by the disturbances they produce on windowpanes and to photograph documents through windows and at great distances. Then, it is not difficult to imagine the large-scale "bugging" of future conversations, which could then be rapidly scanned by computers. These computers would be capable of detecting certain special interest criteria (use of words such as *bet, kill, black power, oppose, revolution*; signs such as angry gestures, threatening voice tones, etc.) indicating whether or not the conversations should be recorded for further analysis. TV monitors both indoors and out may become common as the techniques become cheaper. It may turn out that only those with enormous resources will be able—and then only partly and perhaps only by bribery or political manipulation—to avoid some monitoring or to interfere with transmission of the data. At the minimum, if the monitoring exists, new code languages will develop in efforts to evade some of the consequences.

One standard cliché of the literature of social planning emphasizes that complex societies are more vulnerable to disruption than simple societies. The complex society has greater instantaneous and long-range flexibility, though less useful redundancy; and more bottlenecks could affect it. Thus it may be more affected by major interruptions that overwhelm its instantaneous or short-run adjustment capability before the long-range flexibility has a chance to work. Unlike the simple society, the modern industrial society is highly differentiated and therefore requires great integration in order to function. A disrupted complex society, at least under some important conditions, may not be able even to sustain the low level of productivity that is normal to a simple society.

Greater wealth and improved technology give us a wider range of alternatives; but once an alternative has been chosen, much regulation and imposed order is needed. Thus, geometric increase in the complexity and organization of modern life will necessitate corresponding, even if not directly proportional, increases in the scope and complexity of human and organizational controls. One need not assume the triumph of the police mentality, or the intrusion of motivation that denigrates human dignity, to foresee this. Each restriction will have its valid and attractive rationale, which may even be libertarian. Federal safety regulations for automobile manufacturers and tests for drivers today increase the "freedom" of the license-holding driver to drive in safety. Coercive treatment for the mentally ill raises the probability that they will be able to lead freely constructive lives. Therapeutic abortions, through the death of the fetus, increase the freedom of the mother. And the biological adaptation of man to his ecological niche in an extremely complicated and over populated society will increase his freedom to live a satisfying and useful life.

We have, of course, omitted the crucial qualification, under the existent conditions. It is still possible that the terminus of the process may be inconsistent with anything we would regard as freedom or dignity, or even human. The evolution of society may produce the devolution of man. The adaptability (and superiority) of man has heretofore consisted in his lack of specialized adaptation (as in the case of the lesser animals). Man may, in the not too distant future, be adapted in a specialized sense, while society through the control of genetic science maintains its general adaptability by fitting men to the varying tasks that time and environment provide. (Thus, as Morton A. Kaplan put it, "the survival of the fittest may be replaced by the fitting of the survivors.")

It would be clearly erroneous to compare man to the lemming, but every known animal species on which experimental overcrowding has been carried out is dysfunctionally disorganized. Rules governing mutual adjustment will inevitably be very stringent, and there will be a strong emphasis on adjustment (other-directed orientations) in place of individualism. Resort to drugs, other-world religions, delinquency, crime, and mental disease (as ways of "opting out") could increase significantly, requiring medical, social, and criminal sanctions to prevent or contain those forms of disturbance that are excessively dysfunctional.

The consequences of dislocations and mistakes in the production, logistics (distribution), and control functions of business and government are likely to be so huge that the facilities for coping with them must take precedence over civil liberties or private pursuits and property. The blackout of the east coast in 1965 only suggests what can go wrong in the future. (That particular disturbance need not have occurred with proper control systems, but that is the problem. On the one hand, there could be extremely sophisticated and prudent system designs or, on the other, there could be extensive supervision to avoid the possibility of relatively far-fetched disasters.) Needs for control and surveillance will develop to utilize (or as Parkinson might say, "expand to fill") the technological capabilities that are present in the system. Technological developments will, in addition to meeting environmental requirements, produce needs to satisfy technological capabilities.

As always, the central government would so likely be swamped by the problem of keeping the system functioning properly that it would be concerned only with marginal and immediate problems rather than with long-run, basic issues. In any event there may be no rational or moral feasible solution that does not reject the whole of modern technology or condemn billions of surplus humans to death or deprivation. The twenty-first century would no more be able to return to the world of the twentieth century than we can return to the golden age of Greece.

The Faust legend is a metaphor for a central predicament of modern man. We are interested in it primarily as it gives rise to insights concerning the consequences of the multifold trend characteristic of our culture. For the moment let us set aside the differences in treatments of this legend by several authors, or the same author at different times, as well as divergent critical interpretations. The most popular literary treatments—those by Marlowe and Goethe—do provide at least poetic insight into the problems we have been raising. Marlowe's version is more faithful to the early folk tale, but Goethe's version possesses that poetic ambiguity and complexity that raises the legend to the level of archetype or myth. In both versions, Faust sells his soul to the devil in order to acquire knowledge, power, riches, and women—typical sensate goals.

The object of pragmatic, empirical (sensate) knowledge is to control rather than to comprehend nature—to understand it instrumentally and manipulatively, rather than emphatically, normatively, or mythically. Such knowledge is a tool, not for the philosopher, but for *homo faber*, man the maker or doer, who gambles with fate (Fortuna, or chance, is a woman) to seize those rare opportunities that might never recur. Faustian man, or *homo faber*, is secular, profane, and sensate, rather than theological, philosophical, or theoretical.

The medieval play emphasizes the distinction between the sacred and the secular, between the body and the soul. During performances of the play, or puppet show, Faust would often be prompted from the stage (or even from the audience), "Repent, repent, it is not yet too late." Although he replies to the audience, "I have made a bargain and I will stick with it," he nonetheless vainly attempts to repent in the death scene. The lesson is clear: one may pay too high a price for worldly power, and after the penalty is apparent, repentance is too late. The myths of Prometheus and Icarus—and even the apple of the tree of knowledge—expressed similar misgivings about the potential consequence of striving for prowess with which to transcend human limitations and to subjugate the forces of nature. When Faust builds a new area in which people can find a new life, in which swamps are drained and dikes built to hold back the sea, he rejoices that dikes can never be perfect, since "Freedom and life are earned by those alone who conquer them each day anew."

Faust is not immoral but amoral. He is indifferent to the fate of those who stand in his way rather than brutal; the brutal actions in the play are performed by Faust's agents without Faust's knowledge. However, lest the reader think that Faust would have countermanded this brutality, there is one episode in which an old couple is ruthlessly evicted from their property by Faust himself even though their property is not essential to his scheme. They are in his way, and like a force of nature, he brushes them aside.

We are far from suggesting that the processes once presented by the basic multifold trend can be overcome. Janus, looking both backward and forward, must be the most disillusioned of all. Few of us are likely to return to the naïve optimism of the Enlightenment, to the rationalistic confidence in historical progress that is still dying slowly in both East and West, slowest of all in the U.S., while it continues to gain new adherents in the developing nations and in new nationalistic Communist groups. Some of the social trends, technological innovations, and levels of economic development that forecast a nightmarish twenty-first century are almost surely not reversible by any means short of holocaust.

Yet, if the cycle cannot be stopped, if the warring elements cannot be eliminated (as indeed they could not without the elimination of man), we can perhaps hope that they can be moderated. Just as the economist hopes to avoid not all the phenomena of business cycles, but only their extreme troughs and depressions, so perhaps we can hope with adequate knowledge and intelligence to control the extreme dips and rises of the cultural cycles. If man may never be completely in control of his fate, perhaps at least he may rise to partial control.

We share the prevailing humanistic view that man's increasing capability to alter his environment (not only the outside world but his own physiological and intrapsychic situation as well) amounts to "progress." It would be no more desirable than feasible to attempt to halt permanently the processes of technological and economic development, or to reverse them. Yet our very power over nature threatens to become itself a force of nature that is out of control, as the social framework of action obscures and thwarts not only the human objectives of all the striving for "achievement" and "advancement" but also the inarticulate or ideological reactions against the process. In the last decade of this century, we shall have the power to change the world even more radically than has already been done, but probably we will not develop much ability to restrain our strivings, let alone understand or control the results of these changes. But if we cannot learn to cope with the dangerous responsibilities of our technological success, we may only have thrown off one set of chains —nature-imposed—for another, ostensibly man-made, but in a deeper sense, as Faust learned, also imposed by nature.

If there is any single lesson that emerges from the above, it seems to be this: while it would certainly be desirable and might even be helpful to have a better grasp of how social action may lead to unanticipated or unwanted results, this is not likely to be sufficient. Given man's vastly increased power over his environment, and the unprecedented opportunities for centralization of social control that follows, the effects of social policies—planned or haphazard—are likely to increase drastically, and the consequences of mistakes are likely to grow correspondingly disastrous. While all decisions are in a sense irrevocable, this existential fact must be appreciated increasingly as it becomes an ever more dominant aspect of policy decisions.

Of course, it will be worthwhile to try to improve our understanding of policies and their consequences, but the problem is ultimately too difficult, and these efforts can never be entirely successful. Almost the only safeguard that then remains is to try in general to moderate Faustian impulses to overpower the environment, and to try to decrease both the centralization and the willingness to use accumulating power, or to arrange matters— somehow—so that this power is placed in the hands of people who will respect its disastrous potential and will not centralize it further. What is necessary is an unflagging respect for the world as we find it and for dissent and diversity, even for ornery individual stubbornness, in spite of the mounting impressiveness of the technical-rational structure that bourgeois, sensate society is building. Above all, there must be a concern for perpetuating those institutions that protect freedom of human choice, not only for today's individuals and the pluralistic social groups that would want their views represented, but more important, for those who will follow us—those who in the future may experience their problems differently and would not want to find that we have already foreclosed their choices and altered their natural and social world irretrievably.

II

Technology and Society

Take away the energy distributing networks and the industrial machinery from America, Russia, and all the world's industrialized countries, and within six months more than two billion swiftly and painfully deteriorating people will starve to death. Take away all the world's politicians, all the ideologies and their professional protagonists from those same countries, and send them off on a rocket trip around the sun and leave all the countries their present energy networks, industrial machinery, routine production and distribution personnel, and no more humans will starve nor be afflicted in health than at present.

> —R. BUCKMINSTER FULLER,
> "Man with a Chronofile" (1967)

11

Technology and Society

THE COMPUTER AS AN
INTELLECTUAL TOOL

by SIMON RAMO

THE mass extension of man's intellect by ma-
chine and the partnership of man and machine in the handling of
information may well be the technological advance dominating
this century. As the total information handling capacity of the
world grows through the new partnership, the total brain-power of
man is expanded. Industry, government, education, and all of the
professions will be greatly altered, and so, thus, will be society.

Let us separate into two parts what man or the machine can
do with information. The first involves the relatively simple and
well understood area where we manipulate and exchange information. These operations are performed on information stored in
the mind, in books, or in files, or transferred to a machine to
extend human abilities. Incoming information is added in recognized, specifiable ways to other information, and information is
used in a selection or comparison process controlled by logical,
consistent, and thoroughly describable rules.

The second category of mental activity typically involves what
a human being does in his mind to arrive at his conclusions. It
is often a highly complex process not always thoroughly understood. As a practical matter, by observing today what an executive, an engineer, a lawyer, a military decision-maker, a traffic
controller, or a teacher does in the daily pursuit of his intellectual
activities, we can readily confirm that we are not yet in a position
to set all of these processes down in straightforward mathematical language.

Now in the first category, it is generally possible to design machines that will handle some or all of the intellectual-informational tasks in a superior fashion to that of the unaided human. The electronic computer is better suited than the human brain for handling huge quantities of mundane information. It does this more economically, faster and with less error.

The mind, with all of its versatility and flexibility of internal connections, can add single digit numbers at a rate no higher than perhaps one pair a second, and in a short time its error rate becomes horrible. A modern computer can perform such operations in a millionth of a second with ease. A man could not be expected to memorize and stand ready to recall in an instant more than a small number of telephone numbers. An electronic computer can receive thousands of numbers per second, remember them for an indefinite time and recall them in a fraction of a second.

A book, a file of notes, a blackboard, a slide rule, or a cash register are all extensions to the human brain. These aids prolong memory, increase clarity, expand a number of readily available applicable facts.

Electronic systems constitute broader extensions to the human brain. For the first category of informational tasks mentioned, the computer, once programmed, can handle the assignment with little dependence on its human partner. Moreover, electronic systems have a flexibility and speed for inter-connection at a distance that makes possible large scale interacting networks for information storage, transmission, retrieval and processing that are well beyond man's capabilities. One basic concept then that guides today's application of computers in our man-machine partnership is that the more mundane, but high capacity, information handling tasks are assigned to the machine, while the more contemplative, decision-making, conclusion-drawing intellectual tasks remain for the human mind. Even here, however, the mind can be aided by the machine. And the machine stands ready to sort, categorize, display, search for, and retrieve information, as a willing, tireless, high capacity, partner.

The engineering field has already been revolutionized by the computer. The space program could not have existed if the brains of the designers had not been extended by the computer. Without it, thousands of test flights would have been needed in a clumsy, unacceptable, trial and error approach. As it was, a few dozens of flights proved sufficient to complete the engineering and confirm the design of the space vehicles. The thousands of flights took place in the simulation laboratories made possible by the computer.

Hotels are scheduling their reservations and other operations by electronic interrogating, storage, checking, sorting, and information display devices. Traffic on the ground and in the sky is coming under superior computer control. Chemical and refinery plants are being run better by the use of electronic devices, including computers, to monitor and control complete processes to a degree that is not possible with the unaided brain and senses of the human operators.

In factories, banking, insurance, and industrial operations, longhand records are being replaced by electronically recorded data processed by computers. The higher human intelligence is reserved for the more difficult aspects of these operations. Management control systems are being developed today in which information as to what is happening is electronically compared with the business plans. Deviations automatically produce directives for change as the system quietly covers the routine situations and calls on its human supervisors when the unpredictable non-recurring situations arise.

The next decade or two will see an even broader penetration of the computer and associated electronic systems into every facet of society's endeavors in which informational and intellectual activity exists. In the future, every attorney may be expected to have convenient electronic access to a repository of all the laws, rulings and procedures he needs in his work. In a few seconds the electronic systems will scan, select, and present him with the equivalent results of dozens of trained searchers covering decades of records over the entire nation. The lawyer's intellect will be elevated to the more complex intellectual tasks by supporting him better with the routine aspects of legal practice. Law makers will use computer processing to amass data on the results of enforcement of existing laws and regulations, and of the consequences and shortcomings of these laws. As the world becomes more complicated, every action interacts with an increasing number of other actions. The rules of society are correspondingly becoming highly detailed and the procedures increasingly lengthy. Something new to cope with this situation seems imperative, not just desirable. The electronic system furnishes the answer because of its virtually limitless memory, its speed of sorting, categorizing and comparing, and its ease in communicating information to those who need it.

Before this century nears its end, the physician should have the benefits of electronic networks of "consultative wisdom." He will introduce from his office the recorded history of a patient, the test results, symptoms, complaints, and the physician's diagnosis. The system will return to him quickly a processed and displayed analysis of these facts against the statistics on relative possibilities, complications, effectiveness of various treatments, and a check on some aspects of the diagnosis—in general, a substantial fraction of what a physician could get in theory by consulting with thousands of other physicians who have had similar cases. His treatment of this individual patient would also be recorded and become part of the total file available. With national monitoring of the statistics of medical practice, cause and effect relationships could be studied on a scale not realizable today, and the intellectual effectiveness of the physicians would be raised.

One of the most interesting electronic areas under development today is the automatic translation of natural languages by computer. The machine member of the team provides a crude first translation, identifying double meaning possibilities and weighing alternative translations of phrases based on what has preceded. The human partner aided by such machines can translate effectively with less effort and higher speed than either alone.

The most truly intellectual activity of all must be the education of the human brain. Educators, through computers and related electronic devices, are on the threshold of possessing new tools comparable in importance to the invention of the printed book. The routine material can be in great part machine presented, leaving the more difficult concept for the higher intellect of the human educator.

Programmed electronic machines can stimulate the thinking of a student by the manner of presentation. An electronic presentor can speed up, slow down, add more explanations, skip steps, even as it makes the presentation—all as an automatic result of continually noting the student's responses to questions and then altering the material, or the pace. This "program" would be in accordance with the educator's plan to correspond to the student's apparent rate of comprehension.

A computer network, properly applied in the future to the educational systems, can remember the progress of millions of students, comparing their tested learning with anticipated results, measuring and reporting deviations in progress from what was expected. Yet, remarkably, that same electronic system can be designed to immediately recognize an individual student, examine his record automatically, and provide him an accelerated or other special presentation or test, again as a result of rules that have been set into the system by the wiser human educator. Such a future educational system would involve new large industries employing experts in the subjects to be taught, the design of the programs and the electronic devices. There would have to be new professional groups within an augmented educational profession to provide statistical study, planning, diagnosis, and to match the synthetic machine intelligence with the human brain to achieve the fullest utilization of both.

The human educator will be able to rise to a higher level of intellectual and creative endeavor—relieved of much of the volume of routine work that is so much a part of the teaching profession today. The end result then, as we approach the 21st century, is full use of the computer to extend the human intellect. The biggest single effect could be the general rise of the intellectual level of man. Relieved of routine intellectual tasks, man would be free to concentrate his efforts on higher ones.

Advancing technology often appears a mixed blessing because of the imbalance of technological advance versus social adjustment lag. In a few decades it may be our increased brainpower, itself the result of proper employment of technological advance, that enables us to solve our social problems.

THE MEANING OF AUTOMATION

by BERNARD J. MULLER-THYM

Automation today is bringing us face to face with problems and potentialities beyond our previous experience, and its impact is forcing us to question some of the basic assumptions we have made about the design of machinery, our concepts of organization, and even our basic concepts of work and wealth.

The assumption we made about the design of work done by machines has dominated industrial practice for half a century. Our assumption has been that work will be performed more efficiently if the entire piece of work or the total sequence of operations is broken down into relatively fine pieces, and if our work forms are simpler and more specialized. Although we have achieved a great amount of progress working within this framework, it was actually a curious set of assumptions, since it goes counter to all the rest of our experience with nature. Man, for example, is far more complex than the dinosaur—yet man survives, and the dinosaurs perished. Hands are among the most complex and general-purpose things in nature; with very few elements of specialization, they can perform a tremendous variety of tasks. Yet we made exactly the opposite assumption—that simplification and specialization are more efficient than complexity—when we designed the machines that run our factories all over the world.

As a result, we have had to make our machine tools increasingly larger and more specialized in order to get greater production from them. And as machines get larger, they require

"The Meaning of Automation," by Bernard J. Muller-Thym. Reprinted by permission of the author and *Management Review*, June, 1963. Copyright © 1963 by the American Management Association, Inc.

proportionately greater investments of capital. So in order to get the incremental cost advantage out of a new machine, a company has to use it to produce ever-greater quantities; instead of a run of one hundred, it becomes necessary to have runs of a thousand, ten thousand, or a million of the same item. In consequence, our factories have become larger and more cumbersome, and it has become very difficult to optimize the productive facility. A businessman who bought a machine tool three years ago is at the mercy of a competitor who buys one this year, because the new machine is not only more efficient but incorporates additional technological advances. And even if the three-year-old machine is paid for, the businessman simply does not have the courage to start all over—to tear up his factory and redesign it from scratch.

The new generation of machine tools is not like this at all. It represents a completely different set of assumptions—a complete reversal of past practice. To take a simple example, consider the methods of making automobile tailpipes. The older types of machines with which we are familiar consist of jigs, dies, and fixtures, and once the settings are made, they make a hundred, a thousand, or ten thousand of the same kind of tailpipe. The new type of machine for making tailpipes is small—perhaps the size of a desk—and it has no dies, no fixtures, no settings of any kind. It consists of certain general-purpose things like grippers, benders, and advancers, and it is programmed by tape. On this machine, which costs less than its predecessors, it is possible to make eighty different kinds of tailpipes in succession, just as rapidly and as cheaply as eighty of the same type. This is simple and primitive, but it is an indication that the prototypes of the new generation of machines are already in existence. Their characteristics are general purpose, flexibility, and ability to be programmed with constant changes of program, and hence to be part of a network or society of such machines that form a completely flexible productive array.

By reason of the development of such machines and the development of the concepts and technology of information management, it has become possible to manage the productive matrix directly. In previous years, we have done this in a rather clumsy way by the use of such devices as production control, material control, and the like. What is now within our grasp is a kind of productive capability that is alive with intelligence, alive with information, so that at its maximum it is completely flexible; one could completely reorganize the plant from hour to hour if one wished to do so, and inventories would begin to approach the zero point. It may never be possible to achieve this maximum potential, but it will be possible to come close enough to change radically the allocation of capital as well as the allocation of the productive capabilities themselves.

Automation will also have an impact on our forms of organization, on work structure, and on the institutions of authority and control within the organization itself. Here again, we have been operating for perhaps half a century on the basis of certain assumptions about the organization of work done by human beings. We have always assumed, for example, that there must be someone who is superior over workers, that everyone must have a boss, that no one should have more than one boss, that a limited number of people should report to the same boss, and so on. As a result of these assumptions, we have inevitably created a management work structure illustrated by the classical organization chart—a structure that is pyramidal and many-layered. As a business organized in this way grows larger and larger, not only does the base of the pyramid broaden, but the number of intermediate layers (consisting of supervisors and managers) is multiplied.

We are already, and we have been for some time, beyond the tolerable limits of inefficiency that result from running a business with this kind of organizational structure. There is no need to go into detail about the communications problems and the decay of action that result—not as a consequence of individual incompetence, but as a consequence of the structure itself. Once an organization has grown to any size at all, such a work structure diffuses and dissipates competence and creates organization distances and separations between the parties responsible for action. It results in a decay in action and communication that is directly proportional to the number of intermediaries through whom the action or the message must be transmitted.

It was possible to run our businesses with this kind of work structure one, two, or three generations ago, because businesses were smaller, rates of change in the society and in the economy were slower, and the kinds of competence required to run a business were fewer. This is no longer true. Not only are our businesses larger and more complicated, but the kinds of competence required to run an enterprise have multiplied, and the required competence levels are constantly rising. It has already become impossible to run a large business efficiently with the old kind of structure.

We already have working models of the new kind of organizational structure that increasing complexity will require. If you were to diagram them, they would look somewhat like diagrams of a nervous system, or the kind of diagrams nuclear scientists make. We might consider the present-day organization chart as a two-dimensional Euclidean structure in which any increase in size automatically creates greater distances between the various points. The new type of organization, in contrast, exists in a kind of curved space, where points of competence mobilization, points of decision-making, and points of information management are so arrayed that one can go directly, or almost directly, from any action-taking, decision-making, information-handling point to any other point.

We are fortunate that computer technology has arrived on the scene when its potentials—the capability of handling information nonselectively, totally, and in configurations that can be changed at will—will enable us to be much more daring in designing organization structures. Up to now, business information (e.g., accounting, controls) has been handled piecemeal and selectively. Instead of total information, our information systems have reported samples of business behavior or managerial action, both qualitatively (selected costs, selected money allocations, selected items of sales performance) and in time. These systems were supplemented by having some middle-level manager try to find out what was wrong at a lower level in order to pass the information to his superior, or by managers in a chain trying to force information from the top down through many layers to the point where, hopefully, work would be done. This "bucket brigade" approach is extremely inefficient: There is about a 50 per cent slop, a 50 per cent loss at each transmission.

Analyses of managerial action indicate that people in middle management spend 80 per cent of their time simply handling information—and handling it in a very primitive and inadequate manner. We are fortunate, therefore, that at the very moment when we need to optimize the managerial work structure, we have available to us a computer technology through which we can handle the total information in a system nonselectively, instantaneously, and with random access. This makes it possible for us to create a flexible managerial organizational structure that will enable us to manage the integer of work, the points or concentrations of competence, and the entire business network. And because profit and the creation of wealth is a function of the business network, and is not (as classical economists thought) simply a matter of adding value through production, we now have the capability of managing wealth itself.

This brings us to the third point: the social consequences of automation. We are living in a period in human history that might be considered the end of the Neolithic age. At the very beginning of the Neolithic age (8000–10,000 B.C.) we abandoned our nomadic ways and settled down, and after we became static and attached to the land, we invented the wheel. We also invented property, as defined by an object, primarily land; and we invented ownership as a moral act that focused on and had as its terms such an object.

We are living at the end of the age of the wheel; we are living at the end of the electromechanical age. We have abandoned Neolithic weaponry like spears, arrows, and bullets—selective, single-purpose weaponry that is used to kill the enemy seriatim, one after another—and have adopted nuclear weapons that are total, instantaneous, and with random access. And now we are abandoning property as well.

One of the characteristics of the world in which we live is that property and work are disappearing. This process is going on inexorably; it is further advanced in some parts of the world than in others, but all parts of the world will be involved in it. Automation is accelerating the process, although automation did not bring it about. Property as a thing-type object is disappearing; it is doubtful whether any group of people in the history of the world could measure themselves against their ancestors of comparable wealth and find that they owned so little in comparison.

A house, for example, used to be a thing to be born in, to live in throughout one's life, and to leave to one's son or heir. In recent years, the average length of time a person in the U.S. lives in a particular house has dropped from eight years to five years, and it is still going down. A house today is a kind of space valve in which a married couple and their children live for increasingly shorter periods of time before moving on to another house or to an apartment; it is a place where a family spends the semiprivate part of their lives between trips to the more public centers of worship, work, education, and play.

To take another example: Americans, at a startlingly increasing rate, are leasing personal automobiles rather than owning them. (One of the largest auto manufacturers believes that the majority of our people will have cars through lease within not too many years.) When the leasing company owns the car but does not use it, and the driver uses it but does not own it, the result is something quite different from classic ownership.

One could cite other instances to indicate that property and the thing-element of property are disappearing. (The description of the disappearance of both property and work has already been made eloquently by Gerard Piel in *Consumers of Abundance*, published in 1962 by the Fund for the Republic.) The fact is that we are relatively more wealthy than our Neolithic ancestors; there is an increasingly richer abundance of goods and services for us to enjoy; but there are also increasingly less property and less ownership.

We have brought business into being as the prime wealth-generating organ of our society. The only sources of *new* wealth up to now have been the household of the ancient world, increase from nature, and independent, sporadically occurring invention. Now we have added to the technology of generating wealth by designing a modern business, for a business is a system in which output is greater than input. That output—newly created wealth —is a function of organized innovation and of the total business as a system. But to an increasing extent, the wealth that is created is not so much resident in the hardware as in the competence—the software—of the objects that enter into economic exchanges; and the wealth itself is created at and exists only as a point of intersection in a matrix of economic exchanges.

At the same time, work, in the sense of servile work, is disappearing. It is futile to talk of relieving "chronic unemployment"; the rate is going up, and it is going up much more rapidly than in the past decade. A substantial amount of retraining is going to be necessary, for there is going to be a radical change in the skill mix of people found in a business. But no amount of retraining is going to provide the amount of work that human beings now perform as sources of power, servo-mechanisms, levers, and things of this sort. No amount of work for human beings is going to replace the work that is being destroyed by automation.

In a world in which the prime mechanism for distributing the wealth we have learned to create has been pay for work, the disappearance of work has serious implications. It means that we are able to generate wealth, to invent almost anything we decide to invent, and to achieve command over nature for the first time—yet no one will have money; no one will be able to buy anything.

It would be foolish to try to reverse the direction of this trend; it is basically not bad. It is, in fact, an extension of the noble work of freeing man from slavery, from the curse of Adam, from having to earn his bread by the sweat of his brow. It is a direction that is generally good, and should be regarded by any normal human being as good.

The task before us, therefore, is to invent a new kind of money, new institutions for the distribution of wealth. None of us is ready to describe what these new institutions will be—after all, we have only now identified the phenomenon. But one can describe something of what that society will be like and some of the design criteria for that money or those monies that will replace or supplement pay.

It will be a world in which two of the largest industries will be education and the management of information. Add to these communications—both electronic communication and physical communications in an intricate and sensitive space-time network whose management will require both people and computers. Some factories will produce long rows of standard commodities, but most of them will produce a marvelous variety of different end-products to the requirements of individual customers as well as of markets. (Even buildings—houses, laboratories, and the like—

can be produced this way now, and more cheaply than the inflexible structures we now build.) There will be many more wants and many more goods and services to satisfy them. But while there will be an opportunity for people to be very active and engaged, there will be increasingly less opportunity for them to do the kind of work that has represented the great bulk—perhaps 90 per cent—of the world's work up to now.

The displacement we expect, therefore, will not be like the kind that occurred after the Industrial Revolution—the cycle of temporary employment, followed by greater productivity and then by a greater requirement for workers to satisfy the new orders of demand in a mechanized world. It will rather be a displacement or shift towards kinds of activity, nonservile and sometimes even wealth-producing, that have not been considered work and for which people generally have not been paid in the past.

We know that wealth exists only at a moment of exchange in an economic network. We know that we are also in a society where people are getting married younger, expect to have some children, and look forward to a life of opportunity with a reasonable right to education, health, pleasure, and a life of useful activity in the economy, the society, the polity—and at whatever age may be appropriate. We need, therefore, a kind of "money" that will enable them to have enough such opportunities on a random and timely basis. This would be a money with no thing component: It would be only a language. But the thing part of money—gold, cattle, women—has practically disappeared anyway.

We have barely enough time in which in an evolutionary but planned way to invent such a network and the money-language to make it operational. As a practical strategy, we might use that time to sell our present competences abroad and bring the rest of the world as rapidly as possible to equality with us. A world so dominated by science and electronic communication has to be one world, and economic exchanges can take place in greater volume and with greater enrichment to both parties in such measure as the parties are equal and strong.

This strategy of working simultaneously to design the new networks and to bring the world to our higher level of well-being is the only one we see at the moment to buy our way out of the dislocations that will otherwise occur as we head into an age wherein automation can be either tyrant and malignant, or servant and benign.

CYBERNATION AND HUMAN RIGHTS

by ROBERT THEOBALD

My use of the word cybernation instead of automation does not stem from a desire to *seem* to be saying something new. On the contrary, I use the word cybernation because it represents something quite different from automation. Automation was the process by which you could take a block of metal, put it in at one end of a series of machines and it would come out at the other, as a finished engine block, without the need for human intervention. Automated machinery could do some things fast and well; nevertheless, its potential to organize people out of work was limited because it was inflexible.

Cybernation, however, is highly flexible and will become more so as time passes. Cybernation is the process of linking a computer, which is effectively a machine which will make decisions, and using it to control automated machinery. These interlocking machine-systems can often be controlled by a few people sitting at computers, while the requirements for other workers are very small, for not only will the machines do all the work but the latest ones are being built practically to repair themselves. The potential to organize human beings out of work in order to increase the efficiency of machine-systems is already large and rapidly growing. In other words, the present type of change in

"Cybernation and Human Rights," by Robert Theobald. Reprinted from *Liberation*, August, 1964, by permission of the author.

technology cannot be considered merely a continuation of the organizational process of the last one hundred and fifty years— it means something completely new which is quietly taking place all around us. Cybernation involves a production revolution which has two major consequences. First, in the field of production it is challenging and will increasingly challenge the supremacy of man's mind, and it will do this just as surely as the industrial revolution challenged and overcame the supremacy of man's muscle. In the relatively near future the machine-systems will take over all repetitive physical and mental production tasks and huge numbers of people will be thrown out of work. It has been estimated by some authorities that as little as 10% or even 2% of the labor force will be required for conventional work in the future.

The idea that we can continue to aim at finding a job for everybody is obsolete. A large proportion of those born in the fifties and sixties have no prospect of ever holding an ordinary job. There is no role in today's economy for those teen-agers who are high-school dropouts and there is increasingly little place for those over fifty-five.

Such a picture seems bleak to many: they seem afraid that there will not be enough toil to go round. To me, on the other hand, it appears like the lifting of the curse of Adam, for it will no longer be necessary for man to earn his bread in the sweat of his brow. Machines could perform the productive toil and men could receive the resulting abundance, for machines would not only take over all the toil, they would also make it possible to turn out effectively unlimited quantities of both goods and services. U Thant, Secretary-General of the United Nations, has expressed it in the following terms:

The truth, the central stupendous truth, about developed countries today is that they can have—in anything but the shortest run—the kind and scale of resources they decide to have. . . . It is no longer resources that limit decisions. It is the decision that makes the resources. This is the fundamental revolutionary change—perhaps the most revolutionary mankind has ever known.

There is no need—and no excuse—for poverty in the America of the second half of the twentieth century. Why, then, does it exist, and what can be done? Before I discuss this I want to present a few figures which will show that there is already too much unemployment, that there is the ability to produce more goods and services, and that we will have more unemployment and more ability to produce additional goods and services in coming years.

First, unemployment rates have remained around or above the excessive rate of 5.5% during the sixties. (The last few months have seen a decline to 5.1%.) The unemployment rate for teenagers has been rising steadily, reaching 17% in 1963; the unemployment rate for Negro teenagers was 27% in 1963, while the unemployment rate for teenagers in minority ghettoes often exceeds 50%. Unemployment rates for Negroes are regularly above twice those for whites, whatever their occupation, educational level, age or sex. The unemployment position for other racial minorities is also unfavorable.

These official figures seriously underestimate the true extent of the unemployment problem. In 1962, in addition to the percentage of the labor force who were officially unemployed, nearly 4% of the labor force wanted full-time work but could only find part-time jobs. Methods of calculating unemployment rates—a person is only unemployed if he has actively sought a job recently —ignore the existence of a large group who would like to find jobs but who have not looked for them because they know there are no employment opportunities. Underestimation for this reason is particularly severe for people in groups whose unemployment rates are high—the young, the old and racial minorities. Willard Wirtz, Secretary of Labor, has stated that at least 350,000 young men between 14 and 24 have stopped looking for work. Many people in the depressed agricultural, mining and industrial areas, who officially hold jobs but who are actually grossly underemployed, would move if there were real prospects of finding work elsewhere. It is therefore reasonable to estimate that around eight million people are looking for jobs today as compared to the 3.6 million shown in the official statistics.

Even more serious is the fact that the number of people who have voluntarily removed themselves from the labor force is not static but increases continually. For these people the decision to stop looking for employment and to accept the fact that they will never hold a job or will not hold a job again is largely irreversible, not only in economic but also in social and psychological terms. The older worker calls himself "retired"; he cannot accept work without affecting his social security status. The worker in prime years is forced onto relief: in most states the requirements for becoming a relief recipient bring about such fundamental alterations in an individual's total material situation that a reversal of the process is always difficult and often totally infeasible. The teenager knows that there is no place for him in the labor force but at the same time is unaware of any realistic alternative avenue for self-fulfillment.

Statistical evidence of these trends appears in the decline in the proportion of people claiming to be in the labor force. The recent apparent stabilization, and indeed decline, of the unemployment rate is therefore misleading: it is primarily a reflection of the discouragement and defeat of people who cannot find employment rather than a measure of the economy's success in creating enough jobs for all those who want to find a place in the labor force.

Second, we could produce far more goods and services if we would only find more ways to allow people to buy them—for the past eight years there has been the potential to produce some sixty billion dollars of additional goods and services. We are able every year to produce at least another thirty billion dollars of additional goods and services; this will rise to forty billion dollars per year before the end of the sixties, fifty billion dollars during the first half of the seventies, and at least sixty billion dollars well before the end of the seventies. We will be able to produce an additional one hundred and fifty billion dollars of extra goods and services every year by the end of the century. The children born in 1964 will only be about half way through their lives at this time. I should add that these estimates are certainly conservative.

Third, the forward movement of cybernation is raising the skill level of the machine. If a human being is to compete with such machines, he must *at least* possess a high school diploma. The Department of Labor has estimated, however, that on the basis of present trends as many as thirty per cent of *all* students will be high school drop-outs in this decade.

Fourth, a permanently depressed class is developing in the United States. Scattered throughout the land, some thirty-eight million Americans, or almost one-fifth of the population, are living in a condition of chronic poverty which is daily becoming more evident to the rest of the nation. The percentage of total income received by the poorest 20% of the population has fallen from 4.9% to 4.7% since 1944. Movement out of the ranks of the poor is increasingly difficult, for it depends on an adequate education, while conscription of new and apparently permanent recruits continues.

The best summary of the effects of these trends was perhaps made by the Secretary of Labor at the beginning of 1964:

The confluence of surging population and driving technology is splitting the American labor force into tens of millions of "haves" and millions of "have-nots." In our economy of sixty-nine million jobs, those with wanted skills enjoy opportunity and earning power. But the others face a new and stark problem—exclusion on a permanent basis, both as producers and consumers, from economic life. This division of people threatens to create a human slag-heap. We cannot tolerate the development of a separate nation of the poor, the unskilled, the jobless, living within another nation of the well-off, the trained and the employed.

Is it surprising that the news media are full of reports of violence? There is no need to remind you of these reports nor of the climate which has created them—we all live too close to these problems. But I want to discuss with you the response, or rather the reaction, which is growing among many people. I will quote from the police chief, William H. Parker, in Los Angeles. This report appeared in the magazine *U.S. News and World Report* in April, 1964, in the form of a question and answer interview.

Question: *Has the crime picture changed much in [the last 37 years]?*

Answer: *Not only has the crime picture changed, but the entire attitude of the American people toward crime, I think, has undergone quite a definite change. I think there is a tendency to accept crime as part of the American scene, and to tolerate it.*

Question: *Do you mean that people now feel that wrong-doing is normal?*

Answer: *More than that—they seem to think that we must have a certain amount of crime not only because of man's inherent weakness, but because we are enlarging upon the scope of individual liberty.*

Question: *America might have a choice, eventually, between a criminal state and a police state?*

Answer: *I believe that will become the option before us if crime becomes so troublesome that we are no longer able to control it.*

But Chief Parker did not mention what is to me the most serious aspect of the present situation. He did not deal with the passive apathy of individuals recently demonstrated in several notorious cases in the New York area. In one of these, at least 38 people failed to call the police although they became progressively more aware that a woman was being murdered in the street below their windows. He did not deal with the fact that there is now a desire to witness violence, to participate vicariously, as when a crowd of forty interested spectators remained indifferent to the appeals of an 18-year-old bruised and bloodied office worker as she tried to escape from a rapist. (Only the accidental arrival of two policemen eventually resulted in her rescue.)

It is understandable, if regrettable, when those accidentally present at the scene of a crime or disaster flee through fear. It is incomprehensible as rational behavior when they remain as interested spectators or even active participants. During an attempted suicide which took place in Albany recently, numerous spectators participated in this novel type of sports-event, urging the mentally-disturbed youth to jump to his death and betting on the outcome. Two comments reported in *The New York Times* are hardly believable: "I wish he'd do it and get it over with. If he doesn't hurry up we're going to miss our last bus." And another: "I hope he jumps on this side. We couldn't see him if he jumped over there."

I believe this indifference to violence, and indeed increasing encouragement of it, are products of a society which is rapidly coming to regard inter-race conflict as inevitable; a society which fails to challenge the individual to anything more than economic goals and responsibilities and which has now deprived many people of even an opportunity to achieve the self-respect which would result from reaching these economic goals. Although we are confronted with the symptoms of incipient total breakdown in our society, we are unwilling to face reality. We refuse to recognize that the survival of American values depends on fundamental changes which will reverse the process toward alienation. We refuse to recognize that the economically poor and the culturally alienated, who are the young and the minorities, have and should have little interest in the goals our society presently espouses. Instead of looking for the new and better society that cybernation makes possible we continue the drift into a worse society: we then propose that the way to arrest this drift is through measures which must necessarily be categorized as movements toward a centralized authoritarian state: teen-age curfews and all-day seven-day-a-week retention of children within the confines of the school plant.

Some Proposals

Now I want to set out a program which might suffice to reverse the drift toward a centralized authoritarian state.

The first necessity is to guarantee every individual within the United States a decent standard of living whether he can find work or not. We should provide every individual with an absolute constitutional right to an income adequate to allow him to live with dignity. No governmental agency, judicial body or other organization whatsoever should have the power to suspend or limit any payments by this guarantee. Such an absolute constitutional right to an income will recognize that in an economy where many jobs already represent make-work in any social, and indeed economic, sense and where the requirements for workers will decrease in coming years, it is nonsensical to base the right to an income on an ability to find a job.

Many people have attacked this proposal, but their arguments have failed to convince me. I remain quite sure that the guaranteed income is the first necessary step if we are to achieve the new and better society made possible by cybernation, that it is the only practical means of preserving our fundamental goal of individual freedom, the only method of allowing the individual to make his own decisions and pursue his own interests. The guaranteed income is not one of many solutions to the problems of cybernation: on the contrary it is the economic prerequisite for the solution of the real problems of the second half of the twentieth century, many of which have not yet even begun to be discussed in realistic terms.

The first of these problems is education. One of the key principles of the cybernated era is that society must make an unlimited commitment to produce the conditions in which every individual can develop his full intellectual potential. The acceptance of this principle would make me highly optimistic for the long run. I believe that we have so far developed only a tiny proportion of the potential of most human beings. I believe that acceptance of an absolute right to an income and complete education would allow a flowering of the spirit and mind whose dimensions cannot even be guessed today.

If we are to achieve the complete education of every individual, we must recognize that the student is "working" at least as relevantly as the man in the factory. The time has come when we must introduce the concept of a student salary, starting possibly at 14 and increasing with age, payable to all students attending school or university. This salary would be tangible proof of the recognition by society of the value of this young individual and its acceptance by the child would be a recognition by him of his obligation to the society which has accorded him this right.

Society must not only be concerned with the individual's mental abilities but also with his physical health. We must develop a system which will ensure that everybody can obtain the best medical care—both preventive and curative. Income levels should be seen as totally irrelevant to rights to health and life.

Rights to an income sufficient to live with dignity, to the opportunity to develop oneself fully and to obtain meaningful activity are only extensions of present values, although many people will be shocked by the direction of the proposed extension. However, the coming of the cybernated society not only forces us to live up to past ideals but it also requires the development of new human rights. I want to talk about the need for three rights which seem highly important to me. (There are others which should be mentioned if space permitted.)

The first of these new human rights is for the individual to be provided with guarantees about the quality of all the goods he purchases. It has always been a fundamental principle of marketing in the Western world that the purchaser should discover the quality, condition and quantity of the goods he is purchasing. The seller simply offers a product and it is held to be the responsibility of the purchaser to inform himself as to whether it is satisfactory. This is the famous legal doctrine of *caveat emptor* (let the buyer beware).

Today, the consumer cannot reasonably be expected to examine a television set or any other complex product to discover if it is well made: the makers of many types of goods have recognized this fact and have steadily lengthened their periods of guarantee. We now need to take the next step and acknowledge that the total responsibility for determining whether a product is satisfactory lies with the seller and not with the buyer. Each seller should become responsible for the claims made on behalf of his product and should be forced to refund some multiple of the purchase price if the product does not meet his claims. In some cases, when injury to the purchaser results, the seller should be liable for damages. The manufacturer will therefore have a direct financial interest in living up to the claims made for his product.

In upper Manhattan, we are all used to the shoddy-goods salesman with the foot in the door on a Sunday afternoon or late on a weekday evening. We fail to translate our momentary irritation into terms of national waste. The proposed human right would not only minimize the time wasted by the individual in purchasing repair or replacement: it would also meet desirable social criteria. The time and money the manufacturer saves by selling unsatisfactory products is wasted many times over by the troubles of the user. We need a productive system which will turn out goods which will render the services for which they were designed with the minimum possible number of breakdowns.

In addition, the long-run necessity, if mankind is to survive on this planet, is maximum economy in the use of raw materials. Every pressure should therefore be placed on the manufacturer to maximize the life of the product. This measure would be a first step in this direction.

The second new human right is the right to buy from any seller. Originally the buyer and seller were in close human contact and they naturally wished to choose to whom they would sell and from whom they would buy. Today, business desires to move goods and services at a profit without entangling social problems. As a result it is not only desirable but also necessary for society to state that in return for the right granted the businessman to sell goods and services, he has the obligation to serve all comers. Those who do not want to accept the obligation to sell to all comers should not be granted the right to sell at all.

It is, of course, *only* the establishment of such a principle in law which will provide a completely satisfactory answer to present discrimination practices. It is an answer which must be eventually passed as a constitutional amendment: it must be clearly recognized that private property ceases to be private *just as soon as* the individual or company makes the decision to sell to the public.

It would be naïve, of course, to expect that these new rights, and many others, could be effectively established without a major reform in our legal system. Today, the government has all the resources in a criminal case: the private individual, unless he is wealthy, has no opportunity to hire legal talent of comparable skill. In a civil case, the large corporation controls enough funds to hire a battery of lawyers; the private individual rarely has enough resources to match this ability to spend. We require a new institution: the public defender. Public defenders would be paid by the government and would have the power of government officials but their responsibility would be to take the cases of the private individual whose interests they felt had been unjustly damaged by the use of private and governmental power. They would possess enough resources to challenge the large institution effectively. A system similar to this has already been established in Scandinavia, and Arthur Goldberg has proposed it be introduced into the United States.

The third new human right is that every individual should have the right to receive information undistorted by desires to mislead for the purposes of private gain. This is, in today's world, a very novel proposal for it means that society must develop effective sanctions against individuals and groups who distort information deliberately. That such a proposal seems novel is perhaps a good measure of the degree of malfunction in our society. The framers of the American Constitution intended that the right of free speech and a free press should be a method of achieving free debate, not a justification of deliberate distortion with consequent fragmentation of the society.

What types of distortion am I condemning? I condemn the advertisers who play on the weakness of the individual in order to increase their sales. I condemn the propagandists of any country who unhesitatingly distort the unfavorable and bury the undesirable news. I condemn the academics who distort the truth as they see it in order to gain reputations or power. On the other hand, I do not condemn but resolutely uphold the right of the individual to put forward all the truth as he sees it, however unpalatable it may be. I believe, indeed, that we must smooth the path of individuals who are willing to dissent, for the costs of disagreement with existing social norms are always high. The granting of an absolute constitutional right to an income will be helpful here.

Indeed, I go further. The existence of lively controversy which allows the discovery of the truth in constantly changing circumstances is one of the prime necessities of today. Only a lively democracy can lead to the adoption of appropriate policies to deal with changing situations. Concentration of power in the hands of a few not only is against our past ideals but also fails to meet present necessities.

I would like to suggest that this is, in fact the major role which has been played by the civil rights movement in recent years, and particularly in recent months. The attention of the civil rights groups themselves, and of outside observers, has been concentrated on the degree of success or failure achieved in striving for stated goals. There is a considerable feeling that they have consistently fallen short of their goals and this has been called failure. This is an excessively naïve view of social change. Very few commentators discuss the real success of the civil rights movement—the fact that it has, almost single-handed, wrested America out of the apathy in which it was mired and forced it to face the problems of unemployment and inadequate education, the problems of poverty, and the long-run dangers of cybernation. The drive of the civil rights movement is forcing America to re-examine itself and to recognize that the rights of the Negro cannot be achieved without fundamental social and economic change. The civil rights movement has provided America with another chance, and possibly its last one, to recognize that in conditions of abundance every citizen both can and should be provided with the means to obtain enough food, clothing, shelter, education and health care: in effect to be a first class citizen.

Martin Luther King has taken this theme and proposed in his new book ". . . that the United States launch a broad-based and gigantic Bill of Rights for the Disadvantaged." He adds: "It is a matter of simple justice that the United States, in dealing creatively with the task of raising the Negro from backwardness, should also be rescuing a large stratum of the forgotten white poor. A Bill of Rights for the Disadvantaged could mark the rise of a new era, in which the full resources of the society could be used to attack the tenacious poverty which so paradoxically exists in the midst of plenty."

How can this goal be achieved? Clearly the civil rights movement must be joined by other supporting groups. Only if all those who are concerned with the improvement of our society unite to bring about major change will it be possible to achieve the pace of development in social values which will allow us to benefit from technology and consequent abundance rather than be destroyed by it.

The civil rights and labor movements stand, indeed, at a crossroads. They can become the rallying point for true social change, for demands which in any other period of history would clearly have been Utopian but which are today completely practical and indeed essential. The decision to take the route proposed would deprive the civil rights movement of the support of some sections. It would alienate those who are only concerned with obtaining justice for the Negro, who refuse to recognize that justice for the Negro cannot be secured in a society which does not secure justice for all its citizens; in the same way that present injustice to the Negro is progressively involving injustice to others. In addition, this decision would deprive the unions of the support of those who are concerned solely with people who still are, or might become, union members.

If we plan and carry out the necessary actions our common future has a brighter aspect but we must face up to the unkind fact that much of the potential benefit from cybernation and abundance will be reaped not by us but by our children. We are in many ways the truly lost generation: we are torn adrift from the certainties by which our parents still lived and we will never fully understand the new set of apparent certainties which will seem totally natural to the children growing up today. These children, in their turn, will never understand how we could have allowed our defunct concepts of economics to prevent us from providing everybody with food, clothing, shelter, education, and health care.

In one sense, we will remain chained to our past, unable to enter the promised land. But our generation, and *only* our generation, can bring humanity to this promised land. The challenge is uniquely ours: if we fail to rise to it we will destroy our values, the values of our children and very possibly the whole world. If we succeed we have laid the groundwork for the Great Society.

GUARANTEED INCOME IN THE ELECTRIC AGE

by MARSHALL MCLUHAN

In Shakespeare's day it was a charge against the players that they were little else than beggars and vagabonds because their livelihood derived from direct dependence on the public. They put their hands into people's pockets, as it were. They had no *place* and no stake in society. They had no roles but merely transitory jobs. Decent people, on the contrary, had no merely monetary relation to the society, but were involved in depth relations of loyalty and service. A gentleman could not soon enough or often enough sign himself: "Your obedient and humble servant."

"Guaranteed Income in the Electric Age," by Marshall McLuhan, from *The Guaranteed Income*, edited by Robert Theobald. Copyright © 1965, 1966 by Doubleday & Company, Inc. Reprinted by permission of the publisher.

The growth of social mobility in the sixteenth century raised up a new race of adventuresome men who had skills that they were eager to sell in a changing world. This new breed of rootless men who sold their services, gradually acquired the label "honest." To the ears of established folk "honest" bore some very dubious overtones, as in the case of "honest Iago" in *Othello*. Both Iago and Othello were professional soldiers. They were not gentlemen. They had no place in society. Their salaried position differed little from that of Edmund the bastard (in *King Lear*) or from that of Tom Jones the foundling in Fielding's novel. One of the directions of Renaissance individualism was toward the gradual separation of people from deep commitment to their social situation. This direction was fostered by new facilities for travel by sea and by land, and especially by new studies and new extensions of educational opportunity by means of the printed word.

The quite unexpected psychic and social consequences of the developments in special knowledge and skill during the first onset of typographic technology I have detailed in *The Gutenberg Galaxy* (University of Toronto Press, 1962). The effects on family life are explored in *Centuries of Childhood* by Philippe Ariès (Alfred A. Knopf, 1962). Ariès explains how the very concept of "family" and of "childhood" in our present acceptance of these ideas, was of seventeenth-century origin. Both "family" and "child" had, until the seventeenth century, been so deeply involved in the total communal life as to have no separate existence. As with "nationalism" no theory preceded their arrival.

It may seem unusual to approach the question of guaranteed annual income from such a historical perspective. But guaranteed income as a novelty is so much related to the idea of uniform prices, self-regulating market mechanisms, and salaried "jobs," that it is well to look back to times when such facts were unknown. Until mechanical printing there was no uniform and repeatable commodity that could give rise to uniform pricing patterns. Prior to the printed book the entire book market bore the character of a "secondhand" market. Such is still the character of any market for handmade produce. It was only as typographic technology began to pervade many levels of psyche and society that the organization of work on a fragmented or "job" basis became possible.

Print was the first mechanization of a handicraft. The entire principle of the mechanizing of the work process was implicit in printing from movable types. From Gutenberg types to the Ford assembly lines, from the fifteenth to the twentieth centuries there is a steady progress of fragmentation of the stages of work that constitutes "mechanization" and "specialism." And without an understanding of the ancient processes and techniques of mechanization it is unlikely that anybody could obtain insight into the quite contrary patterns of work and remuneration that are coming into play in the electronic age. For the electronic age is not a mechanical age; nor will the procedures of mechanical fragmentation and specialism serve for survival or sanity in this new time.

Even today we are inclined to look at new situations through the preceding one. No age until ours has imagined that there was any alternative to this habit of seeing one's own time through the preceding age. The reason is simply that environments are as total as they are imperceptible. Each new age creates an environment whose content is the preceding age. The content is perceptible. The environment is not. This principle of human perception extends to our technologies as well. At present TV is environmental and imperceptible. Its "content" is the movie, which was the preceding environment. The movie is now being processed by the new TV environment into a most perceptible art form. It is the peculiar fate of all environments formed by new technologies that they are imperceptible during their initial reign, while conferring an eminent degree of visibility upon their predecessors. When the movie was dominant and environmental its content was the book and the press. Both book and newspaper were elevated to art forms by poets and painters of the 1920s. The book became an art form when it ceased to be environmental. When the printed book was newly dominant as a psychic and social environment, in the sixteenth century, it took as its "content" the preceding medieval environment of manuscript and iconographic culture. The Middle Ages became an art form to the Renaissance. The "medieval world view" that had been imperceptible when it was dominant became luminously present to the new age of print and individualism.

When the process of mechanization, and the industrial specialism of human tasks and functions, had first created a novel environment, it surrounded the older environment of agricultural labor and handicrafts. Nature became an art form for the first time when it became the content of industrialized society. People began to puzzle over the failure of previous ages to note the spiritual and aesthetic qualities of the natural scene. Wordsworth spoke for his time:

> *And I have felt*
> *A presence that disturbs me with the joy*
> *Of elevated thoughts; a sense sublime*
> *Of something far more deeply interfused,*
> *Whose dwelling is the light of setting suns,*
> *And the round ocean and the living air,*
> *And the blue sky, and in the mind of man.*

When the mechanical environment first became enveloped by the new electric technology, men began to enjoy abstract mechanical forms as iconic art. It was in this later part of the nineteenth century that the Renaissance itself became perceptible as an art form to artists, philosophers, and historians alike. It is possible to pinpoint the arrival of a new environmental technology at the moment when any preceding set of forms and activities begin to be appreciated as a work of art. By the same token, such belated awareness is the mark of the failure to apprehend the character of the emergent new environment. The only "control" exercised over the new forces would seem to consist of a fascinated withdrawal of perception from the new constitutive forces together with a panicky concern for the receding configurations. Such is the significance of the Goldwater mood and the rhetoric of Ayn Rand.

The fact that the mechanical age ends with the advent of electric technology has not been widely noted. The new electric environment has as its content the old mechanical technology and work organization. As a result of being processed by the new electric environment the mechanical age has become luminously perceived as a galaxy of art forms. *Mechanization Takes Command* by Sigfried Giedion (Oxford University Press, 1948) is a monumental study of the application of mechanical principles to many areas of human endeavor. Giedion is an art historian who, in the electronic age, finds it quite congenial to study the development of machines and industry as art forms. Indeed the rise of management consulting in this century depends upon viewing the entire configuration of a business as a unified work of art. The new electronic environment enables us to be aware of the older environment of enterprise and of fragmented production techniques, as never before. When mechanism was itself an environmental and all-pervasive process, it was much less visible than now. Today it is the all-pervasive environment of electric information movement that is invisible.

In moving from the age of the mechanical wheel to the age of circuitry and feedback, man has suddenly made a break with the several-thousand-year span that is called the Neolithic age. When man the hunter settled down to specialize his production into crops and handicrafts he began a process of fragmentation of his interests and activities that continued until the arrival of electric technology. If we think of neolithic man as dedicated to the increase of his powers by tools and techniques that extended his physical being, we can designate the electronic age as the environmental extension, not of various parts of our bodies, but of the nervous system. Instead of affording a superior means of locomotion or transport, electricity moves information. Light and power become modes of information as much as information becomes a direct form of power and decision-making in all matters affecting merchandising and production.

It is above all the organic character of the loop or feedback that is involved in circuitry that constitutes the revolution of our time. It is not only in industry and economics that we persist in seeing our age through the spectacles of the older time of mechanism. Even in the communication industries the concept of broadcasting continues to be that of "transmission" rather than of feedback. But a century ago Poe and Baudelaire had fully recognized that communication is not transmission but feedback, not message but participation of the audience in the making process. This salutary perception derived from the new electric environment alters the conception of the role of art in society as much as it changes the relation of producer and market or man and the state. Art suddenly became not a privileged possession for elites but the indispensable means of perception and awareness for whole populations. Art was suddenly seen to be a prepared environment, or anti-environment, created to liberate human faculties from the universal numbing operation of environments as such. It was natural that some of this new vision of man's power to free himself from the perceptual servitude to environments, should have carried over into social and economic life. Ironically this new vision of perceptual liberation, through art as anti-environment, seemed quite at odds with the industrial environment that had recently arisen with a promise to free men from scarcity. For many it has seemed that the alienation both from life and from work, which arose with the age of the iron horse and the iron mills, was amply offset by the promise of abundance. Ugly surroundings and fragmented, repetitive toil were to be endured until there could be plenty for all.

Alienation occurs in any situation to the degree that there is specialism and fragmentation. The obsession with "involvement" that now pervades our culture is closely related to electric technology. Circuitry means that every situation must fold back into itself much in the pattern of cognition and its playback, which is "recognition" in the action of human perceiving and knowing. The new technology mimes the prime procedure of human learning and knowing. The electronic environment is swiftly processing the mechanical one into forms of organic unity. As Teilhard de Chardin observed, electromagnetism came into a mechanized world as "a prodigious biological event." It imposes its own modes and ground rules. It moves us out of a world of products into a world of processes. It stresses the exchange of services in place of things. It supplants artifacts with facts and production with learning and programming. After the nineteenth-century stress on produce and hardware, we move into a world of information and images. In such an environment the older technologies, including money, take on new functions and meanings. Above all, the patterns of work undergo total change.

What we call "jobs" represent a relatively recent pattern of work. When a man is using all his faculties we think he is at leisure, or at play. The artist doesn't have a job because he uses all his powers at once. Were he to pause to work out his income tax, he would be using only a few of his powers. That would be a "job." A mother doesn't have a "job" because she has to do forty jobs at once. So with a top executive or a surgeon. Under conditions of electric circuitry all the fragmented job patterns tend to blend once more into involving and demanding forms of work that more and more resemble teaching and learning and "human service" in its older sense of dedicated loyalty.

To the analytic observer of change the growth of the advertising industry in the past fifty years is very revealing. Its size helps us to understand why the moving of information is itself a principal industry of the electric age. A.T.&T. far overshadows any other enterprise, yet it moves mainly information. The rationale of advertising also heralds the age of automation. Automation is not gimmickry or gadgetry so much as programmed information. On an inclusive social basis, advertising aims at the orchestrating of all enterprises with all human needs and aspirations. As an adjunct to the mechanisms of the market, advertising serves to translate produce into information and images. The entire trend of advertising is away from the product to the process, from the separate item to the corporate image. And the corporate image is the most involving of effects for it is really made up of public attitudes.

Precisely because advertising moves toward the involving of the public in the production and distribution process, it is a self-liquidating institution. Computers now afford means of enabling the public to participate in product selection and design to the point at which current ad messages become irrelevant and superfluous. It seems likely that markets and the pricing system, as we have known them, are already obsolescent in relation to the computerized programming and processing of materials and the organization of work.

One way to get at this matter is to note how in the eighteenth century the rise of markets and pricing systems took on a new character when the supply of uniformly manufactured goods began to create a new image of the economy. Even by 1800 the proportion of the English economy that had been mechanized was small. It was a process seen mostly in the areas of iron and cotton. Quantitatively, the amount of social action subjected to mechanization was small. The amount of new mechanical hardware in relation to the entire traditional scene was insignificant. Yet the image that men had of their age was shifting. New models of perception had begun to invade the military and educational establishments. As for the arts, they had already proclaimed a revolution. Nature rather than the man-made artifact was now to be regarded as the prime source of aesthetic nourishment and inspiration. As the age of mechanized production gathered to an environmental or inclusive image, the arts announced themselves as an "anti-environmental" control system. As mechanical precision of repetitive production became a new pattern of work and organization, the arts turned to stress spontaneity of action and uniqueness of perception.

Similar contradictions on an even larger scale beset us in the new era of information processing and automation programming. The place of prices and markets and jobs and salaries necessarily assumes a very different relation to an economy based on electronic information movement from the relation they had as controls for a mechanized system of production. For electricity is not mechanical nor fragmented, nor is automated production necessarily oriented toward uniform and repeatable products. Indeed, it is as easy and economical to produce, via computer programming, unique variants of any product as to produce identical repetitions of the same. The custom-built and specially designed can be achieved at the same cost as the mass-produced. Yet such custom-made produce is not envisaged as a goal of automated production. The fact that it is possible draws attention to the wide differences between the old mechanization based on fragmentation of processes, and automation based on information circuits. More germane to the theme of salaries and guaranteed income, the information aspect of automation causes us to heed the new kinds of markets and pricing systems that must come into play as controls for the information environment.

Uniform pricing is a procedure quite meaningless without uniform commodities. Even as an organized system for quantifying information, money is of little use when there is an insufficiency of objects available for translation via the money technology. Money is a technology devised to perform the role of translating one kind of service into another. It is an information system that is now being subjected to special strains in the electronic information age. Money was never devised for electric speeds of transactions. In its private uses it is being pushed ever further in the credit card direction today. That means that money cannot persist indefinitely as a monolithic, uniform system of quantified data, under the conditions of electric information movement that include automation. We have already reached the multi-money phase. The decentralization of money into groupings of graded credit cards has already gone some distance. This is a development that corresponds very much to the natural thrust of electric technology away from uniformity and pyramidal centralism. It was the mechanical, fragmented technology and society that felt the need for centralism as a principle of order and power.

My chapter on "Automation" in *Understanding Media* begins with this theme, that electric integration creates multiplicity, autonomy, and diversity rather than sameness, dependence, and conformity:

A newspaper headline recently read, "Little Red Schoolhouse Dies When Good Road Built." One-room schools, with all subjects being taught to all grades at the same time, simply dissolve when better transportation permits specialized spaces and specialized teaching. At the extreme of speeded-up movement, however, specialism of space and subject disappears once more. With automation, it is not only jobs that disappear, and complex roles that reappear. Centuries of specialist stress in pedagogy and in the arrangement of data now end with the instantaneous retrieval of information made possible by electricity. Automation is information and it not only ends jobs in the world of work, it ends subjects in the world of learning. It does not end the world of learning. The future of work consists of learning a living in the automation age. This is a familiar pattern in electric technology in general. It ends the old dichotomies between culture and technology, between art and commerce, and between work and leisure. Whereas in the mechanical age of fragmentation leisure had been the absence of work, or mere idleness, the reverse is true in the electric age. As the age of information demands the simultaneous use of all our faculties, we discover that we are most at leisure when we are most intensely involved, very much as with the artists in all ages.

In creating a vast anti-environment to the mechanical age that began with printing from movable types, electromagnetism and circuitry have involved people and their interests in one another to an extreme degree. It is this interplay, or involvement in common circuits, that creates information and wealth and diversity alike. It is the condition of fragmentation and specialism that creates competitiveness and uniformity. Those who are assured of their uniqueness are much less inclined to be competitive.

The question of guaranteed income when viewed in relation to a fragmented economy of mechanical production and uniform prices, can indeed be considered with reference to scarcity and abundance. The question is then one of discovering a means of maintaining a correspondence between income and prices, and between products and customers. An insufficiency in any one of these sectors tends to be designated as "scarcity." Prices can then be seen as a kind of corporate social computer for working out relations between supply and demand, production and consumption. The same social "computer" function, applied to a wide area of fragmented factors of prices, products, and varied satisfactions was, in the eighteenth century, designated as the "hedonistic calculus." This mysterious, equilibrating action among a great array of objective and subjective components mystified the Age of Reason as much as the force of gravity. Until a high degree of fragmentation had come into the society such a "calculus" could not have occurred. Today it is natural to observe of the self-regulating functions of the market with regard to supply and demand, that it is with the factor of insufficiency that demand increases rapidly, as under rationing. In the first place a certain level of supply is needed to create demand at all. Three motorcars in a nation do not suffice for "demand." A motorcar "environment" has first to be created. After that process has been established, for any product, a decrease in supply creates a phenomenal flow of information. Advertising then occurs spontaneously without benefit of advertisers. Today advertising aims at creating the environmental dimension for each product. Information alone is now expected to do what the product did in previous times to create a milieu for itself.

A native society beset by "scarcity" of some single factor of supply will take vigorous action, making masks and doing dances to correct the cosmic imbalance. Looking on from the outside at this self-regulating mechanism of man and cosmos, we would be inclined to say that their "scarcity" was in the order of information rather than of products. As information levels rise the principle of substitutibility or transformation comes into play. Subsistence can then be won from an ever wider range of resources, until information itself becomes the principal commodity in function and in bulk.

Under conditions of electric information technology, "scarcity" can only accidentally and temporarily characterize any single sector or factor in the economy. The very concept of "scarcity" now begins to undergo a great change. We encounter the new concept in such phrases as "the problem of the culturally disadvantaged child." Such phrases result from an integral awareness of social viability. The older fragmented and specialist notions are not to be found here. At present, for example, "the culturally disadvantaged child" is as much a feature of the upper-middle-class world as of the "slum." He is a child who has failed to acquire that visual orientation of his sensory life that is still vital to the bureaucratic routines of school and market place.

The "scarcity" that typically afflicts men in the full current of electronic information play is that of time and energy to cope with the available information. "Information overload" is the abundance that creates the really traumatic scarcity of our age. There is, above all, scarcity of insight into the processes—physical, psychic, and social—whose control we now realize to be mandatory. With the sheer increase of the speed of information the entire social process enters a state of ever-enriching ferment and transformation of goals. As our technology eliminates insufficiency of products and means in all the private and public sectors, social man encounters the scarcity that has always haunted the rich—the scarcity of life itself to enjoy the opulence provided by nature and achieved by talent and genius. The social conflicts bred from hunger and from competition for limited resources, can now be resolved. The inner conflicts may become the more severe for all that, calling, it would seem, for an orchestration of resources in relation to our human faculties. Is it not from the occasionally achieved orchestration and harmony of our inner powers in relation to our outer problems that the big breakthroughs occur?

Guaranteed income must increasingly include the satisfaction we gain from effective involvement in meaningful work. "Leisure," which the artist always enjoys, is created by the fullest possible employment of the faculties in creative activity. In the same way a guaranteed income results from a coordination of community resources such as only electric automation can make possible. The orchestration and involvement of corporate resources that become natural with automation, create for the community the kind of "leisure" that has always been known to the individual artist and creative person: the leisure of fulfillment resulting from the fullest use of one's powers. It is this "leisure" that dissolves the existing job structure with its fragmentary and repetitive noninvolvement of the integral powers of man. The guaranteed income that results from automation could therefore be understood to include that quite unquantifiable factor of joy and satisfaction that results from a free and full disclosure of one's powers in any task organized to permit such activity. Guaranteed income, therefore, can indeed be thought of as relating to the obsolescent technology of machines and products and price, or it can be thought of more meaningfully in relation to learning and understanding and discovery through dialogue in human encounter, which are the work patterns of the electronic age.

THE ELECTROMAGNETIC SOCIETY

by OLIVER L. REISER

We are coming to an even more speculative part of the present theory of social cybernetics. Our hypothesis may be stated in the form of a question: If there is an analogy

---

(or homomorphic image) between electronic machines and brain machines, so that if you have a brain you can scan and when you can scan you have an essential feature of a brain, *does it not follow that as the world becomes more tightly knit into the interlacing network of radio, television, and telephonic systems, we human cells of the social organism are actually in the process of creating a world sensorium?*

Let us explore the possibilities. The hypothesis is based on the fundamental idea that as social evolution progresses and becomes ever more intimately interwoven with the proliferating spiderwebs of telephony, radio, television, radar, telegraphy, and other media of communication, we are in fact constructing what may be termed the electromagnetic society.

In order that the world may be integrated into an electromagnetic society, we shall require as a physical basis for world unity, a unified and world-wide symbolism such as C. K. Bliss has given us in his *Semantography*. We are all familiar with the integrative power of symbols (flags, dramas, parades, folkways, science notations, and the like), which secure this cohesive power from the potency of symbolism as a common denominator for ideational and emotional responses within and among humans. At the present time it looks as if the semantography of the coming world organism might start with the simple picture language of Bliss. If somehow it were possible to shrink all knowledge and all human history so that an all-world drama could be put on a universal symbolism basis for invariant transfer across the social whole, and if it were possible to use the full play of global techniques in a unified semantography for television sets, the epic space-time drama curving the planetary field and bending the arc of human evolution into the spiral of a time-binding synthesis would lift up the inner lives of peoples everywhere by sheer evocation of latent powers. Thus history would be salvaged from the dark domain of futility and despair.

Social Physics

Social physics is an empirical social science which is interested in relating a number of separate sciences: mathematics, physics, sociology, economics, linguistics, and others. Contributors to this field include George K. Zipf, John Q. Stewart, Stuart Carter Dodd, John von Neumann, W. F. Sutherland, and N. Rashevsky. An important concept in social physics is the notion of *demographic energy*. As a working hypothesis, *demographic energy* refers to the *number of human relationships per unit of time* thought of not as static but as an impulse which happens like a wave along the string. The *accumulating total* of such happenings is the integral of the energy with respect to time, and seems to resemble *action* in physics.

Demographic energy defines the relation of N_1 people who are at a distance d from N_2 people. Hence the formula, $N_1 \cdot N_2/d$, worked out by Zipf, has for example been applied to the interchange of telephone calls between pairs of cities. The appearance in this formula of the factor of inverse distance (the d in the denominator) is theoretically reasonable, for the further apart people are the less interaction with each other, and has much empirical evidence in its favor. This demographic energy can be computed from a map showing *contours of potential* as these have been worked out at Princeton University.

To those who are versed in the science of electrical engineering, this has an element of familiarity because the formula, "potential equals population divided by distance," is analogous to Ohm's law, "current equals voltage divided by resistance." Some persons might think this isomorphism is accidental—but not the social physicists! Two lines of supporting evidence may be introduced, one practical and one theoretical. Let us consider them.

Some indication of the fantastic developments in electrical integration, inspired largely by military needs, is the "push button" system of defending the United States against possible air attacks. The system (called SAGE) involves the use of electronic brains at radar sites to count the approaching enemy planes, determine their altitudes, distances, flying speeds, etc., and flash this information to sub-sectors of the Direction Center. All the information from all centers is recorded on IBM-type cards which speed this information into a computer. On the basis of the total information, appropriate counter-measures are taken—the decisions being made by "thinking machines" which even specify what types of weapons are to be used in counter-measures. A similar development for commercial air transportation will soon be required by civil airports to control planes of the jet age as they streak through the sky lanes at supersonic speeds. This spreading network of radar-controlled airports will require new kinds of computers with electronic memory devices to minimize the human element in the dawning air and ether age.

All this is but a hint of what is coming in all areas of communication, including television, radio, radar, and other media where we are moving into a situation in which sub-centers (ganglia) know everything about what is going on in their convolutions of the world brain, with higher-level integrations giving decisions at appropriate times based on information from the interwoven areas. One can be sure that if the "West" is committed to such an electromagnetic pattern of integration, the "East" will also follow suit with similar radar networks. One can only hope that global television programs will become the civilian peace-time substitutes for the military electromagnetic integrations.

On the theoretical side, a measure of support for the thesis that an electromagnetic society is emerging is provided by Mr. W. F. Sutherland's investigations. In a paper on "The Dynamics of Economic Growth," presented at the meeting of the AAAS in December, 1950, Mr. Sutherland (of the Toronto Hydro-Electrical System) showed in detail how laws regulating the human behaviorial economy resemble those of electrophysics. After noting the manner in which variations of current or voltage in an electric circuit follow patterns similar to those of the logistic curve, Mr. Sutherland indicated the way in which it is possible to define and measure "economic force," "economic resistance," and other parameters on the basis of the similarities between economic and electrical action patterns.

It is true that Mr. Sutherland's argument that the behavior of the economic system as a whole can be dealt with by the same equations which are used for the dynamo is based on reasoning by analogy, but the similarities between electrical machines and our electromagnetic society are certainly suggestive of reliable isomorphisms. Even the parallel between the non-linearity of brain physiology and social electrophysiology carries over, for as Mr. Sutherland points out, the growth potential (demographic energy) of a community is more than the sum of the individual potentials. This point is sufficiently important to justify a fuller statement.

The Non-Linearity of Field Physics

While the social physicists share in unity of viewpoint, there is one place where differences of opinion crop up. In the foregoing paragraph, I mentioned the analogy between the non-linearity of brain physiology and social electrophysiology. In our own theory of emergent evolution we have constantly emphasized that our field-theoretical approach, by way of levels of organization associated with new or emergent dimensionalities, specifically provides for gestalt properties which are transposable across the social (macroscopic) wholes. In such cases, where non-linear equations are appropriate, a function of the sum is not a sum of the functions.

We have also insisted that this type of situation appears in biology, psychology, and sociology, no less than in physics. A brief quotation will illustrate this idea in physics. In the Appendix to the 1953 edition of his book, *The Meaning of Relativity,* Albert Einstein announced that he had worked out equations which gave unity to gravitational and electromagnetic forces. These equations are "non-linear partial differential equations"—much more complicated than those of the original relativity theory. This unified field theory cannot at present be tested because no one knows how to verify the equations.

In an article by Einstein and Infeld, the requirements of the situation in physics are clearly set forth as follows:

A linear law always means that the motion of singularities is arbitrary. If to a world-line of a singularity with mass m_1 there belongs a field F_1 and if to a world-line of a singularity with mass m_2 there belongs a field F_2, then the superposition of these two fields, that is $F_1 + F_2$, is also a solution of the linear equations. In such a solution the same two world-lines would appear together that appeared singly. Therefore the field with its linear laws cannot apply to any interaction between the singularities. Thus only non-linear field equations can provide us with equations of motion because only non-linearity can express the interaction between singularities.

If the reader will now substitute the term *neuron* for *singularity,* and *circuit* for *world-line* in this quotation, we have an analogue for the microscopic and macroscopic levels of the brain. And if, in relativity theory, the field constitutes a non-linear continuum wherein the familiar additive formula for the compounding of velocities and addition of vectors is set aside because of the non-linearity of the situation, how much more so do brain processes and social phenomena manifest non-linear, non-additive, or gestalt-wholistic properties?

This latter is my own extrapolation. It may be noted that this isomorphism in the non-linearity of physical fields, biological fields, cortico-mental fields, and psycho-social fields is neither accepted nor rejected by contemporary science, simply because the question is not even considered in current theorizing. However, a few investigators are beginning to realize the presence of the problem. Recently several social scientists have raised the question of whether the socio-cultural field is a non-linear field. One author has used the term "macro-economics" to refer to situations wherein the properties of the whole are not a sum of the properties of the parts.

The Limitations of Contemporary Social Science

Some of the difficulties encountered in current social science are certainly due to the inadequate conceptual foundations on which these "sciences" rest. Economics, politics, and psychology are missing out because they deal with partial systems rather than wholes. Moreover, the newer quasi-sciences, mainly in the social domain, have not passed beyond the empirical stage because they have not yet derived their basic general laws. When these laws are formulated, they may approximate those of the physical sciences. The problem of "analogies" among the sciences needs to be restudied in the light of *homomorphic images* analysis. To make this point more specifically, let us return to the subject of social physics.

The work in the area of social physics is in one sense a direct application of physical laws to physical things and events, and in another sense it is a study of isomorphic relations. Dr. John Q. Stewart, for example, considers "mass" as being the sheer physical mass of the things mankind accumulates around itself, and also as being *analogous* to the idea of mass when society is treated as a gas subject to gas laws. Mr. Frank Sutherland also employs the concept of mass in this dual manner. He recognizes that physical space is important, but there is also the idea of economic organization as constituting a kind of economic (non-physical) space. The virtue of this is evident, since the consequence is a coherent set of dimensions which suffices to give homogeneity to the economic equational system—a higher kind of isomorphism than the merely analogical. In a more general way, the new science of social cybernetics will furnish us with a bridge of isomorphism whereby certain archetypal forms may be given greater universality.

The right road is indicated by Sutherland when he points out that economic space is not physical space, nor is economic force the same as physical force. They are both isomorphic, though not identical. The electrical theory is used as a stepping stone to economic theory and, once established, this latter is able to stand on its own feet with its own set of dimensions and definitions. Both levels, however, are still "organismic."

The fact is that organismic action fields have not yet been recognized and dealt with adequately. Even feed-backs are essentially organismic since they occur only in action fields that are something more than linear. *Structure* is necessary in such cases. The living body contains a whole host of such action-fields, as do the economic and political domains. Most of these are of the negative variety, but positive feed-backs also occur. The cybernetics analysis should recognize this, especially when dealing with wholistic situations. But the forthright acceptance of an isomorphism between lower and higher dimensions carries us far beyond the old Aristotelian-Euclidian-Newtonian three-dimensional framework for the physical world, and this is clearly discernible in dimensional analysis as applied to higher function spaces. To the electrical engineer the foregoing ideas will come as old friends. In their own area the work they have done is considerable. To be sure, the application of such analysis to social systems has not gone very far, but when the coming electrical-social system attains its emergent being, electrodynamics will find its proper place in the new social science.

In these references to field-physics sociology we find support for our conception of gestalt properties of a macroscopic whole. Surely in time the social scientists will come to grips with this problem. Meantime, we must formulate our answer to the question: Is the psychic field which characterizes the world sensorium the product of the individual mental fields, or is it a wholistic, non-linear field which is *sui generis*? But in the latter case, how can it be an "emergent"? Or is it possible that these alternatives are not mutually exclusive of each other?

Admittedly the hypothesis of a Psychic Field for the World Sensorium is highly speculative, but by long tradition philosophers are permitted to explore far beyond the already charted territories of knowledge. However, to confer upon our visions some measure of confirmation, let us for a moment return to the realm of established facts by quoting the following passage, which will then be used as a kind of springboard for another leap into a world of imagination. In his masterly work, *Man on his Nature*, Sir Charles Sherrington pictures the brain when it is asleep and awake. He asks us to imagine:

A scheme of lines and nodal points, gathered together at one end into a great ravelled knot, the brain, and at the other end trailing off to a sort of stalk, the spinal cord. Imagine activity in this shown by little points of light. Of these some flash rhythmically, faster or slower. Others are travelling points streaming in serial lines at various speeds. The rhythmic stationary lights lie at nodes. The nodes are both goals whither converge, and junctions whence diverge, the lines of travelling lights. Suppose we choose the hour of deep sleep. Then only at sparse and out-of-the-way places are nodes flashing and trains of light points running. The great knotted headpiece lies for the most part quite dark. Occasionally at places in it lighted points flash or move but soon subside.

Should we continue to watch the scheme we should observe after a time an impressive change which suddenly occurs. In the great head end which had been mostly darkness spring myriads of lights, as though activity from one of these local places suddenly spread far and wide. The great topmost sheet of the mass, where hardly a light twinkled or moved becomes now a sparkling field of rhythmic flashing points with trains of travelling sparks hurrying hither and thither. It is as if the milky way entered upon some cosmic dance. Swiftly the head mass becomes an enchanted loom where millions of flashing shuttles weave a dissolving pattern, always a meaningful pattern though never an abiding one. The brain is awake and with it the mind is returning.

In the foregoing comparison the distinguished physiologist depicts the brain asleep and awake. Our problem—somewhat different—is to evolve a world brain which can then be "awakened." But since, for us, the cells are individual human beings, the "awakening" will consist in linking the "cell tubes" functionally through a communication system whereby messages that have an all-world meaning (that is, represent a gestalt picture like scanning in television) are transmitted. In other words, the awakening of a world sensorium corresponds to the fabrication of a social cortex because the interlacing networks of electrical proliferations are the transmission channels of the social nervous system. In order to provide the physical basis for world-level meanings, the world cortex spiderweb of action patterns must be synchronized by a central clocking device which arranges the "program" in a temporal sequence. The immensely simple message to be written into the form of a universal picture language will be spelled out over a planetary network of interlacing lines uniting the peoples of the world into an electromagnetic society. This will be the incarnation of a planetary civilization with unified symbolism providing the physical basis for a higher-level unity. In such a case, communication is not person-to-person, but person-to-world-mind-to-person.

III

Enterprise and

Remuneration

Perhaps the most significant aspect of the middle
third of the twentieth century has been the sustained economic growth achieved in the post-
World War II era. This has raised the real possibility of world-wide industrialization and of the
emergence in more advanced industrial nations
of what has been called a post-industrial culture.
—HERMAN KAHN AND ANTHONY J. WIENER,
The Year 2000 (1967)

THE MANAGEMENT OF BUSINESS

by BERNARD J. MULLER-THYM

THE same kinds of changes are going on in business, as pervasive, as revolutionary, and as profound as are going on in the quality of education, in science and technology.

I thought I would try to talk of three types of points: one, the change in the nature of business as a system, and specifically about the goal of business as a wealth-creator in our society: two, changes in the nature of work, organization and structure of work; three, changes in the nature and uses of authority and power.

Now prior to about 1950, or at least prior to the end of World War II, those things we called business were rather simple and rather naïve. You had a business, for example, if you had something to sell. In a world of relative scarcity you supposed that there was a market and supposed that there were people ready to buy your product if you could somehow meet them or find them. You assembled a few people with a relatively low order of skill who knew how to make something, a few people who knew how to persuade others to buy it, and somebody to watch the figures to make sure you didn't run out of money. If you combined these few skills of a very low order with a high energy influx, you had a business. If at the end of any given period of time you had taken in more money than you had paid out, you'd call this a profit, and you were all right. This concept of a business and this approach to running a business was generally all right—for the pre-World War II type world.

Actually, the role of business in the total economy was not to create wealth, but to manipulate it, to regulate it, to redistribute it. The only sources of excellent newness in the world were two.

The first was nature, so that from the planting of a seed we could multiply a hundredfold, or from husbandry, the mating of animals, sheep, slaves and so forth, one would get absolute increase. The other source was from what the economists called technological advance, but it's really invention, where invention is considered to be the work of independent, sporadically occurring geniuses. Leonardo da Vinci invented submarines, and Watts the steam engine, and Whitney the cotton gin, and somebody else the computer.

But these are all regarded as acts of some mysteriously occurring thing in isolation, and the work of the entrepreneur was to take the invention and pay the inventor for 17 years for his work (our patent laws all work in this way). Then the entrepreneur exploited the invention, and by way of making it available to large numbers of people he spread around the increase in wealth which the invention itself made possible.

The classic economists, like Karl Marx and Adam Smith, said that profit was a reward to the entrepreneur for doing this kind of thing. But, basically, it is a closed universe in which there is only a certain amount of wealth which is manipulated; the role of business is to keep shuffling this stuff around, reallocating it, and so forth.

Two things happened just about 1950. First, we invented the organization of invention; the most interesting newly invented institution has been this. Where we don't have a body of existing knowledge, we now know how to invent it, as General Electric did when they invented the whole business of the behavior of liquid sodium in a high temperature range. They took a couple of months off and invented a branch of physics.

We know that the process of invention basically works backwards. In the kind of world in which we live you decide what you're going to invent, and then you mobilize the competencies which are required to invent this; then you simply move forward to invent it. This mode of progress is not limited. You don't get results by accretion or by addition, for the way in which a system-type project develops is something like the development which takes place at conception from zygote, embryo, fetus, infant, child, adult and so on. Here, the total reality is being designed at the very beginning, and the mode of progress is from the immature to the mature.

We invented the organization of invention, and then we deliberately plugged this into a business complex in the form of a research and development department, or of some department for the management of innovation. How many companies in America, in 1950, had a formally organized research and development group? There weren't very many.

It's commonplace today for a company to have an organized research faculty. Now there can be only one reason for this organized kind of research, and that is to take a business which has a system we have conceived of as a closed system (one which was in balance, and in which output was equal to input) and to punch a hole in it, to inject imbalance, to create disturbance. As a result of disturbance and a subsequent functioning of the business as a total system, it will have reached that point where it is able to re-create its relationship with customers. Then something will have happened as a result of which there is absolutely more in the sum of the outputs than was in the sum of the inputs.

This is something absolutely new, and the result is that it has turned most businesses into systems which, in our society, have the role of being a wealth-generator, not simply a wealth-manipulator.

Now I am talking about something that is commonplace in the lives of managers and presidents of companies who are making decisions. Managers make decisions today in terms of a kind of economics which has yet to be written, and which very few economists recognize for anything like this. The implications of this new economics are simply tremendous, and one cannot foresee the limits at all. A business has really become a machine for generating wealth. It has been an organization for mobilizing competences. It has become an organization for channeling intelligence in such a way that some new kind of economic reality, called wealth, will be brought into big business. Therefore the manager becomes a designer of complex systems—in the sense that the Polaris is a system or that the DNA molecule is a system—which have their own inner dynamics, laws, and parameters which interact with each other. The manager is much more concerned with the dynamics of the interplay of the systems than he is with the optimization within the framework of a single system itself.

Therefore, a manager has to become very proficient today in

the use of many logics, such as the array of operations-research techniques, the knowledge of how to build models, the use of information systems and computers, and so forth. All of these things prepare him for that moment, which is discontinuous with its antecedent, in which he has to bring something into existence. This is something different from what managers have done prior to 1950.

The second thing that has happened has been a radical change in organization and the nature of work. Prior to about 1950, we assumed that the work of workers, people like meal-getters, valve-washers, rope-pullers, symbol-recorders, and information processors, could be done better if we would take the sequence of operations, the process, and break it down by some analytical method into units which we would arrange linearly so as to shove the work in here and hopefully have it come out at the other end. This is not basically an efficient way of getting work done, for you cannot get work that has any kind of skill requirements done in this fashion. I would like to point out to you that the reason we organize work this way in the textbooks has not been because it is more efficient to do so. The real author of the invention of this type of work array was not Henry Ford or Frederick Winslow Taylor; it was probably some one no later than the ancient scribes who invented the phonetic alphabet and writing on paper.

Since we invented work around 7500 years ago, we have had a work habit based on somebody who invented a tool like a spade. Then we have a slave who will take the spade and dig something; we stand a man over the slave to make sure he's digging; then we create a third person, like an auditor, to watch these two to make sure that they are doing it. Thus, we created this basic cell or this basic component of a worker. So, having designed work of workers in this fashion and having made the concomitant design commitments, we have to have somebody working over these people, whether he be a slave or a free man or a member of management.

These are the sort of assumptions we've made about organization and the way it was working. I don't think there's a single company represented in this group, whatever way it may draw its organization chart, which is not operating outside the precepts of that chart. An organization chart doesn't tell you where the components are. It doesn't give one any clue as to the requirements of an actions communication network for getting things done.

What happened was that as we turned business into a wealth-creating organ of our society, there began to be all these massive inputs from the many human bodies of knowledge which were developing. It would be a rash man who would single out any substantive body of human knowledge on which the manager of a modern business may not have to call in the running of his business. And the competence level required is going up all the time.

Our organizational shapes are no longer pyramidal in character; we are living with kinds of work structures which, if you diagram them, would look like diagrams of a nervous system, or a circuit model for a computer. A total business system will be made up of a complex of centers that have very high concentration of skills; these centers are united by communication networks in which ideally one could go from any action-taking, decision-making, information-handling center to any other. What is coming into existence is a kind of complex in which there are many centers. For example, here will be a chemical plant with all kinds of engineers, productive capabilities, people on part applications, people who keep the equipment running sweetly. These people perform in an automated way, or with combinations of human beings and machines, various families of productive work; combined with them are people who manage markets, and who manage relationships with different customer groups. The complex here is a simple, successful chemical company which almost defies description.

Now we have not gone as far as this, organizationally, until now, because the technical problem of managing the total information of the system with manual technologies on a sampling basis made it emotionally too difficult to do. We can now manage such networks with computers, more accurately, more sensitively, and in totality.

This is something of the nature of the organizational forms coming into existence, where servile work is disappearing; along with this, the inconvenience of pay is disappearing. The ironic thing is that the moment when we really want to get rid of slavery, at the moment when for the first time in history we know absolutely how to create wealth (we know that wealth and value are not added by production, but they are a function of innovation, marketing, research and of the total business of a system), we are losing what has been the only mechanism in our society for distributing wealth: wages. It's up to us to invent another kind of money, another mechanism for distributing wealth.

But whether we do that well or not, the requirements of a manager to make decisions and run such a network is a present-day requirement. And so the manager should know about computers in order, first of all, not to be baffled by the computer experts. One must know the limits of a class logic, and the optimizations they present; also what it means to live in an electronic world, because contrary to what many people will tell you, the computer is not simply something for performing linear functions faster. A computer belongs to a radically different order of existence. It is not electro-mechanical; things in it do not happen sequentially; it does not belong to the age of the wheel. It belongs to an age when we can deal with things in totality, instantaneously, at 186,000 miles per second, and using randomness as a resource. Now the minute you begin to use randomness as a resource, you can integrate at will and you can redesign at will. And this is not cultivating energy, but quite the contrary. It is the ability to use any available bit of human competence, rearranging this to one's own purposes in relationship to what one decides to do. This is what managers are now about to do and are just starting to do.

And so this puts a very special requirement on managers, but what has happened to them in terms of our work force is that no longer in a business do we really have any one person making a decision. Whether this was ever good or not, I don't know. And there are some times and some situations which human beings are faced with when you do want one man to call a signal. For example, I want only one man doing this in a control tower at an airport. I want only one traffic cop on a corner, and I don't want him if the lights are operating; because the way you cause traffic jams is to have a cop out there making counter-signals to the lights.

When you do have one man to make a goal, where by the simple injection of his decision to do something you now create a variable which has not existed in the array of variables you considered prior to this. And sometimes you make the thing right by doing it, as for example what happened the time I was driving out to LaGuardia Airport. It was raining, and a dump truck had overturned in such a way that only one lane was left open. Some man, who had no blue suit, no star, no symbols of authority, got out of his car and directed traffic. Do you know that every single motorist obeyed him; temporarily, he had whatever validation and authority were necessary to perform this task.

When there are circumstances like this in a business, what we have are multiple centers of decision-making, very powerful, all working together. If you want to call functioning in such a network making a group decision, you can; but the language and the models on which the group decision is based don't fit this example too well. But if you have a system like this in an identical-type company, and you have programs for the business' organization and information systems, the requirement for information here is one of openness, totality, and the ability to integrate at will.

Each of these centers operates with a high degree of skill, with a maximum of economy, and this corresponds with the maximum of dependence upon the network. Now this is a paradox in which the manager is caught. It's one of those of authority and freedom which have been bouncing around in our discussions recently. Multiple centers are action-taking, decision-making, and information-handling. The requirements for a high degree of competence, a maximum of autonomy and freedom correspond with the maximum dependence upon a network itself.

Now this will be frightening only if you try to put it against the folklore of management which is in all the books. If you just think of it in terms of the requirements of the work to be done, it's not hard at all. It does clash with the old clichés about delegation (that you can delegate authority, but you can't delegate responsibility), which is absolutely meaningless; you can accept this remark only if you don't think about it.

If you'll think of this in terms of the actual requirements of running the system, the problems aren't so great; they are very much like typical human problems. They are a sign of excellence and perfection, rather than imperfections, because as systems in nature become more perfect, they become more complex and more independent; at the same time they require and even create the requirement of greater dependence upon other systems.

In this sense the manager today can no longer operate in isolation from the rest of the world. He has not only to be aware of his environment, to keep his business relevant to the culture, to the society, to the polity, to the world in which it functions, but he has to do this in such a way that he can see himself interacting, if possible, with somebody in Ghana, in Troy, New York, and Asia Minor, and wherever it is that these centers of interaction are likely to take place. This supposes that we have, along with the requirement for greater sophistication in managing networks, an exponentially increasing requirement as managers, not for information turned out linearly with computers, but for information presented in its totality. In order to function in such a world, the world itself must be loaded with intelligence and mutually interacting information.

A SYSTEM OF SOCIAL ACCOUNTS

by DANIEL BELL

T HE development of national economic accounting provides us with an instructive picture of the workings of a modern economy. There are, at present, for example, four types of accounting systems which allow us to measure different kinds of economic phenomena and transactions: (a) National Income and Product Accounts sum up the total value of goods and services transacted in the economy and the allocation of net income among households, government, business, and foreign units; (b) National Moneyflow Accounts trace the flow of funds between financial and non-financial units, including households and gov-

Excerpted from "Notes on the Post-Industrial Society (I)," by Daniel Bell, in *The Public Interest* # 7 (Spring, 1967). Copyright © 1967 by *National Affairs, Inc.* Reprinted by permission.

ernment; (c) National Interindustry Accounts set forth the value of purchases and sales of goods and services between variously "disaggregated" units of business, government, household and foreign sectors; (d) National Wealth Accounting, in effect a national assets inventory, evaluates the reproducible assets and resources of the nation.

Yet these and other economic concepts, particularly the now familiar Gross National Product, are limited in their use, and sometimes—more by popular opinion than by professional economists—give us a distorted picture of the social economy. GNP measures the sum total of goods and services transacted within the *market* economy. It is immediately apparent that services performed within a household—by a wife, for example—are not "valued." (The British economist A. C. Pigou, a pioneer of welfare economics, once remarked that if a widowed vicar paid his housekeeper a weekly wage, this was an addition to the national income; if he married her, it became a subtraction.) The point at stake is that "income" in rural areas (where a substantial amount of food may be produced at home) is often "under-valued" as against urban income—a fact neglected not only in some discussions about poverty in the U.S., but in the international comparisons between the U.S. and some well-to-do agrarian countries (e.g., Denmark, New Zealand) who, on the scale of GNP, rank lower than their real income would put them.

Moreover, if national income is understated by considering GNP alone, the sense of progress can be exaggerated by the "additive" nature of GNP accounting. Thus, when a factory is built, the new construction and the new payroll are an addition to the GNP. If, at the same time, the factory pollutes a stream and builds a filtration plant to divert the wastes, these expenditures, too, become an addition to the GNP.* True, more money

---

* In a similar vein, Victor Fuchs of the National Bureau of Economic Research, in writing of the expansion of the service sector of the economy, remarks: "There has been a presumption [among economists] that the more highly developed the economy the more useful the [real GNP as a] measure becomes. . . . But the trend may now be in the other direction, because at very high levels of GNP per capita, a large fraction of productive effort is devoted to the services (where real output is very difficult to measure) and to other activities (that are not measured at all)." Among the activities that are not measured today, in fact, are many government services, since these cannot be valued at market prices.

has indeed been spent in the economy; but the gross addition simply masks an "offset cost," not a genuine contribution to economic progress. The definition of what is an addition and what is an offset clearly is a difficult task, but one insufficiently recognized in the popular discussion of national economic accounting, and in the widespread acceptance of GNP as a "welfare" or "growth" measuring device.

One can have a meaningful sense of progress only by knowing its costs, direct and indirect. A difficulty in national economic accounting today is that of assigning the costs generated by one group which often are borne by others (e.g., the costs to the community of strip mining, gouging out a countryside).* But the problem is not one that can be handled on an *ad hoc* basis. We need a broader cost matrix.

In effect, what we need is a System of Social Accounts which would broaden our concept of costs and benefits, and put economic accounting into a broader framework. The eventual purpose would be to create a "balance sheet" that would be useful in clarifying policy choices.

What would a system of social accounts allow us to do? The word "accounts," as it stands now, is perhaps a misnomer. Sociologists have been able to establish few completely consistent sets of relationships (such as the relationship, say, between unemployment and delinquency). Even where sophisticated social analysis can establish relationships, it is difficult to establish these in measurable terms. But we can begin by seeking to establish a conceptual framework.

A System of Social Accounts would begin with a series of social indicators that would give us a broader and more balanced reckoning of the meaning of economic progress as we know it. This

---

* A "far-out," but still telling, example is that of New York City, which in order to reduce the "costs" of snow removal no longer hires additional private trucks to cart away the snow but has its sanitation department push the snow into the middle of the busy streets where passing taxis, busses and cars grind it into slush that is then hosed down the sewers. The city reduced its costs, but the amount of slush which splattered on the trousers, coats, and dresses of the passersby increased the cleaning and dyeing bills in the city by a substantial amount. From the point of view of the city and the cleaning industry there was a distinct gain; but this surely was an "irrational" way of distributing the extra costs involved.

effort to set up a System of Social Accounts would move us toward four goals:

(a) the measurement of the social costs and net returns of innovations,

(b) the measurement of social ills (e.g., crime, family disruption),

(c) the creation of "performance budgets" in areas of defined social needs (e.g., housing, education),

(d) indicators of economic opportunity and social mobility.

The following elaboration of the four problems referred to above is meant to be merely illustrative.

(a) *Social Costs and Net Return:* Technological advances create new investment opportunities. These investments are expected to be paid for by the enhanced earnings they produce. But clearly there are losses as well. The major loss is the unemployment created by technological change, particularly in those instances where the advanced age of the worker of the particular skill that is displaced makes it difficult for him to find new employment. Or, a new plant in an area may create new employment opportunities, yet its by-products—water pollution and air pollution—may create additional costs for the community. Long ago, Professor A. C. Pigou demonstrated, in his *The Economics of Welfare*, that there is frequently a divergence between the private cost borne by an entrepreneur and the social costs. Into the cost account of the private entrepreneur goes only those items for which he has to pay, while such items as maintenance of the unemployed, provisions for the victims of industrial accidents or occupational diseases, costs of access roads, etc. are borne, in the old phrase of J. M. Clark, as "social overhead costs."

The question of which costs should be borne by the firm and which by the community is clearly a matter of public policy. Increasingly, for example, firms responsible for polluting the waters of a river are asked to bear the costs of filtration. The Ruhr, flowing through West Germany's most dense industrial region, is at present less polluted than it was twenty years ago. Swimming and boating are commonplace. This happy circumstance is the result of a cooperative arrangement between 259 municipalities and 2,200 industries along the river who have developed a system of effluent fees calculated to encourage the construction of waste disposal systems. In this case the entire cost of pollution is assigned to the source. On the other hand, certain costs of severence pay or maintenance of an older labor force on a firm's payroll may be so huge as to inhibit the introduction of useful technological devices, and such costs might more efficiently be borne by the community than by the firm itself. But these questions of public policy can only be decided when we have a clearer picture of the actual social costs and returns of particular innovations.*

(b) *The Measurement of Social Ills:* Every society pays a huge price for crime, juvenile delinquency, and disruption of the family. The costs of child care and mental health are also high. There are no simple causes, such as unemployment, of such social ills. Yet such ills and social tensions do, in a measurable way, have significant effects on the economy (from loss of able-bodied workers because of mental illness, to direct losses of property because of thefts and riots). Although data on crime, on health, dependent children and the like are collected by U.S. Government agencies, there is rarely any effort to link these problems to underlying conditions; nor is there a full measure of the cost of these ills. Systematic analysis of such data might suggest possible courses of remedial action.

(c) *Performance Budgets:* The American commitment is not only to raise the standard of living, but to improve the quality of life. But we have few "yardsticks" to tell us how we are doing. A system of social accounts would contain "performance budgets" in various areas to serve as such yardsticks. A national "housing budget," for example, would indicate where we stand in regard to the goal of a "decent home for every American family." It would also enable us to locate, by city and region, the areas of greatest needs and so provide the basis for effective public policy.

---

* Andrew Shonfield, in his book *Modern Capitalism*, points out that the construction of a new subway line in London was held up for over a decade on the premise that it couldn't pay its way—until someone demonstrated that the secondary benefits resulting for the people *not* using the line (in speeding taxi and private vehicular flow and the like) would result in a true return on investment which was 10 percent over the capital cost of the project. Andrew Shonfield, *Modern Capitalism* (Oxford University Press, 1965), pp. 227-229.

A series of community health indices would tell us how well we are meeting the needs of our people in regard to adequate medical care.

(d) *Indicators of Economic Opportunity and Social Mobility:* More than twenty-five years ago, in *An American Dilemma*, Gunnar Myrdal wrote: "We should . . . have liked to present in our study a general index, year by year or at least decade by decade, as a quantitative expression of the movement of the entire system we are studying: the status of the Negro in America. . . . But the work of constructing and analyzing a general index of Negro status in America amounts to a major investigation in itself, and we must leave the matter as a proposal for later research."

Two decades later, we still have no "general index" of the status of the Negro in America. In a strict methodological sense, no "comprehensive indexes" are perhaps possible; but we *can* assemble specific indicators. Thus, where once it seemed impossible to conceive of a "value" figure for "human assets," the creation of recent years of a "lifetime-earning power index" gives us a measure to reflect the improvements in income which come with increased education, improvement in health, and reduction of discrimination. And economists have a term, "opportunity costs," which allows us to calculate not only direct costs but also the gains foregone from the use of those resources elsewhere.

DOLLARABILITY

by R. BUCKMINSTER FULLER

Money was devised primarily as an abstract means by which man might convert his specific-work (energy conversion) into the acquisition of those products of the work of others necessary to his completeness of growth.

The more industrialized man has become in harnessing his environment for mutual inter-service, protection, routine and growth, the more specialized—that is, the more scientifically coöperative—he has also become.

The main difference between the agrarian world, with its dominant animate slavery, and the industrial world, which is characterized by the inanimate servitude of abstract power, is that in the former man could—and did—essentially consume and support himself out of the direct products of his work, whereas today's industrial worker could not possibly survive by the consumption of the glass bulb turned out by the machine he tends, or of an electric winding.

In the agrarian era of local intercourse, man could barter his surplus product directly with the local producer of other necessities. Money, as an abstract interpolation medium, was unnecessary. Such money as was then in circulation functioned as a means of product conversion in the export, by the landlord, of the surplus products of his serfs. In foreign lands these were converted into tangible forms of intrinsic wealth for the landlord's account.

In the current industrial era, the "dollar" is an utter necessity for the worker in the interpolation of his specialized work into essential goods and services; not, however, the metallic dollar, which is a relic from the buccaneering age when exporting landlords had little knowledge of the value of goods to be received in exchange for their produce. They were trading, as have, also, frontiersmen, even up to now, with unknown people and toward whom they had not by experience established credit. In the course of early trading, a metallic money was developed as a concentrate medium of exchange and a *belief* grew up as to its potentially direct value, which in due course was improperly termed "credit." Money, metallically, was relatively the safest medium of temporary value maintenance, being almost non-corrosive and non-substitutable due to its rarity. Moreover, because of its high concentration it was easily stowable and defendable.

This metallic characteristic of money is no longer a primarily essential part of the internal U.S. dollar. Not only is the industrial worker of America willing to interpolate his work stint into a paper dollar—an intrinsically worthless medium—but actually prefers it to a metallic dollar, since he credits every worker in the United States with an understanding of, and belief in, the integrity of coöperation that obviates a metallic specie in favor of the far more efficiently transportable "greenback." He goes even further. He writes his own dollars in the form of checks, signifying integrity in a still higher degree.

In the course of his employment by an industrial establishment, the American worker often receives a check for his services which says, in effect, that he has industrially done his stint on the basis of so many hours of precise energy conversion, the value of his length of service being at least theoretically amplified in direct proportion to the technical nicety of his precision-ability in the process of energy conversion.

This check, which represents an account of his work, is usually deposited in an accounting-storage for subsequent conversion into whatever services and goods he needs within the limits of this storage. Very often the check is immediately exchanged by the "bank" for dollar bills, for efficient reasons, a few of which we shall relate.

If a worker's accounted total of work is small and his requirements minimal, the individual value of the goods and services of which he is in immediate need is low, the true value being *basically* determined by the quantum of converted energy involved in the product of service, despite popular misconceptions of value due to a "royalty"-to-"royalty" or "profit" superimposition.

Coins of small denomination represent a particularly useful

work conversion medium for the individual in the interpolation of work into low value goods and services since cash sales minimize "overhead." Such coins, however, seldom represent the real intrinsic, or open market, value of the metal out of which they are stamped; for instance, a dollar in pennies may be worth only about 15¢ as copper metal. Coins of small denomination are denominationally valid only by *popular credit*. As fractional units of paper dollars (by man's habit of thinking) they are so quickly and therefore so efficiently handled that their use eliminates the costly accounting necessarily involved in the acquisition of minor goods and services through the medium of a paper check.

It costs the accounting agent ("bank") approximately 5¢ to handle a check. This charge is now in process of being shifted directly to the accountee in various systems such as the "master checking account." In these plans a balance need not be kept by the depositor, who simply pays 5¢ for every check or sum of cash deposited to, and 5¢ for every check drawn against his account. Should this practice become general the banking system's necessity of making hidden-from-the-populace profit for existence would be eliminated.

Accounting is quite as definitely an energy conversion process as is any other physical work, involving our three "satisfaction" factors: Energy available, Time, and Precision. It may be accomplished efficiently in relation to large operations and highly complicated energy conversion problems, where there is a uniform sequence of events permitting the use of mechanical calculators, but it cannot be efficiently utilized in highly variable, small transactions in which the whimsy and opinions of men are involved.

Whim is most specifically involved at the present moment in the matter of WHERE and WHEN and into WHAT man is going to convert small portions of his time-energy credits, particularly in the field of low value products and services, for the acquisition of which empirical fractional metallic equivalents are efficiently essential. For instance, in the 5¢ and 10¢ store where, seeing a lamp shade or writing pad for only 10¢ which he "might" want, he "whimsicalizes" his small credit of 10¢ for one or the other—or for another beer.

The fact that exploitation of this naïve, whimsical intercoursing and trans-acting of man, granted a job, or a "relief" sense of any security still exists in "credit-storage-establishments," does not minimize the importance of the factual trend *from* metallic specie *to* abstracted credit certificates—progressive ephemeralization of the expanding universe.

This exploration confusion is due to the physical (though otherwise non-identical) relationship between metallic money—efficiently still necessary to "small changing"—and the distinctly different international trading requirements for actual metal not only in ounces and pounds but often in tons of gold and silver bullion to be stored in continental banks as collateral in the international export-import trade.

Such export collateral is still necessitated by dissimilarity of languages, especially money languages (remembering that our definition of language involves sympathetic understanding), and the numerical and symbological variance of the accounting systems of various nations, just as in earliest trading days. The difference between Roman and Arabic numerals provided "cause" for profitable misunderstanding. None of the nations whose monetary policies are locally dominated by self-interested metallic bullion holders has, as yet, signified its willingness to standardize, or, as they call it, "stabilize" in relation to any other nation. Why? Because they do not as yet have to, by virtue of any laws of physics, except those of ballistics, and there are fortunes to be made overnight in the guessing game fluctuations developed by world-wide important "chance" events. Among such factors are obviously the vagaries of season, storms—a million "Chinks" drowned by a flood—which make international stabilization almost impossible. Nationalism itself is the big "fly in the ointment."

There is still current a scarcity of rare metals with which to cover the volume of international export and import trade. This scarcity can be increased in any locality by shipment of the metals from any one country to another by those who own the dominant "units." Wherefore the international money game is one of chess playing, bullion being the pawn. The great variable occurs through an admixture of interlocking directorates who have their hands in all four pockets, both sides and back and front, money and commerce, manufacture and transport. When one of these players finds that he has goods to sell and the buyer has too little bullion to handle the trade, the former is in the market to buy bullion. When both have made a profit through the transaction the bullion which they induced into the trade, provided either has no further goods immediately for sale, is put on the market, the collateralizer becoming a seller.

International metallic money traders are the direct descendants of the parasitic underwriters of the buccaneering might-makes-right fighting world of old. It is quite likely that none of its current representatives will succumb to stabilization without an actual fighting showdown. Searching analysis reveals that the current militaristic world activity is specifically fanned by, and indirectly originated by an intramural "big shot" fight over metallic money's stabilization dominance among the advocates of divergent policies in the matter of exploitation of man's needs by virtue of the legalized status of their intermediary.

The international metallic money group early usurped, through their feudal dominance of workers, the credit storage mechanisms (banks) of the workers. They are now fighting to retain their hold on these because there is an intrinsic-wealth turnover value in the utilization, for their own gain, of the workers' credit while it remains stored with them. Bankers use people's credit when entrusted to them with no more moral equity than a storage warehouse proprietor has to use for himself the automobiles and furniture of people stored with him.

The metallic money bankers have, by dint of the *obscurity* requisite to the pursuance of their legalized and tradition-"honored" racket, blinded the populace to a true interpretation of the meaning and all-mighty power of their dollar or work unit equivalents. Given the opportunity to understand the truth, the populace will no longer be willing to have their banks run as they are at present, but will infinitely prefer that the government run them; i.e., they will run themselves, emancipated entirely from management by metallic money racketeers who, as "compensation" for their services, assign to themselves a credit "take-out" of some 10% of all that the workers produce. In full consideration of these facts, the workers may *insist* on government management of their credit storage and credit interpolation with a fixed overhead charge through affixed stamps.

When government handling of personal credit accounts is incepted (it has already been willy-nillied into taking over the bulk of major utility, R.R., and realty credit handling) an efficient means for the elimination of "small change" transactions will unquestionably and inevitably have to be evolved, certainly at least for the conversion of an individual's work into goods and services of immediate true necessity.

Irrespective of the myriad of trade names for specific food products that have won preferment through poetic and dramatic advertising, every man, woman and child can—and should—consume a specific average amount of standard foods per annum.

It would be an highly efficient move on the part of the government, as the representative of a specific number of people for whom goods and services in satisfaction of every essential need are now produced, and are continuously more abundantly producible, to accredit *basic* rations on Bureau of Standards classifications. This would obviate the multitudinous accounting intricacies of the present method, with a high supercharge for legal enforcement involved in the rightful acquisition by the people of essential goods and services produced by the one for the other. It would eliminate, also, the daily three trips to the grocer's, if he is near, and the once-a-week trip if he is far away. This elimination could be accomplished by the bold stroke of automatically accrediting each and every human being with the acquisition-ability of those essentials of survival and growth which have attained "plenitudinous" status—grade "B" milk, for instance—just as the government has already accredited primary education with a bookkeeping system reduced to simple arithmetic. There is no problem in education of necessity to account for the high "take" of the student who is a glutton for knowledge against the child who eschews it. Similarly, the food balance would be maintained because no stomach is so big that it could upset the credit system.

Lest such an accounting efficiency provoke stagnation and retrogression, the government need only reserve the right of decision of placement monthly, or other progressive time-unit contracts, with the industrial groups competing for the provision of staples. The basis of arriving at such decisions would be that of competitive bidding for the furnishing of the required goods and services, relative to an itemization of standards scientifically determined.

It would be even more preferable if the individuals of the

populace, having been accredited at their central bank, be allowed to place their own contracts monthly at the local A. & P. or Reeves, *et cetera*, thus indicating an authentic vote as to the quality of service provided by the suppliers, whom the government will accredit centrally at their bank on the basis of *per capita* contract placement.

This credit of the people, by the people, and for the people, through the medium of government (themselves) could be inaugurated and maintained without changing the present industrial and banking systems. It would be necessary only to eliminate the monetary *entrepreneurs* from these inevitable basic functions.

It is not suggested that this method of accounting simplification should supersede the present procedure of credit-storing by individuals of EXCESS credits EARNED by them from their industrial service by reason of ingenuity and super-to-minimum-stint activity.

This is not a new plan. The government already acts similarly in the matter of awarding monthly contracts for the furnishing of goods and services to government establishments, such as the Army, Navy, Panama Canal, *et cetera*. It does not do this, however, as a blanket United States contract. The awards are made locally by the supply officers at the Brooklyn Navy Yard, Boston, Pearl Harbor, and elsewhere, which allows for adjustment to local conditions and meritorious branch service. This system has not been confined simply to governmental contracting. It has been demonstrated in partial effect and to a high degree of efficiency in the great coöperatives of England and the Scandinavian countries, where the accounting efficiency, however, has been fouled by the fact that it is not an all-people's accounting, which would eliminate the actual mark-up of the individual item of every bill of goods currently adding 2¢ to every loaf of bread.

This system is not to be confused with the "bread lines" of the purely communistic meal ticket because, as advocated, this plan would apply in the first place only to basic food stuffs and not to the caviare of the scarcity category, and, secondly, it would promote competition among the purveyors. That there is a great surge toward such a system is demonstrated not only in the ever normal granary types of solution of mal-distributed products, but also in the several thousand coöperatives that have mushroomed up in the U. S. and which have been attempting to organize consumers, but which will never be highly effectual as compared to the efficiency involved in the foregoing governmental, all people's, energy-credit interpolating procedure.

At present the value of super-to-stint service is appraised haphazardly by operating managers who are in a dilemma or "on the mat" between *enterpreneuring*-for-unearned-increment directors, on the one hand, the workers on another, and, kicking them in the pants from behind, the engineers and scientists indicating increased efficiencies of operation to be obtained by the continual change of process, instrument, management and distribution.

These "on the mat" industrial operating managers are controlled, through fear of job loss, by the "directors" of profit extraction and are dealt with, by the latter, also on an OPINION basis. "Directors" are continually of the OPINION that greater profits should be produced, and no improvements instituted. This attitude makes it generally impossible for managers to listen to the scientific rationalization of ingenious and willing-to-work, super-to-minimum-stint people. It is impossible for them to listen to and rationalize (ratio-analyze) the efficiencies urged upon them in the name of science or equity of worker-credit.

The fact remains, however, that improvements of service and product ARE reducible to a *specific energy conversion* terminology. Furthermore, it is not only possible but highly efficient and facile to determine, in advance, the precise energy and time-saving involved in any improvement of industrial operation. This is already being done, in a degree, by industry in the flow sheets of its research departments.

Were managers relieved of the necessity of justifying their decisions to the OPINION of directors, they could calculate scientifically, in terms of precise time and energy saving, the specific value of the ideas evolved by any person, whether or not the latter is fortified by an academic diploma.

In this connection, the therblig studies of the Link Belt Company are important. A therblig is the lowest common denominator of human mechanical motion, the therbligs are now actually in use for basic "cost" determination in many scientifically managed industrial establishments.

A mechanical study was made of the human structure (somewhat as in our phantom captain analysis). So many "cranes," *et cetera*, were catalogued, together with the limiting swings and balance of the cranes, for checking up, turning, addressing work to external machines for forming, polishing, *et cetera*. Slow motion camera studies showed whether the total energy available was being efficiently articulated or whether the "crane" under consideration was describing an inefficient arc further complicated by interspersed unnecessary muscular contractions and expansions.

It was thus possible to determine what the simplest crane *motion* could be and how much energy it would require. Consequently it was possible to demonstrate the efficient motion to the worker in such a manner that any worker, after two days of learning, irrespective of educational advantage (provided he was not deformed), could perform the operation within the specific energy and time equation indicated by the advanced theoretical analysis. It was found that, after two days' experience, there was virtually no variation between the performance by a worker who had been skilled in one of various arts and the man of no tutoring or skill, when reduced to this "simplest" operation. The flow of work was then composed of these completely segregated simplest motions.

This system, which was developed for simplification, for the safety of the worker, and to provide every physical worker with an EQUAL ADVANTAGE to any other, involved the employment, if properly followed, of a vast number of workers, due to the multiple segregation. It has never been widely applied, however, as it was "too theoretical" for profit-directed management. It did not constitute a "speed up" of the individual, but was a natural, rhythmic and safe motion that did not deplete the worker's energy storage or mental balance.

A further purpose of the therblig studies was the idea that such a system, if carried out in full, would make it possible to inter-account work activity, not only between departments of an industry but between whole industries, with the same accuracy that costs can be determined where inanimate electric power and machines alone are concerned. The cost could be determined with the accuracy with which power production itself is now determined: to the millionth of a cent. Such a system would automatically provide a yardstick of basic energy conversion for every worker and every product cost throughout the world, and furthermore would completely segregate his *super-to-stint* activity which emanates individually from his abstract or initiative and rationalizing activity.

These therblig studies are of true scientific determination and are in no way to be confused with the Bedaux or "B" (B-damned) system or any other of the speed-up or piece-work schemes that have been promoted for the specific purpose of higher profit. The therblig unit is a basic motion unit beyond which no speed-up can be made. It is something like Einstein's "c^2," i.e., TOP *efficient* speed. Therefore no speed-up system could be imposed upon the therblig *studies*. The latter brings us to the determination of a basic physical work unit, involving no invention or mental resourcefulness. These units make up into a yardstick or basic rate in the terms of which the worker's TRUE dollar is interpolated: "A dollar an hour" for basic energy conversion into work without recourse to initiative, which anyone can perform if scientifically instrumented and instructed.

No legislative peg of minimum wages and maximum hours, even on an annual pay basis, can be of any value to the worker until his dollar is standardized upon this unit physical energy conversion rate, instead of upon a basic metal unit, which unit in turn is subject to scarcity manipulation and to monopoly. Individual "work" belongs to all men, is in the plentitudinous category, and cannot be taken from them except by a political system that countenances slavery in one form or another. The democratic theory is the only political theory thus far advanced that does not, on the one hand, countenance "slavery" and yet, on the other, is complementary to "industry."

Once this basic rate of conversion-of-energy to products is established, then super-to-stint activity of the individual with initiative can come into account to be reckoned and rewarded very specifically as mechanical inventions that may be demonstrated to convert energy by inanimate mechanics into work in a more efficient manner than already demonstrated in the particular field involved.

Compensation for such activities as acting or playwriting, seemingly foreign to the production of essentials, will always be determined on the basis of pure demand and supply, or by acclaim.

When the basic pure physical energy activity, as above related, is compared with the supplying of man's basic survival essentials, a balance sheet can easily be taken off which will certify the opportunity of work to all healthy people. It is sheer guess to estimate what the basic annual stint requirements to pay off annual basic supply would be, but it may be reasonably hazarded to be in the nature of a month's service *per annum*.

This area of man's occupation in production and consumption IS socializable, but only by straight engineering and science. All other activities of man are super-to-stint, to be rewarded, either by mechanical analysis or by popular acclaim. If you happen to be Mrs. Gotrocks, and think you have plenty of dollars to avoid basic stint, okay. This is not a social system involving tearing the top down. If you have enough dollars to last the rest of your life, fine! This system does, however, allow the nomination of a dollar on which all people of the world can be self-supporting—a basic rate to which all other service is not only relative, but relative-plus.

Now, what is our true dollar?

We have already determined that a worker can develop .13 k.w.h. a day. What is the electrical production industry's charge for a k.w.h.? It has been charging all that the traffic will bear. But the k.w.h. costs the electrical industry delivered within a 150 mile radius of the dynamo approximately $.006, when produced from fuels, and approximately $.003, when produced hydraulically.

In view of the fact that the 30 watts per hour maximum life-average energy-conversion-to-work by man from sun and stars, direct and indirect, is worth, on the basis of 1938 U. S. hydraulic power cost ($.003 per k.w.h.) but $.000906 per hour, and his day's work $.00039, year's work $.1425, and his total lifetime's work $4.30, it is obvious that an hourly wage rate must be established, which, in addition to man's energy output, will compensate him for self and mechanical extension control ability, responsibility of parenthood, and for his legacy of literacy, knowledge in general, and civilized attitude toward voluntary cooperation.

If we adhere to today's intuitively integrated "dollar" value as a unit, in order to evolute instead of revolute, we find, after calculating the total cost of man's arriving at the age of mature service and of maintaining himself thereafter during his 30 years of social usefulness, that, in order to "break even" man must receive a $1 an hour BASE-WAGE. How do we arrive at this?

We will make an appraisal of all work and time-energy conversion cost involved in spontaneous family continuity based not only on work done for others for money, which is all that is now legally accounted in U. S. "income," but upon home duties, farm activities, voluntary direct prosocial activity, and self preparation for greater service.

It now costs U. S. society approximately $10,000 to nurture and educate the average child until the age of 18. This not only includes his education, but all other costs, direct or indirect, as, for example, food, clothing, shelter, as well as the paving of the streets the child walks to and from school upon and the policing and lighting of the same. On reaching maturity the average U. S. human will, at present writing, have 30 years' expectancy in which to refund society for this investment in him. Each average individual, therefore, must amortize himself at $333 per annum. (Succeed by intelligent design in increasing "expectancy" and the rate will decrease proportionately.)

The amortization for two parents is: currently	*$666.00 per annum*
Cost of maturing 2 children, at the "now" rate of $10,000 each for 18 years	*1110.00 " "*
(This figure might be greatly reduced with increased efficiency of end result by television education)	
Maintenance of the parents, including shelter, food, clothing, industrial and government services in general, at $1500 each (decency standard)	*3000.00 " "*

$4776.00

The average American family consists of the parents and two children. In accounting the work of the family, the mother's labor in the home must be included, as equal to the father working either at home or for someone else, in the pertinent aspects of energy, ingenuity, time, and precision involved, as must also that of the children as helpers during non-educational and play periods, the work of the two latter being assumed to be the equivalent of one adult. This makes a total of three adult equivalents. The average energy-work of an adult per day in a life-time's span, as we have previously determined, is 4.3 hours a day, 365 days to the year, a total of 1570 hours each per annum. Three adults would represent 4710 hours of work a year. If we will acknowledge that man's TRUE CAPITAL is his TIME and that his true dollarability is an objectivized hour of that time and not a chip of metal in somebody else's pocket or in a Kentucky mountain vault, then a true hour accounting of average intelligent effort, farm, factory, or fireside, would adequately balance "costs" as now determined by our abstracted fear-longing-and-credit poised dollars which total up to $4710 minimum annual family output.

If Murph or his wife work "out" on a 40 hour-week basis, they can accomplish their 1570 hour social-stint in 39 weeks and take a 3 months annual vacation; if they work on a 30 hour-week basis 52 weeks will be consumed, ergo no vacation. If they use their "bean" a bit one or two months a year of "out work" might get them "by."

There are many $50,000 a year executives in the U.S. If they were paid at the hydraulic power rate, they would have to develop an efficient energy-management-ability of 16,500,000 k.w.h. per annum, or the equivalent of a 2000 k.w. hydroelectric turbo-generator, running 24 hours a day for a year, or a 20,000 k.w. generator on the basis of the present running time of power equipment. Our $50,000 executive, *granted he is worth this*, is the equivalent, as an energy-articulation-motor, of the 4 combined 1000 horse power motors of the Boeing "Flying Fortress" when turning-up at full roaring speed, hypothetically engaged in a non-stop flight of 110 trips around the world at the equator within one year. "Some" executive! Yet Mr. Ford is probably demonstrating 10 times this power management ability ('tho, allowing it to compound, he has never "cashed in").

Compare this power interpretation with our overall-accounted $4710 a year by-guess-by-God-and-by-love work of the average family, or with the $1569 of the man of the family if he is hiring out at the rate of $1 an hour for "pickanshovel, passthe-buck labor." At that rate of pay, as an energy articulating mechanism, he is at least equivalent to an 80 h.p. Ford motor running 24 hours a day for a year; while as a moron-prime-mover he *or the executive* would be but the equivalent of a ½ candle power flash light bulb glimming for a year.

Ten million unemployed American workers considered only as tread-mill power producers, Roman galley slaves, or pyramid stone-elevators, sum totally as a team of 10 million, are but the mechanical power equivalent of a 67 h.p. or "little Ford" motor running 24 hours a day for a year. En masse, as pure might, the 10 million are worth less than one man at our base rate of a dollar-hour—to such a dominant equation has *right* progressed over *might*. We have indeed developed a long way from slave days in actual mechanical, energy, and brain fact, and it is either to be: man's hour yardsticks the dollar; or the metallic dollar will have to be deflated 99.999% to have tactical meaning. Gamblers who have set their traps for the "great inflation" might well apprentice in stenography while waiting.

The *overage* momentarily in favor of that relay of executives who really earn $50,000 a year, represents compensation for the latter's investment in self-training, time speculation, and the mastery of knowledge which brought them to the point of proven and accredited compositional ability of the activities of man with his mammoth mutual mechanical extensions and inanimate power harnessings to a total equivalent of 16½ million k.w.h. per annum harmonic group articulation.

In view of the $4.30 life-time energy conversion value of men as moron-prime-movers, we understand clearly why evolution spontaneously banished animate slavery throughout the British Empire, the U.S. and elsewhere within the immediate 10 years which simultaneously broadcast the invention of the dynamo and production steel.

Many are the "economics" professors who have told us with a grin or a smirk that CAPITAL IS, after all, TIME, but now we, involuntarily born into time, perceive, through mechanical attainment, that conversely TIME IS CAPITAL, to be articulated by us individually after our own progressive evaluations, at least cost to society on minimum-standard relief, or as often and as broadly amplified as we self-controlledly and all-inclusively may comprehend the phenomenon.

In an improved system of industry, freed from non-scientific director control the inventor responsible for work-saving equivalents—not only for one but indirectly for all since industry is so highly integrated that the slightest ripple of improvement reaches the farthest shore—would be accredited on the basis of his precise energy-time-saving contribution. If he saved 1/3 of a million k.w. *per annum* (this would be "some" invention) he would be accredited with $1,000. This would be payable, however, only as the time-saving accrues, thus allowing for adjustment of the invention's contiguous aptitudes. The invention *per se* might theoretically save time, but it must be logically synchronized with contiguous inventions and conditions before the inventor can be accredited in accurate terms. If the credit were $1,000, the inventor would be free to convert this sum into goods and services super to those of prime necessity, with which he would already have been automatically accredited.

In such manner, wealth—which should be pure credit for pro-social ability super-to-minimum-stint—would become the specific utility of the articulator, not at the cost of any human but through super-specific benefit to all humans. In this scientific economy, wealth would not have the characteristics of feudal intrinsic wealth. That kind of wealth was based on a you-or-me survival philosophy, and, being material, was theoretically bequeathable in perpetuity through an extension of the principle of the "divine right of kings," as finite property for the privilege of the heirs of the original feudal profiteer. But its values were physical and anything physical "wears out" relative to TIME. Time does not "wear out" so long as there is life. Time is directly available to all. Controlled time is our true wealth.

The degree to which we control and are masters of our time and have harnessed our environment to our will and weal, by our time *use*, determines our numerically specific relative wealth as individuals, or as a social unit comprised of individuals of any number.

No one in our proposed economy of scientific service and efficiency could justifiably resent vast amplifications of individual credit as directly proportional to pro-social service entailing in no way deprivation of others' time-control wealth, but, contrariwise, signifying the provision of greater time-control means for others. The amplification of individual credit for thoughtful-service would obtain during and only for the life of the individual. Such credit is specifically individual and abstract, though readily able to render puny by comparison the fortunes of today, or of any time in the past.

If a man were so scientifically able as to evolve a practical thought that would eliminate cancer forever from the human mechanism, surely none would resent his interpolation of his popularly accrued credit for such thoughtful and beneficial service as the acquisition of the most able boat to sail the seven seas, or of an aeroplane to fly to Mars. Indeed, the individual evolving so able a thought might possibly be expected, through enlarged perspective and contemplation, in his aeroplane flying to Mars, or in his boat on the Indian Ocean, or in his private laboratory at the North Pole if that were his preference, to evolve further vastly efficient pro-social thought. If a thousand guests on his yacht would accelerate such thought, then let him have a thousand guests if they are spontaneously willing. It is certain that his yacht would not be run by coal-slinging slaves.

How would the saving to humanity be accounted?

In terms of government-collected figures, which, in the present hypothetical instance, would compare the aggregate previous number of cancer victims and numerical value energy depletion caused by the disease with the subsequent dwindling average loss. Although assumed averages would have to be used at first, these would continually be corrected by census findings, the system becoming progressively more equitable with increasing uniform, universal knowledge. A vast amount of data already exists in the actuarial departments of the great quasi-cooperative insurance corporations upon which the original postulates of every saving by cancer or analogous cures may be determined.

Today in the accounting branches of an industrial establishment, the simplest over-all annual accounting system is employed. No moneys are exchanged—not even dollar bills. This is true not only intramurally in a single industry, but obtains between many corporate entities in industry.

In the economy herein proposed it would be unnecessary for Mr. Murphy to *deposit* his work-representative checks. The work performed by him could be automatically and more simply industrially inter-accounted and, consequently, far more efficiently.

Workers would not be able to overdraw their accounts, for the check-up on the accrued excess of credit of the super-to-minimum stint of any individual would be but a matter of seconds' determination. The one desiring goods and services, super to automatically accredited essentials, need only signify his desire at some point of distribution contact, where facilities would exist to determine, possibly by telegraphic exchange to a central bureau, the dollarability of the acquirer in proportion to the energy conversion value of the product or service desired.

There would be no place, in such an economy, for an opinionated appraisal of the purchaser by any *salesman*, that unfortunate being of today. This would obviate current risks on either side of a transaction, growing out of opinionated personality perquisites of the purchaser or equally opinionated "claims" for the product. The elimination of opinion would be succeeded by true scientific appraisal and credit of both product and purchaser. No more "bad account" merchants—no more process servers.

With such an improved system would come the welcome elimination of an infinity of traditional stupidities regarding dress and all the fallaleries of "keeping up with the Jones's" essential to opinionated credit "build-up." Gone would be the temptation to stretch the opinionated and, therefore, unknown quantity credit of individuals either by themselves or by others. No "overdrawn" accounts, indeed.

At present Mr. Murphy's opinion that he has given freely and well of his thoughts and acts to society has to be articulated by "finger-in-the-fire" or trial-and-error wanderings.

Despite his inability, under our current scarcity-and-profit economy, to convert his "gifts" from himself to society into dollars that *he* considers commensurate with his service, this failure does not preclude his continuing to believe that he does contribute goods and services beyond the dollars he receives. He assumes that he has that much credit, and often seeks to interpolate it into goods and services for his own consumption. If he over-accredits himself by his opinion, he finds himself in "hot water" even though his erroneous appraisal was sincerely attempted.

This self-opinion accrediting leads, in the aggregate, to threats and claims beyond all calculation and provokes continuous woeful court proceedings, and wide nervous debility, all of which would vanish in a system of truly scientific credit.

The "dollar" is already practically employed as a measure of energy conversion despite this fact's obscurity at the hands of the profit-manipulation system. This impending time-energy based economy is precisely the eruptive force against which "manipulation" is today aggressively articulating.

How is this known?

If it were not so, the financier would not still be fighting for "recovery" and would not be resistant to every step toward socialization of the obvious plenitudes. Neither would he be fighting his "partners-in-crime" for a division of what is left of the spoils of the old racket. Such a conflict would no longer be necessary because the financier and the "boys" would, under the new economy, be getting "plenty" out of the people in full measure of their worth. Albeit many astonishing salaries might be drastically reduced if service were scientifically appraised.

The "attractiveness" of war to Finance would diminish. There would be no war in China or in Spain. Wars are an "out" and "out" manifestation of the resistance of the old profit system to the rise of worker well being and the world-wide demand by the workers to be heard effectively in politics.

The old profit system has too little imagination to foresee universal wealth and comfort implicit in the trends which the "new" deal has allowed to become popularly visible. Equally unimaginative must the workers also be who scare off the profit system operators from any possibility of envisionment of the mutually delightful commonwealth now looming up, by their suppression-born subversiveness which infers pulling down the top and the revolutionary guillotine for all financial aristocracy. To such a perverted frame of mind have many active so-called "Communists" arrived that, indeed, they would refuse an open gate to the promised land and would only enter through a bombed breech in the wall. Fortunately, the over-all chronology of industrial scientific history indicates that, despite the extreme hostility of these extreme out-camps, the commonwealth of "you AND me" is willy-nilly approaching. The speed of the approach is thrilling.

Technocracy? No. Technocracy failed because it made no allowance for passion, fashion, chance, change, intuition, the mysticism of harmony, and, most important of all, for—"*it happens.*"

Technocracy called for an autocracy of engineers to fulfill its scheme. Political movements that call for an autocracy of a special viewpoint are ever doomed to failure as the trend indicates segregation of issues and a recomposed balance of all-time forces. SPECULATION and INITIATIVE in the acceleration of CHANGE, are ALL-TIME FORCES, and are as essential in a scheme of realism as suffrage and the socialization of essentials and plenitudes.

Superstition is another important all-time force, but it was derisively dismissed by the technocrats as mystic pish posh, allowing man to fall into the piteous pathologic condition that they sneeringly considered engulfs so many men. Many world-wide superstitions, however, are scientifically rationalizable and sustainable as of high importance.

The superstition that singing too early in the morning is a forerunner of tears in the evening is universally current in primitives and among supposedly highly developed, socially cultured people. This superstition is actually—in view of the wave phenomenon and unit of energy output clearly measured and charted in emotional attitudes—an indication of man's ultimate anticipation of the necessary balancing of lows and highs. In it, therefore, is a distinctly scientific proclivity. Yet emotion, so essential to selective growth and survival, was denied by technocracy as a social factor.

As power systems become integrated and the network pool becomes more balanced by invention in the matter of greater distance transmission we shall eventually come to a point where there is attained a balanced power pool available at equal cost at any point in the land. Then man, eschewing any "brain work" and working only as a "prime power," will be able to earn but $4.30 in a life time, on the basis, as stated above, of present hydropower cost. Not until this continentally pooled power condition has arrived, however, will the system of integration of man's energy conversion rate on a basis of *time* dollarability be possible.

Until that time, granted raw materials for conversion to end product and the fabricating machinery for that conversion, the dollar rate of the worker as a simple animated energy conversion medium for activation of the fabricating machinery will be directly proportional in amount to the ratio of the distance-cost increase of the inanimate, potentially competitive, power source from the specific factory under consideration.

A worker's time-energy-dollar credit is not representative merely of his maximum limit of personal physical servitude, i.e., .13 k.w. hours a day. It also represents a compound of .13 k.w. hours' serviceability to others, and the precise application of this serviceability (with understanding and credit of its original significance) to the management of his 21 inanimate, electrical slaves, the work of which is articulated with varying efficiency by means of man's self-extension.

These machines have amplified the ability of the inanimate electrical slaves somewhere near a thousandfold above the original caveman's precision and leverage ability. The progression is geometrical. The choice of machines and the place consideration—that is, where man will have them work-serve him—are thought-occupation-necessities of each and every individual, as a result of which one is able to arrive at a preferential "contact" for maximum relative efficiency of individual specific service to the whole of the human family.

This last consideration immediately brings to the fore the vital role of EDUCATION and complete unbe-tampered news dissemination as a primary means for society's egress from exploitation to active self-captaincy. It emphasizes the importance of maintaining a teleologic attitude when acquiring an education for one's self and when educating others.

An example of teleologic rationalization has been given in the presentation of this new concept of a scientific economy. It began with a consideration of the starry universe and ended with an analysis of the time-energy conversion dollarability of the individual.

Einstein's equation "$E = Mc^2$" may now be teleologically translated to Energy $\bowtie$ Man $\times$ Intellect, the latter being true rate maker of energy conversion. Thus Einstein has served us, by providing, through his simple statement of the meaning of the physical universe, a formula for developing uncompromisable and untaintable dollarability.

IV

Architecture and City Planning

Whatever the causes, from the earliest plans of the modern kind, seeking to remedy the evils of nuisance factories and urban congestion, and up to the most recent plans for regional development and physical science fiction, we find always the insistence that reintegration of the physical plan is an essential part of political, cultural, and moral reintegration.

—PAUL AND PERCIVAL GOODMAN,
Communitas (1960)

LAYING THE FOUNDATIONS

by CONSTANTINOS A. DOXIADIS

In order to lay the foundations for the architecture of the future and prepare the proper programme of action, we have to start with a definition of our subject which can be generally accepted. We must, that is, find out what architecture is and what it is trying to do.

We must first remind ourselves that architecture is the discipline not of designing houses or buildings, much less of designing monuments, but of building the human habitat. As such it consists of a science, a technique and an art. In order to create a better architecture—that is, a better habitat—we have to assist in the creation of a better way of living. Although this is not the task of the architect alone, the architect can certainly play a very important role in several aspects of this great problem.

How great this problem is can be understood if we think of how little attention we pay today to the notion of living, as against the notion of moving, in several industrialized countries. The most characteristic example of this new trend is the great importance attached by many people to their car, in contrast to their relative indifference towards their house. The new trends, the new problems, which arise in this field can be seen also in the increasing number and importance of caravan camps, of people living in trailer homes; these are the first signs of a new drift, the drift to nomadism in our society. Architecture has to contribute to the solution of these problems and especially to the concept of a proper way of living which will lead to the proper type of human habitat.

"Laying the Foundations," abridged from *Architecture in Transition*, by Constantinos A. Doxiadis. Copyright © 1963 by Constantinos A. Doxiadis. Reprinted by permission of Oxford University Press, Inc., Hutchinson and Company, Ltd., and the author.

In order to achieve these ends architecture has to be seen as a discipline meant to serve everyone, to house everyone, to create the proper habitat for every citizen of the world. Much more, it has to be seen as a service provided for the people of the world, and not as an art or a mental exercise in the abstract. Furthermore, we must be aware that we cannot limit architecture to the creation, much less to the design, of buildings to be put together on a layout which has nothing to do with their conception and their creation.

For this purpose we have to reunite the conception and creation of the layout with the conception and creation of the buildings. To do this, we have to divide the human habitat not into special aspects of the same physical unit, but into units of different sizes. This means specifically that we cannot afford to leave the layout as the exclusive domain of a certain speciality—let us say town planning—and the buildings to another, say architecture. This is like letting one architect design the plan and another the elevation of a building. We have to entrust the same man or group of men with the creation of a total unit.

Such a unit can no longer be the single building. It has to be a community of a minor class, a community within which the architect will have full responsibility for the conception and the creation of the proper human habitat. It seems to me that such a unit should be one which is controlled by the human scale, and such is only the human community, within which man alone is the controlling factor.

Architecture and Ekistics

In defining architecture as the discipline of building the human habitat, we especially noted two points: that the architect has to contribute to the conception of the human habitat, and also that he has to limit himself to minor units of that habitat up to a certain size. Both these points are necessary in order to define the real limitations of our discipline, for architecture cannot answer all problems of the human habitat.

In more specific terms, this means that architecture has to find a physical solution to the problem of the human habitat, conceiving this in collaboration with a number of other disciplines included within the broader framework of ekistics, the total science of human settlements. Architecture gives the final physical answer for minor units of the human habitat up to the human community. In this respect, architecture has to be seen as a part of ekistics, no longer as regards the differentiation between the layout of a city and the creation of buildings in it, but rather as regards the differentiation between conceiving the whole human habitat (ekistics) and giving expression to the smallest reasonable units of it (architecture). In this spirit a number of units of architecture taken together form a city or an urban area; but these areas are in the domain of urbanism where the role of architecture is clearly an auxiliary one.

If we move from the urban area to the conception and creation of the region where we have a balance of urban and rural development, then the role of architecture becomes even smaller, and it is regionalism which takes on the overall responsibility.

In this way we have defined architecture as a part of ekistics, having to deal with a series of units in the following way:

(a) *with rooms (non-subdivided, built-up spaces designed and built by the architect with or without the contribution of the interior decorator). These units do not grow, but are static in size;*

(b) *single houses or buildings, which are created by the architect but can be conceived as growing, expandable and changing units;*

(c) *the human community, which is designed and created by the architect and does not grow;*

(d) *the cities, growing organisms created by the urbanists, but with only a minor degree of collaboration from the architect; and*

(e) *the regions, which do not grow and within which architecture plays an even more minor role than in cities.*

The order we have taken brings out the fact that the physical units with which the architect deals form an alternating series— one not growing, one growing, one not growing, one growing, one not growing—as rooms, buildings, human communities, dynamic cities and regions succeed one another.

Architecture in space plays a great role in minor units and a diminishing one as the units grow large. The development of architecture in the future will regulate the degree of its inter-relation and interdependence with other disciplines. The influence of architecture should not be missing even from the synthesis of the largest unit, that is from ecumenopolis; but before it can play this role architecture has to mature in its role and respon-sibilities.

* * *

From Local to Ecumenic

We have already seen that architecture moves from local to ecumenic expressions and that this, being the result of much greater forces which are related to the evolution of our civiliza-tion, is an unavoidable trend. We are sure, that is, that the general trends are all leading to an ecumenic architecture; yet we do not know how, where and what kind of ecumenic archi-tecture we are going to have.

When are we going to reach this phase of an earth covered by an ecumenic architecture? Evidently, when we are able to have the same type of industry everywhere, the same economic con-ditions, as well as the same type of prefabrication, the same organization of production and the same type of society. This implies that differences in technological development from area to area will be minimized as a result of an equalization of in-come. It also means that there will be a dense system of trans-portation so that all localities can be supplied with prefabricated architectural elements with equal facility.

When speaking in such terms we shall have to be realistic, and accept that this means that, even if we wished, we could not achieve a totally ecumenic architecture before the end of the twenty-first century. In the meantime there will be countries and parts of countries exhibiting definite progress towards an ecu-menic architecture.

Such an evolution in some countries will have an impact on the rest which, although not economically or industrially ripe for an ecumenic architecture, will still tend towards one because of the tendency to imitate, if for no other reason. We shall therefore have some hybrid solutions between local and ecumenic which will, however, as ecumenic forces increase and spread, tend to be more and more consistent, more and more honest in their expression.

It now seems that before humanity can reach the phase of an ecumenic architecture it is likely to pass through several phases, during which we shall find our world divided into the following zones of architecture:

(a) zones of ecumenic architecture under development;
(b) zones of local architecture as yet untouched by the ecumenic trends; and
(c) zones of hybrid architecture.

The success of the architectural solution in each case, during this period of transition, will depend on the ability of the architect to:

(a) recognize the phase of evolution through which the locality he serves is passing; and
(b) at the same time respect, as far as possible, the requirements of both ecumenic and local nature, in order to find the best possible balance between them at that particular moment in time.

What is ecumenic architecture going to be? And is it going to be the same everywhere? If we take the view that present trends will continue it certainly seems that way. But this will not be true if, in spite of the unifying forces (tendency to similar incomes, industrialization, prefabrication, organization, etc.), there are local factors, such as climate, sun, light and landscape, which cannot be changed. This means that the orientation of buildings, the architectural synthesis (less dense in the colder climates, more dense in the hotter climates) and the desire for the greatest possible economy for the achievement of a practical project, are going to force us to respect the local requirements more and more.

This means that our architecture will have the same ecumenic character overall, but that the solutions will vary from locality to locality and thus create a different impression in each.

All these factors lead to the general conclusion that we are tending towards ecumenic architecture. But if we allow trends to continue as at present we shall find ourselves disregarding local forces and moving towards an architecture which will be controlled 100 per cent by ecumenic forces. This would be an unfortunate development, and we have to be careful to preserve as far as possible all those local forces which should have an influence on architecture. Only in this way will we achieve the proper balance between ecumenic and local forces.

From Traditional to Contemporary

In contrasting the local with the ecumenic, we are in fact also contrasting the traditional with the contemporary, since traditional architecture is bound to a locality whilst contemporary architecture is mainly influenced by ecumenic trends. We should not be misled into believing, however, that the problem of the local as against the ecumenic is the same as the problem of the traditional as against the contemporary, because, although local expression is very much related to tradition, ecumenic expression is not necessarily contemporary. It is true that future solutions will tend to be ecumenic but we have two basic points to keep in mind, viz.:

(a) *even in the far distant future architecture should not be influenced only by ecumenic forces, and*
(b) *it will take us quite a long time to reach the phase in which ecumenic forces will control the architecture of the whole world.*

This means that we have to pay attention to the relationship between traditional and contemporary in every instance of architectural creation.

Moreover, we shall have to turn our attention much more to the traditional solutions, for they have a lot to teach us not only about the locality we are working for, but also about the ecumenic architecture which is developing throughout the world. The fact is that we know very little about the experience which has been accumulated by many local civilizations over thousands of years.

Our desire for that which is new, our desire for discovery, has cut the long threads which connected us with our past. Yet this desire for the new is misplaced in many respects. We should not worry so much about new solutions as about right solutions. If the right solutions lead us back to tradition we should not be afraid.

If we now compare the relationship between traditional and new solutions, then we shall see that the percentage of traditional solutions is probably higher than the percentage representing the influence of local forces. This is because almost all the local forces which will prevail in the future are connected with tradition. But in addition to that there are also ecumenic forces, which will be preserved and will play a role in the future, although they are not new but have emerged from the past. In this respect we should be careful in the future to recognize the relationship between the traditional and the new forces. As an example I would like to mention the notion of space and the dimensions of space within buildings (rooms, etc.) and outside them (minor squares, roads for pedestrians, etc.) where the human scale is concerned.

When contrasting the traditional with the new in the formation of the contemporary we must not imagine that there will be a clear-cut distinction, and that we are going to have areas of traditional solutions and areas of new solutions. On the contrary, we shall witness the emergence of both traditional and new solutions within the same civilization, even within the same urban area, the same locality, even the same project. This will come about because we are creating many types of architectural space for many types of people of different income groups, professional and social classes; moreover it will depend on the degree to which every such class or group of people absorbs the new forces and adopts the new solutions as well as on the level of architectural creation. For example if we are inside an old house, a building, a small street or square, we will then recognize the traditional element, as we have come closer to the factors which have conditioned the traditional solutions. On the contrary, if we reach the size of a metropolis, then location, order of magnitude and formation are the same all over the world. But one metropolis still differs from another in its minor elements and can differ much more the farther we move on the micro-scale of the city towards the house. Thus, one metropolis can differ from another in its micro-patterns of land use, free spaces and green, in the formation of the human or minor communities or sectors within it and in the micro-space created within and between houses.

Is this kind of differentiation valuable? I think it is. It serves the people best as it gives them a better solution to a large number of problems which are conditioned by local people and local forces. There is no need to transfer the international contemporary forces to the micro-space of our living if we don't have special reasons for doing so. Certainly, though, if some day this also proves necessary, if some day people will feel happier by having air-conditioning everywhere and they can afford to have it, then even this reservation may no longer hold good. But since that is really something in the distant future, and since we must have great reservations about living in an artificial climate, I think we should speak of the need to keep as many of the local traditional forces in play as we can.

But is this in fact possible? The answer is a positive "yes." This is because the infiltration of international elements really starts at the outskirts of the city, at the harbour, the airport or the railway station where the internationally conceived machines play the greatest role. These elements infiltrate from there into the main arteries of the city, where cars play the greatest role and into the heart of the city where foreign forces play a certain role. But they do not infiltrate into our private lives very quickly. The external factors really influence a city from the elements of the highest order downwards, whilst the elements of a lower order are not so directly influenced. We may import solutions for a steel bridge, but there is no need for us to do the same for our houses.

Some day, perhaps years or even decades or a century hence, these forces will even have infiltrated as far as every single house. This time lag constitutes the breathing space in which we can try to alter the present trend and create the proper urban frame for our architecture. Such an urban frame will have:

(a) international characteristics in its main elements; and
(b) local-traditional characteristics in its micro-space.

What might these latter be? I think I could mention several. First, the neighbourhood, the small community with internal cohesion and even administrative expression. This we can keep, controlled by the pedestrian, retaining its own character, its own micro-climate, its own micro-society—a micro-community, in fact.

We can also keep the human scale where people walk about unimpeded by cars, and we can even create a micro-climate within our cities by appropriate use of gardens, open spaces and water.

In some cases, as in hot climates, we can keep the internal courtyard for the houses, open or covered. This is an element which could survive to the benefit of houses that may even be air-conditioned some day, when air-conditioning is far more economically feasible.

On the other hand, the new forces are by necessity breaking into certain other patterns, such as those of international transportation, of main transportation lines, means of communication, industrial production, etc. But it would be worse than stupid to allow, without careful consideration, these same forces to break unconditionally the patterns which are of such importance in our lives as the patterns of our houses.

When confronted with this problem of the coexistence of different patterns we must try to see whether such a solution is perhaps only a compromise between new and traditional patterns; if it is, then it can promise only a temporary solution and as such would not have any permanent value. What we need, however, is a solution which would be no meaningless compromise but a *synthesis* of the existing with the new forces, each category of which will operate at a different level. If we can achieve this synthesis, then we shall have made an enormous contribution to the future of architecture. What is more, we shall have rendered a useful service to the people, since such a synthesis would constitute an expression of its own forces. It would also be a service to humanity because, by preserving some of the natural forces of civilization, and by demonstrating this necessity for all areas, we could help lead to a civilization which would become ecumenic not by suppressing the national-local civilizations, but by bringing them into the free synthesis of a single ecumenic civilization.

From Subjective to Objective

Architecture has until now been based on subjective methods of approach. We usually relate a whole architectural creation to the subjective approach, basing this approach on an enormous amount of subjective information which is itself very often completely misleading.

In dealing with such important questions as that of how we want to live, however, we cannot rely solely on subjective methods of approach. We need a much more objective methodology.

We have already spoken of ekistics as the science of human settlements and of our attempts to develop it, but we must recognize that it is still very young as a science. We have to intensify our search for an objective, scientific approach to all problems related to human settlements and architectural creation. The fact that we are now beginning to understand phenomena such as the dynamic growth of the city—leading to the new concept of dynapolis—should not satisfy us. On the contrary, it should frighten us by showing how much we have overlooked and how long and difficult is the task on which we have embarked.

Thinking of architecture and our methods of approach, we should not overlook the fact that humanity is gradually acquiring the ability to study many phenomena such as economic development and biological evolution, and to proceed to a synthesis as in a modern musical composition in a much more analytical manner. There are two basic reasons for this:

(a) *Many of these phenomena (for example the economies of countries) are becoming more and more complicated, which makes such analytic study imperative; and*
(b) *humanity itself is becoming better equipped to discover and investigate the secrets of these phenomena.*

In order to reach more objective solutions in architecture we have to carry out proper research. It is only through such research that we can get to the point of understanding the differences between the total architectural activity which is not influenced by the architects, the architectural activity of the architects and the hybrid solutions in between. It is only through such research that we can be sure of finding ways to merge the natural solutions with those given by the architects, so as to eliminate the hybrids and achieve a continuous and consistent effort throughout the spectrum of architectural creation.

Another advantage we may expect from research is that new theories may help us understand our failures and then arrive at more suitable solutions. One of our great problems in present-day architecture, for example, is the uniformity towards which we are being led by standardization, prefabrication, etc.; a uniformity which is reaching a point at which we can no longer distinguish our own house from our neighbour's. We have reached the point at which it might well be profitable to apply the modern communication theory to the study of such phenomena of uniformity; this may prove to us what variety of messages we should receive from an architectural synthesis in order to satisfy all our needs. This, as well as cybernetics and other new theories, will gradually facilitate our better understanding of the complex problems we are facing.

Yet objective analysis will not provide the final solution to the problems of architectural synthesis, for it is unquestioned that the final solution itself must be subjective. It is very dangerous, however, to proceed towards subjective solutions of such complicated problems with only a subjective analysis of the situation. The proper method would be to base our thinking on an objective analysis of the architectural problems, and work out a series of objective solutions; but we must then proceed to a final solution which should be subjectively related to every specific case for any given problem and for any given locality. It is the proper balance between objective and subjective methods that is going to make an architecture of the future worthy of its name. To rely on subjective solutions will mean a move backwards, but to rely only on objective solutions will, on the contrary, mean the end of architectural creation.

From Utilitarian to Monumental

Before closing this discussion, however, it seems necessary to stress again how dangerous it is that the whole attention of our present era should be directed towards the non-repeated types of buildings, which usually tend to become monuments.

People taking this road think that they are simply repeating what has happened in history, from which we only remember the non-repeated monumental buildings. But this is wrong. It is true that those historical buildings were the ones representative of the architectural creation of their time, but that was simply because they were at the top of the cone of the total architectural creation and because our cultures were different.

The proper road is to start from the utilitarian buildings and be concerned only with them, to develop a utilitarian architecture and let it gradually grow into a monumental one. No reasonable effort towards architectural creation in the future can begin unless it is based on utilitarian buildings. They are the buildings that everybody is concerned about, it is to them that the greatest forces of industry, of government and of private individuals should be allocated, and it is at this level that we can create an architecture which may some day find its monumental expression in some few buildings of extraordinary importance, if our culture creates a content and a meaning for them.

If monumental buildings will be required by our culture, then, in progressing from utilitarian buildings which are to be repeated towards similar buildings which are not often repeated, almost without being aware of it, we shall in due time find ourselves creating monumental buildings.

In this way we shall move gradually from the commonplace and the temporary towards the exceptional and the lasting; but this cannot take place overnight, within a short period, or even on the basis of a prescribed time-schedule. We must stop our desperate efforts to create a style. If we let architecture develop properly it will almost naturally be led towards a new ecumenic style, the architect of which will be the whole of humanity. When it is created it will no more be possible for a future historian of art to name the architect of the new style than we can today name the architect of the Classical Greek, the Mogul, the Gothic, the Japanese, the Renaissance or of any other great style of humanity.

It is only by thinking in these terms, by getting our role into its proper perspective, that we can justify our present creation and play our proper role as the agents of the human civilization and culture which is developing.

HABITAT '67

by MOSHE SAFDIE

O<small>F</small> the forces which are bringing about change in our urban patterns, some are obvious and much discussed: population growth, changing economic base, and general expansion of the economy. Some are more subtle and have to do with the desires and aspirations of the population.

We want to live in a small intimate community; yet we want to have all the amenities of the great metropolis. We want a dwelling with privacy, identity; yet we want the setting of a rich social life. We want to be near open country; yet we let the city spread endlessly. We want all the things suburbia has to offer; but we also want the amenities of the downtown area. What we really want is Utopia, but we are not clear about what Utopia is. The planner's and the architect's task today is to resolve these contradictions.

There is, of course, no economic reason why, particularly on this continent, we should not achieve Utopia. There is no reason why every family should not live in a spacious dwelling, why every dwelling should not have a view and sunlight. There is no reason why a pedestrian should ever have to cross the path of a car, nor why a car should ever have to stop for a red light.

Five decades ago, the wealthy North American descending to the slums within his city disassociated himself—he did not feel responsible. Twenty years later, descending to the slums, he did not feel responsible but he did feel compassionate. Today, he has learned to share a moral responsibility—he cannot disassociate.

The political realities of our time add another force which we must satisfy in conceiving our Utopian environment. In the past, it was possible to consider the environment in terms of national economy and resources. Today, it is essential to consider these in terms of global economy and resources. Just as it is no longer possible today within a country to justify an extremely uneven distribution of wealth which results in slums on the one hand and mansions on the other, so it is becoming impossible to justify extreme wealth and prosperity in one country and poverty in another. As we have evened out the distribution of wealth within national boundaries in the past, we are now entering a phase in which this is taking place globally. Consequently, the need for economy in using land, labor, and natural resources becomes even more critical. The image of Utopia must have universal application. To the planner and the architect today, economy is a moral obligation.

But do we have the image?

Our democracy operates through selection. Our environment is a result of selection and inertia. To exercise selection, there must be an image so simple and clear that a pressure is created upon our system to achieve it. After the Second World War, we had such an image in North America. It was the image of the single-family house, detached on its own lot in the green suburb. So simple, clear, and strong was the image that our entire system of legislation and of financing was transformed to make it possible to obtain our dream. But the image was limited. It did not take into account many facets which are essential aspects of the environment's totality and survival. It did not take account of the concentration of business and industry. It did not take account of our social needs and the variety demanded in daily life. It did not relate to our land resources or to our transportation systems. But the image was clear and it was pushed through. Today, through experience, we have become aware that we must evolve a more concentrated environment; that we must transform technically to achieve economies in the construction of the environment, such as we have achieved in other industries through mass production and automation. But we are unable to exercise selection because we have no clear image of what we want.

We must explore in two directions: the potentials of urban systems on a regional scale—the pattern of settlement that determines the environment. This involves transportation systems; the relationship between communities; between the open country and urbanized country; between industrial and agricultural facilities. From these considerations must grow the new form of our regional cities.

And then, we must explore the scale of construction itself. No longer can we think of the city as a two-dimensional pattern consisting of detached buildings. The city is evolving into a continuous three-dimensional system in which all the land uses that make up the environment are integrated. A mass-produced system must be designed to satisfy an infinity of "structures," that is: stability, sunlight, air movement, circulation, grouping of elements, service, sense of location, and others.

In the process of achieving this, we are undergoing two revolutions. One is in the field of transportation, and the other is in the field of construction. The revolution in the field of transportation will expand the mobility of man. It will expand the limits of the size of cities from the one-hour travel limit of 20 or 30 miles to 300 or 400 miles. This will make it possible for the regional city, made up of many smaller interdependent communities, to group 10 or 20 million people sharing all facilities. It will make it possible to integrate the agricultural and industrial segments of the environment, as well as the open recreational space, with the built-up urban space. These new means of surface transportation will be the primary determinants of the regional urban pattern.

The development of three-dimensional building systems would permit the reorganization of the land uses within the environment from a two-dimensional pattern to a three-dimensional pattern in space. This would permit a more concentrated environment without losing the amenities which we consider essential.

It is with this conviction that Habitat '67 has evolved, and it was in recognition of this that three Canadian governments, federal, provincial, and municipal, who are building Habitat, have supported it. They have considered it as a research project where the aspects of a mass-produced building system will be explored. As a building system, Habitat '67 attempts to find and offer solutions to the problems of the environment today:

1. Habitat attempts to provide appropriately for families within a high-density development and to preserve the amenities of the single-family house in a multistory urban structure.

2. Habitat attempts to integrate within a community all the

urban functions: residential, commercial, industrial, institu-ional, and recreational. These functions are rearranged from the conventional city pattern into a three-dimensional structure with each function attempting to complement the others.

3. Habitat attempts to introduce a building system which utilizes mechanization and mass production methods already used by other industries toward the achievement of a more economical construction of higher quality, capable of production in volume to answer global housing needs.

4. Habitat is located so that it will affect the growth of the city of Montreal. It is a beachhead, a catalyst on the riverfront which would accelerate the redevelopment of the waterfront of Montreal and bring about the reopening of the city toward the St. Lawrence River, now separated by industry and the harbor.

CITIES AND CULTURE

by EDWARD T. HALL

The implosion of the world population into cities everywhere is creating a series of destructive behavioral sinks more lethal than the hydrogen bomb. Man is faced with a chain reaction and practically no knowledge of the structure of the cultural atoms producing it. If what is known about animals when they are crowded or moved to an unfamiliar biotope is at all relevant to mankind, we are now facing some terrible conse-quences in our urban sinks. Studies of ethology and comparative proxemics should alert us to the dangers ahead as our rural popu-lations pour into urban centers. The adjustment of these people

"Cities and Culture," from *The Hidden Dimension* by Edward T. Hall. Copy-right © 1966 by Edward T. Hall. Reprinted by permission of Doubleday & Company, Inc., and the author.

is not just economic but involves an *entire way of life*. There are the added complexities of dealing with strange communication systems, uncongenial spaces, and the pathology associated with an active, swelling behavioral sink.

The lower-class Negro in the United States poses very special problems in his adjustment to city living, which if they are not solved may well destroy us by making our cities uninhabitable. An often overlooked fact is that lower-class Negroes and middle-class whites are culturally distinct from each other. In many respects, the situation of the American Negro parallels that of the American Indian. The differences between these minority groups and the dominant culture are basic and have to do with such core values as the use and structuring of space, time, and materials, all of which are learned early in life. Some Negro spokesmen have gone so far as to say that no white man could possibly understand the Negro. They are right if they are referring to lower-class Negro culture. However, few people grasp the fact that cultural differences of the type that many Negroes experience as isolating, while exacerbated by prejudice, are not the same as prejudice, nor are they inherently prejudicial. They lie at the core of the human situation and they are as old as man.

A point I want to emphasize is that in the major cities of the United States, people of very different cultures are now in contact with each other in dangerously high concentrations, a situation which brings to mind a study of pathologist Charles Southwick. Southwick discovered that peromyscus mice could tolerate high cage densities until strange mice were introduced. When this occurred there was not only a significant increase in fighting but an increase in the weight of the adrenal glands as well as the blood eosinphil count (both of which are associated with stress). Now even if it were possible to abolish all prejudice and discrimination and erase a disgraceful past, the lower-class Negro in American cities would still be confronted with a syndrome that is currently extremely stressful: the sink (popularly referred to as "the jungle"), the existence of great cultural differences between himself and the dominant white middle class of America, and a completely foreign biotope.

Sociologists Glazer and Moynihan in their fascinating book, *Beyond the Melting Pot*, have clearly demonstrated that in fact there is no melting pot in American cities. Their study focused on New York but their conclusions could apply to many other cities. The major ethnic groups of American cities maintain distinct identities for several generations. Yet our housing and city planning programs seldom take these ethnic differences into account. Even while writing this chapter I was asked to consult with an urban planning agency which was considering the problem of urban life in 1980. The entire plan under discussion was predicated on complete absences of both ethnic and class differences by this date. Nothing in man's past indicates to me that these differences will disappear in one generation!

The Need for Controls

Lewis Mumford states that the primary reason for Hammurabi's code was to combat the lawlessness of the people flocking into the early Mesopotamian cities. Since then a lesson repeatedly brought home about the relationship of man to the city is the need for enforced laws to replace tribal custom. Laws and law enforcement agencies are present in cities all over the world, but at times they find it difficult to cope with the problems facing them and they need help. An aid to law and order that has not been used to the fullest extent possible is the power of custom and public opinion in the ethnic enclaves. These enclaves perform many useful purposes; one of the most important is that they act as lifetime reception areas in which the second generation can learn to make the transition to city life. The principal problem with the enclave as it is now placed in the city is that its size is limited. When membership increases at a rate greater than the capacity to turn rural peoples into city dwellers (which is the number that moves out of the enclave), only two choices remain: territorial growth or overcrowding.

If the enclave cannot expand and fails to maintain a healthy density (which varies with each ethnic group), a sink develops. The normal capacities of law enforcement agencies are not able to deal with sinks. This is illustrated by what has happened in New York City with its Puerto Rican and Negro populations. According to a recent *Time* report, 232,000 people are packed into three and a half square miles in Harlem. Apart from letting the sink run its course and destroy the city, there is an alternative solution: *introduce design features that will counteract the ill effects of the sink but not destroy the enclave in the process.* In animal populations, the solution is simple enough and frighteningly like what we see in our urban renewal programs as well as our suburban sprawl. To increase density in a rat population and maintain healthy specimens, put them in boxes so they can't see each other, clean their cages, and give them enough to eat. You can pile the boxes up as many stories as you wish. Unfortunately, caged animals become stupid, which is a very heavy price to pay for a super filing system! The question we must ask ourselves is, How far can we afford to travel down the road of sensory deprivation in order to file people away? One of man's most critical needs, therefore, is for principles for designing spaces that will maintain a healthy density, a healthy interaction rate, a proper amount of involvement, and a continuing sense of ethnic identification. The creation of such principles will require the combined efforts of many diverse specialists all working closely together on a massive scale.

This point was stressed in 1964 at the second Delos conference. Organized by the Greek architect, town planner, and builder C. A. Doxiadis, the Delos conferences annually assemble an impressive array of experts from all over the world whose knowledge and skills can contribute to the proper study of what Doxiadis has termed ekistics (the study of settlements). The conclusions reached by this group were: (1) Both the New Town programs in England and Israel are based on inadequate, century-old data. For one thing, the towns were too small, yet even the greater size now proposed by English planners is based on very limited research. (2) Although the public is aware of the desperate situation of the ever-growing megalopolis, nothing is being done about it. (3) The combination of the catastrophic growth of both the number of automobiles and the population is creating a chaotic situation in which there are no self-correcting features. Either automobiles are precipitated to the heart of the city by freeways (leading to the choked-up effect present in London and New York City) or the town gives way to the automobile, disappearing under a maze of freeways, as is the case with Los Angeles. (4) To keep our economies growing, few activities would promote such a wide spectrum of industries, services, and skills as rebuilding the cities of the world. (5) Planning, education, and research in ekistics must be not only co-ordinated and underwritten but raised to the highest level of priority in governments.

Psychology and Architecture

To solve formidable urban problems, there is the need not only for the usual coterie of experts—city planners, architects, engineers of all types, economists, law enforcement specialists, traffic and transportation experts, educators, lawyers, social workers, and political scientists—but for a number of new experts. Psychologists, anthropologists, and ethologists are seldom, if ever, prominently featured as permanent members of city planning departments but they should be. Research budgets must not be whimsically turned on and off as has happened in the past. When good, workable plans are developed, planners must not be forced to witness a breakdown in implementation which is so often excused on the grounds of politics or expediency. Also, planning and renewal must not be separated; instead, renewal must be an integral part of planning.

Consider the public housing constructed for low income groups in Chicago which has tended to dress up and hide but not solve the basic problem. Bear in mind that the low income population which is pouring into Chicago and many other American cities is largely Negro and comes from rural areas or small towns in the South. Most of these people have had no tradition or experience in urban living. Like the Puerto Ricans and Appalachian whites, many of the Negroes also suffer from a totally inadequate education. Row after row of high-rise apartments is less distressing to look at than slums but more disturbing to live in than much of what it replaced. The Negroes have been particularly outspoken in their condemnation of high-rise housing. All they see in it is white domination, a monument to a failure in ethnic relations. They joke about how the white man is now piling Negro on top of Negro, stacking them up in high rises. The high rise fails to solve many basic human problems. As one tenant described his building to me: "It's no place to raise a family. A mother can't look out for her kids if they are fifteen floors down in the playground. They get beaten up by the rough ones, the elevators are unsafe and full of filth (people in defiance against the buildings use them as toilets), they are slow and break down. When I want to go home I think twice because it may take me half an hour to get the elevator. Did you ever have to walk up fifteen floors when the elevator was broken? You don't do *that* too often. . . ."

Happily, some architects are beginning to think in terms of two-, three-, and four-story developments designed with a view to human safety. There is very little data, however, on what kind of spaces are best suited to the Negro. My own experience dates back to World War II when I served with a Negro engineer general services regiment. The regiment assembled in Texas, and participated in all five European campaigns. However, it wasn't until we reached the Philippines that the men found a life on a *scale* that suited them. They could easily see themselves adapting to the Philippine society and economy where a man could set himself up in business in a bamboo stall no bigger than two telephone booths. The open market place with all its activity seems more suitable to the proxemic needs of the Negro than crowded American stores which are enclosed by walls and windows.

In other words, I think that it will ultimately be proved that *scale* is a key factor in planning towns, neighborhoods, and housing developments. Most important, urban scale must be consistent with ethnic scale, since each ethnic group seems to have developed its own scale.

There are in addition class differences, which are reported in the work of psychologist Marc Fried and sociologists Herbert Gans, Peggy Gleicher, and Chester Hartman, in a series of important publications on Boston's West End.

The Boston plans for slum clearance and urban renewal failed to take into account the fact that the working-class neighborhoods were quite different from those of the middle class. The West End residents were highly involved with each other; to them the hallways, the stores, the churches, and even the streets provided an essential part of living together in a community. As Hartman points out, in computing population density in the West End there was actually several times the living space available than would be apparent if judged by middle-class standards based solely on the dwelling unit. An additional point was made about the "urban village" (Gans's term). The Boston West End was a device for turning immigrant villagers into city dwellers, a process which required about three generations. If it had to be "renewed" a more satisfactory solution would have been renovation rather than destruction of the entire neighborhood, which encompassed not only buildings but social systems as well. For when urban renewal forced removal to more modern but less integrated spaces, a significant number of Italians became depressed and apparently lost much of their interest in life. Their world had been shattered, not through malice or design but with the best of intentions, because in Fried's words: " '. . . home' is not merely an apartment or a house but a local area in which some of the most meaningful aspects of life are experienced." The relationship of the West Enders to their urban village was in addition to everything else a matter of scale. The "street" was both familiar and intimate.

While very little is known about something as abstract as scale, I am convinced that it represents a facet of the human requirement that man is ultimately going to have to understand, for it directly affects the judgment of what constitutes proper population density. In addition, setting standards for healthy urban densities is doubly difficult because the basic rules for estimating the proper size of the family dwelling unit are unknown. In the last few years the sizes of dwelling spaces have had a way of slipping unnoticed from barely adequate to completely inadequate as economic and other pressures increase. Not just the poor but even the well-to-do find themselves squeezed by high-rise speculative builders who shave six inches here and a foot there to lower costs and increase profits. Nor can individual units be considered out of context. An apartment which is barely adequate becomes uninhabitable to some people at the exact moment that a rising apartment house next door cuts off the view.

Pathology and Overcrowding

Like the link between cancer and smoking, the cumulative effects of crowding are usually not experienced until the damage has been done. So far, most of what is known of the human side of cities are the bare facts of crime, illegitimacy, inadequate education, and illness; our most crying need at present is for imaginative research on a massive scale. Although there are many studies of urban life that will prove to be relevant once the relationship of the urban sink to human pathology has been accepted, I know only one which relates directly to the consequences of insufficient space. This research was done by the Chombard de Lauwes, a French husband-and-wife team who combine the skills of sociology and psychology. They produced some of the first statistical data on the consequences of crowding in urban housing. With typical French thoroughness the Chombard de Lauwes collected measurable data on every conceivable aspect of the family life of the French worker. At first they recorded and computed crowding in terms of the number of residents per dwelling unit. This index revealed very little and the Chombard de Lauwes then decided to use a new index to establish crowding— *the number of square meters per person per unit*. The results of this index were startling; when the space available was below eight to ten square meters per person social and physical pathologies doubled! Illness, crime, and crowding were definitely linked. When the space available rose *above* fourteen square meters per person, the incidence of pathology of both types also increased, but not so sharply. The Chombard de Lauwes were at a loss to explain the latter figure except to say that families in the second category were usually upwardly mobile and tended to devote more attention to getting ahead than they did to their children. A note of caution must be introduced here. There is nothing magic about ten to thirteen square meters of space. This figure is only applicable to a very limited segment of the French population at a particular time and has no demonstrable relevance to any other population. To compute crowding for different ethnic groups it is necessary to recall for a moment the earlier research dealing with the senses.

The degree to which peoples are sensorially involved with each other, and how they use time, determine not only at what point they are crowded but the methods for relieving crowding as well. Puerto Ricans and Negroes have a much higher involvement ratio than New Englanders and Americans of German or Scandinavian stock. Highly involved people apparently require higher densities than less involved people, and they may also require more protection or screening from outsiders. It is absolutely essential that we learn more about how to compute the maximum, minimum, and optimum density of the different cultural enclaves that make up our cities.

Monochronic and Polychronic Time

Time and the way it is handled have a lot to do with the structuring of space. In *The Silent Language*, I described two contrasting ways of handling time, monochronic and polychronic. Monochronic is characteristic of low-involvement peoples, who compartmentalize time; they schedule one thing at a time and become disoriented if they have to deal with too many things at once. Polychronic people, possibly because they are so much involved with each other, tend to keep several operations going at once, like jugglers. Therefore, the monochronic person often finds it easier to function if he can separate activities in space, whereas the polychronic person tends to collect activities. If, however, these two types are interacting with each other, much of the difficulty they experience can be overcome by the proper structuring of space. Monochronic northern Europeans, for example, find the constant interruptions of polychronic southern Europeans almost unbearable because it seems that nothing ever gets done. Since order is *not* important to the southern Europeans the customer with the most "push" gets served first even though he may have been the last to enter.

To reduce the polychronic effect, one must reduce involvement, which means separating activities with as much screening as necessary. The other side of the coin is that monochronic people serving polychronic customers must reduce or eliminate physical screening so that people can establish contact. This often means physical contact. For the businessman who serves Latin Americans the success of the settee as contrasted with the desk is an example of what I mean. We have yet to apply even simple principles such as these to the planning of urban spaces. The highly involved polychronic Neapolitan builds and uses the Galeria Umberto where everyone can get together. The Spanish plaza and the Italian piazza serve both involvement and polychronic functions, whereas the strung-out Main Street so characteristic of the United

States reflects not only our structuring of time but our lack of involvement in others. Inasmuch as our large cities now incorporate significant elements of both of the types represented above, it might have a salutary effect on the relationships between the two groups if both types of spaces were provided.

City planners should go even further in creating congenial spaces that will encourage and strengthen the cultural enclave. This will serve two purposes: first, it will assist the city and the enclave in the transformation process that takes place generation by generation as country folk are converted to city dwellers; and, second, it will strengthen social controls that combat lawlessness. As it is now, we have built lawlessness into our enclaves by letting them turn into sinks. In the words of Barbara Ward, we have to find some way of making the "ghetto" respectable. This means not only that they will be safe but that people can move on when the enclave has performed its functions.

In the course of planning our new cities and revamping our old ones, we might consider positively reinforcing man's continuing need to belong to a social group akin to the old neighborhood where he is known, has a place, and where people have a sense of responsibility for each other. Apart from the ethnic enclave, virtually everything about American cities today is sociofugal and drives men apart, alienating them from each other. The recent and shocking instances in which people have been beaten and even murdered while their "neighbors" looked on without even picking up a phone indicates how far this trend toward alienation has progressed.

The Automobile Syndrome

How did we reach this state of affairs? One knows intuitively that there are many explanations in addition to the design and layout of buildings and spaces. There is, however, a technical artifact built into our culture which has completely altered our way of life upon which we are now so completely dependent on to satisfy so many needs that it is difficult to conceive of our ever giving it up. I am referring, of course, to the automobile. The automobile is the greatest consumer of public and personal space yet created by man. In Los Angeles, the automobile town par excellence, Barbara Ward found that 60 to 70 per cent of the space is devoted to cars (streets, parking, and freeways). The car gobbles up spaces in which people might meet. Parks, sidewalks, everything goes to the automobile.

There are additional consequences of this syndrome that are worth considering. Not only do people no longer wish to walk, but it is not possible for those who do wish to, to find a *place* to walk. This not only makes people flabby but cuts them off from each other. When people walk, they get to know each other if only by sight. With automobiles the opposite is true. The dirt, noise, exhaust, parked cars, and smog have made the urban outdoors too unpleasant. In addition, most experts agree that the flabby muscles and reduced circulation of the blood that come from lack of regular exercise make man much more prone to heart attacks.

Yet there is no inherent incompatibility between man in an urban setting and the automobile. It's all a matter of proper planning and built-in design features which separate cars from people, a point stressed by the architect Victor Gruen in *The Heart of Our Cities*. There are already numerous examples of how this can be done by imaginative planning.

Paris is known as a city in which the outdoors has been made attractive to people and where it is not only possible but pleasurable to stretch one's legs, breathe, sniff the air, and "take in" the people and the city. The sidewalks along the Champs-Elysées engender a wonderful expansive feeling associated with a hundred-foot separation of one's self from the traffic. It is noteworthy that the little streets and alleys too narrow to accept most vehicles not only provide variety but are a constant reminder that Paris is for *people*. Venice is without a doubt one of the most wonderfully satisfying cities in the world, with an almost universal appeal. The most striking features of Venice are the absence of vehicular traffic, the variety of spaces, and the wonderful shops. San Marco Square with automobiles parked in the middle would be a disaster and totally unthinkable!

Florence, while different from Paris or Venice, is a stimulating city for the pedestrian. The sidewalks in the central portion of town are narrow so that walking from the Ponte Vecchio to Piazza della Signoria one meets people face to face and has to step aside or go around them. The automobile does not fit in with the design of Florence and if the townspeople were to ban vehicular traffic from the center of town, the transformation could be extraordinary.

The automobile not only seals its occupants in a metal and glass cocoon, cutting them off from the outside world, but it has a way of actually decreasing the sense of movement through space. Loss of the sense of movement comes not only from insulation from road surfaces and noise but is visual as well. The driver on the freeway moves *in a stream of traffic* while visual detail at close distances is blurred by speed.

Man's entire organism was designed to move through the environment at less than five miles per hour. How many can remember what it is like to be able to see everything nearby quite sharply as one walks through the countryside for a week, a fortnight, or a month? At walking speeds even the nearsighted can see trees, shrubbery, leaves and grass, the surfaces of rocks and stones, grains of sand, ants, beetles, caterpillars, even gnats, flies and mosquitoes, to say nothing of birds and other wildlife. Not only is near vision blurred by the speed of the automobile but one's relationship to the countryside is vastly altered. I realized this once while riding my horse from Santa Fe, New Mexico, to the Indian reservations in northern Arizona. My route took me north of Mt. Taylor, which I knew well because I had passed its southern edge fifty times on the highway from Albuquerque to Gallup. Driving west at automobile speeds one watches the mountain rotate as different faces are presented. The whole panorama is finished in one or two hours and ends with the red-walled Navajo sandstone cliffs outside of Gallup. At walking speed (which is all one can do on a horse if great distances are to be covered) the mountain does not appear to move or rotate. Space and distance and the land itself have more meaning. As speed increases, sensory involvement falls off until one is experiencing real sensory deprivation. In modern American cars the kinesthetic sense of space is absent. Kinesthetic space and visual space are insulated from each other and are no longer mutually reinforcing. Soft springs, soft cushions, soft tires, power steering, and monotonously smooth pavements create an unreal experience of the earth. One manufacturer has even gone so far as to advertise his product by showing a car full of happy people *floating on a cloud above the road!*

Automobiles insulate man not only from the environment but from human contact as well. They permit only the most limited types of interaction, usually competitive, aggressive, and destructive. If people are to be brought together again, given a chance to get acquainted with each other and involved in nature, some fundamental solutions must be found to the problems posed by the automobile.

Contained Community Buildings

Many factors in addition to the automobile are combining to gradually strangle the hearts of our cities. It is not possible to say at this time whether the flight of the middle class from the city can be reversed, or what the ultimate consequences will be if this trend is not reversed. There are, however, a few small encouraging spots on the horizon well worth watching. One of them is Marina City, Bertrand Goldberg's circular apartment towers in Chicago. The towers occupy a city block downtown on the edge of the Chicago River. The lower floors spiral upward and provide open-air, off-street parking facilities for the apartment residents. Marina City has many other features that answer the needs of city dwellers: restaurants, bars and taverns, a super market, liquor store, theater, ice skating rink, a bank, boat basins, and even an art gallery. It is safe, protected from weather and possible city violence (you don't need to go outside for anything). If tenant turnover isn't too great because of the small spaces in the apartments, some tenants may actually get to know each other and develop a sense of community. The view of a city, especially at night, is a delight and one of its greatest assets, yet how few people get to appreciate it? Visually, the design of Marina City is superb. Viewed from a distance, the towers are like the pine trees on the ridges around San Francisco Bay; the balconies stimulate the fovea and beckon the viewer to come closer, promising new surprises with each shift in the visual field. Another promising approach to civic design is that developed by Chloethiel Smith, an architect in Washington, D.C. Miss Smith, always concerned with the human side of architecture, has managed to create interesting, esthetically satisfying, and humanly congenial solutions to problems in urban renewal. Automobiles are handled as inconspicuously as possible and kept away from people.

City planners and architects should welcome opportunities to experiment with radically new, integrated forms that will hold an entire community. One of the advantages of Marina City, apart from the excitement it generates visually, is that it represents a definite, well-delineated amount of contained space without the killing effect of long corridors. There will be no spilling out or spreading or sprawling from this structure. Its principal defect is the cramped living space, which a number of the tenants I have talked to experience as unduly confining. In the heart of the city one needs more space in the home, not less. The home must be an antidote for city stresses.

As now constituted, the American city is extraordinarily wasteful, emptying itself each night and every weekend. One would think that efficiency-minded Americans could do better. The result of the suburbanization of our cities is that the remaining residents are now predominantly the overcrowded impoverished and the very rich, with a sprinkling of holdouts from the middle class. As a result, the city is very unstable.

Prospectus for City Planning of the Future

The city has existed in various forms for some five thousand years and it seems unlikely that there will be a ready-made substitute for it. There is no doubt in my mind that the city is in addition to everything else an expression of the culture of the people who produced it, an extension of society that performs many complex, interrelated functions, some of which we are not even aware of. From the perspective of the anthropologist one approaches the city with some degree of awe and the knowledge that we do not know nearly enough to plan intelligently for the city of the future. Yet plan we must because the future has caught up with us. There are several points which are crucial to the solutions of the numerous problems facing us today. They are:

1. Finding suitable methods for computing and measuring human scale in all its dimensions including the hidden dimensions of culture. The proper meshing of human scale and the scale imposed by the automobile presents us with a great challenge.

2. Making constructive use of the ethnic enclave. Somehow there is a close identification between the image that man has of himself and the space that he inhabits. Much of today's popular

literature devoted to the search for identity reflects this relationship. A very real effort should be made to discover and satisfy the needs of the Spanish American, the Negro, and other ethnic groups so that the spaces which they inhabit are not only compatible with their needs but reinforce the positive elements of their culture that help to provide identity and strength.

3. Conserving large, readily available outdoor spaces. London, Paris, and Stockholm are models which if properly adapted could prove useful for American city planners. The great danger in the United States today is the continuing destruction of the outdoors. This can prove extraordinarily serious, if not fatal, to the entire country. Solving the problem of the outdoors and man's need for contact with nature is complicated by the increasing incidence of crime and violence associated with our city sinks. Parks and beaches are daily becoming more dangerous. This only intensifies the sense of crowding which urban residents experience when they are cut off from recreational facilities. In addition to city recreation areas and green belts, setting aside large sections of primitive outdoors is one of our greatest needs. Failure to take this step now could mean catastrophe for future generations.

4. Preserving useful, satisfying old buildings and neighborhoods from "the bomb" of urban renewal. Not all new things are necessarily good nor are all old things bad. There are many places in our cities—sometimes only a few houses or a cluster of houses—which deserve to be preserved. They afford continuity with the past and they lend variety to our townscapes.

In this brief review I have said nothing about the very great strides the English have made in urban renewal under the London Plan, first set forth by Sir Patrick Abercrombie and Mr. J. H. Foreshaw in 1943. By the building of their "new towns," the English have characteristically demonstrated that they are not afraid to plan. Also, by preserving barriers of open country (green belts) separating major centers, they have insured future generations against the megalopolis pattern which we experience in the United States when cities merge. There have been mistakes, of course, but by and large our own city governments could learn from the British that planning must be co-ordinated and courageously applied. It must be emphasized, however, that using the English plans as a model is a matter of policy, not practice, for their plans would not in any case be applicable to America. Ours is a very different culture.

No plan is perfect, yet plans are necessary if we are to avoid complete chaos. Because environment structures relationships and planners cannot think of everything, important features will inevitably be omitted. To reduce the serious human consequences of planning errors, there must be built-in research programs which are adequately staffed and soundly financed. Such research is no more a luxury than are the gauges in an airplane cockpit.

THE CITY AS A SYSTEM

by JOHN P. EBERHARD

To attempt a systems definition of anything as complex as a city has two difficulties. One is how to describe such systems in terms of manageable packages. Yet, at the same time, the package—or the market—must be large enough to be attractive. In fact, the market should be as large as the market for an equivalent space system or weapons system. The other difficulty is how to describe the system in a way which breaks imaginary boundaries tied to existing technological solutions. I choose to do this by resorting to analogy. I suggest a double analogy: one of the human body, because the dynamics of growth are also characteristic of the requirement for adaption by human systems; and the other of the computer, in order to differentiate between "hardware" systems and "software" systems of the city.

Building on this analogy, then, there are four major "hardware" systems:

(1) The metabolic system: the technological network which

provides for the ingestion each day of huge quantities of water, supplies, food, and fuel and the consequent production of waste in the form of sewage, garbage, trash, and air pollutants. The systems character here suggests the futility of working on the pollution problem alone while ignoring the technology of the input or the processing mechanisms. Like the vital organs of the body, there are key technological mechanisms for the metabolism of the city. These include filtration plants, reservoirs, power stations, garbage dumps, supermarkets, sewage treatment plants, etc., but these too are only *parts* of the system.

(2) The cardio-vascular system: the horizontal and vertical paths of movement and the objects which move along them, like subways and trains, highways and automobiles, sidewalks, elevators, stairways and people. The movement of objects and people along the pathways of movement is dynamic, but the "veins" and "arteries" themselves are technologically static; they have little inner resilience for adapting to shifts in demand.

(3) The nervous system: the information-communication network of the city which makes it possible for its many parts to keep in touch, for it to be (at least potentially) managed as an entity, or for signals to be emitted at the proper time in order for the other systems to remain under control. Telephone switching centers, electrical distribution networks, television, street signs, and traffic control signals are all parts of the existing technological solutions.

(4) The enclosure system: the combination of skeletal or structural subsystems and surface subsystems that surround the hollow places of the city in which the life of the city goes on. Present solutions are mostly individual buildings—houses, apartments, schools, churches, offices, etc., or enclosures like subway stations, sports stadiums, playgrounds. They are mostly discontinuous entities designed as lonely pieces of art. Henceforth, they should be conceived as *total* systems; they should be constructed as organic wholes. When we speak of the enclosure system, we should not think of buildings; we must think more broadly, for this makes it possible to speculate on new technological processes, the end products of which will not be "buildings" in the conventional sense of the word.

These four systems represent a view of the major hardware

system of the city. I do not have any short list of software systems that is as nearly all-inclusive, but I can suggest four that might come close—the economic system, the political system, the educational system, and the life support system. These four major systems might include, by definition, such subsystems as the money system, the health system, the recreational system, the safety system, and others.

I would also find it important to include those aspects of life that are philosophical or religious, or to wish that any such categorization would take into account what essayist Conrad Knickerbocker called "the emotional calculus of American life—the frantic rhythms and morals that make our urban existence unlike anything city dwellers have experienced ever before." Because the software systems cannot be seen, the relationship of these qualities of life to the hardware of the city is difficult to describe. In what follows, I would like to suggest their interdependence and how this interdependence demands systems of major dimensions which will be opportunities for high-tendency companies.

Taking what I have said thus far, I want you to envision your own model of an enclosure system for 250,000 people. I will impose one rule, reflecting what I said a moment ago: You are *not* permitted to envision a model which is simply a collection of buildings. Rather, you must create an enclosure system which is a *total* system—in other words, one which integrates *all* the systems we have been talking about, including the movement system, the metabolic system, and the information-communications system.

Looking at your imaginary model, you now can appreciate that it would have to be planned and produced as an integrated whole. If it is going to function as effectively as you want it to, you cannot allow it to be created bit by bit, with a different organization responsible for each element and no coordinating concepts to provide a total system approach. Each subsystem will need to be integrated with the others, rather than generated at random as in the past.

But what sort of organization *can* perform this coordinating function? Certainly the scope of such systems development is beyond the capacity of most companies we consider traditionally as members of the building industry. I believe this responsibility will fall to the enterprises possessing capabilities in high-technology and in systems work. Indeed, I think there is enormous potential for such companies in designing and producing these future urban complexes. Moreover, this ought not to hurt the producers of traditional building products. On the contrary, these traditional companies could have their markets enhanced by the high-technology companies which create the more sophisticated hardware systems that will be needed to tie an urban complex together. Because of this, the resistance to innovations of the scale envisioned here should be greatly reduced. Building codes, zoning ordinances, and trade practices are not designed to cope with systems designs of this magnitude, so that such regulations will have to be mitigated; if not altogether set aside. The proposed Demonstrations Cities Project of the Department of Housing and Urban Development, which I will discuss later, could help create the market for such projects.

If existing building codes, zoning ordinances, and other forms of minimum design requirements for housing are to be set aside for such large-scale undertakings, then what will we use for guidelines? In my view, the systems approach to the design of city systems of this scale properly begins by addressing ourselves to the *user requirements*. By user requirements, I mean more than a system's functional requirements, such as FHA's minimum requirements for closets or plumbing fixtures, and more than simple engineering design requirements, such as a building's capacity to carry live load. Neither do I consider user requirements to be properly developed if they are simply the result of observing how existing building components perform. These may be useful in preparing performance specifications, once the user requirements have been identified, but true user requirements must *also* consider the values of the society into which the new city system is to be placed. The values of the society, and those qualities of life determined by such values, are the requirements which make the systems-development process for cities more difficult and more challenging than space or weapons systems.

The development of user requirements for a city system will be a large and complicated problem of analysis. We lack much of the knowledge of a fundamental kind that we need to do the job adequately. As an illustration of the kinds of performance requirements which hardware systems will have to meet, let me suggest a few requirements for the enclosure system. Some of these will contain new challenges; others are constants which we need only be reminded of.

As an example of new performance requirements: enclosure systems which have an unrelenting and paramount need to be *dynamic*. They must be capable of adapting *quickly* to user needs; they must also be capable of adapting over a *long period of time*. When an enclosure fails to meet this latter requirement, there is no alternative but for the occupants to adapt to the enclosure, however inconvenient this may be. The Harlem area of New York is a good example. The area has been the home of many ethnic cultures over a long period of time. The limitations of the *buildings* in Harlem to adapt is one of the contributing factors to the present discontent of those who live there.

Just as crucial, but little understood, is the need for building spaces to adapt quickly to new needs. Educational programs and research programs require that people assemble and reassemble throughout the day in different-size groups for different purposes. A classroom which meets the needs of 100 students attending a biology lecture is not likely to be well adapted to a class of 15 students in mechanical drawing. In most such cases, people are now required to adapt to available spaces, because the space is not adaptable itself.

Second, let us take an example of a performance requirement which becomes more comprehensive when one takes a systems view: Enclosure systems need a supply of skilled workmen and replacement parts to maintain them in operating condition. This is the same back-up capability that is recognized and given appropriate emphasis in present systems designs of all military and space programs. Today, we seldom impose such a requirement when we build. The producers of building components traditionally end their responsibility when they have delivered the product to the contractor. A systems view requires that this more comprehensive performance requirement be imposed.

Next, let us look at one of those *constant* requirements that must be considered: in any true systems design, the elements of the total system must be compatible with one another. For one example: when a structural system is not designed to be compatible with a mechanical system, the cost of the latter will be higher than it ought to be. For another: if a rail-line roadbed is not designed for high speed, it is foolish to try to increase the technological performance of the trains.

Having looked at some of the performance requirements of the hardware system, let us look now at the interdependence of the hardware systems and the software systems. What do we want these systems to do together? At minimum, the hardware systems should not impose unnecessary constraints. For example, the ability to gain access to places of work should not be constrained by the performance of the movement system. In emergency, the paths of movement should not constrain the ability to gain access to medical services.

These potentially negative aspects of the imposition of the hardware system on the software system are clear enough to show the necessity for considering their design as a part of the total system. But there are also positive aspects. For example:

• A well-functioning, publicly owned transportation system, designed as an integral part of such a complex, could encourage a greater degree of participation in common events.

• A community's money-credit-exchange system could be modified if all stores were linked to a computer-based system which recorded purchases against banking accounts.

• The information system of a community could be enhanced by a linkage between the telephone and an information bank containing data on weather, transportation schedules, schedules of current events.

• Advanced education programs could be designed based on programmed instruction and home consoles.

• Live music—open air concerts and marching bands—could be woven into the fabric of the movement paths, as could displays of arts and crafts of various kinds.

In looking at the total systems potential, therefore, it is possible to gain improvements either through new hardware technologies that increase the scope of the software systems, or to use new software concepts as a basis for developing new hardware technology. In either case the opportunities are immense.

V

People and Resources

The real evolutionary unit now is not man's mere body; it is 'all-mankind's-brains-together-with-all-the-extrabodily-materials-that-come-under-the-manipulation-of-their-hands'. . . . Man, with tools as his projected body and machines the prosthetic creatures of his hands, is not merely a promising animal biologically; he makes every other animal wholly obsolete, except as they serve *his* purposes or prosthetic metabolism, locomotion, manufacture of materials and of biological medicines.

—WESTON LA BARRE,
The Human Animal (1954)

THE POPULATION TRAP

by KENNETH E. BOULDING

ONE of the most difficult problems facing mankind in the present historical era is the control of its own population. The problem has two aspects: an immediate short-run aspect involving the relation of population growth to the dynamics of a developing society, and a long-run aspect involving the ultimate population equilibrium. Both these problems are of great importance and both of them are fundamentally unsolved.

The short-run aspect of the problem is largely the result of the sudden introduction of malaria control and other public health measures in tropical societies which previously have had a high rate of infant mortality. We can regard this if we like as the incursion of certain postcivilized techniques into what are essentially societies in the stage of classical civilization. The results are usually dramatic. With the aid of DDT, it has been possible to reduce the crude death rate from its "civilized" level of about twenty-five per thousand down to nine or ten in a matter of a year or two. The exact physiological causes of this phenomenon are still imperfectly understood. The eradication of malaria seems to be the main contributing factor, though probably not the sole cause. Whatever the cause, however, the facts are clear and the results, alas, can easily be disastrous. There is no more tragic irony than this, that a sudden improvement in the health of the people and especially in the health of children could prove to be a disaster. Nevertheless in the absence of an equally sharp decline in the birth rate these societies may easily find themselves faced with an unmanageable problem which may actually prevent their economic development altogether.

The problem arises because a sudden change in infant mortality, without a corresponding change in the birth rate, results in a shift in the age distribution of the society toward the younger ages with great rapidity, so that they have an unusually large proportion of children. This means correspondingly that the proportion of the population of working age is diminished. Thus in 1955 the proportion between the ages of fifteen and fifty-nine was an almost uniform 61 per cent in Europe, North America, and Oceania—that is, the developed part of the world—whereas in tropical Africa it was only 49 per cent, and in Asia about 55 per cent. This is in spite of the fact that in the developed part of the world there is a much larger proportion of old people. In Africa and Southeast Asia 43 per cent of the population were under the age of fifteen. In part this is due to adult mortality, so that a smaller proportion of the population live to be sixty. In part it is also a result of the tremendous decline in infant mortality which hit most of these countries in the late 1940's.

This situation, in which infant mortality declines without a corresponding decline in the birth rate, and before an expansion of adult longevity, is a recipe for demographic and economic disaster. A constantly declining proportion of the population of the working age has to support the constantly increasing proportion of population of nonworking age, and the ability of the society to spare resources for a growth industry is correspondingly impaired. The problem is made doubly difficult because a major element in the growth industry itself is the education of the young. When there is a very large proportion of children and young people, it becomes increasingly difficult to provide the resources for the kind of education which is necessary if the society is to pass over into the modern world.

One of the essential differences between civilized and post-civilized society is that in civilized society a relatively small proportion of resources of the adult working population need to be devoted to the upbringing and education of the young. Children are raised and educated in the casual spare time of their mother, whose time mainly has to be devoted to the productive work of the peasant farm, the small shop, or the industrial household. In a postcivilized society the amount of learning which must be performed by the average individual is so great that the task of education cannot possibly be done by the family. There therefore has to be an increasing proportion of resources devoted to formal education, and as we move toward postcivilization we move toward a society in which virtually every child and young person receives formal education for the first twenty years or so of his life. This deliberate investment in the human resource is the main key to the transition from civilized to postcivilized society. And in those civilized societies which are suffering the great demographic upheaval the problem of the transition is enormously intensified because of the burden of the large proportion of children.

For the developed countries the dynamic problem of the demographic upheaval is not so severe, though even in many of these countries the remarkable upsurge in the birth rate from about 1940 on has created a serious problem for education. All countries, however, whether developed or undeveloped, face the problem of long-run equilibrium of population. There is no country in the world whose population is stationary. The average rate of increase of the world population at a very modest estimate is about 1.6 per cent a year, and over the next forty years this may be 2 per cent a year. This means a doubling of the world population in something under forty years. It is little wonder that the present century is called the age of population explosion. In the whole of its history the human population has never expanded at this rate, and it is clear that this rate of expansion cannot go on for very long. At present rates of population expansion it will take only a little over three hundred years for a whole land area of the world to become a single city. It takes only seven or eight hundred years before we have standing room only over the whole face of the planet! Just in case anyone thinks we can solve the problem by shooting people to outer space, it would take only about eight thousand years at the present rate of population increase before the whole astronomical universe, two billion light years in diameter, is packed solid with humanity!

A generation ago it seemed reasonable to suppose that this problem would solve itself with the increase in income. It was observed that the richer countries had lower birth rates than the poorer countries and that the richer classes within each country had a lower birth rate than the poorer classes. The recipe for the control of population then seemed merely to be to make everybody rich. Then it was argued that people would become aware of the high cost of having children and would automatically restrict their families to the numbers which would not diminish their income. In the 1930's, indeed, there were many areas in Europe and many sections of the population in North America where the net reproduction rate was so low that there was a fear of race suicide. The net reproduction rate may be roughly thought of as the ratio of each generation to the numbers of its parents. If this ratio is one, then each generation as it dies off leaves an exactly equal generation to replace it. If it is more than one, the population is bound to increase; if it is less than one, the population is bound to diminish. In the 1930's in many parts of the developed societies the net reproduction rate was actually less than one. In the 1940's, however, there was a change, perhaps caused by rising incomes, coupled with a more favorable attitude toward children. This may signify a retreat into the family as the one island of security in a world in which the state has become a monster incapable of providing security or of attracting true affection. Whatever the reasons, the facts are clear. In almost all societies today, the net reproduction ratio is much greater than one. At its present rate of increase, for instance, the United States will reach a billion people in a little over a hundred years. It is therefore quite possible that our great-grandchildren will look back on this as a golden age of spacious living and will inhabit a planet in which there is no room to move and no place to go.

Mankind is therefore faced with a hideous problem in terms of sheer arithmetic. It is an arithmetic, moreover, which cannot be denied even though we nearly all try to deny it. The arithmetic is simply this: *any* positive rate of growth whatever eventually carries a human population to an unacceptable magnitude, no matter how small the rate of growth may be, unless the rate of population growth can be reduced to zero before the population reaches an unacceptable magnitude. There is a famous theorem in economics, one which I call the dismal theorem, which states that if the only thing which can check the growth of population is starvation and misery, then the population will grow until it is sufficiently miserable and starving to check its growth. There is a second, even worse theorem which I call the utterly dismal theorem. This says that if the only thing which can check the growth of population is starvation and misery, then the ultimate result of any technological improvement is to enable a larger number of people to live in misery than before and hence to increase the total sum of human misery. These theorems can of course be restated in a cheerful form—that if something other than starvation and misery can check the growth of population before it reaches an unacceptable magnitude, then the population does not have to grow until it is miserable and starved. The cheerful forms of these theorems, however, require work and conscious effort and social organization. In the absence of these, the dismal theorems take over.

For the theorems to be cheerful we must face another piece of arithmetic. This is, that in an equilibrium population the birth rate and death rate must not only be equal, but must be equal to the reciprocal of the average age at death—or what is the same thing, of the average expectation of life at birth. If the average age at death is twenty-five, then the birth rate and the death rate will be forty per thousand in an equilibrium population. If the average age of death is seventy, as it will be in a postcivilized society, then the birth rate and the death rate cannot be more than about fourteen. If there is no birth control—that is, the limitation of the number of births below the natural limit of fecundity—then there can be no death control. If the birth rate is allowed to rise to the limit of natural fecundity, which is something between forty and fifty per thousand, the death rate will also eventually rise to this level, and this means that the average age at death will be only twenty-five years or even less. This indeed is the typical condition of classical civilization. If we want to have death control, and if we want to raise the average age of death to seventy, then we must face the limitation of birth. Any moral principle which states otherwise is false morality, for no morality can be true which attempts to deny the sheer fact of arithmetic.

Having said this, we must hasten to add that there are many different methods of achieving limitation of births. Contraception is one method and an important one but by no means the only one, and indeed it is almost certainly not sufficient. As in the case of economic development, the motto in population control seems to be "where there's a will there's a way." The will is all-important, the way is secondary. Many of the ways, however, which are most effective are also unpleasant and indeed unacceptable. Infanticide and abortion are probably still the most certain methods of population control. Infanticide is repugnant to a developed moral sensitivity and can hardly be practiced without destroying certain intangible values which are important to a high quality of human life. Abortion is undoubtedly preferable to infanticide, though we know too little about the physiological and psychological damage which it may cause to recommend it without serious qualms. If this is the only method for successful population control, however, the moral prejudice against it may have to be waived in the light of the unmitigated human misery which will result from inability to control population altogether. This is one place where we have to reckon the moral cost against the moral returns.

Contraception certainly seems preferable to abortion, and indeed the moral objection to contraception in principle seems to be confined to a single major branch of the Christian church. Even here the difference in practice between this church and the rest of society is much smaller than the difference in precept. Contraception, however, also has its problems, and it is by no means an automatic solution to the problem of population control. Even with full knowledge and practice of contraception parents may still decide, voluntarily, to have more children, on the average, than are required to keep the population in a stable equilibrium. Furthermore existing methods are by no means certain in operation, and even if, for instance, most parents decide to have two children but end up by accidentally having a third, this is enough to upset the population equilibrium.

The fact that we must recognize is that it is social institutions which are dominant in determining the ability of a society to control its population, not the mere physiology of reproduction. A classic example of this proposition is Ireland. The Irish learned the Malthusian lesson the hard way. In 1700 they had a population of about two million. They were living in misery on small grains. Then someone introduced the potato, which was a great technical improvement, enabling a larger amount of food to be grown per acre, and indeed per man, than before. For a while the standard of life of the Irish improved, infant mortality declined, and there was a great increase in population. By 1846 there were eight million people living in misery on potatoes. Hardly any better example of the utterly dismal theorem can be found. Then came the failure in the potato crop and the great famine. Two million people died of starvation. Two million emigrated and the four million who remained had learned a lesson. The population of Ireland has increased very little in over a hundred years, partly as a result of continued emigration, but more as a result of limitation of births. In this case the limitation was achieved through late marriages and the imposition of a strongly puritan ethic upon the young people which seems to have the effect of strongly limiting the number of children born out of wedlock. It is striking that one of the most successful examples of population control should have taken place in a Roman Catholic country, one, however, in which Catholicism takes an unusually puritanical form.

But the great variety of possible solutions to this problem becomes apparent when we look at Japan, which is almost the only other country where the deliberate limitation of population growth has had much success. Here the machinery of population control seems to have been abortion rather than late marriages. The precariousness of these solutions, however, is indicated first by the fact that neither of them has been totally successful, for in neither Ireland nor Japan has the net reproduction rate actually been reduced to one, and in the second place even the existing solutions can easily break down under the impact of social change or economic development.

On a world scale this whole problem is enormously complicated by the different rates of population growth of different regions and nations. The first fruits of the technological revolution were enjoyed by Europe, and the period from 1500 to the early twentieth century can well be regarded as dominated by the expansion of European power and European populations to other parts of the world. The entire continents of North and South America and Australia were in fact populated largely from Europe, at least in their temperate regions. The mosquito saved most of tropical Africa from European immigration, and Asia was already reasonably full of people at the beginning of the era. We now find ourselves in the twentieth century with this period of expansion come to an end and very few open spaces left in the world. The geographical distribution of the world population is probably set for a long time to come, excluding wars of biological extermination.

Under these circumstances the problem of migration as a solution to the population problem becomes one of great difficulty. It is clear that migration is no longer a general solution for the population problem, and indeed on a world scale may actually intensify it. A region which is under genuine Malthusian pressure, for instance, can easily become a perpetual source of emigrants. If the population is really being limited by the food supply, then every person who emigrates releases food which enables another child or even two to survive. Even in the relatively short run, migration then provides very little alleviation of severe population pressure. Furthermore emigration often has a bad qualitative effect on the society which is losing people in this way, for it is usually the young, the ambitious, and the energetic who migrate. Hence in a society which has a substantial volume of emigration it is the old, the children, the sick, and the unambitious who remain behind not only to carry on the work of the society but also to produce the next generation. A society or a region which has a long-continued emigration therefore becomes depleted in human resources. It usually lacks leadership and sometimes becomes completely incapable of reorganizing itself. The southern Appalachian region in the United States is a good case in point. In these societies even the education system often turns into a funnel to drain off all the best young people, and so benefits the society which is receiving the migrants rather than the one that is educating and then losing them. The tragic truth of the principle that "to him that hath shall be given" is dramatically illustrated by this principle. The rich areas or the rich countries tend to attract the abler people from poorer areas, and this perpetuates or even increases the disparities of income.

The different rates of growth of different populations also comprise an important long-run force producing international and internal political tension. The idea of population pressure as a cause of war is too crude to be taken very seriously. Population pressure itself is a result of a large number of social factors, some of which may increase and some of which may diminish the propensities to make war. Nevertheless differential rates of population growth unquestionably increase the difficulty of the problem of stable peace. The unwillingness of many countries and many subgroups within countries to face the problem of population control is closely connected with their unwillingness to seem to weaken their relative position in the world. The inability of the United Nations, for instance, even to get this problem on its agenda is a reflection of the fact that the fears of relative changes in population are sufficient to prohibit any rational discussion of the total problem.

Ability to handle this problem intelligently is further handicapped by the fact that there are some short-run exceptions to the principles outlined above. The example of Puerto Rico, for instance, suggests that in a poor, small country which is already suffering from severe population pressure the ability to find a temporary outlet for its surplus population can be an important aid in its development. Certainly if Puerto Rico had not been able to send over half a million people to the mainland of the United States its development over the last twenty-five years would have been much more difficult. It is therefore hard to say to a country like Haiti or Indonesia or even China, "You must not export your surplus population, for this will do you no good in the long run." Indeed if a process of internal reorganization is going on, this proposition may not be true. It is not even always true that an increase in population is an enemy of development. There are some societies indeed in which population increase is the first step toward development. A decline in infant mortality upsets the old family structure, tends to destroy the extended family, provides a labor force for new cities, and may indeed provide precisely the disequilibrating influence which will throw the society off its old equilibrium of stable poverty and create an ongoing process of development.

It is very hard to avoid a certain pessimism in this area. Nowhere are such strong forces laid against the learning of realistic images of the future of mankind. All existing solutions to this problem are either disagreeable or unstable, and yet solutions must be found if postcivilized society is not to end in disaster and if our great technological accomplishments are not to result in enormous increase in the total sum of human misery. There is need to devote a substantial intellectual resource to this problem, and this we are not doing. We need to expand our knowledge of physiology, psychology, sociology, economics, and ethics in this whole area. There is a strong temptation for "folk wisdom" to refuse to face this problem or to try to brush it off with partial solutions. The Communist and the Catholic are curiously alike, though for different ideological reasons, in this particular respect, and they both seem to be almost incapable of developing a realistic appraisal of the nature of the problem and the need for its solution. On this particular point my perception of truth requires me to say that I think both the Communist and the Catholic are, at present, enemies of man's future, although I think it is also possible for both of them to reform and to take a more realistic attitude. I am deeply conscious furthermore that the "liberal" attitude toward the subject, while it may recognize its importance, has contributed very little toward its solution. We are all guilty of ignorance, frivolity, and blindness, and the accusing fingers of billions of the unborn are pointed angrily toward us.

I have only one positive suggestion to make, a proposal which now seems so farfetched that I find it creates only amusement when I propose it. I think in all seriousness, however, that a system of marketable licenses to have children is the only one which will combine the minimum of social control necessary to the solution to this problem with a maximum of individual liberty and ethical choice. Each girl on approaching maturity would be presented with a certificate which will entitle its owner to have, say, 2.2 children, or whatever number would ensure a reproductive rate of one. The unit of these certificates might be the "decichild," and accumulation of ten of these units by purchase, inheritance, or gift would permit a woman in maturity to have one legal child. We would then set up a market in these units in which the rich and the philoprogenitive would purchase them from the poor, the nuns, the maiden aunts, and so on. The men perhaps could be left out of these arrangements, as it is only the fertility of woman which is strictly relevant to population control. However, it may be found socially desirable to have them in the plan, in which case all children both male and female would receive, say, eleven or twelve decichild certificates at birth or at maturity, and a woman could then accumulate these through marriage.

This plan would have the additional advantage of developing a long-run tendency toward equality in income, for the rich would have many children and become poor and the poor would have few children and become rich. The price of the certificate would of course reflect the general desire in a society to have children. Where the desire is very high the price would be bid up; where it was low the price would also be low. Perhaps the ideal situation would be found when the price was naturally zero, in which case those who wanted children would have them without extra cost. If the price were very high the system would probably have to be supplemented by some sort of grants to enable the deserving but impecunious to have children, while cutting off the desires of the less deserving through taxation. The sheer unfamiliarity of a scheme of this kind makes it seem absurd at the moment. The fact that it seems absurd, however, is merely a reflection of the total unwillingness of mankind to face up to what is perhaps its most serious long-run problem.

EXPERIMENTAL GENETICS AND HUMAN EVOLUTION

by JOSHUA LEDERBERG

Planning based on informed foresight is the hallmark of organized human intelligence, in every theater from the personal decisions of domestic life to school bond elections to the world industrial economy. One sphere where it is hardly

"Experimental Genetics and Human Evolution," by Joshua Lederberg. Reprinted by permission of the author and publisher from *The American Naturalist* 100: 519–531, 1966.

ever observed is the prediction and modification of human nature. The hazards of monolithic sophistocratic rationalization of fundamental human policy should not be overlooked, and medicine is wisely dedicated to the welfare of individual patients one at a time. However, though lacking machinery for global oversight, we must still find ways to cope with the population explosion, environmental pollution, clinical experimentation, the allocation of scarce resources like kidneys (transplant or artificial), even a convention on when life begins and ends, which confounds discussion of abortion and euthanasia. Concern for the biological substratum of posterity, i.e., eugenics, is divided by the same cross-purposes. Nevertheless, whether or not he dares to advocate concrete action, every student of evolution must be intrigued by what is happening to his own species (what else matters?), and especially the new evolutionary theory needed to model a self-modifying system that makes imperfect plans for its own nature.

Repeated rediscovery notwithstanding, the eugenic controversy started in the infancy of genetic science. More recently, the integration of experimental genetics and biochemistry has provoked a new line of speculation about more powerful techniques than the gradual shift of gene frequencies by selective breeding for the modification of man. This article will first recapitulate a widely held skepticism about the criteria for the "good man" who is the aim of eugenic policy. The strategic impasse will not deter tactical assaults, but favors those with the most obvious, short-run payoff. I will then show how this points to an impending revision of the experimental design of human evolution, based on precedents already established in other species of animals and plants.

The debate needed to ventilate these issues has started in a few conferences: *Man and his future* (G. Wolstenholme, ed.), Ciba Foundation Symposium, 1962; *Control of human heredity and evolution* (T. M. Sonneborn, ed.), Macmillan, 1965; and *Biological aspects of social problems* (Meade & Parkes, eds.), Plenum Press, 1965, which document many other ideas and references to primary literature. I would refer especially to Dobzhansky (1962) and Harris (1964)* for outlines of the philosophical and technical foundations of the discussion.

---

* See references at conclusion of essay. Ed.

Despite every intention of generality, the outlook of this article is unavoidably culture-bound; many of my allusions pertain to academic life in the United States and might seem utterly absurd to the vast majority of the world's population, of which we are hardly an unbiased sample. The futility of discussing the patterns of human evolution without fairer representation of its actual components is the most cogent criticism of any simplicistic definition of eugenic goals.

1) Human culture has grown so rapidly that the biological evolution of the species during the last hundred generations has only begun to adjust to it. Microscopic processes of human evolution go on, but the instability of the historical milieu obscures any coherent pattern of biological adaptation since the paleolithic. Cultural cohesion tends to mute strident biological innovation, by the exclusion of deviants (whether "positive" or "negative"). But of course it generates its own biases, with many short-term fluctuations in the selective value of different genotypes and the long-term cancellation of many advantages irrelevant to civilized life.

2) Even on the time scale of the cultural revolution, we must acknowledge a singularity in the history and evolution of the planet: the emergence of scientific insight and technological power in the present era. In one lifetime, the parish has become the solar system.

3) The historical examples of the application of technology such as armaments and the population explosion are premonitions of the future. The hazards of imbalance as between technical power and social wisdom are well advertised, but technology itself is out-of-balance. For example, the technology of arms control has only recently attracted a fraction of the scientific attention devoted to its politics.

4) There has been considerable discussion of the supposed hazard to the human gene pool from the sheltering of the tacitly "unfit" by medicine or social welfare. Not so widely understood is the futility of negative-eugenic programs: most deleterious genes are represented and maintained in the population mainly by normal (conceivably sometimes supernormal?) heterozygotes. If we attack the heterozygotes as well as overtly afflicted homozygotes, almost no human being will qualify. In addition, many well-established institutions, such as the comfort of the auto-

mobile, and of heated shelters, war, and inheritance of unearned wealth or power, are equally suspect as dysgenic. It is very difficult to see how we can reconcile any aggressive negative eugenic program with humanistic aspirations for individual self-expression and the approbation of diversity. Positive eugenic programs can be defended roughly in proportion to their ineffectiveness: applied on a really effective scale they would state the same dilemmas. At present the main hazard of these proposals is the oblique even if unintended weight they may appear to give to the enforcement of negative eugenics on outcast groups.

Genetic counseling can nevertheless play an important role within the framework of personal decision and foresight for the immediate family. It can offer grave negative cautions about inbreeding and recurrence of genetic disease; it might also encourage optimists to look for compatibility or complementarity of positive attainments as a factor in mating preference. However, the public advertisement of "superior germ plasm" (sperm banks) is open to so many distortions—like most manipulations of mass taste—that its implementation would probably run very differently from its sponsors' hopes. As in adoption proceedings, the anonymity of third parties can be set aside only at great risk to the stability of family life.

5) The cultural revolution has begun its most critical impact on human evolution, having generated technical power which now feeds back to biological nature. The last decade of molecular biology has given us a mechanistic understanding of heredity, and an entry to the same for development. These are just as applicable to human nature as they are to microbial physiology. Some themes of biological engineering are already an inevitable accompaniment of scientific and medical progress over the next five to 20 years.

The sharpest challenges to our pretensions about human nature are already in view—and may be overlooked by too farsighted focussing on more sophisticated possibilities, like "chemical control of genotype." (To save repeating a phrase, let me call this genetic alchemy, or *algeny*.) Algeny is diversionary, not because I doubt its eventual realization, but because the obvious difficulties provide a too convenient refuge for evading sooner anxieties. Perhaps I might point to some analogous history. Some years ago, I suggested that the genetics of somatic cells of mammals could be worked out most directly by exploiting precedented interactions of cells in fusion, coalescence of karyotypes, and segregation. This was already being brilliantly realized, but much more energy has still been spent in vain pursuit of DNA- and virus-mediated transfer of genes in mammalian cells. These algenical visions still dominate the imagination of most of my colleagues, and may of course ultimately succeed.

The realization of applied biology is, simply, medicine; a more effective slogan on which to focus an alternative to eugenics is "euphenics." Euphenics means all the ameliorations of genotypic maladjustment, including liability to any disease, that could be brought about by treatment of the affected individual, more efficaciously, the earlier in his development. Disease is any deficit relative to a desired norm, and with its shots to accelerate brain growth, the next generation or two will surely have an even more dismal clinical appreciation of our intellectual capacity than we as students did for our professors.

The eventual impact of molecular biology on medicine should be self-evident. An immediate point of application follows from the clarification of immunity. It is now certain that the next few years will see the development of tissue and organ transplantation on a large scale. It would be a mistake to think of this as merely the repair of catastrophic defects in kidney or heart. Many more of us have slighter imbalance in our homeostats, muscles, teeth, stomachs or scalps, whose amenability to exchange will add up more weightily for standards of human performance. These implants will compete with their mechanical counterparts, which already prove the eminence of the trivial. The automobile is evolving into an all-purpose exoskeleton now augmented not only with locomotors but also a variety of sensors, effectors, and communicators. As it can also be equipped with auxiliary blood-pumps, gas-bubblers, and a laundry (kidney), much of the effort that goes into making these medical devices implantable may be already irrelevant to contemporary man.

Embedded in molecular biology are the crucial answers to grave and basic questions about aging, the major degenerative diseases, and cancer; and it seems an easy gamble that very consequential changes in lifespan and the whole pattern of life are in the offing, provided only that the momentum of existing scientific effort is sustained. Quite apart from the glimpses of the bizarre that mechanical and transplanted organs may offer, this is a general issue of the utmost importance to the fabric of human relationships; we have hardly begun to face it.

It is already a very heavy burden on the conscience of our physicians that the ebbing of life is a gradual process; that the spontaneous beating of the heart is no longer the uncontrollable axiom of human life; indeed that many a "person" could be maintained indefinitely as an organ culture if there were any motive for it. Biological science already has a great deal to say and more questions to ask about the foundations of personality and its temporal continuity, which we have not begun to apply to the disposition of our own lives. The whole issue of self-identification needs scientific reexamination before we apply infinite effort to preserve a material body, many of whose molecules are transient anyhow. Inevitably, biological knowledge weighs many human beings with personal responsibility for decisions that were once relegated to divine Providence. In mythical terms, human nature began with the eating of the fruit of the Tree of Knowledge. Curiously, Genesis correlates this with the pain of childbirth, an insight that the growth of man's brain has gone beyond the safe and comfortable. However, the expulsion from Eden only postponed our access to the Tree of Life.

If the limit to a brain volume of 1500 ml is dictated by the proportions of the female pelvis—and obstetrics testifies how marginal the adaptation is—the simple practice of cesarean section could set us on a new evolutionary track. Very little is now known of the embryological homeostat for size and complexity of the brain. However, the few hints from early effects of some hormones, and the "NGF" regulator of the sympathetic ganglia warrant the expectation of prophylactic control of the development of the growing brain. As such techniques become available, the responsibility for their administration can no more be evaded than for sending a child to school. Unfortunately, there are bound to be serious risks on both sides of the equation.

The elaboration of euphenics is, however, not the main purpose of a discussion of human evolution, except for the one point—the added difficulties it creates for any measure of human value. If this subject were not at the heart of the eugenic controversy, it would be arrogant to insist on the discussion of it.

Reconsider how we must reevaluate the cumulative score of a human genotype regarded over a lifetime, and for its contribution to the human future. Besides present perplexities, look to future perturbations:

1) Durability. The mere extension of lifespan alters the scores. Performance must be measured over the whole term of life, not based only on youthful precocity.

2) The euthenic context. Educational opportunity and practice are changing rapidly. Consider

a) Recognition of individual diversity. Educators have begun to learn, and exercise the knowledge, that children vary widely in the details of their information-processing machinery, e.g., the relative acuity of their sensory modalities. Many "dull" children must be reclassified as over-specialized; we might well make virtue out of necessity in enabling each child to exploit his inherent skills. This can be accomplished realistically by

b) Computer-assisted teaching. The computer display is perhaps just an extension of the printed book, but we need a much more versatile adjustment of the information channels to the subtle requirements and performance of each child. This can hardly be achieved where each teacher must deal with any number of children simultaneously. In fact, the apparent value of a genotype will fluctuate according to the current status and the availability of the teaching programs and their relevance to the values of the community! Human teachers remain indispensable for developing and guiding these programs and for their insights into motivational and social sides of their students' behavior. In the long run, the individuation of the euthenic environment can only accentuate the importance of genotypic variation.

c) Within the United States and in other ways throughout the world, we observe an unprecedented experiment in equality of opportunity without regard to race. The uncontrollability of environments has left no room for the scientist to embrace any conclusions whatever about the genetic basis of differences in racial performance. Community attitudes have made genes for dark skin handicaps to academic achievement, often overriding superior brains. Many other genes play on the interaction of child and community, and ultimate human performance, just as deviously. As our knowledge of, and more to the point, the community's response to, these idiosyncrasies evolves, there will be a corresponding revision of the value equation.

d) Job skills change. Neat handwriting and mental arithmetic once crucial for white-collar work are now obsolete. Tolerance for assembly line tedium is following muscular power onto the wasteheap of redundant skills. Social skills, leadership, and esthetic breadth are becoming the criteria of job success in many fields as machines take over the more routine tasks, in which logical rigor may soon be encompassed.

e) Western culture and its limited population is being succeeded by a much broader world culture. Is there much point in setting eugenic standards relevant only to a small minority of the world's population even as we watch the unprecedented breakdown of intercultural barriers? The jet airplane has already had an incalculably greater effect on human population genetics than any conceivable program of calculated eugenics.

3) The world situation. The central problem for the species must bias any momentary evaluation. Until recently, this was perceived as agricultural efficiency. Hunger still haunts the earth, but we might just manage to marshal the technical resources to assuage it. The specter of the industrialized world is suddenly nuclear suicide, and this has already led to some concern as to the biological adaptation of the species most appropriate to an age dominated by nuclear power. Political institutions are likely to change course much more rapidly than any biological response. As has been pointed out repeatedly, adaptability is man's unique adaptation.

This begs the question how to anticipate future needs, how far adaptability can be generalized, and how well it can compete, in any well-defined microniche, with more rigorous specialization. To put it another way, how do we identify the most adaptable genotypes now living and what is the price, to the detriment in special skills, of this adaptability?

4) Response to euphenics. The medico-technological context of human performance is more predictable than the socio-political. We are already committed to the attempted eradication of infectious agents like malaria, tuberculosis, cholera, variola, and

poliovirus. In consequence, any breakdown of public health services can be catastrophic by exposing large, imperfectly immunized populations to these parasites. If the interplay of Hemoglobin S and malaria is a useful model, genetic adaptations to a germ-free environment are taking place too; chemical pollution might replace germs as a major selective factor except that its cumulative impact on adults is less cogent than acute infanticide. The context of modern man, in fact, includes steadily increasing reliance on medicine, i.e., euphenics, from ovulation onwards. It makes as little sense to decry genetic adaptations to this as to other components of civilized life. The quality of a genotype cannot now be evaluated in terms of a hypothetical state of nature (wherein we would quickly grunt in chilly displeasure at our unfurred skins), but must match the pragmatic expectations of the milieu of the individual and his descendants. In fact selection is so slow, especially for rare genes, as to make this a theoretical issue for some time. It would be a tour de force to demonstrate any change in the frequency of a specific deleterious gene in a human population that could be unambiguously traced to a relaxation of natural selection against it. In comparison to the pace of medical progress, these exigencies are trivial.

As medical practice evolves so does the evaluation of health and vigor. What has happened to pancreatic diabetes is happening to phenylketonuria, and is bound to happen to many other biochemical and developmental diseases. Indeed, it would be no surprise to find compensating advantages, in certain contexts, for some of these genotypes.

The availability of transplants and prosthetics is an extension of the social process which relaxes the demands placed on a single genotype. We can imagine the systematic use of chimerism as another way of merging the best that each of a variety of genotypes can offer.

Recall that the most successful exercises in plant breeding have not established pure lines of vigorous individuals. Instead, somewhat over-specialized strains are nurtured and the latent resources of individually unpromising parents are merged in vigorous hybrid offspring. (A good farmer has learned how common sense conflicts with reality when he tries to use ears of hybrid corn as seed for another generation.)

5) Social adjustment. We are on the shakiest ground trying to sort out the genetic basis of such social diseases as crime and delinquency. In any case we have a long way to go in elucidating how nature and nurture interact in this field; e.g., what penalty the species would suffer by extirpating every gene that might in some environment contribute to crime and rebellious behavior.[1] Instability of family life, the estrangement of the generations, and the shallowness of human communication are more prevalent and cumulatively more serious diseases than violent crime, and must be given equal account in any effort to define the "good man," or in any lament of human deterioration.

Who will toss the first stone?

6) The sexual dimorphism. Most eugenic discussions have been overwhelmingly male-oriented, as is academic life. Western culture is more paradoxical than ever in its assignment of roles to women, and thereby in the design of their education and the advertised criteria of feminine success, stressed by conflicting demands for decoration and utility, dependence and initiative. The lack of useful occupation for many older women is a premonition of the leisure society where "work may become the prerogative of a chosen elite." Half the beneficiaries of eugenic design will be women. Will their creativity and happiness be augmented in a genotype that recombines XX and a set of male-oriented autosomes? Or shall we bypass the dimorphism and evolve a race where this does not matter? To shout *"Vive la différence"* and then ignore it is hypocrisy.

Occupational discrimination by sex has been outlawed as a byproduct of the civil rights movement in the United States, which raises nice biological questions. The sexual dimorphism is one of the most primitive of genetic differentials. Yet, in forthcoming attempts to enforce and evade the law, we shall see how thin the scientific groundwork is to answer how far the statistics of female performance in industrial society are biologically vs. socioculturally determined. In some ways this may be even harder to answer objectively than for the racial counterpart, since we are even less able to perform a meaningful experiment. What finesse it will take to design genotypes optimized for both sexes, i.e.,

---

[1] Professor Walter Bodmer proposes labelling this concept "the social load."

properly rechanneled by the developmental switch with respect to the full set of desiderata, besides the primary sex characteristics!

7) The leisure society. This discussion has been dominated by criteria of performance at work. The whole framework may be obsolescent on the time scale of a few generations. As machines come to do almost all of the work, and this must include managerial and inventive tasks as well as clerical and manual, what are the relevant human values? Will not boredom be the most pernicious disease, and a zest for life without the compulsion of labor the rare essential for the species? Play rather than work will be the substratum of human activity, and the transmutation of play into cultural progress will replace the underpinning by industrial and military technology of its superstructure of basic science.

Perhaps the scientist who works for his joy in it is the most nearly preadapted for that topsy-turvy world, obviously an impeccable criterion for eugenic choice.

This leads us finally to algeny. Man is indeed on the brink of a major evolutionary perturbation, but this is not algeny, but *vegetative propagation.* (No one will be surprised that Haldane had anticipated this reasoning years ago.)

For the sake of argument, suppose we could mimic with human cells what we know in bacteria, the useful transfer of DNA extracted from one cell line to the chromosomes of another cell. Suppose we could even go one step further and sprinkle some specified changes of genotype over that DNA. What use could we make of this technology in the production as opposed to the experimental phase?

Repair genetic-metabolic disease? Indeed, if a diffusible hormone or enzyme were involved; but the same virtues are more readily available by transplantation. The advantage is consequential only if some nondiffusible product or irreversible developmental commitment (like a neuronal pattern) were involved. However, it is utterly unreasonable to anticipate the correct reprogramming of every treated cell. Then we must perform the algeny on gamete or zygote, but in so doing we face the difficulty of testing the consequences of the intervention! If the purpose is a better human being, by any standard, we would need 20 years to prove that the developmental perturbation was the intended, or in any way a desirable one. And if it were, we would face the same hazards generation after generation. The premise of this argument is that the inherent complexity of the system precludes any merely prospective experiment in algeny. It is bound to fail a large part of the time, and possibly with disastrous consequences if we slip even a single nucleotide.

To recapitulate, if the desired effect is achieved by modifying some somatic cells, the same end is available by transplanting cells already known to have these properties. In general this should be much easier than systematically changing the existing ones. If the zygote or a gamete needs to be altered, the operation is bound to have an uncertain outcome, and needs some kind of retrospective test. This ability to manipulate zygote nuclei should depend on prior capacity for nuclear transplantation and vegetative proliferation of the involved cells—both as part of the operation, and for the experimental calibration of the results.

If we have efficacious methods for testing and selecting new genotypes, do we have much need for algeny? Would not recombination and mutation give ample material for test? Perhaps for some time. But I would credit the possibility of designing a useful protein from first premises, replacing evolution by art. It would then be requisite to implant a specified nucleotide sequence into a chromosome. This would still be useless without retrospective inspection and approval of the result, e.g., in a clone of somatic cells. What to do with the mishaps needs to be answered before we can believe that these risks will be undertaken in the fabrication of humans. But, during an experimental phase, algeny may be as useful for the generation of designed genotypes, especially if they can be verified in cell culture, as other combinatorial tricks in the geneticists' repertoire.

Vegetative reproduction, once we are reminded that it is an indispensable facet of experimental technique in the microbial analogy, cannot be so readily dismissed. In fact there is ample precedent for it, and not only throughout the plant and microbial kingdoms, but in many lower animals. Monozygotic twins in man are accidental examples. Experimentally, we know of successful nuclear transplantation from diploid somatic as well as germline cells into enucleated amphibian eggs. There is nothing to suggest any particular difficulty about accomplishing this in mammals or man, though it will rightly be admired as a technical tour de force when it is first implemented (or will this sentence be an anachronism before it is published?). Indeed I am more puzzled by the rigor with which apogamous reproduction has been excluded from the vertebrate as compared to the plant world, where its short-run advantages are widely exercised. If the restriction is accidental from the standpoint of cell biology, nevertheless a phylum that was able to fall into this trap might be greatly impeded in its evolutionary experimentation towards creative innovation.

Vegetative or clonal reproduction has a certain interest as an investigative tool in human biology, and as an indispensable basis for any systematic algenics; but other arguments suggest that there will be little delay between demonstration and use. Clonality outweighs algeny at a much earlier stage of scientific sophistication, primarily because it answers the technical specifications of the eugenicists in a way that Mendelian breeding does not. If a superior individual (and presumably then genotype) is identified, why not copy it directly, rather than suffer all the risks of recombinational disruption, including those of sex. The same solace is accorded the carrier of genetic disease: why not be sure of an exact copy of yourself rather than risk a homozygous segregant; or at worst copy your spouse and allow some degree of biological parenthood. Parental disappointment in their recombinant offspring is rather more prevalent than overt disease. Less grandiose is the assurance of sex-control; nuclear transplantation is the one method now verified.

Indeed, horticultural practice verifies that a mix of sexual and clonal reproduction makes good sense for genetic design. Leave sexual reproduction for experimental purposes; when a suitable type is ascertained, take care to maintain it by clonal propagation. The Plant Patent Act already gives legal recognition to the process, and the rights of the developer are advertised "Asexual Reproduction Forbidden."

Clonality will be available to and have significant consequences from acts of individual decision—Medawar's piecemeal social engineering—given only community acquiescence or indifference to its practice. But here this simply allows the exercise of a minority attitude, possibly long before its implications for the whole community can be understood. Most of us pretend to abhor the narcissistic motives that would impel a clonist, but he (or she) will pass just that predisposing genotype intact to the clone. Wherever and for whatever motives close endogamy has prevailed before, clonism and clonishness will prevail.

Apogamy as a way of life in the plant world is well understood as an evolutionary cul-de-sac, often associated with hybrid luxuriance. It can be an unexcelled means of multiplying a rigidly well-adapted genotype to fill a stationary niche. So long as the environment remains static, the members of the clone might congratulate themselves that they had outwitted the genetic load; and they have indeed won a short-term advantage. In the human context, it is at least debatable whether sufficient latent variability to allow for any future contingency were preserved if the population were distributed among some millions of clones. From a strictly biological standpoint, tempered clonality could allow the best of both worlds—we would at least enjoy being able to observe the experiment of discovering whether a second Einstein would outdo the first one. How to temper the process and the accompanying social frictions is another problem.

The internal properties of the clone open up new possibilities, e.g., the free exchange of organ transplants with no concern for graft rejection. More uniquely human is the diversity of brains. How much of the difficulty of intimate communication between one human and another, despite the function of common learned language, arises from the discrepancy in their genetically determined neurological hardware? Monozygotic twins are notoriously sympathetic, easily able to interpret one another's minimal gestures and brief words; I know, however, of no objective studies of their economy of communication. For further argument, I will assume that genetic identity confers neurological similarity, and that this eases communication. This has never been systematically exploited as between twins, though it might be singularly useful in stressed occupations—say a pair of astronauts, or a deep-sea diver and his pump-tender, or a surgical team. It would be relatively more important in the discourse between generations, where an older clonont would teach his infant copy. A systematic division of intellectual labor would allow efficient communicants to have something useful to say to one another.

The burden of this argument is that the cultural process poses contradictory requirements of uniformity (for communication) and heterogeneity (for innovation). We have no idea where we stand on this scale. At least in certain areas—say soldiery—it is almost certain that clones would have a self-contained advantage, partly independent of, partly accentuated by the special characteristics of the genotype which is replicated. This introverted and potentially narrow-minded advantage of a clonish group may be the chief threat to a pluralistically dedicated species.

Even when nuclear transplantation has succeeded in the mouse, there would remain formidable restraints on the way to human application, and one might even doubt the further investment of experimental effort. However several lines are likely to become active. Animal husbandry, for prize cattle and racehorses, could not ignore the opportunity, just as it bore the brunt of the enterprises of artificial insemination and oval transplantation. The dormant storage of human germ plasm as sperm will be replaced by the freezing of somatic tissues to save potential donor nuclei. Experiments on the efficacy of human nuclear transplantation will continue on a somatic basis, and these tissue clones used progressively in chimeras. Human nuclei, and individual chromosomes and genes of the karyotype, will also be recombined with cells of other animal species—these experiments now well under way in cell culture. Before long we are bound to hear of tests of the effect of dosage of the human 21st chromosome on the development of the brain of the mouse or the gorilla. Extracorporeal gestation would merely accelerate these experiments. As bizarre as they seem, they are direct translations to man of classical work in experimental cytogenetics in Drosophila and in many plants. They need no further advance in algeny, just a small step in cell biology.

My colleagues differ widely in their reaction to the idea that anyone could conscientiously risk the crucial experiment, the first attempt to clone a man. Perhaps this will not be attempted until gestation can be monitored closely to be sure the fetus meets expectations. The mingling of individual human chromosomes with other mammals assures a gradualistic enlargement of the field and lowers the threshold of optimism or arrogance, particularly if cloning in other mammals gives incompletely predictable results.

What are the practical aims of this discussion? It might help to redirect energies now wasted on naïve eugenics and to protect the community from a misapplication of genetic policy. It may sensitize students to recognize the significance of the fruition of experiments like nuclear transplantation. Most important, it may help to provoke more critical use of the lessons of history for the direction of our future. This will need a much wider participation in these concerns. It is hard enough to approach verifiable truth in experimental work; surely much wider criticism is needed for speculations whose scientific verifiability falls in inverse proportion to their human relevance. Scientists are by no means the best qualified architects of social policy, but there are two functions no one can do for them: the apprehension and interpretation of technical challenges to expose them for political action, and forethought for the balance of scientific effort that may be needed to manage such challenges. Popular trends in scientific work towards effective responses to human needs move just as slowly as other social institutions, and good work will come only from a widespread identification of scientists with these needs.

The foundations of any policy must rest on some deliberation of purpose. One test that may appeal to skeptical scientists is to ask what they admire in the trend of human history. Few will leave out the growing richness of man's inquiry about nature, about himself and his purpose. As long as we insist that this inquiry remain open, we have a pragmatic basis for a humble appreciation of the value of innumerable different approaches to life and its questions, of respect for the dignity of human life and of individuality, and we decry the arrogance that insists on an irrevocable answer to any of these questions of value. The same humility will keep open the options for human nature until their consequences to the legacy momentarily entrusted to us are fully understood. These concerns are entirely consistent with the rigorously mechanistic formulation of life which has been the systematic basis of recent progress in biological science.

Humanistic culture rests on a definition of man which we already know to be biologically vulnerable. Nevertheless the goals of our culture rest on a credo of the sanctity of human individuality. But how do we assay for *man* to demarcate him from his isolated or scrambled tissues and organs, on one side, from experimental karyotypic hybrids on another. Pragmatically, the legal privileges of humanity will remain with objects that look enough like men to grip their consciences, and whose nurture does not cost too much. Rather than superficial appearance of face or chromosomes, a more rational criterion[2] of human identity might be the potential for communication with the species, which is the foundation on which the unique glory of man is built.

Coda. Recent discussions of controlled human evolution have focussed on two techniques: selective breeding (eugenics) and genetic alchemy (algeny). The implementation will doubtless proceed even without an adequate basis of understanding of human values, not to mention vast gaps in human genetics.

Eugenics is relatively inefficacious since its reasonable aims are a necessarily slow shift in the population frequencies of favorable genes. Segregation and recombination vitiate most short-range utilities. Its proponents are therefore led to advocate not only individual attention to but the widespread adoption of its techniques, and a minority of them would seek the sanction of law to enforce the doctrine. Most geneticists would insist on a deeper knowledge of human genetics before considering statutory intrusion on personal liberties in this sphere. Meanwhile there is grave danger that the minority view will lead to a confusion of the economic and social aims of rational population policy with genocide. The defensive reaction to such a confusion could be a disastrous impediment to the adoption of family planning by just those groups whose economic and educational progress most urgently demands it.

Algeny presupposes a number of scientific advances that have yet to be perfected; and its immediate application to human biology is, probably unrealistically, discounted as purely speculative. In this paper, I infer that the path to algeny already opens up two major diversions of human evolution: clonal reproduction and introgression of genetic material from other species. Indeed, the essential features of these techniques have already been demonstrated in vertebrates, namely nuclear transplantation in amphibia, and somatic hybridization of a variety of cells in culture, including human.

Paradoxically, the issue of "subhuman" hybrids may arise first,

---

[2] On further reflection I would attack any insistence on this suggestion (which I have made before) as another example of the intellectual arrogance that I decry a few sentences before—a human foible by no means egregious.

just because of the touchiness of experimentation on obviously human material. Tissue and organ cultures and transplants are already in wide experimental or therapeutic use, but there would be widespread inhibitions about risky experiments leading to an object that could be labelled as a human or parahuman infant. However, there is enormous scientific interest in organisms whose karyotype is augmented by fragments of the human chromosome set, especially as we know so little in detail of man's biological and genetic homology with other primates. This is being and will be pushed in steps as far as biology will allow, to larger and larger proportions of human genome in intact animals, and to organ combinations and chimeras with varying proportions of human, subhuman, and hybrid tissue (note actual efforts to transplant primate organs to man). The hybridization is likely to be somatic, and the elaboration of these steps to make full use of nuclear transplantation to test how well these assorted genotypes will support the full development of a zygote.

Other techniques may well be discovered as shortcuts, especially how to induce the differentiation of a competent egg from somatic tissue, bypassing meiosis. This process has no experimental foundation at present, but plenty of precedent in natural history.

These are not the most congenial subjects for friendly conversation, especially if the conversants mistake comment for advocacy. If I differ from the consensus of my colleagues it may be only in suggesting a time scale of a few years rather than decades. Indeed, we will then face two risks, (1) that our scientific position is extremely unbalanced from the standpoint of its human impact, and (2) that precedents affecting the long-term rationale of social policy will be set, not on the basis of well-debated principles, but on the accidents of the first advertised examples. The accidentals might be as capricious as the nationality, batting average, or public esteem of a clonont, the handsomeness of a parahuman progeny, the private morality of the experimenters, or public awareness that man is part of the continuum of life.

LITERATURE CITED

Dobzhansky, T. 1962. *Mankind Evolving*. Yale University Press, New Haven, Conn.

Harris, M. 1964. *Cell Culture and Somatic Variation*. Holt, Rinehart
   and Winston, Inc., New York.
Meade, J. E., and A. S. Parkes (eds.). 1965. *Biological Aspects of
   Social Problems*. Plenum Press, New York.
Sonneborn, T. M. (ed.). 1965. *Control of Human Heredity and
   Evolution*. The Macmillan Co., New York.
Wolstenholme, G. (ed.). 1962. *Man and His Future*. Ciba Founda-
   tion Symposium. Little, Brown & Co., Boston, Mass.

DELIBERATE EFFORTS TO CONTROL HUMAN BEHAVIOR AND MODIFY PERSONALITY

by GARDNER C. QUARTON

RECENT developments in pharmacology and
neurophysiology have focused attention on technological possibilities for controlling behavior and changing personality in radical
ways. If a new technology of this type is developed, it could
have a marked influence on the lives of some individuals. Systematic applications of these techniques would have broad social
implications.

The very idea of manipulating human behavior seems to stir up
both fears and wishful fantasies. These interfere with a commonsense evaluation of the issues. This emotional reaction to the idea
of behavior manipulation must be evaluated at three different
levels: first, as a barrier to the collecting of facts and to sensible
assessment of the social problem; second, as a factor in the social
acceptance of the technology; and, third, as a manipulative tool

"Deliberate Efforts to Control Human Behavior and Modify Personality," by
Gardner C. Quarton. Reprinted by permission from *Dædalus, Journal of the
American Academy of Arts and Sciences*, Vol. 96, No. 3. Copyright © 1967
by the American Academy of Arts and Sciences.

for modifying human behavior in its own right. The first of these must be considered before any other discussion. An emotional reaction to the idea of behavior control seems to lead to a short circuiting of the process of evaluation. Most discussion of behavior control begins with the possibility of a new technology and then either jumps to the desirability of an application of such techniques in the immediate future or to a possible mechanism of control of the technique to prevent its abuse. In these short-circuited discussions the leap from the idea to plans for immediate social action omits a review of the factual issues that would seem to be necessary for a more deliberate evaluation. Very often there is a failure to distinguish between facts and predictions, between facts and values, and between values and proposals for social action. This smearing of the status of propositions limits the usefulness of many such discussions.

The current state of the "art" can be summed up by saying that it is, in fact, possible to alter behavior by drugs, neurosurgical intervention, and systematic stimulus control. At present, the techniques are crude, not necessarily reliable, and not based on a sound and complete theoretical understanding of the underlying mechanisms. But, in a sense, since they are at least partially effective even without this full understanding, we should not delay an evaluation of the social implications until complete understanding is achieved.

Certain trends of the past fifteen years suggest an increase in the importance of the problem of behavior manipulation in the immediate future. Until quite recently the medical doctor was one of the few professionals with both a major interest in modifying human behavior and personality, and a biological interest in the brain. His concern arose directly from his therapeutic activities. He knew, understood, and presumably liked his neighbors and patients. He was, however, usually so busy with the demands of practice and so compelled to act with inadequate knowledge that he seldom reflected on alternate explanations of behavior and rarely conducted systematic experiments. As a result, scientific knowledge of the determinants of human behavior has developed very slowly. With the development of modern academic medicine, the concept has spread that doctors can be investigative human biologists. In the last few years this idea has been extended to psychiatry, neurology, and neurosurgery. This has led to a rapid increase in research effort and has supplied a group of highly skilled technicians who have extended the findings of animal biology and psychology by human experiments. During the same period, with the development of molecular genetics, biology—as it is taught in the universities—has become less naturalistic and more experimental. Not only are careers in experimental biology possible outside medicine, but much of the really significant progress has occurred there. Psychology as a laboratory science has developed apace. Many dedicated, full-time investigators are working intensively on the determinants of human behavior. It seems very likely, then, that we can expect a rapid increase in the scientific knowledge about the way in which the brain works and the way in which environmental factors interact with biological events to produce complex behavior. It also seems likely that many of those doing research will be specialists with little knowledge of or interest in the human consequences of the applications of their research.

We can expect increasingly effective methods for modifying personality and controlling behavior. What will these techniques be? Who will use them? And for what purposes?

The Technological Possibilities

Although there have been many new suggestions for modifying human behavior, some methods go back thousands of years. Both the new and the old deserve some kind of systematic consideration.

There are a number of methods for categorizing technological possibilities. No schema is completely satisfactory because the determinants of behavior are not themselves well understood and because they interact in very complex ways. For instance, it is obvious that genes are determinants of behavior and that environmental factors available as stimuli are also critical. But it is no longer profitable to argue that one of these general classes is more important than another. Both are necessary; each is insufficient alone; and they interact in a complex nonlinear fashion.

In discussions of this type there is often a problem with the word *control*. In order to speak of a technological intervention as controlling some aspect of behavior, it is not necessary to assume that total control is achieved. It may be that a very slight shift in the probabilities of a response at a certain critical period will produce an important effect.

A distinction can be made between interventions affecting the development of mechanisms that determine behavior in the adult organism and those that manipulate an already mature mechanism. For instance, hormones can be administered early in the life of an animal so that development is modified, and the later repertory of behavior altered as a result of this early intervention. When administered to a mature animal, hormones change the probabilities of responses in quite a different way.

In classifying determinants of behavior change, it is sometimes convenient to assume that they act either on the organism or on the environment in which the organism lives. But this simplifying distinction may break down since the organism is in constant interaction with the environment. If we disturb the flow of information from the organism to the environment and back to the organism, it is not necessarily clear whether we are acting on the organism or on the environment. For instance, if we cut the legs off an animal, we prevent certain types of behavior by modifying the organism. But because the behavior repertory is reduced, the environmental patterns perceived by the animal are also reduced, and behavior is influenced by the censorship of stimuli.

Some techniques for modifying behavior are relatively reversible (drugs, prostheses) ; others are in some sense irreversible (destructive brain operations, college educations). This distinction partially accounts for that made in the title between control of behavior and modification of personality. More is involved in modifying personality, however, than in the production of irreversible changes. I use the word *personality* to refer to patterns of behavior in which there are not only simultaneous and sequential complexities, but also recurring features that are characteristic for that individual. A brain operation that reduces anxiety and increases spontaneous impulsive behavior is, in this sense, a technique that modifies personality.

A rational and exhaustive categorization of ways of influencing behavior would concern itself with issues like reversibility, the effect on the maturation process, and so forth. It might even ignore differences between technological devices if the type of effect were similar. For instance, certain drugs and electrical stimulation might both alert an individual by similar action on arousal mechanisms in the brain. But for the purposes of this discussion, the best schema to use in surveying available methods of behavior manipulation seems to be in terms of the techniques themselves.

Modification of the Genetic Code

Developments in the molecular biology of the gene have raised the possibility that the DNA code might be radically altered by the substitution of new genetic material for that already existing in a cell. In 1928 it was discovered that the addition of heat-killed cells of a pathogenic strain of diplococcus pneumoniae to a suspension of live nonpathogenic pneumonia cells caused a small fraction of the live bacteria to become pathogenic. This genetic recombination has been given the name "transformation," and in recent years attention has focused on the possibility that it might be feasible in mammals, especially man. Since the genes make a major contribution to all kinds of behavior, the rather wild speculation has been made that genetic recombination might constitute a device for eliminating undesirable behavior traits. I shall mention this possibility only to set it aside. So far, all experiments on transformation in mammals have been negative except for special cases in which viruses transform normal cells into cancer cells. Furthermore, relatively little is known of the location on the chromosomes of those genes that are vital for different types of behavior. It seems unlikely that human behavioral genetics will advance sufficiently in the next fifty years to make this method of behavior modification worthy of serious consideration. Moreover, the contributions of the genes to behavior and personality are exceedingly complex. It is almost certain that geneticists would turn their attention first to the elimination of disorders due to single genes.

Gene Selection by Controlled Mating

Selective breeding of animals has been carried on for years to produce desired behavioral traits. These techniques are certainly available for application to human behavior. These methods also will not be considered in detail, partly because they seem unlikely to be extensively used due to the opposition of our current society, and also because, if they were applied, the effect would not be demonstrable until several generations had passed.

Nutritional Influences

An adequate diet is necessary for normal human growth and development and, incidentally, for normal behavior. A limited diet, particularly the absence of certain vitamins, can lead to deficiency syndromes characterized by abnormal behavior. A good example of this is pellagra, which is due to a deficiency of nicotinic acid. The search for nutritional factors that can correct behavior abnormalities will obviously continue. This is not likely, however, to be a technological device used in the manipulation of normal individuals except under extreme conditions when persuasion techniques utilizing food and water deprivation are employed.

Hormones

Recent information developing from investigation of the effect of hormones on a wide variety of mechanisms shows that hormones can modify human behavior in many different ways. Neural tissues differentiate one way if certain sexual hormones are present and another way if they are absent. The organizing influence of hormones often depends on their presence during a particular stage of development as well as upon the amount. For instance, sexual hormones act not only to influence the development of effector systems making adult sexual performance possible, but influence the intensity of sexual drive and the nature of sex-related behavior. In adult life, sexual hormones alter the intensity of drive and modify the reception of stimuli which influence sexual performance. The adrenocortical hormones, thyroxin, and epinephrine also modify behavior. Relatively few studies have been done on humans by withholding and administering hormones to modify behavior, chiefly because other effects of hormones have held greater interest, and because side effects are often more important than the behavioral effects.

The Use of Drugs

Alcohol and other similar drugs have, of course, been used for thousands of years to modify behavior and subjective experience. Interest in psychopharmacology has been greatly increased with need for anesthetics, analgesics, and a wide variety of sedatives and stimulants. The earlier studies of these agents were empirical in the sense that the goal of the investigation was merely to determine whether or not the drug produced an effect, and the type of effect obtained. In recent years there has been extensive interest in the chemical organization of the nervous system, particularly in the effort to clarify the role of chemicals as possible transmitter substances used in the actual transfer of information from one neuron to another. Although no substance has been proved with absolute certainty to be a transmitter in the central nervous system, information is rapidly being collected concerning the synthesis, storage, transport, utilization, and mode of breakdown of many substances in the brain that probably function as transmitters or as modulators of transmission. In the next twenty-five years, this information is likely to revolutionize pharmacology by supplying a whole new group of drugs, discovered not by accident, but through systematic research into basic brain mechanisms. For instance, in the last decade there has been a very large amount of research on the catecholamines such as norepinephrine. Many drugs that act upon the central nervous system are now believed to act by influencing the availability of norepinephrine. This system is increasingly considered to be important in the mechanisms that determine mood. It is certainly reasonable to guess that control of mood in man may be possible by pharmacological means in the next fifty years.

The mechanism and purpose of sleep remain great scientific mysteries. Recent investigations have demonstrated, however, many neural and chemical mechanisms necessary for initiating and maintaining sleep. It is quite possible that investigations of these phenomena will progress rapidly and lead to new drugs.

Although there have been many attempts recently to demonstrate that RNA and protein synthesis are essential for learning and memory, evidence of a breakthrough in this area is not available at this time. Some drugs are known to enhance slightly the efficiency of certain types of learning in animals. Research in this area is certain to continue at a rapid rate, but its outcome is not predictable at present.

Drugs that "expand consciousness," such as LSD, require close attention. These agents produce a subjective experience that combines an intensification of sensation with some confusion and with heightened emotions, including elation and fear. They have been used in combination with psychotherapy to treat various mental disorders. The most dramatic aspect of these "psychedelic" agents is that they have escaped from the control of the scientific community and are distributed and used by sub-cultures within our society. The scientific use of LSD has recently been much curtailed by evidence that a prolonged psychosis can follow a single, very small dose. It is not possible to predict the future of these drugs because new scientific discoveries can radically alter utilization patterns, and because use of drugs for kicks is complicated by other very complex social phenomena.

The future will probably bring entirely new classes of drugs into prominence. It is not easy to speculate on the possible social consequences.

Neurosurgical Interventions

Psychosurgery, defined as surgical operations on the intact brain performed for the relief of mental symptoms, was conceived by Egas Moniz in Lisbon in 1933 and first carried out under his direction in 1935. During the 1950's there was considerable use of these techniques, particularly with operations to remove the frontal lobes or to sever the connection of the frontal lobes with the rest of the brain.

These procedures depend for their effectiveness on knowledge of the function of the different parts of the brain. Investigation of human brain function is quite naturally slow because experimental studies on living human brains are not considered ethical. With the recent upsurge of interest in the brain and the availability of primates, many studies of the localization of brain function have been carried out. With this newer information there has come additional interest in brain destruction in the frontal and temporal lobes, in the cingulate gyrus, and in certain subcortical centers that will alter some aspects of behavior without radically crippling the subject.

More recently behavior in animals has been modified by inserting electrodes into the brain. Small currents are passed through the electrodes while the animals or humans are awake and behaving relatively normally. This current flow stimulates a small group of neurons to produce nerve impulses, and these impulses in turn produce, modify, or arrest behavior. It is sometimes argued that this stimulation is not physiological or that we do not know whether the behavioral effect is produced by adding or subtracting messages in the brain. Also, scientists are often not exactly sure where electrodes are placed in the brain since they must be implanted with complex stereotactic devices, using bony landmarks and "brain atlases" as guides. The mechanism of action of brain stimulation is not fully understood, and there is some difficulty in producing reliable effects through repeated efforts to duplicate a single phenomenon. In spite of this, brain stimulation does modify behavior and will be increasingly investigated.

Brain stimulation in animals can be used to elicit fragments of behavior that appear organized, to produce alertness, drowsiness, and sleep, to arrest any ongoing behavior, to modify the urgency of biological drives such as sex and maternal tendencies, to increase or decrease aggressive behavior, and so forth. Certain placements of electrodes in the brain will cause an animal to continue to press a bar indefinitely if pressing that bar produces stimulation. Conversely, animals with other electrode placements will immediately press bars to turn off stimulation. This has led to acceptance of the notion that there are centers of the brain that elicit "pleasant" or "unpleasant" sensations. These can be stimulated to reward or punish behavior, and, in fact, this type of stimulation can be a substitute for externally delivered reinforcements. Recently the devices used to produce brain stimulation have been made smaller and simpler, and stimulation can now be carried out by radio without connecting cables.

Dr. Jose Delgado, who has done much of the research on brain stimulation in monkeys, has shown that stimulation of the brain of one monkey will modify the social behavior of a group. Monkeys without brain electrodes can even learn to activate an electrode in the brain of an aggressive companion to reduce the effectiveness of his attacks on them. In the last few years experiments with implanted electrodes in humans have shown that most of the effects obtained with other mammals are probably quite feasible in humans.

Small direct currents passing through the brain from electrodes outside the skull and scalp have also been used to alter mood. These effects are quite variable from occasion to occasion, but further investigation will almost certainly be carried out. Chemicals can be placed in very limited areas of the brain by means of small cannulae, making possible a combination of neurosurgical and pharmacological methods of altering behavior.

Surgery Outside the Brain

Surgery outside the brain deserves brief mention. Removal of glands can be used to alter the endocrine system. Research on techniques in which mechanisms are attached to the body to increase effectiveness can be considered likely. Prostheses have only been used so far to help those crippled by accidental injury, but, in principle, such devices could extend the range of function of normal individuals.

Environmental Manipulations

It is obvious that many social institutions, such as the family, the school, the church, and the psychiatrist, play an important role in shaping and controlling the behavior and personality of individuals. I have considered these influences as outside the scope of this discussion. There are, however, relatively specific methods that bring behavior under stimulus control and, therefore, deserve consideration along with the biological technologies.

Pavlov and Skinner and their followers have demonstrated how relatively simple techniques involving the pairing of stimuli with rewards and punishment can modify behavior. There has been much recent interest in extending such techniques to humans and in investigating applications in situations reasonably close to everyday life. Because humans are so much more complex than animals, and their past experiences and various motivations make them less predictable, there is some disagreement about the interpretations of these extensions. In spite of these reservations, a fairly precise technology exists and will be extensively applied in the next fifty years.

Interest in well-timed and well-placed "reinforcement" has obscured the fact that other methods of behavioral manipulation are also quite readily available. Some of these are quite simple, and modern systems analysis and flow-charting schemes permit them to be extensively applied if society allows it. For instance, the behavior of an individual is much influenced by the opportunities that are made available or denied to him. Much greater control of opportunity to act is possible using modern communication and control techniques. Similarly, behavior is readily modified by supplying or withholding maps or models of how other individuals behave. This type of control is more difficult to achieve. Hypnosis also deserves mention because it is now being studied by serious, scientifically trained investigators.

Monitoring

It is important in any type of behavior control to know how an individual behaved before and after the application of behavior-control techniques. Thus, efficient monitoring devices greatly increase the effectiveness of any method of control. Modern communication equipment and rapid computational devices increase the number and range of surveillance devices and the methods of getting information in a useful form to a person or machine engaged in behavior control. Radio transmitters can be implanted in human subjects. Behavior can be observed by television cameras and listened to by microphones. Routine behavior can be recorded at check points in computer procedures, commercial activities, and at toll gates. Most of these possibilities are fortunately not exploited under present circumstances.

Mixed Methods

The most efficient utilization of behavior-control technology would involve mixing techniques. If, for instance, a human subject had electrodes implanted in such a way that any ongoing action could be rewarded, punished, or prevented, and if micro-transmitters and receivers made external wires and apparatus unnecessary, he could be placed in a learning situation, and selected patterns of behavior could be encouraged or discouraged automatically. With effective monitoring and computing equipment, much of the process could be controlled automatically. Let us take another example. Assume a great increase in the efficiency of a governmental taxation program. If taxes were collected more frequently, if taxation policies were altered over short intervals to serve immediate policy needs, and if the individual were made acutely aware of the effect of taxation on his life, a high degree of control of the behavior of the individual would be possible. Such a program would make use of modern data processing and monitoring, reinforcement techniques, and certain display procedures.

Social Acceptance of Technological Change

The impact of technological change upon society depends not only on the nature of the technology, but also upon its acceptance by society. In no area is this more important than in the area of manipulation of behavior. Social attitudes may be so strong and of such a character that in spite of technological possibilities, no utilization by society can occur. At the opposite extreme a totalitarian government might use such techniques extensively. A sober prediction of events in the next thirty-five years would suggest some intermediate possibility.

It would be extremely useful if one could examine in a careful way instances of social acceptance of behavior manipulation and extrapolate from these. Unfortunately, the instances of behavior manipulation have been scattered and are so crude that the pattern of social acceptance itself has been difficult to assess. There is a literature on the reaction of the citizens of the United States to brainwashing in Red China, and there are, of course, written documents protesting almost all of the behavior-control techniques. Most people seem to be frightened but fascinated. A systematic study of these attitudes might be a very useful tool in making projections into the future.

Psychiatrists and educators, the prime candidates to use manipulation techniques, appear to be quite ambivalent concerning their development and application. Psychiatrists, particularly, often have value systems of their own that stress the importance of individual differences, the resolution of social conflict by increases in interindividual communication and group insight, and a gradual replacement of irrational explanations of events by ideas tested against reality in a personal and practical way. Psychiatrists trained in this way dislike therapeutic techniques that involve manipulation of the patient by any method, including environmental modification or drugs. They use manipulative techniques only when other methods fail, but it is important that they do use them on occasion, and that other psychiatrists, with or without qualms, sometimes use drugs and neurosurgery to relieve anxiety after only a brief analysis of the patient's over-all life problem. During the period of major interest in frontal lobotomy, hundreds of transorbital frontal leucotomies were performed in some state hospitals in periods of time so short that it is hard to believe the cases were thoroughly analyzed. Casual but well-intentioned use of these techniques is a reality today. It would, therefore, be naïve to think it will not occur to a significant degree in the future.

One abuse of drugs that occurs today in some places is the use of tranquilizers in hospitals for the mentally ill and the aged primarily to keep troublemaking patients from annoying the staff. This use of drugs may actually prevent the life experiences necessary for social recovery, and in the future this type of abuse will be possible to an even greater extent.

More important than the attitudes of people in the general population are the opinions and decisions of individuals who are in a position to pass on research projects that explore behavior manipulation. We know very little about how the critical decisions are made. One gets the impression that such decision-making bodies have been, on the whole, quite conservative. Experiments on stimulus and reinforcement control have been restricted to studies in the field of education with normal and retarded children and to scattered work with other groups of abnormal individuals. Experiments in which electrodes are implanted in human subjects have just begun and, as a rule, have been restricted to situations in which a clear therapeutic gain could be anticipated from the implantation—for example, in victims of epilepsy and severe motor disorders who could be helped by brain stimulation and destruction. The practical problem raised by research on mood control will soon be more pressing.

Another important factor in anticipating social acceptance involves the fragmentation of the society. Some sections of society may accept a new technology even though the society as a whole rejects it. Let us suppose, for instance, that new and effective drugs become available. It will be very important whether or not control of distribution and use is encouraged or inhibited by large private manufacturing industries, by secret and semicriminal distributing groups, or by government and nonprofit organizations operating under full public scrutiny. I have already mentioned that some methods of manipulating behavior are likely to slip from the control of those who originate them. It seems likely, for instance, that certain kinds of drugs which are easily and cheaply produced and which can be manufactured by relatively inexperienced chemists can be made and used by individuals in spite of disapproval by society at large and the institutions set up by the government to control use. Other methods of behavior manipulation, such as those involving major brain surgery, are not likely to be possible except under reasonable public scrutiny.

A cautious general extrapolation from present acceptance of behavior-manipulation techniques suggests that a limited extension of use of surgical techniques and stimulus-control methods will proceed under fairly close supervision by the public and by academic institutions. Many new drugs will undoubtedly be developed both in academic institutions and by large private drug houses. Advertising will probably continue to exaggerate the need for drugs in order to promote sales. If we argue by analogy from current difficulties in control of drugs, we can assume that new drugs will be accepted, at least by certain parts of our society, and will pose serious problems for society and for those institutions of government that are attempting control. Because drugs can be used easily, it is also quite likely that they will constitute the most common technique for manipulating behavior with full social approval—for instance, increasingly in the handling of behavior deviants.

SYNTHETIC FOOD FOR TOMORROW'S BILLIONS

by ARCHIBALD T. MCPHERSON

THE major problem facing the world today is twofold: population and food. Modern medicine and improved sanitation have brought about a spectacular increase in the average life-span while the birthrate in many countries remains practically unchanged. In Europe, the British Commonwealth, and the U.S., the birthrate is about 20 per thousand population per year while the death rate is about 10 per thousand. In the less developed countries of Asia, Africa, and South America, which contain the larger part of the world's population, the birthrate, for the most part, is 40 to 45 per thousand while the death rate is about 20 per thousand, and is dropping rapidly. The data for Mainland China (about which there may be some doubt) show a birthrate of 34 per thousand and a death rate of 11. Mexico has a birthrate of 45 per thousand and a death rate of only 10.

Efforts to check the birthrate and to increase the food supply are severely handicapped by lack of education, restrictive customs, and lethargy from malnutrition and undernutrition. Little can be accomplished without mass education and a significant increase in the standard of living in the countries having the highest birthrates. The standard of living, however, cannot be raised without markedly increasing the production of food and simultaneously freeing a part of the agricultural population to engage in the manufacture of agricultural and other equipment and to provide services. Furthermore, this massive increase in food

"Synthetic Food for Tomorrow's Billions," by Archibald T. McPherson, is reprinted with permission from the September 1965 issue of the *Bulletin of the Atomic Scientists.* Copyright 1965 by the Educational Foundation for Nuclear Science.

supply must be accomplished in so short a time that the additional food will not be consumed by the natural increase in the population.

Conventional methods to provide more food—improved agricultural practices, increased fertilizer production and use, avoidance of waste in handling and distributing food, opening new lands for cultivation—have been practiced for many years and are responsible for the fact that food production has thus far kept pace with the expanding population. But there is little prospect that conventional methods can produce enough food to provide a minimum adequate diet for the ever-hungry half of the world's population, and at the same time feed the rapidly mounting numbers. The ultimate solution of the problem must lie in a totally new source of food that will relieve the world's population from virtually sole dependence on agriculture.

The problem of population and food is not new; it has confronted man for most of the millions of years that human beings have been on the earth. The present problem differs only in its magnitude and intensity.

Nine thousand years ago, just before the dawn of civilization, the earth was populated by only one or two persons per square mile of good hunting and fishing territory. The total population of the world was somewhere between one and five million. The major occupation was food gathering—hunting; fishing; collecting fruit, roots, seeds, leaves, grubs, and insects. Early man lived precariously and in many parts of the world he spent a life of hardship in fertile areas of unrealized potential.

The population and food problem of prehistoric man was solved through the development of agriculture, which brought about a radically different way of life and made possible our present-day civilization. Agriculture afforded a reasonably assured supply of food from one season to the next; it made possible a fixed abode; it gave man freedom from continual food gathering which enabled him to develop arts and crafts; and it permitted the discoveries and advances of one generation to be passed to the next, first by tradition and soon after by writing.

One region of the earth that provided both plants and animals suitable for domestication was the hilly country and adjacent areas flanking the "fertile crescent" that bounds the Tigris-

Euphrates Valley. The grain which was subsequently domesticated to become wheat was emmer; the animals were sheep and goats; the time was soon after the last glacial period. The early agricultural developments led to the formation of village farming communities around the fertile crescent. Two such early communities whose sites have been excavated and studied were at Jarmo on the northeast and Jericho on the west. Jarmo has been dated at about 7000 B.C. and its population has been estimated at about 700.

The development of agriculture, with the great increase in food supply, permitted a very rapid increase in the population of the world. By 4000 B.C.—only 3,000 years after Jarmo—Mesopotamia and Egypt were thickly populated in comparison with pre-agricultural times, and the growth of cities and empires had begun. By 3000 B.C., writing had been invented, complex governments had evolved, and great engineering projects had been undertaken, such as the irrigation systems of the Tigris-Euphrates Valley and the pyramids of Egypt. All of these developments were possible because, as in America today, a fraction of the people could produce enough food for the entire population.

The population of the ancient world undoubtedly increased almost explosively with the initial discovery and spread of agriculture, but became stabilized as the great empires matured. From the beginning of the Christian era to about A.D. 700, the world population remained approximately stable at about 200 or 300 million. During the Dark Ages the population decreased, particularly during the devastating plagues. By the year 1650, which marks the beginning of the scientific age, the population curve had risen again and the world population is estimated to have been 470 to 545 million. In the 200 years between 1650 and 1850 the population approximately doubled. In the next 100 years from 1850 to 1950 the population more than doubled. In the 30 years from 1950 to 1980 it will have doubled again. Today the population of the world is increasing by a number of people equal to the entire population of the U.S. every three years. Many factors since 1650 have combined to bring about this rapid increase in population, but no factors have had such great effects as the advances in medicine and the improvements in sanitation which have so greatly lengthened man's life-span.

The phenomenal increase in population would make the problem of food for the future a difficult one, even if present food supplies were adequate. The difficulty is compounded, however, by widespread hunger and malnutrition throughout the greater part of the world today. In the light of the world food picture, the present abundance of food and crop surpluses in the U.S. are a minor and, probably, a transitory phenomenon. If by some miracle of distribution our surpluses could be made available to the ever-hungry millions of India, Pakistan, and China, they would all be consumed within a few weeks.

The world food supply is deficient not only in quantity but also in quality. The quantity index is calories per person per day; the quality index is grams of protein, particularly animal protein (meat, milk, and eggs), per person per day. On these indices, the countries of the world fall rather sharply into two groups. In one group are the economically developed countries, including those of Europe and parts of the British Commonwealth, Argentina, Uruguay, and the U.S. In the other group are the economically underdeveloped countries that make up most of Asia, Africa, Central America, and South America. The contrast between the average nutritional status in these two groups of countries is shown by the following data:

	In the developed countries	In the underdeveloped countries
Calories, daily per person	2,941	2,033
Total protein, daily grams per person	84.0	52.4
Animal protein only, daily grams per person	38.8	7.2
Population (1959–61), in millions	1,089	1,923

Source: "World Food Budget, 1970," Economic Research Service, U.S. Department of Agriculture, Washington, D.C. All figures are averaged for base years 1959–61.

The difference in calories is quite marked, but of even more significance is the difference in protein and, in particular, the difference between 39 grams of animal protein per person per day for the favored countries and seven grams for the others.

The relation of caloric intake to the amount of work that an individual can do is well known, but it is not so well understood that a sufficient number of calories may not be enough. Calories alone may be "empty" if they are provided by sugar and starchy foods without the necessary proteins, fats, minerals, and vitamins.

Proteins in the diet provide amino acids which the body utilizes in the building and repair of tissues and in a variety of important body functions. Proteins in excess of these needs merely serve as a source of energy. Plant and animal proteins contain about twenty-two different amino acids in varying proportions. Of these twenty-two amino acids, eight are essential in the adult diet; if they are provided, the body can synthesize the remaining fourteen as required. The essential amino acids are isoleucine, leucine, lysine, methionine, phenylalanine, threonine, tryptophane, and valine. A ninth amino acid, histidine, is regarded as necessary to maintain growth during childhood. Furthermore, the body must have these essential amino acids in a definite proportion in order to utilize them efficiently. If any one is in short supply, the remainder can be utilized only in proportion to the amount in which that one is present. The degree of utilization on this basis is termed the efficiency of a protein.

The animal proteins (meat, milk, and eggs) contain the amino acids in about the proportion needed by the human body, but the vegetable proteins of both the cereals and the legumes are deficient in certain of the amino acids, particularly lysine and methionine. Lysine is deficient in all of the common cereals—wheat, rice, rye, oats, barley—and methionine is deficient in the legumes—peas, beans, soy beans, peanuts. The addition of lysine to cereals and methionine to legumes in amounts of about one-half of one per cent to one per cent greatly increases the efficiency of the proteins contained and renders them much more nearly equivalent to animal proteins. (A still greater protein efficiency could probably be attained by adding small amounts of other amino acids, but the additional gain would be small.) In the U.S. most of the methionine and lysine produced are used in the feeding of poultry and swine. However, one brand of bread is enriched by the addition of about one half of one per cent of l-lysine, which is said to double the efficiency of the protein of the wheat.

Protein deficiency in the diet in the underdeveloped countries contributes very significantly to the high mortality of children and to the poor development of those that survive. In one survey, malnutrition was found to be responsible for 36 per cent of the deaths of children in their second year, 40 per cent of the deaths in the third year, and 19 per cent in the sixth and seventh years. In addition, malnutrition was undoubtedly a contributing factor to deaths from other causes.

Two diseases are caused by malnutrition: kwashiorkor and marasmus. Kwashiorkor is characterized by puny development, a distended abdomen, apathy, and lassitude. A child with marasmus is dwarfed and acutely emaciated. Except in very advanced cases, spectacular cures can be effected by correct feeding with a diet rich in proteins.

In the underdeveloped countries, food and population are caught in a desperate circle. Small, slow gains are made in productivity, but there is no relief from hunger because there are always more mouths to be fed. Agricultural production could be markedly increased by the adoption of western methods, but tools, fertilizers, and other resources are lacking and, most of all, people suffering from hunger and malnutrition are lethargic and they lack the energy to adopt new ways that would improve their lot.

The situation calls for a critical increase in the quantity and quality of food to outrun the increase in population and provide a standard of living that will permit education and, in turn, make possible the intelligent control of population. The experience of western countries has shown that when the standard of living is raised and education is provided the birthrate falls spontaneously, without government pressure. Thus the paradox is that small and slow increases in food production are accompanied by a proportionate increase in the population, while large and rapid increases may result in decreasing the birthrate and stabilizing the population.

Conventional methods of increasing food production, for example through agriculture and fisheries, cannot be expanded rapidly enough to provide this critical increase. Too many people are involved, and in many places the profound social changes required cannot be brought about quickly. We must turn from agriculture to the production of food by synthesis. Synthesis of large quantities of food that are basically identical with natural food can be achieved by relatively small numbers of people using readily available raw materials in facilities that can be set up and duplicated almost anywhere in the world.

All substances essential for human nutrition have been identified. Their chemical composition and molecular structure have been determined, and their synthesis has been effected. The scientific basis for the synthesis of food has thus been well established; only the engineering remains to be done. Synthetic food products are not inferior imitations or substitutes for food products of plant or animal origin; they are essentially the same substances, although they may be in different forms. They are synthesized in ways that give promise of being quicker, cheaper, and more efficient than their production by living organisms.

Evidence for the practicality of the direct synthesis of food is provided by the highly successful, large-scale synthesis of non-food agricultural products. In the U.S. today, almost all dyes, resins, plastics, and drugs are synthetic products. More than half of the paints, soaps, detergents, and rubber are synthetic. Man-made textiles are gaining rapidly over cotton, wool, and silk, and a replacement has been developed for leather. Only tobacco remains as a nonfood agricultural product without a synthetic counterpart.

Today, unheralded by publicity, synthetic foods are being produced in the U.S. in quantities of millions of pounds a year at prices that insure a ready market. The principal products are vitamins, flavoring materials, and amino acids. Except for flavoring materials they are principally marketed for animal rather than human consumption.

Two methods of production are commonly used—direct synthesis and biosynthesis. Methionine, for example, is produced by direct chemical synthesis, whereas lysine has been produced both by chemical synthesis and by biosynthesis, which involves the use of special cultures of micro-organisms growing on substrates of carefully controlled composition. (It is understood that the product now on the market is made by the latter method.)

In order to show what might be done in providing synthetic food to supplement the present inadequate supply of food from agriculture, let us consider specifically the problem of Asia and the Far East—the most critical area in the world today from the standpoint of food, population, and political unrest. Walter H. Pawley, in a study for the United Nations, gives the 1958 rates of food consumption in this area and makes recommendations for the year 2000 that would represent minimum levels for adequate nutrition (Walter Pawley, "Possibilities of Increasing World Food Production," Freedom from Hunger Campaign, Basic Study No. 10, [United Nations, New York, 1963]). It is instructive to compare Pawley's figures with those for the consumption of food in the U.S. in 1958:

	In Asia and the Far East		In the U.S.
	1958	2000	1958
Calories, daily per person	2,070	2,400	3,120
Vegetable protein, daily grams per person	48	55	28
Animal protein, daily grams per person	8	20	66

With the world in turmoil and hunger riots already having taken place in India, it is by no means certain that the Asiatic peoples will wait patiently until the year 2000 for an increase of 330 calories per day. The year 1980 would be a much more reasonable date to set for Asia and the Far East to attain a minimum adequate diet, and by the year 2000 food should be as plentiful as it is in the U.S. today.

The most important need shown by Pawley's estimates is for an increase in animal protein from eight to 20 grams per person per day. (Proteins and calories are the major items considered by Pawley and others, but it should be recognized that there are deficiencies in other items as well—certainly in vitamins and probably in minerals.) Animal protein (which contains the eight or nine essential amino acids) is better termed a "complete protein." For practical purposes a complete protein can be largely, and perhaps entirely, replaced in the diet by a mixture of the essential amino acids in the correct proportion, since proteins are broken down to the constituent amino acids in the process of digestion.

The first step in improving the Asiatic diet by the use of synthetic materials would be to supplement the inadequate protein of the grains and legumes by the addition of small percentages of two amino acids: lysine and methionine. Since production methods for both lysine and methionine are already available, it would be necessary only to build the facilities and to develop methods for incorporating the amino acids in the diet.

Such supplementation would improve the efficiency of the protein in the diet, but the total amount of protein would still be inadequate. It would still be necessary to synthesize all of the essential amino acids in a total quantity sufficient to make up or to provide additional protein by other means—as from biosynthesis by microorganisms. From other developments in the chemical industry it would seem entirely possible to work out production methods for the amino acids now made only in laboratory or pilot plant quantities, and build large-scale manufacturing facilities by 1980.

In 1980 it is estimated that the population of Asia and the Far East will be 2.268 billion. Assuming that the agricultural production barely keeps pace with the increase in population, the animal protein per capita per day by that date will still be eight grams per person, which must be increased to 20 grams to provide what Pawley regards as the minimum for an adequate diet. To supply the difference between eight grams and 20 grams per person per day in 1980 in terms of a mixture of the essential amino acids would require the quantity $12 \times 366 \times 2.268$ billion grams, or 9.96 million metric tons. (By way of comparison, this is about five times the annual production of synthetic rubber in the free world.) Taking the average cost of the amino acids at the high figure of four dollars per kilo, the total cost would be about $40 billion per year or about $18 per person per year. With a major research and development effort the cost of amino acids could probably be brought below the estimated cost. However, meat contains only about 20 per cent protein, so that pure amino acids at four dollars per kilogram would be equivalent to meat at 35 cents or 40 cents a pound.

An inspection of the Asiatic diet indicates that fats, rather than additional carbohydrates, would be a welcome and a nutritionally desirable means of supplying the needed calories. Fat provides a concentrated form of food energy, so that to increase the daily calorie consumption from 2,070 to 2,400 would require only 36.6 grams of fat. (The amount of fat consumed per person per day in the U.S. in 1954 was 142.6 grams, as compared with 25.3 grams in India.) On this basis the annual requirement for the 1980 population of Asia and the Far East would be 30.4 million metric tons. This estimate neglects the calories that would be provided by the 12 grams of protein per person per day which would reduce the amount by roughly 10 per cent. From the standpoint of the chemical industry the production of 30 million tons a year, though large, would be within the capability of a fifteen-year research and development program.

The chemist can build up organic substances from any form of the elements that may be conveniently available. Coal is used to a considerable extent, and even wood is occasionally employed, but at present natural gas and liquid petroleum are preferred for all manner of organic synthesis. Nitrogen in the atmosphere is utilized by first fixing it as ammonia, which may be employed directly in the synthesis of amino acids. Sulfur and phosphorus are needed in foods in only small amounts which are readily obtainable from inorganic sources. Hydrogen is, of course, present in hydrocarbons and in water, and oxygen may be obtained from water and from the atmosphere.

The synthesis of food from petroleum would require at most only a small fraction of the amount of petroleum used for fuel, and would not, as is often suggested, deplete a valuable and diminishing natural resource. The synthetic amino acids and fats proposed here for Asia and the Far East would require about 18 kilograms of petroleum per person per year whereas the consumption of petroleum is 104 kilograms per person per year and is rising at a rate of about 10 per cent per year.

Thanks to the misguided humor of the cartoonist, the mention of synthetic food brings to mind the picture of tasteless food pills. The facts are, of course, that the composition and quantity of the basic constituents of food are the same whether the food is synthesized by plants and the plants are eaten by man; whether the plant food is collected and concentrated by an animal and the animal is eaten by man; or whether the basic constituents of the food are directly synthesized by man.

Nevertheless, age-old food habits are slow to change and synthetic foods must be introduced in a way that will make them sought after rather than merely tolerated. The first prerequisites to acceptance are pleasing odors and tastes. Most natural materials that appeal to the senses of smell and taste, as well as many not known in nature, have already been synthesized. Over 63 million pounds of natural and synthetic flavoring materials and perfumes were produced in the U.S. in 1961 at an average price of $1.24 per pound; this indicates that there should be no major problem in this area.

Another prerequisite to acceptance is a variety of desirable consistencies. Many organic materials, including amino acids, can be polymerized or converted into polymers in combination with other substances. By varying the molecular weight and structure, a polymer of a given basic composition can usually be prepared with a wide range of properties from soft to brittle. Once the food processor and distributor are provided with the basic synthetic materials for an adequate diet, there are almost endless possibilities for preparing and marketing these basic materials.

There are many advantages to the direct synthesis of otherwise scarce food materials such as amino acids and vitamins. Production can be expanded rapidly once large-scale manufacturing methods have been developed, and can be geared to the demand with neither costly surpluses nor unfulfilled requirements. The man-power requirements for chemical manufacture are low; a relatively small number of persons could manufacture synthetic food for a large population with no necessity for the slow mass education and changes of custom that are essential for the improvement of agriculture. Food production could be undertaken in any part of the world that possessed coal or petroleum as the necessary raw material and fuel. This would permit countries now dependent on importing food to achieve self-sufficiency, and would make possible a radically different distribution of industry and population throughout the world.

For the immediate future all of the resources of both agriculture and synthetic production will be taxed to provide enough food of adequate quality. When a sufficient output is attained, agriculture and synthesis may coexist for a long time, often supplementing each other, but sometimes competing. Synthesis of food materials will inevitably continue to gain as it has for nonfood agricultural products, but some agricultural pursuits will persist, just as hunting and fishing have persisted in the modern world.

What are the alternatives? Are there other means of increasing the world's food supply that will both meet the present deficit and provide enough or more to constitute adequate nutrition for everyone? If more food is not supplied—and supplied soon—what may happen, and what choices do we in the U.S. have?

Efforts are being made by the Food and Agriculture Organization of the United Nations and many other organizations and agencies to improve crop yields and increase animal production. The problem seems simple if one looks at the disparity between yields per acre in many parts of Asia and the Far East and the yields achieved in the U.S. with modern methods. Progress is being made, but not rapidly. The principal factor is the human. Many of the people concerned are both undernourished and malnourished, and consequently lack the initiative and vigor to undertake new methods. Much time and patience will be required to change the practices and habits of centuries. Many of the newly independent governments, far from being helpful, are more concerned with the acquisition of steel mills and nuclear reactors as status symbols than they are with improvements in their agricultural or fishing practices. Great modern cities are springing up all over Asia, Africa, and South America, but life and practices in the villages on which the cities depend for their food go on unchanged, and sometimes changed for the worse. Grain from the U.S. cannot serve as a stop-gap measure for long because there will not be enough. In less than 15 years the increase in population in India and Pakistan will equal the entire population of the U.S.

Widespread famine is clearly foreseen by authorities and mention of it is being made, from time to time, in the daily press. Famine is not new to Asia and the Far East. In times past, millions have been carried away by starvation and disease and occasional waves of pestilence. The masses of people in the villages have submitted passively and quietly to famine and starvation, with only passing notice from the West. Now, however, there is a new group of people to be reckoned with—those who have migrated to the cities and work in the new industries. They have had a taste of western living; their income, though low by our standards, has brought them more food and a higher standard of living than they ever dreamed of in their villages. These city workers will not passively submit to hunger and privation. The food rioters of India seen in the newsreels were not gaunt and emaciated; they were well-muscled, vigorous, and determined. With only a part of the population in this category a government might be forced to resort to war to take food by force rather than submit to widespread famine. Any such war could become a world war with the "have" nations and their superior resources pitted against the "have-not" nations and their greater numbers driven to desperation by their plight.

Thus, the synthesis of food is not merely a possible development at some distant time. A crisis is approaching. A new, little-known, untried, but feasible solution is available. The question is whether the leaders of nations will recognize and avail themselves of this solution in time.

THE NATIONAL POLLUTION SCANDAL

by GAYLORD NELSON

THE natural environment of America—the woods and waters and wildlife, the clear air and blue sky, the fertile soil and the scenic landscape—is threatened with destruction. Our growing population and expanding industries, the explosion of scientific knowledge, the vast increase in income levels, leisure time, and mobility—all of these powerful trends are exert-

"The National Pollution Scandal," by Gaylord Nelson. Reprinted by permission from *The Progressive*, February 1967.

ing such pressure on our natural resources that many of them could be effectively ruined over the next ten or fifteen years. Our overcrowded parks are becoming slums. Our birds and wildlife are being driven away or killed outright. Scenic rural areas are blighted by junkyards and billboards, and neon blight soils the outskirts of most cities. In our orgy of expansion, we are bulldozing away the natural landscape and building a cold new world of concrete and aluminum. Strip miners' shovels are tearing away whole mountains and spreading ugly wastes for miles around. America the affluent is well on the way to destroying America the beautiful. Of all these developments, the most tragic and the most costly is the rapidly mounting pollution of our lakes and streams.

Perhaps the pain is more intense for a Senator from a state like Wisconsin, bordered on three sides by the Great Lakes and the Mississippi, blessed with 8,000 inland lakes and hundreds of rivers and trout streams. Actually, our state seems rather fortunate at the moment. A yachtsman on Lake Superior can raise a bucket of water still crystal-clear and cold enough to drink with delight. Canoeists on the St. Croix or Wolf Rivers still shoot through frothing rapids of sparkling water, and catch fish in the deep, swirling pools.

But the bell is tolling for Wisconsin just as for all the nation. A recent survey of twelve major river basins in southeastern Wisconsin found not a single one fit even for the partial body contact involved in fishing or wading. A competent governmental agency concluded that 754 miles of rivers in this region had been turned into open sewers. Beaches along Lake Michigan, a vast blue sea with seemingly limitless quantities of fresh water, are being closed to swimmers. A sordid ocean of pollution is pouring into the Mississippi from the Minneapolis-St. Paul urban complex. The first serious signs of pollution are soiling Lake Superior, and our small inland lakes are, one by one, becoming murky and smelly and choked with algae.

Elsewhere, all across the nation, the same tragedy is being enacted, although in many areas the curtain already has come down. The waters are already ruined. Every major river system in America is seriously polluted, from the Androscoggin in Maine to the Columbia in the far Northwest. The rivers once celebrated in poetry and song—the Monongahela, the Cumberland, the Ohio, the Hudson, the Delaware, the Rio Grande—have been blackened with sewage, chemicals, oil, and trash. They are sewers of filth and disease. The Monongahela, which drains the mining and industrial areas of West Virginia and Pennsylvania, empties the equivalent of 200,000 tons of sulfuric acid each year into the Ohio River—which in turn is the water supply for millions of people who use and re-use Ohio River water many times over.

National attention has been centered on once beautiful Lake Erie, the great lake which is the recreational front yard of Buffalo, Cleveland, Toledo and Detroit, and which supplies water for ten million Americans. A Public Health Service survey of Lake Erie made the shocking discovery that, in the 2,600 square mile heart of the lake, there was no dissolved oxygen at all in the water. The lake in this vast area could support no desirable aquatic life, only lowly creatures such as bloodworms, sludgeworms, sowbugs, and bloodsuckers.

Along with the germs and industrial acids which pour into Lake Erie are millions of pounds of phosphates, a major ingredient in detergents. Each pound of phosphate will propagate 700 pounds of algae. Beneath the waters of this great lake, largely hidden from sight, a hideous cancer-like growth of algae is forming. As algae blooms and dies, it becomes a pollutant itself. It robs the lake of still more oxygen—and it releases the phosphate to grow another crop of algae. Lake Erie is a product of its tributaries. A Public Health Service study of these American sewers is horrifying to read.

The Maumee River flows from Fort Wayne, Indiana, through Defiance and Napoleon, Ohio, and on to Toledo, where it joins the lake. Even as far upstream as Fort Wayne, the river has insufficient oxygen to support anything but trash fish and lower organisms, and as it flows toward Lake Erie conditions get steadily worse. The count of coliform bacteria runs as high as 24,000 times the allowable maximum under Federal drinking water standards. The concentration of carbolic acid, a byproduct of steelmaking, runs up to 137 times the allowable maximum. A packing company dumps 136 pounds of oil per day into the Maumee River. A plating company dumps thirty-eight pounds of cyanide per day. Defiance, Ohio, closes its sewage plant entirely for one or two months each year, and all its raw sewage goes directly into the Maumee. Below Defiance, a foundry dumps cinders and ashes into the river. The Maumee is joined by the Auglaize River, which is even more polluted than the Maumee, and is especially rich in ammonia compounds. At Napoleon, Ohio, the city draws its drinking water from the sordid Maumee, and a soup company draws off ten million gallons a day for soup processing. (The firm assures me that its modern water treatment plant, complete with carbon filters, can "polish the water to a high quality.") Below Napoleon, things get really bad. Forty per cent of samples taken by the Public Health Service showed presence of salmonella, an intestinal bacteria that can cause severe illness. As the Maumee flows into Lake Erie at Toledo, it gets its final dose of pollution—the effluent from the Toledo sewage plant and what the Public Health Service describes as "oil, scum, metallic deposits, and toxic materials."

Another Lake Erie tributary—the Cuyahoga—which flows into the lake at Cleveland, is described by the Public Health Service as "debris-filled, oil-slicked, and dirty-looking throughout." It is loaded with coliform bacteria and salmonella. It is so polluted with oil that it frequently catches fire. Structures known as "fire breaks" have been built out into the river to fight these blazes. In the Cleveland harbor, the Public Health Service could find virtually no conventional aquatic life. However, the sludgeworms which thrive on organic matter were well represented—400,000 per square meter on the harbor bottom.

That is the story of Lake Erie, and although it is so shocking and disgusting as to deserve urgent national attention, it is not unique. Southern Lake Michigan, ringed with oil refineries, steel mills, and municipal sewage outfalls, may be even worse. Scientists estimate that it would take 100 years to replace the polluted water of southern Lake Michigan, and some consider the pollution in this area irreversible.

We have our own Wisconsin pollution scandal in Green Bay, a magnificent recreational body of water in northeastern Wisconsin, widely known as a yachtsman's paradise and site of a multimillion dollar resort industry. This "Cape Cod of Wisconsin" is threatened with ruin by a tide of pollution which is moving up the bay at the rate of more than one mile per year. The pollution comes from rivers such as the Fox, the Peshtigo, the Oconto, and the Menominee, which drain large areas of Wisconsin and northern Michigan.

The experience in Lake Erie, Lake Michigan, and Green Bay has convinced many experts of this chilling fact: It is a definite possibility that the Great Lakes—the greatest single source of fresh water in the world—could be effectively destroyed by pollution in the years ahead. If this were to happen, it would be the greatest natural resource disaster in modern history.

That is the outline of this new American tragedy. The obvious question now is, what can be done about it? First, I think we must learn what a complex and widespread problem we face in water pollution. Like crime, like death on the highway, pollution is a social problem which extends throughout our society. There is no single villain, and there is no simple answer. It must be attacked for what it is—a sinister byproduct of the prosperous, urbanized, industrialized world in which we live. We must take care not to ride off in pursuit of just one villain—such as city sewage, or industrial waste, or detergents, or toilet wastes from boats; this is a battle which must be fought with skill and courage on many different fronts. Nor should we be fooled by the strategy of many polluters, who argue, in effect: "The pollution which we cause is minor compared to the big, nation-wide problem. Why not leave us alone and go after the big offenders?" Even some of the lesser offenders in the pollution crisis could ruin us in time.

The primary sources of pollution are these:

MUNICIPAL SEWAGE—Despite heroic efforts and heavy investments by many cities, our municipal sewage treatment plants are woefully inadequate. Some cities have no treatment at all; others remove only part of the pollutants found in sewage. As a result, the effluent discharged by our cities today (treated and untreated) is equivalent to the *untreated* sewage from a nation of seventy-five million people.

INDUSTRIAL POLLUTION is roughly twice as big a problem as municipal sewage. Despite tremendous investments in research and treatment plant construction by some industries, the overall record is terrible. Some industries feel they cannot remain competitive if they spend heavily for treatment plants. Communities and states are reluctant to push them too far. As a result, industrial wastes (treated and untreated) now discharged into our waters are presently equal to the *untreated* sewage of a nation of 165 million people.

SEPTIC TANKS—Vast sections of the nation have no sewer collection or treatment system at all. In such areas, underground septic tanks, often poorly made and undersized, are expected to distribute wastes into the soil. They overflow into natural watercourses, they leak bacteria and detergents into underground wells, and they are destroying lakes by filling them with nutrients that foster heavy growths of algae.

SHIPS AND MARINE TERMINALS—In selected areas, the discharge of toilet wastes, oil, garbage, and rubbish from ships and shoreline installations is a major problem. For some reason, this form of pollution is widely tolerated and enforcement of laws forbidding it is virtually nonexistent.

PESTICIDES—The terrifying prospect of spreading poison all over the globe confronts us. We now use more than 700 million pounds a year of synthetic pesticides and agricultural chemicals of 45,000 varieties. This volume is expected to increase tenfold in the next twenty years. Many of these poisons persist forever in the environment, and their concentration builds up geometrically as they progress through the food chain (water, seaweed, fish, birds, mammals). DDT residue has been discovered in penguins in Antarctica, in reindeer in Alaska, in seals, and in fish caught in remote areas of the Pacific Ocean. One part of DDT in one billion parts of water will kill blue crabs in eight days.

SILT—One of the most serious pollutants all over the world is the dirt which washes into our waters from off the land. This somewhat natural problem is disastrously aggravated by contemporary trends—widespread clearing of land for subdivisions and shopping centers; construction of highways and parking lots (which cause rapid runoff) and the intensive development of lakeshores and riverbanks. Controlling surface runoff and the siltation which it causes is complicated by our patchwork of political boundaries and the lack of coordinated government planning.

DETERGENTS, FERTILIZERS, AND OTHER CHEMICALS—Some of these commonly used substances pass through even good waste treatment systems and become persistent pollutants. Such pollution can be eliminated only by changing the composition of such substances, regulating their use, or devising new removal techniques.

Obviously, any nationwide problem made up of so many elements is extremely difficult to attack. Yet I believe that the rapidly accelerating destruction of our natural resources is our number one domestic problem, and the greatest of all our resource problems is water pollution. If we are to meet this pollution threat, if we are to save the waters of America and preserve this most indispensable part of our natural environment, we must make the war on pollution a high priority matter at every level of government—local, state and Federal—and we must insist that private industry do likewise. Baffling and complicated as the pollution problem is, it is not insoluble. There is no reason in the world why a great and prosperous nation, with the money and know-how to shoot man to the moon, cannot prevent its lakes and rivers from being destroyed and its life-giving water supplies endangered. Just as there is no single cause of pollution, so is there no single solution to the problem.

Consider the question of what to do about municipal sewage and industrial wastes. Why do we tolerate a situation where these two sources alone pour into our waters each year the equivalent of the completely untreated sewage of a nation of 240 million persons? Here it is largely a matter of lack of money, aggravated in some cases by a shocking lack of public concern. There are now more than 1300 communities which have sewer systems but discharge their wastes into the waters without any treatment at all. These communities have a population of more than eleven million people. How such a condition could exist in the year 1966—when it is generally illegal to throw a gum wrapper out of a car window—is inconceivable.

We have another 1300 communities—with almost seventeen million population—which treat their wastes but in a completely inadequate manner. In most cases, these are communities which use what is known as "primary" treatment. They screen their sewage and let the solids settle out, but they do not remove dissolved solids, salts, chemicals, bacteria, and special problems such as detergents. Every community should have what is known as "secondary" treatment, under which sewage—after primary treatment—is held in holding tanks, brought into contact with air and biologically active sludge, so that bacteria have a chance to consume the pollutants.

The Conference of State Sanitary Engineers estimates that it would cost $1.8 billion to provide adequate sewage collection and treatment for these communities which now have no treatment or completely inadequate treatment. But even this would still leave us with a massive municipal pollution problem. Even good secondary treatment removes only eighty per cent to ninety per cent of the pollutants. Chicago, for instance, with a good secondary treatment plant, discharges treated effluent which is equivalent to the untreated, raw sewage of one million people. It dumps 1,800 tons of solids per day into the Illinois waterway. At the rate the pollution load is increasing it is estimated that even if all communities have secondary treatment plants by 1980, the total amount of pollutants reaching watercourses would still be the same as today. Obviously, we need a massive program to build highly effective city sewage treatment plants.

It is also obvious that local property taxes cannot support such a gigantic investment, and that if we wait for communities to do this on their own, it will never be done. Most state budgets also are severely strained, so much of this burden is going to have to be borne by the Federal government—if we want the job done early enough to be effective. The Senate Air and Water Pollution subcommittee estimates that it will cost $20 billion to provide secondary treatment in plants serving eighty per cent of the population and more advanced treatment in plants serving the other twenty per cent. We have had a Federal program to assist communities in building such treatment plants for the past ten years, but it has been inadequate. It has recently been greatly improved, but it is still inadequate. In the past it has provided grants of up to thirty per cent within the limits of available funds. The most recent act—the Clean Waters Restoration Act of 1966—authorizes a total of about $3.6 billion over the next five years ($150 million in 1967, $450 million in 1968, $700 million in 1969, $1 billion in 1970, and $1.25 billion in 1971). A community can get a grant for up to fifty per cent of the cost of a project, provided the state pays twenty-five per cent and provided water quality standards have been established.

New York needs an estimated $1.7 billion for new sewage plants. The new law would give it a total of only $307 million.

Ohio needs $1 billion and would get $180 million. Wisconsin needs $286 million and would get $75 million. If we are serious about the Federal government paying fifty per cent of the cost of eliminating municipal pollution, then Washington must provide $10 billion—not $3.6 billion—and even then we will be expecting our hard-pressed states and communities to come up with another $10 billion. Personally, I think it is unrealistic to expect the states and localities to assume a burden of this size. And I do not think the nation can sit by and wait while its communities struggle to build up the financial resources and the political courage needed to do the job. I think we should get sewage treatment plants built the way we are getting interstate highways built—by offering ninety per cent Federal financing. I have introduced legislation which would establish such a program.

The municipal sewage problem is complicated by another problem—combined storm and sanitary sewers. By combining storm water and human wastes in one sewer system, many cities build up such a tremendous load during rainstorms that their sewage treatment plants cannot handle it. They have had to install automatic devices which divert the combined sewer load directly into lakes or streams whenever it gets above a certain level. In this manner, sixty-five billion gallons of raw, untreated sewage goes into our lakes and rivers each year. Most cities are separating storm and sanitary sewers in new subdivisions, but the task of separating the sewers in the older areas is a staggering one. Complete separation would cost an estimated $30 billion. It would cost $160 per resident in Washington, D.C., $215 in Milwaukee, $280 in Concord, New Hampshire. It would cost Wisconsin an estimated $186 million, Indiana $496 million, Michigan $970 million, New York and Illinois about $1.12 billion each. These are only general estimates of the direct costs and they do not take into account the disruption of traffic and the local economy caused by ripping up miles of underground sewers. In the hope of avoiding such costs, the Federal government has underwritten several research projects to see if this problem cannot be met in some other way—through temporary underground storage of sewer overflows, for instance, or by building smaller sanitary sewer pipes inside existing storm sewers.

The staggering problem of *industrial* pollution is virtually untouched today by our Federal anti-pollution programs, even though industry contributes twice as much pollution to our waters as do municipalities. If we do not step up our industrial waste treatment plant construction, the pollution effect of industrial wastes alone by 1970 will be equal to the untreated, raw sewage from our entire population. Industries are widely criticized for dumping wastes into our waters, and this criticism is often justified. They are pressured by local, state, and Federal officials. But some industries are able to avoid a serious crackdown against them by threatening to move. Most industries argue—sometimes effectively—that they cannot be expected to make massive investments in treatment plants if their competitors—often in different parts of the country—are not forced to do so.

I have come to the conclusion that the threat of enforcement alone is not going to solve our industrial pollution problem. We must provide direct financial assistance to see to it that the plants are built. I have introduced legislation to provide both loans and grants of up to fifty per cent to industries whose size and economic circumstances prevent them from assuming the full burden of providing their own facilities. I think such assistance should be carefully limited and should be for a short period, but I do not think we can avoid it. We are going to pay the cost of industrial pollution in one way or another—in the cost of the manufactured product, in taxes, or in ruined water resources.

But massive construction programs alone are not going to solve our municipal and industrial pollution problems. We need a tremendous expansion of Federally supported research to find completely new answers. Our whole waste disposal system, from the household toilet to the municipal sewage treatment plant, is a holdover from another era. The system should be studied and redesigned, using the latest scientific techniques, and fitted into a coordinated, nationwide system of waste disposal. Research grants should be made to private industry and universities to develop new methods and devices to refine, use, neutralize, or destroy pollutants. We should compute what our present waste disposal systems are costing us—including the loss in natural resources destroyed—and what alternative systems would cost.

Compared with municipal and industrial pollution, the other pollution problems I have mentioned are statistically small. For that reason, they are often ignored. But we cannot safely do that.

Even if we managed to contain the flood of municipal and industrial pollution, the other sources could do fatal damage to our environment. Septic tanks must be controlled at the state and local level, and in many areas I think we must forbid new installations and work to replace existing ones with sewer systems. For instance, once an inland lake is ringed with cottages with septic tanks, it is doomed. Septic tanks must drain somewhere and in most lakeshore settings the natural drainage flow is into the lake. At the very least, this drainage will fertilize the lake, cause the rapid growth of algae, and turn the lake into a murky, foul-smelling mess.

Ship pollution is certainly serious enough to justify Federal action, even though such suggestions cause howls of protest from those who insist it "isn't practical." Why is it practical to install retention facilities on buses, house trailers, and aircraft but not on boats and ships? Obviously, we are willing to allow wastes to be dumped into our water supplies which we would never tolerate being dumped onto the land. We need Federal laws to require suitable facilities on all vessels using our navigable waters, and we need a better enforcement system to crack down on such disgraceful practices as dumping oil and pumping out oily ballast tanks on the Great Lakes and in our rivers.

The siltation problem can be controlled only through strict zoning and land use controls. We have got to prevent intensive development of our shorelines if we are to save our waters. Once a large portion of the natural vegetative cover is destroyed, the water resource is in danger. I believe that the Federal government should provide financial assistance to those willing to carry out soil conservation practices along our lakes and streams on a scale large enough to be meaningful:

Pesticides, detergents, and exotic new chemicals will plague us for years to come. New treatment systems may offer some hope for removing these substances, but I think they must be controlled directly. Those which cannot be removed safely in normal treatment processes, and those which have chemical structures which cause them to persist in our environment and to threaten fish, wildlife, and human health, should be banned or their use strictly regulated.

In speeches in some twenty-three states in the past four years, I have called for an emergency, crash program to fight water pollution. I have offered my estimate of the cost of conquering water pollution as $50 to $100 billion over the next decade. It now appears I may have been conservative. The Public Health Service now estimates that it will cost some $20 billion to clean up the Great Lakes alone, and the total national cost is now estimated at $100 billion. But everywhere I have gone I have found the public willing to pay this cost to save their waters. In fact, I think the public is far ahead of local, state, and Federal officials in facing up to this crisis. I think that citizens in most communities would support a sharp crackdown on local polluters of every variety. I think they want their states to establish high water quality standards, and then enforce them. I think they can be shown the need for bold regional action to deal with those vast interstate pollution problems (such as on the Mississippi and the Great Lakes) which obviously are too big for any community or any state to handle. And I think that the citizens of America now recognize that the destruction of the major river networks of the nation, the threatened destruction of the Great Lakes, and the slow ruination of our treasured inland lakes and trout streams is a calamity of such gigantic proportions as to deserve the urgent attention of all citizens and prompt action by the national government.

THE NEW MUTANTS

by LESLIE A. FIEDLER

A REALIZATION that the legitimate functions of literature are bewilderingly, almost inexhaustibly various has always exhilarated poets and dismayed critics. And critics, therefore, have sought age after age to legislate limits to literature—

"The New Mutants," by Leslie A. Fiedler. Reprinted from *Partisan Review*, Fall, 1965, Vol. XXXII, No. 4, by permission of the author and *Partisan Review*. © 1965 by *Partisan Review*.

legitimizing certain of its functions and disavowing others—in hope of insuring to themselves the exhilaration of which they have felt unjustly deprived, and providing for poets the dismay which the critics at least have thought good for them.

Such shifting and exclusive emphasis is not, however, purely the product of critical malice, or even of critical principle. Somehow every period is, to begin with, especially aware of certain functions of literature and especially oblivious to others: endowed with a special sensitivity and a complementary obtuseness, which, indeed, give to that period its characteristic flavor and feel. So, for instance, the Augustan Era is marked by sensitivity in regard to the uses of diction, obtuseness in regard to those of imagery.

What the peculiar obtuseness of the present age may be I find it difficult to say (being its victim as well as its recorder), perhaps toward the didactic or certain modes of the sentimental. I am reasonably sure, however, that our period is acutely aware of the sense in which literature, if not invents, at least collaborates in the invention of time. The beginnings of that awareness go back certainly to the beginnings of the Renaissance, to Humanism as a self-conscious movement; though a critical development occurred toward the end of the eighteenth century with the dawning of the Age of Revolution. And we may have reached a second critical point right now.

At any rate, we have long been aware (in the last decades uncomfortably aware) that a chief function of literature is to express and in part to create not only theories of time but also attitudes toward time. Such attitudes constitute, however, a politics as well as an esthetics; or, more properly perhaps, a necessary mythological substratum of politics—as, in fact, the conventional terms reactionary, conservative, revolutionary indicate: all involving stances toward the past.

It is with the past, then, that we must start, since the invention of the past seems to have preceded that of the present and the future; and since we are gathered in a university at whose heart stands a library[1]—the latter, like the former, a visible monument to the theory that a chief responsibility of literature is to

[1] "The New Mutants" is a written version of a talk given by Mr. Fiedler at the Conference on the Idea of The Future held at Rutgers, in June, 1965. The conference was sponsored by Partisan Review and the Congress for Cultural Freedom, with the cooperation of Rutgers, The State University.

preserve and perpetuate the past. Few universities are explicitly (and none with any real degree of confidence) dedicated to this venerable goal any longer. The Great Books idea (which once transformed the University of Chicago and lives on now in provincial study groups) was perhaps its last desperate expression. Yet the shaky continuing existence of the universities and the building of new college libraries (with matching Federal funds) remind us not only of that tradition but of the literature created in its name: the neo-epic, for instance, all the way from Dante to Milton; and even the frantically nostalgic Historical Romance, out of the counting house by Sir Walter Scott.

Obviously, however, literature has a contemporary as well as a traditional function. That is to say, it may be dedicated to illuminating the present and the meaning of the present, which is, after all, no more given than the past. Certainly the modern or bourgeois novel was thus contemporary in the hands of its great inventors, Richardson, Fielding, Smollett and Sterne; and it became contemporary again—with, as it were, a sigh of relief—when Flaubert, having plunged deep into the Historical Romance, emerged once more into the present of Emma Bovary. But the second function of the novel tends to transform itself into a third: a revolutionary or prophetic or futurist function; and it is with the latter that I am here concerned.

Especially important for our own time is the sense in which literature first conceived the possibility of the future (rather than an End of Time or an Eternal Return, an Apocalypse or Second Coming); and then furnished that future in joyous or terrified anticipation, thus preparing all of us to inhabit it. Men have dreamed and even written down utopias from ancient times; but such utopias were at first typically allegories rather than projections: nonexistent models against which to measure the real world, exploitations of the impossible (as the traditional name declares) rather than explorations or anticipations or programs of the possible. And, in any event, only recently have such works occupied a position anywhere near the center of literature.

Indeed, the movement of futurist literature from the periphery to the center of culture provides a clue to certain essential meanings of our times and of the art which best reflects it. If we make a brief excursion from the lofty reaches of High Art to the humbler levels of Pop Culture—where radical transformations in literature are reflected in simplified form—the extent and nature of the futurist revolution will become immediately evident. Certainly, we have seen in recent years the purveyors of Pop Culture transfer their energies from the Western and the Dracula-type thriller (last heirs of the Romantic and Gothic concern with the past) to the Detective Story especially in its hard-boiled form (final vulgarization of the realists' dedication to the present) to Science Fiction (a new genre based on hints in E. A. Poe and committed to "extrapolating" the future). This development is based in part on the tendency to rapid exhaustion inherent in popular forms; but in part reflects a growing sense of the irrelevance of the past and even of the present to 1965. Surely, there has never been a moment in which the most naïve as well as the most sophisticated have been so acutely aware of how the past threatens momentarily to disappear from the present, which itself seems on the verge of disappearing into the future.

And this awareness functions, therefore, on the level of art as well as entertainment, persuading quite serious writers to emulate the modes of Science Fiction. The novel is most amenable to this sort of adaptation, whose traces we can find in writers as various as William Golding and Anthony Burgess, William Burroughs and Kurt Vonnegut, Jr., Harry Mathews and John Barth—to all of whom young readers tend to respond with a sympathy they do not feel even toward such forerunners of the mode (still more allegorical than prophetic) as Aldous Huxley, H. G. Wells and George Orwell. But the influence of Science Fiction can be discerned in poetry as well, and even in the polemical essays of such polymath prophets as Wilhelm Reich, Buckminster Fuller, Marshall McLuhan, perhaps also Norman O. Brown. Indeed, in Fuller the prophetic–Science-Fiction view of man is always at the point of fragmenting into verse:

> *men are known as being six feet tall*
> *because that is their tactile limit;*
> *they are not known by how far we can hear them,*
> *e.g., as a one-half mile man*
> *and only to dogs are men known*
> *by their gigantic olfactoral dimensions. . . .*

I am not now interested in analyzing, however, the diction and imagery which have passed from Science Fiction into post-Modernist literature, but rather in coming to terms with the prophetic content common to both: with the myth rather than the modes of Science Fiction. But that myth is quite simply the myth of the end of man, of the transcendence or transformation of the human—a vision quite different from that of the extinction of our species by the Bomb, which seems stereotype rather than archetype and consequently the source of editorials rather than poems. More fruitful artistically is the prospect of the radical transformation (under the impact of advanced technology and the transfer of traditional human functions to machines) of *homo sapiens* into something else: the emergence—to use the language of Science Fiction itself—of "mutants" among us.

A simpleminded prevision of this event is to be found in Arthur C. Clarke's *Childhood's End*, at the conclusion of which the mutated offspring of parents much like us are about to take off under their own power into outer space. Mr. Clarke believes that he is talking about a time still to come because he takes metaphor for fact; though simply translating "outer space" into "inner space" reveals to us that what he is up to is less prediction than description; since the post-human future is now, and if not we, at least our children, are what it would be comfortable to pretend we still only foresee. But what, in fact, are they: these mutants who are likely to sit before us in class, or across from us at the dinner table, or who stare at us with hostility from street corners as we pass?

Beatniks or hipsters, layabouts and drop-outs we are likely to call them with corresponding hostility—or more elegantly, but still without sympathy, passive onlookers, abstentionists, spiritual catatonics. There resides in all of these terms an element of truth, at least about the relationship of the young to what we have defined as the tradition, the world we have made for them; and if we turn to the books in which they see their own destiny best represented (*A Clockwork Orange*, say, or *On the Road* or *Temple of Gold*), we will find nothing to contradict that truth. Nor will we find anything to expand it, since the young and their laureates avoid on principle the kind of definition (even of themselves) for which we necessarily seek.

Let us begin then with the negative definition our own hostility suggests, since this is all that is available to us, and say that the "mutants" in our midst are non-participants in the past (though our wisdom assures us this is impossible), drop-outs from history. The withdrawal from school, so typical of their generation and so inscrutable to ours, is best understood as a lived symbol of their rejection of the notion of cultural continuity and progress, which our graded educational system represents in institutional form. It is not merely a matter of their rejecting what happens to have happened just before them, as the young do, after all, in every age; but of their attempting to disavow the very idea of the past, of their seeking to avoid recapitulating it step by step—up to the point of graduation into the present.

Specifically, the tradition from which they strive to disengage is the tradition of the human, as the West (understanding the West to extend from the United States to Russia) has defined it, Humanism itself, both in its bourgeois and Marxist forms; and more especially, the cult of reason—that dream of Socrates, redreamed by the Renaissance and surviving all travesties down to only yesterday. To be sure, there have long been anti-rational forces at work in the West, including primitive Christianity itself; but the very notion of literary culture is a product of Humanism, as the early Christians knew (setting fire to libraries), so that the Church in order to sponsor poets had first to come to terms with reason itself by way of Aquinas and Aristotle.

Only with Dada was the notion of an anti-rational anti-literature born; and Dada became Surrealism, i.e., submitted to the influence of those last neo-Humanists, those desperate Socratic Cabalists, Freud and Marx—dedicated respectively to contriving a rationale of violence and a rationale of impulse. The new irrationalists, however, deny all the apostles of reason, Freud as well as Socrates; and if they seem to exempt Marx, this is because they know less about him, have heard him evoked less often by the teachers they are driven to deny. Not only do they reject the Socratic adage that the unexamined life is not worth living, since for them precisely the unexamined life is the only one worth enduring at all. But they also abjure the Freudian one: "Where id was, ego shall be," since for them the true rallying cry is, "Let id prevail over ego, impulse over order," or—in negative terms—"Freud is a fink!"

The first time I heard this irreverent charge from the mouth of a student some five or six years ago (I who had grown up thinking of Freud as a revolutionary, a pioneer), I knew that I was already in the future; though I did not yet suspect that there would be no room in that future for the university system to which I had devoted my life. Kerouac might have told me so, or Ginsberg, or even so polite and genteel a spokesman for youth as J. D. Salinger, but I was too aware of what was wrong with such writers (their faults more readily apparent to my taste than their virtues) to be sensitive to the truths they told. It took, therefore, certain public events to illuminate (for me) the literature which might have illuminated them.

I am thinking, of course, of the recent demonstrations at Berkeley and elsewhere, whose ostensible causes were civil rights or freedom of speech or Vietnam, but whose not so secret slogan was all the time: *The Professor Is a Fink!* And what an array of bad anti-academic novels, I cannot help reminding myself, written by disgruntled professors, created the mythology out of which that slogan grew. Each generation of students is invented by the generation of teachers just before them; but how different they are in dream and fact—as different as self-hatred and its reflection in another. How different the professors in Jeremy Larner's *Drive, He Said* from those even in Randall Jarrell's *Pictures from an Institution* or Mary McCarthy's *Groves of Academe*.

To be sure, many motives operated to set the students in action, some of them imagined in no book, however good or bad. Many of the thousands who resisted or shouted on campuses did so in the name of naïve or disingenuous or even nostalgic politics (be careful what you wish for in your middle age, or your children will parody it forthwith!); and sheer ennui doubtless played a role along with a justified rage against the hypocrisies of academic life. Universities have long rivaled the churches in their devotion to institutionalizing hypocrisy; and more recently they have outstripped television itself (which most professors affect to despise even more than they despise organized religion) in the institutionalization of boredom.

But what the students were protesting in large part, I have come to believe, was the very notion of man which the universities sought to impose upon them: that bourgeois-Protestant version of Humanism, with its view of man as justified by rationality, work, duty, vocation, maturity, success; and its concomitant understanding of childhood and adolescence as a temporarily privileged time of preparation for assuming those burdens. The new irrationalists, however, are prepared to advocate prolonging adolescence to the grave, and are ready to dispense with school as an outlived excuse for leisure. To them work is as obsolete as reason, a vestige (already dispensable for large numbers) of an economically marginal, pre-automated world; and the obsolescence of the two adds up to the obsolescence of everything our society understands by maturity.

Nor is it in the name of an older more valid Humanistic view of man that the new irrationalists would reject the WASP version; Rabelais is as alien to them as Benjamin Franklin. Disinterested scholarship, reflection, the life of reason, a respect for tradition stir (however dimly and confusedly) chiefly their contempt; and the Abbey of Theleme would seem as sterile to them as Robinson Crusoe's Island. To the classroom, the library, the laboratory, the office conference and the meeting of scholars, they prefer the demonstration, the sit-in, the riot: the mindless unity of an impassioned crowd (with guitars beating out the rhythm in the background), whose immediate cause is felt rather than thought out, whose ultimate cause is itself. In light of this, the Teach-in, often ill understood because of an emphasis on its declared political ends, can be seen as implicitly a parody and mockery of the real classroom: related to the actual business of the university, to real teaching only as the Demonstration Trial (of Dimitrov, of the Soviet Doctors, of Eichmann) to real justice or Demonstration Voting (for one party or a token two) to real suffrage.

At least, since Berkeley (or perhaps since Martin Luther King provided students with new paradigms for action) the choice has been extended beyond what the earlier laureates of the new youth could imagine in the novel: the nervous breakdown at home rather than the return to "sanity" and school, which was the best Salinger could invent for Franny and Holden; or Kerouac's way out for his "saintly" vagrants, that "road" from nowhere to noplace with homemade gurus at the way stations. The structure of those fictional vaudevilles between hard covers that currently please the young (*Catch 22*, *V.*, *A Mother's Kisses*), suggest in their brutality and discontinuity, their politics of mockery something of the spirit of the student demonstrations; but only Jeremy Larner, as far as I know, has dealt explicitly with the abandonment of the classroom in favor of the dionysiac pack, the turning from *polis* to *thiasos*, from forms of social organization traditionally thought of as male to the sort of passionate community attributed by the ancients to females out of control.

Conventional slogans in favor of "Good Works" (pious emendations of existing social structures, or extensions of accepted "rights" to excluded groups) though they provide the motive power of such protests are irrelevant to their form and their final significance. They become their essential selves, i.e., genuine new forms of rebellion, when the demonstrators hoist (as they did in the final stages of the Berkeley protests) the sort of slogan which embarrasses not only fellow-travelers but even the bureaucrats who direct the initial stages of the revolt: at the University of California, the single four-letter word no family newspaper would reprint, though no member of a family who could read was likely not to know it.

It is possible to argue on the basis of the political facts themselves that the word "fuck" entered the whole scene accidentally (there were only four students behind the "Dirty Speech Movement," only fifteen hundred kids could be persuaded to demonstrate for it, etc., etc.). But the prophetic literature which anticipates the movement indicates otherwise, suggesting that the logic of their illogical course eventually sets the young against language itself, against the very counters of logical discourse. They seek an anti-language of protest as inevitably as they seek anti-poems and anti-novels, end with the ultimate anti-word, which the demonstrators at Berkeley disingenuously claimed stood for FREEDOM UNDER CLARK KERR.

Esthetics, however, had already anticipated politics in this regard; porno-poetry preceding and preparing the way for what Lewis Feuer has aptly called porno-politics. Already in 1963, in an essay entitled *"Phi Upsilon Kappa,"* the young poet Michael McClure was writing: "Gregory Corso has asked me to join with him in a project to free the word FUCK from its chains and strictures. I leap to make some new freedom. . . ." And McClure's own "Fuck Ode" is a product of this collaboration, as the very name of Ed Saunders' journal, *Fuck You,* is the creation of an

analogous impulse. The aging critics of the young who have dealt
with the Berkeley demonstrations in such journals as *Commentary*
and the *New Leader* do not, however, read either Saunders' porno-
pacifist magazine or *Kulchur*, in which McClure's manifesto was
first printed—the age barrier separating readership in the United
States more effectively than class, political affiliation or anything else.

Their sense of porno-esthetics is likely to come from deserters
from their own camp, chiefly Norman Mailer, and especially his
recent *An American Dream*, which represents the entry of anti-
language (extending the tentative explorations of "The Time of
Her Time") into the world of the middle-aged, both on the level
of mass culture and that of yesterday's ex-Marxist, post-Freudian
avant-garde. Characteristically enough, Mailer's book has occa-
sioned in the latter quarters reviews as irrelevant, incoherent,
misleading and fundamentally scared as the most philistine responses to the Berkeley demonstrations, Philip Rahv and Stanley
Edgar Hyman providing two egregious examples. Yet elsewhere
(in sectors held by those more at ease with their own conserva-
tism, i.e., without defunct radicalisms to uphold) the most obscene
forays of the young are being met with a disheartening kind of
tolerance and even an attempt to adapt them to the conditions
of commodity art.

But precisely here, of course, a disconcerting irony is involved;
for after a while, there will be no Rahvs and Hymans left to
shock—anti-language becoming mere language with repeated use
and in the face of acceptance; so that all sense of exhilaration
will be lost along with the possibility of offense. What to do then
except to choose silence, since raising the ante of violence is ultimately self-defeating; and the way of obscenity in any case leads
as naturally to silence as to further excess? Moreover, to the
talkative heirs of Socrates, silence is the one offense that never
wears out, the radicalism that can never become fashionable;
which is why, after the obscene slogan has been hauled down,
a blank placard is raised in its place.

There are difficulties, to be sure, when one attempts to move
from the politics of silence to an analogous sort of poetry. The
opposite number to the silent picketer would be the silent poet,
which is a contradiction in terms; yet there are these days non-

singers of (perhaps) great talent who shrug off the temptation to song with the muttered comment, "Creativity is out." Some, however, make literature of a kind precisely at the point of maximum tension between the tug toward silence and the pull toward publication. Music is a better language really for saying what one would prefer not to say at all—and all the way from certain sorts of sufficiently cool jazz to Rock 'n' Roll (with its minimal lyrics that defy understanding on a first hearing), music is the preferred art of the irrationalists.

But some varieties of skinny poetry seem apt, too (as practiced, say, by Robert Creeley after the example of W. C. Williams), since their lines are three parts silence to one part speech:

> *My lady*
> *fair with*
> *soft*
> *arms, what*
> *can I say to*
> *you— words, words . . .*

And, of course, fiction aspiring to become Pop Art, say, *An American Dream* (with the experiments of Hemingway and Nathanael West behind it), works approximately as well, since clichés are almost as inaudible as silence itself. The point is not to shout, not to insist, but to hang cool, to baffle all mothers, cultural and spiritual as well as actual.

When the Town Council in Venice, California, was about to close down a particularly notorious beatnik cafe, a lady asked to testify before them, presumably to clinch the case against the offenders. What she reported, however, was that each day as she walked by the cafe and looked in its windows, she saw the unsavory types who inhabited it "just standing there, looking— nonchalant." And, in a way, her improbable adjective does describe a crime against her world; for non-chaleur ("cool," the futurists themselves would prefer to call it) is the essence of their life-style as well as of the literary styles to which they respond: the offensive style of those who are not so much *for* anything in particular, as "with it" in general.

But such an attitude is as remote from traditional "alienation," with its profound longing to end disconnection, as it is from ordinary forms of allegiance, with their desperate resolve not to admit disconnection. The new young celebrate disconnection—accept it as one of the necessary consequences of the industrial system which has delivered them from work and duty, of that welfare state which makes disengagement the last possible virtue, whether it call itself Capitalist, Socialist or Communist. "Detachment" is the traditional name for the stance the futurists assume; but "detachment" carries with it irrelevant religious, even specifically Christian overtones. The post-modernists are surely in some sense "mystics," religious at least in a way they do not ordinarily know how to confess, but they are not Christians.

Indeed, they regard Christianity, quite as the Black Muslim (with whom they have certain affinities) do, as a white ideology: merely one more method—along with Humanism, technology, Marxism—of imposing "White" or Western values on the colored rest of the world. To the new barbarian, however, that would-be post-Humanist (who is in most cases the white offspring of Christian forebears) his whiteness is likely to seem if not a stigma and symbol of shame, at least the outward sign of his exclusion from all that his Christian Humanist ancestors rejected in themselves and projected mythologically upon the colored man. For such reasons, his religion, when it becomes explicit, claims to be derived from Tibet or Japan or the ceremonies of the Plains Indians, or is composed out of the non-Christian sub-mythology that has grown up among Negro jazz musicians and in the civil rights movement. When the new barbarian speaks of "soul," for instance, he means not "soul" as in Heaven, but as in "soul music" or even "soul food."

It is all part of the attempt of the generation under twenty-five, not exclusively in its most sensitive members but especially in them, to become Negro, even as they attempt to become poor or pre-rational. About this particular form of psychic assimilation I have written sufficiently in the past (summing up what I had been long saying in chapters seven and eight of *Waiting for the End*), neglecting only the sense in which what starts as a specifically American movement becomes an international one, spreading to the *yé-yé* girls of France or the working-class entertainers of Liverpool with astonishing swiftness and ease.

What interests me more particularly right now is a parallel

assimilationist attempt, which may, indeed, be more parochial and is certainly most marked at the moment in the Anglo-Saxon world, i.e., in those cultural communities most totally committed to bourgeois-Protestant values and surest that they are unequivocally "white." I am thinking of the effort of young men in England and the United States to assimilate into themselves (or even to assimilate themselves into) that otherness, that sum total of rejected psychic elements which the middle-class heirs of the Renaissance have identified with "woman." To become new men, these children of the future seem to feel, they must not only become more Black than White but more female than male. And it is natural that the need to make such an adjustment be felt with especial acuteness in post-Protestant highly industrialized societies, where the functions regarded as specifically male for some three hundred years tend most rapidly to become obsolete.

Surely, in America, machines already perform better than humans a large number of those aggressive-productive activities which our ancestors considered man's special province, even his *raison d'être*. Not only has the male's prerogative of making things and money (which is to say, of working) been preempted, but also his time-honored privilege of dealing out death by hand, which until quite recently was regarded as a supreme mark of masculine valor. While it seems theoretically possible, even in the heart of Anglo-Saxondom, to imagine a leisurely, pacific male, in fact the losses in secondary functions sustained by men appear to have shaken their faith in their primary masculine function as well, in their ability to achieve the conquest (as the traditional metaphor has it) of women. Earlier, advances in technology had detached the wooing and winning of women from the begetting of children; and though the invention of the condom had at least left the decision to inhibit fatherhood in the power of males, its replacement by the "loop" and the "pill" has placed paternity at the mercy of the whims of women.

Writers of fiction and verse registered the technological obsolescence of masculinity long before it was felt even by the representative minority who give to the present younger generation its character and significance. And literary critics have talked a good deal during the past couple of decades about the conversion of the literary hero into the non-hero or the anti-hero; but they have in general failed to notice his simultaneous conversion into the non- or anti-male. Yet ever since Hemingway at least, certain male protagonists of American literature have not only fled rather than sought out combat but have also fled rather than sought out women. From Jake Barnes to Holden Caulfield they have continued to run from the threat of female sexuality; and, indeed, there are models for such evasion in our classic books, where heroes still eager for the fight (Natty Bumppo comes to mind) are already shy of wives and sweethearts and mothers.

It is not absolutely required that the anti-male anti-hero be impotent or homosexual or both (though this helps, as we remember remembering Walt Whitman), merely that he be more seduced than seducing, more passive than active. Consider, for instance, the oddly "womanish" Herzog of Bellow's best seller, that Jewish Emma Bovary with a Ph.D., whose chief flaw is physical vanity and a taste for fancy clothes. Bellow, however, is more interested in summing up the past than in evoking the future; and *Herzog* therefore seems an end rather than a beginning, the product of nostalgia (remember when there were real Jews once, and the "Jewish Novel" had not yet been discovered!) rather than prophecy. No, the post-humanist, post-male, post-white, post-heroic world is a post-Jewish world by the same token, anti-Semitism as inextricably woven into it as into the movement for Negro rights; and its scriptural books are necessarily *goyish*, not least of all William Burroughs' *The Naked Lunch*.

Burroughs is the chief prophet of the post-male post-heroic world; and it is his emulators who move into the center of the relevant literary scene, for *The Naked Lunch* (the later novels are less successful, less exciting but relevant still) is more than it seems: no mere essay in heroin-hallucinated homosexual pornography—but a nightmare anticipation (in Science Fiction form) of post-Humanist sexuality. Here, as in Alexander Trocchi, John Rechy, Harry Mathews (even an occasional Jew like Allen Ginsberg, who has begun by inscribing properly anti-Jewish obscenities on the walls of the world), are clues to the new attitudes toward sex that will continue to inform our improbable novels of passion and our even more improbable love songs.

The young to whom I have been referring, the mythologically representative minority (who, by a process that infuriates the mythologically inert majority out of which they come, "stand for" their times), live in a community in which what used to be called the "Sexual Revolution," the Freudian-Laurentian revolt of their grandparents and parents, has triumphed as imperfectly and unsatisfactorily as all revolutions always triumph. They confront, therefore, the necessity of determining not only what meanings "love" can have in their new world, but—even more disturbingly —what significance, if any, "male" and "female" now possess. For a while, they (or at least their literary spokesmen recruited from the generation just before them) seemed content to celebrate a kind of *reductio* or *exaltatio ad absurdum* of their parents' once revolutionary sexual goals: The Reichian-inspired Cult of the Orgasm.

Young men and women eager to be delivered of traditional ideologies of love find especially congenial the belief that not union or relationship (much less offspring) but physical release is the end of the sexual act; and that, therefore, it is a matter of indifference with whom or by what method one pursues the therapeutic climax, so long as that climax is total and repeated frequently. And Wilhelm Reich happily detaches this belief from the vestiges of Freudian rationalism, setting it instead in a context of Science Fiction and witchcraft; but his emphasis upon "full genitality," upon growing up and away from infantile pleasures, strikes the young as a disguised plea for the "maturity" they have learned to despise. In a time when the duties associated with adulthood promise to become irrelevant, there seems little reason for denying oneself the joys of babyhood—even if these are associated with such regressive fantasies as escaping it all in the arms of little sister (in the Gospel according to J. D. Salinger) or flirting with the possibility of getting into bed with papa (in the Gospel according to Norman Mailer).

Only Norman O. Brown in *Life Against Death* has come to terms on the level of theory with the aspiration to take the final evolutionary leap and cast off adulthood completely, at least in the area of sex. His post-Freudian program for pan-sexual, non-orgasmic love rejects "full genitality" in favor of a species of indiscriminate bundling, a dream of unlimited sub-coital intimacy which Brown calls (in his vocabulary the term is an honorific) "polymorphous perverse." And here finally is an essential clue to the nature of the second sexual revolution, the post-sexual revolution, first evoked in literature by Brother Antoninus more than a decade ago, in a verse prayer addressed somewhat improbably to the Christian God:

Annul in me my manhood, Lord, and make
Me woman sexed and weak . . .

> *Make me then*
Girl-hearted, virgin-souled, woman-docile, maiden-meek . . .

Despite the accents of this invocation, however, what is at work is not essentially a homosexual revolt or even a rebellion against women, though its advocates seek to wrest from women their ancient privileges of receiving the Holy Ghost and pleasuring men; and though the attitudes of the movement can be adapted to the anti-female bias of, say, Edward Albee. If in *Who's Afraid of Virginia Woolf?* Albee can portray the relationship of two homosexuals (one in drag) as the model of contemporary marriage, this must be because contemporary marriage has in fact turned into something much like that parody. And it is true that what survives of bourgeois marriage and the bourgeois family is a target which the new barbarians join the old homosexuals in reviling, seeking to replace Mom, Pop and the kids with a neo-Whitmanian gaggle of giggling *camerados*. Such groups are, in fact, whether gathered in coffee houses, university cafeterias or around the literature tables on campuses, the peace-time equivalents, as it were, to the demonstrating crowd. But even their program of displacing Dick-Jane-Spot-Baby, etc., the WASP family of grade school primers, is not the fundamental motive of the post-sexual revolution.

What is at stake from Burroughs to Bellow, Ginsberg to Albee, Salinger to Gregory Corso is a more personal transformation: a radical metamorphosis of the Western male—utterly unforeseen in the decades before us, but visible now in every high school and college classroom, as well as on the paperback racks in airports and supermarkets. All around us, young males are beginning to retrieve for themselves the cavalier role once piously and class-consciously surrendered to women: *that of being beautiful and being loved*. Here once more the example to the Negro—the feckless and adorned Negro male with the blood of Cavaliers in his veins—has served as a model. And what else is left to young men, in any case, after the devaluation of the grim duties they had arrogated to themselves in place of the pursuit of lovelinesss?

All of us who are middle-aged and were Marxists, which is to say, who once numbered ourselves among the last assured Puritans, have surely noticed in ourselves a vestigial roundhead rage at the new hair styles of the advanced or—if you please—delinquent young. Watching young men titivate their locks (the comb, the pocket mirror and the bobby pin having replaced the jackknife, catcher's mitt and brass knuckles), we feel the same baffled resentment that stirs in us when we realize that they have rejected work. A job and unequivocal maleness—these are two sides of the same Calvinist coin, which in the future buys nothing.

Few of us, however, have really understood how the Beatle hairdo is part of a syndrome, of which high heels, jeans tight over the buttocks, etc., are other aspects, symptomatic of a larger retreat from masculine aggressiveness to female allure—in literature and the arts to the style called "camp." And fewer still have realized how that style, though the invention of homosexuals, is now the possession of basically heterosexual males as well, a strategy in their campaign to establish a new relationship not only with women but with their own masculinity. In the course of that campaign, they have embraced certain kinds of gesture and garb, certain accents and tones traditionally associated with females or female impersonators; which is why we have been observing recently (in life as well as fiction and verse) young boys, quite unequivocally male, playing all the traditional roles of women: the vamp, the coquette, the whore, the icy tease, the pure young virgin.

Not only oldsters, who had envisioned and despaired of quite another future, are bewildered by this turn of events, but young girls, too, seem scarcely to know what is happening—looking on with that new, schizoid stare which itself has become a hallmark of our times. And the crop-headed jocks, those crew-cut athletes who represent an obsolescent masculine style based on quite other values, have tended to strike back blindly; beating the hell out of some poor kid whose hair is too long or whose pants are too tight—quite as they once beat up young Communists for revealing that their politics had become obsolete. Even heterosexual writers, however, have been slow to catch up, the revolution in sensibility running ahead of that in expression; and they have perforce permitted homosexuals to speak for them (Burroughs and Genet and Baldwin and Ginsberg and Albee and a score of others), even to invent the forms in which the future will have to speak.

The revolt against masculinity is not limited, however, to simple matters of coiffure and costume, visible even to athletes; or to the adaptation of certain campy styles and modes to new uses. There is also a sense in which two large social movements that have set the young in motion and furnished images of action for their books—movements as important in their own right as porno-politics and the pursuit of the polymorphous perverse—are connected analogically to the abdication from traditional maleness. The first of these is nonviolent or passive resistance, so oddly come back to the land of its inventor, that icy Thoreau who dreamed a love which ". . . has not much human blood in it, but consists with a certain disregard for men and their erections. . . ."

The civil rights movement, however, in which nonviolence has found a home, has been hospitable not only to the sort of post-humanist I have been describing; so that at a demonstration (Selma, Alabama, will do as an example) the true hippie will be found side by side with backwoods Baptists, nuns on a spiritual spree, boy bureaucrats practicing to take power, resurrected socialists, Unitarians in search of a God, and just plain tourists, gathered, as once at the Battle of Bull Run, to see the fun. For each of these, nonviolence will have a different sort of fundamental meaning—as a tactic, a camouflage, a passing fad, a pious gesture—but for each in part, and for the post-humanist especially, it will signify the possibility of heroism without aggression, effective action without guilt.

There have always been two contradictory American ideals: to be the occasion of maximum violence, and to remain absolutely innocent. Once, however, these were thought hopelessly incompatible for males (except, perhaps, as embodied in works of art), reserved strictly for women: the spouse of the wife-beater, for instance, or the victim of rape. But males have now assumed these classic roles; and just as a particularly beleaguered wife occasionally slipped over the dividing line into violence, so do the new passive protesters—leaving us to confront (or resign to the courts) such homey female questions as: *Did Mario Savio really bite that cop in the leg as he sagged limply toward the ground?*

The second social movement is the drug cult, more widespread among youth, from its squarest limits to its most beat, than anyone seems prepared to admit in public; and at its beat limit at least inextricably involved with the civil rights movement, as the recent arrests of Peter DeLissovoy and Susan Ryerson revealed even to the ordinary newspaper reader. "Police said that most of the recipients [of marijuana] were college students," the U.P. story runs. "They quoted Miss Ryerson and DeLissovoy as saying that many of the letter packets were sent to civil rights workers." Only fiction and verse, however, has dealt with the conjunction of homosexuality, drugs and civil rights, eschewing the general piety of the press which has been unwilling to compromise "good works" on behalf of the Negro by associating it with the deep radicalism of a way of life based on the ritual consumption of "pot."

The widespread use of such hallucinogens as peyote, marijuana, the "mexican mushroom," LSD, etc., as well as pep pills, goof balls, airplane glue, certain kinds of cough syrups and even, though in many fewer cases, heroin, is not merely a matter of a changing taste in stimulants but of the programmatic espousal of an anti-puritanical mode of existence—hedonistic and detached —one more strategy in the war on time and work. But it is also (to pursue my analogy once more) an attempt to arrogate to the male certain traditional privileges of the female. What could be more womanly, as Elémire Zolla was already pointing out some years ago, than permitting the penetration of the body by a foreign object which not only stirs delight but even (possibly) creates new life?

In any case, with drugs we have come to the crux of the futurist revolt, the hinge of everything else, as the young tell us over and over in their writing. When the movement was first finding a voice, Allen Ginsberg set this aspect of it in proper context in an immensely comic, utterly serious poem called "America," in which "pot" is associated with earlier forms of rebellion, a commitment to catatonia, and a rejection of conventional male potency:

America I used to be a communist when I was a kid I'm not
  sorry.
I smoke marijuana every chance I get.
I sit in my house for days on end and stare at the roses in the
  closet.
When I go to Chinatown I . . . never get laid . . .

Similarly, Michael McClure reveals in his essay, "*Phi Upsilon Kappa*," that before penetrating the "cavern of Anglo-Saxon," whence he emerged with the slogan of the ultimate Berkeley demonstrators, he had been on mescalin. "I have emerged from a dark night of the soul; I entered it by Peyote." And by now, drug-taking has become as standard a feature of the literature of the young as oral-genital love-making. I flip open the first issue of yet another ephemeral San Francisco little magazine quite at random and read: "I tie up and the main pipe [the ante-cobital vein, for the clinically inclined] swells like a prideful beggar beneath the skin. Just before I get on it is always the worst." Worse than the experience, however, is its literary rendering; and the badness of such confessional fiction, flawed by the sentimentality of those who desire to live "like a cunning vegetable," is a badness we older readers find it only too easy to perceive, as our sons and daughters find it only too easy to overlook. Yet precisely here the age and the mode define themselves; for not in the master but in the hacks new forms are established, new lines drawn.

Here, at any rate, is where the young lose us in literature as well as life, since here they pass over into real revolt, i.e., what we really cannot abide, hard as we try. The mother who has sent her son to private schools and on to Harvard to keep him out of classrooms overcrowded with poor Negroes, rejoices when he sets out for Mississippi with his comrades in SNCC, but shudders when he turns on with LSD; just as the ex-Marxist father, who has earlier proved radicalism impossible, rejoices to see his son stand up, piously and pompously, for CORE or SDS, but trembles to hear him quote Alpert and Leary or praise Burroughs. Just as certainly as liberalism is the LSD of the aging, LSD is the radicalism of the young.

If whiskey long served as an appropriate symbolic excess for those who chafed against Puritan restraint without finally challenging it—temporarily releasing them to socially harmful aggression and (hopefully) sexual self-indulgence, the new popular drugs provide an excess quite as satisfactorily symbolic to the post-Puritans—releasing them from sanity to madness by destroying in them the inner restrictive order which has somehow survived the dissolution of the outer. It is finally insanity, then, that the futurists learn to admire and emulate, quite as they learn to pursue vision instead of learning, hallucination rather than logic. The schizophrenic replaces the sage as their ideal, their new culture hero, figured forth as a giant schizoid Indian (his madness modeled in part on the author's own experiences with LSD) in Ken Kesey's *One Flew Over the Cuckoo's Nest*.

The hippier young are not alone, however, in their taste for the insane; we live in a time when readers in general respond sympathetically to madness in literature wherever it is found, in established writers as well as in those trying to establish new modes. Surely it is not the lucidity and logic of Robert Lowell or Theodore Roethke or John Berryman which we admire, but their flirtation with incoherence and disorder. And certainly it is Mailer at his most nearly psychotic, Mailer the creature rather than the master of his fantasies who moves us to admiration; while in the case of Saul Bellow, we endure the theoretical optimism and acceptance for the sake of the delightful melancholia, the fertile paranoia which he cannot disavow any more than the talent at whose root they lie. Even essayists and analysts recommend themselves to us these days by a certain redemptive nuttiness; at any rate, we do not love, say, Marshall McLuhan less because he continually risks sounding like the body-fluids man in *Dr. Strangelove*.

We have, moreover, recently been witnessing the development of a new form of social psychiatry (a psychiatry of the future already anticipated by the literature of the future) which considers some varieties of "schizophrenia" not diseases to be cured but forays into an unknown psychic world: random penetrations by bewildered internal cosmonauts of a realm that it will be the task of the next generations to explore. And if the accounts which the returning schizophrenics give (the argument of the apologists runs) of the "places" they have been are fantastic and garbled, surely they are no more so than, for example, Columbus' reports of the world he had claimed for Spain, a world bounded—according to his newly drawn maps—by Cathay on the north and Paradise on the south.

In any case, poets and junkies have been suggesting to us that the new world appropriate to the new men of the latter twentieth century is to be discovered only by the conquest of inner space: by an adventure of the spirit, an extension of psychic possibility, of which the flights into outer space—moonshots and expeditions to Mars—are precisely such unwitting metaphors and analogues as the voyages of exploration were of the earlier breakthrough into the Renaissance, from whose consequences the young seek now so desperately to escape. The laureate of that new conquest is William Burroughs; and it is fitting that the final word be his:

"This war will be won in the air. In the Silent Air with Image Rays. You were a pilot remember? Tracer bullets cutting the right wing you were free in space a few seconds before in blue space between eyes. Go back to Silence. Keep Silence. Keep Silence. K.S. K.S. . . . From Silence re-write the message that is you. You are the message I send to The Enemy. My Silent Message."
The Naked Astronauts were free in space. . . .

VI

Education

The student need not feel that he is dealing with cold machines in the place of warm teachers any more than he feels that way today when he reads a book by himself instead of listening to an oral presentation by a human teacher.

—SIMON RAMO,
"A New Technique of Education" (1957)

VI

Education

TECHNOLOGY AND EDUCATION

by R. BUCKMINSTER FULLER

THE big question is how are we, as educators, going to handle the enormous increase in the new life. How do we make available to these new students what we have been able to discover fairly accurately about the universe and the way it is operating? How are we going to be able to get to them the true net value won blindly through the long tradition of ignorant dedications and hard-won lessons of all the unknown mothers and all the other invisibly heroic people who have given hopefully to the new life, such as, for instance, the fabulous heritage of men's stoic capacity to carry on despite immense hardships?

The new life needs to be inspired with the realization that it has all kinds of new advantages that have been gained through great dedications of unknown, unsung heroes of intellectual exploration and great intuitively faithful integrities of men groping in the dark. Unless the new life is highly appreciative of those who have gone before, it won't be able to take effective advantage of its heritage. It will not be as regenerated and inspired as it might be if it appreciated the comprehensive love invested in that heritage.

The old political way of looking at things is such that the political machine says we first must get a "school house" for our constituents, and it must look like Harvard University, or it must be Georgian and a whole big pile of it. "We see that the rich kids went to school in automobiles; so let's get beautiful buses for our kids." "Harvard and Yale have long had football; our school is going to have football." There is nothing boys used to have that they are not going to "get" from their politicians,

A selection from *Education Automation: Freeing the Scholar To Return to His Studies*, by R. Buckminster Fuller. Copyright © 1962 by Southern Illinois University Press. Reprinted by permission of the Southern Illinois University Press.

who, above all, know best how to exploit the inferiority complex which they understand so well as handed down from the ages and ages of 99 per cent have-not-ness of mankind. There is a sort of class inferiority amelioration battle that goes on with the politicos in seeking the favor of their constituents to get into or back into office, and little if any attention is paid to the real educational problems at hand.

In thinking about these problems, I have thought a lot about what I have learned that may be useful as proven by experiments in my own self-discipling. I have met some powerful thinkers. I met Dr. Einstein. I wrote three chapters in a book about Dr. Einstein, and my publishers said that they wouldn't publish it because I wasn't on the list of people who understood Einstein. I asked them to send the typescript to Einstein, and they did. He then said he approved of it—that I had interpreted him properly—and so the chapters did get published. When Einstein approved of my typescript he asked me to come and meet him and talk about my book. I am quite confident that I can say with authority that Einstein, when he wanted to study, didn't sit in the middle of a school room. That is probably the poorest place he could have gone to study. When an individual is really thinking, he is tremendously isolated. He may manage to isolate himself in Grand Central Station, but it is *despite* the environment rather than because of it. The place to study is not in a school room.

Parents quite clearly love their children; that is a safe general observation. We don't say parents send their children to school to get rid of them. The fact is, however, that it is very convenient for mothers, in order to be able to clean the house for the family, to have the children out of the way for a little while. The little red school house was not entirely motivated by educational ambitions.

There is also a general baby-sitting function which is called school. While the children are being "baby sat," they might as well be given something to read. We find that they get along pretty well with the game of "reading"; so we give them more to read, and we add writing and arithmetic. Very seriously, much of what goes on in our schools is strictly related to social experiences, and that is fine—that's good for the kids. But I would say we are going to add much more in the very near future by taking advantage of the children's ability to show us what they need.

I have taken photographs of my grandchildren looking at television. Without consideration of the "value," the actual concentration of a child on the message which is coming to him is fabulous. They really "latch on." Given the chance to get accurate, logical, and lucid information at the time when they want and need to get it, they will go after it and inhibit it in a most effective manner. I am quite certain that we are soon going to begin to do the following: At our universities we will take the men who are the faculty leaders in research or in teaching. We are not going to ask them to give the same lectures over and over each year from their curriculum cards, finding themselves confronted with another roomful of people and asking themselves, "What was it I said last year?" This is a routine which deadens the faculty member. We are going to select, instead, the people who are authorities on various subjects—the men who are most respected by other men within their respective departments and fields. They will give their basic lecture course just once to a group of human beings, including both the experts in their own subject and bright children and adults without special training in their field. This lecture will be recorded as Southern Illinois University did my last lecture series of fifty-two hours in October 1960. They will make moving picture footage of the lecture as well as hi-fi tape recording. Then the professor and his faculty associates will listen to this recording time and again.

"What you say is very good," his associates may comment, "but we have heard you say it a little better at other times." The professor then dubs in a better statement. Thus begins complete reworking of the tape, cleaned up, and cleaned up some more, as in the moving picture cutting, and new illustrative "footage" will be added on. The whole of a university department will work on improving the message and conceptioning of a picture for many months, sometimes for years. The graduate students who want to be present in the university and who also qualify to be with the men who have great powers and intellectual capability together with the faculty may spend a year getting a documentary ready. They will not even depend upon the diction of the original lecturer, because the diction of that person may be very inadequate to his really fundamental conceptioning and information, which should be superb. His knowledge may be very great, but he may be a poor lecturer because of poor speaking habits or false teeth. Another voice will take over the task of getting his exact words across. Others will gradually process the tape and moving picture footage, using communications specialists, psychologists, etc.

For instance, I am quite certain that some day we will take a subject such as Einstein's Theory of Relativity, and with the "Einstein" of the subject and his colleagues working on it for a year, we will finally get it reduced down to what is "net" in the subject and enthusiastically approved by the "Einstein" who gave the original lecture. What is *net* will become communicated so well that any child can turn on a documentary device, a TV, and get the Einstein lucidity of thinking and get it quickly and firmly. I am quite sure that we are going to get research and development laboratories of education where the faculty will become producers of extraordinary moving-picture documentaries. That is going to be the big, new educational trend.

THE NEW LANGUAGES

by *EDMUND CARPENTER*

> *Brain of the New World,*
> *What a task is thine,*
> *To formulate the modern*
> *. . . to recast poems, churches, art*
>
> WHITMAN

ENGLISH is a mass medium. All languages are mass media. The new mass media—film, radio, TV—are new languages, their grammars as yet unknown. Each codifies reality differently; each conceals a unique metaphysics. Linguists tell us it's possible to say anything in any language if you use enough words or images, but there's rarely time; the natural course is for a culture to exploit its media biases.

Writing, for example, didn't record oral language; it was a new language, which the spoken word came to imitate. Writing encouraged an analytical mode of thinking with emphasis upon lineality. Oral languages tended to be polysynthetic, composed of great, tight conglomerates, like twisted knots, within which images were juxtaposed, inseparably fused; written communications consisted of little words chronologically ordered. Subject became distinct from verb, adjective from noun, thus separating actor from action, essence from form. Where preliterate man imposed form diffidently, temporarily—for such transitory forms lived but temporarily on the tip of his tongue, in the living situation—the printed word was inflexible, permanent, in touch with eternity: it embalmed truth for posterity.

This embalming process froze language, eliminated the art of ambiguity, made puns "the lowest form of wit," destroyed word

"The New Languages," by Edmund Carpenter, from EXPLORATIONS # 7. Reprinted by permission of the author.

linkages. The word became a static symbol, applicable to and separate from that which it symbolized. It now belonged to the objective world; it could be seen. Now came the distinction between being and meaning, the dispute as to whether the Eucharist *was* or only *signified* the body of the Sacrifice. The word became a neutral symbol, no longer an inextricable part of a creative process.

Gutenberg completed the process. The manuscript page with pictures, colors, correlation between symbol and space, gave way to uniform type, the black-and-white page, read silently, alone. The format of the book favored lineal expression, for the argument ran like a thread from cover to cover: subject to verb to object, sentence to sentence, paragraph to paragraph, chapter to chapter, carefully structured from beginning to end, with value embedded in the climax. This was not true of great poetry and drama, which retained multi-perspective, but it was true of most books, particularly texts, histories, autobiographies, novels. Events were arranged chronologically and hence, it was assumed, causally; relationship, not being, was valued. The author became an *authority;* his data were serious, that is, *serially* organized. Such data, if sequentially ordered and printed, conveyed value and truth; arranged any other way, they were suspect.

The newspaper format brought an end to book culture. It offers short, discrete articles that give important facts first and then taper off to incidental details, which may be, and often are, eliminated by the make-up man. The fact that reporters cannot control the length of their articles means that, in writing them, emphasis can't be placed on structure, at least in the traditional linear sense, with climax or conclusion at the end. Everything has to be captured in the headline; from there it goes down the pyramid to incidentals. In fact there is often more in the headline than in the article; occasionally, no article at all accompanies the banner headline.

The position and size of articles on the front page are determined by interest and importance, not content. Unrelated reports from Moscow, Sarawak, London, and Ittipik are juxtaposed; time and space, as separate concepts, are destroyed and the *here* and *now* presented as a single Gestalt. Subway readers consume everything on the front page, then turn to page 2 to read, in incidental order, continuations. A Toronto banner headline ran: TOWNSEND TO MARRY PRINCESS; directly beneath this was a second headline: *Fabian Says This May Not Be Sex Crime.* This went unnoticed by eyes and minds conditioned to consider each newspaper item in isolation.

Such a format lends itself to simultaneity, not chronology or lineality. Items abstracted from a total situation aren't arranged in causal sequence, but presented holistically, as raw experience. The front page is a cosmic *Finnegans Wake.*

The disorder of the newspaper throws the reader into a producer role. The reader has to process the news himself; he has to co-create, to cooperate in the creation of the work. The newspaper format calls for the direct participation of the consumer.

In magazines, where a writer more frequently controls the length of his article, he can, if he wishes, organize it in traditional style, but the majority don't. An increasingly popular presentation is the printed symposium, which is little more than collected opinions, pro and con. The magazine format as a whole opposes lineality; its pictures lack tenses. In *Life,* extremes are juxtaposed; space ships and prehistoric monsters, Flemish monasteries and dope addicts. It creates a sense of urgency and uncertainty: the next page is unpredictable. One encounters rapidly a riot in Teheran, a Hollywood marriage, the wonders of the Eisenhower administration, a two-headed calf, a party on Jones beach, all sandwiched between ads. The eye takes in the page as a whole (readers may pretend this isn't so, but the success of advertising suggests it is), and the page—indeed, the whole magazine—becomes a single Gestalt where association, though not causal, is often lifelike.

The same is true of the other new languages. Both radio and TV offer short, unrelated programs, interrupted between and within by commercials. I say "interrupted," being myself an anachronism of book culture, but my children don't regard them as interruptions, as breaking continuity. Rather, they regard them as part of a whole, and their reaction is neither one of annoyance nor one of indifference. The ideal news broadcast has half a dozen speakers from as many parts of the world on as many subjects. The London correspondent doesn't comment on what the

Washington correspondent has just said; he hasn't even heard him.

The child is right in not regarding commercials as interruptions. For the only time anyone smiles on TV is in commercials. The rest of life, in news broadcasts and soap operas, is presented as so horrible that the only way to get through life is to buy this product: then you'll smile. Aesop never wrote a clearer fable. It's heaven and hell brought up to date: Hell in the headline, Heaven in the ad. Without the other, neither has meaning.

There's pattern in these new media—not line, but knot; not lineality or causality or chronology, nothing that leads to a desired climax; but a Gordian knot without antecedents or results, containing within itself carefully selected elements, juxtaposed, inseparably fused; a knot that can't be untied to give the long, thin cord of lineality.

This is especially true of ads that never present an ordered, sequential, rational argument but simply present the product associated with desirable things or attitudes. Thus Coca-Cola is shown held by a beautiful blonde, who sits in a Cadillac, surrounded by bronze, muscular admirers, with the sun shining overhead. By repetition these elements become associated, in our minds, into a pattern of sufficient cohesion so that one element can magically evoke the others. If we think of ads as designed solely to sell products, we miss their main effect: to increase pleasure in the consumption of the product. Coca-Cola is far more than a cooling drink; the consumer participates, vicariously, in a much larger experience. In Africa, in Melanesia, to drink a Coke is to participate in the American way of life.

Of the new languages, TV comes closest to drama and ritual. It combines music and art, language and gesture, rhetoric and color. It favors simultaneity of visual and auditory images. Cameras focus not on speakers but on persons spoken to or about; the audience *hears* the accuser but *watches* the accused. In a single impression it hears the prosecutor, watches the trembling hands of the big-town crook, and sees the look of moral indignation on Senator Tobey's face. This is real drama, in process, with the outcome uncertain. Print can't do this; it has a different bias.

Books and movies only pretend uncertainty, but live TV

retains this vital aspect of life. Seen on TV, the fire in the 1952 Democratic Convention threatened briefly to become a conflagration; seen on newsreel, it was history, without potentiality.

The absence of uncertainty is no handicap to other media, if they are properly used, for their biases are different. Thus it's clear from the beginning that Hamlet is a doomed man, but, far from detracting in interest, this heightens the sense of tragedy.

Now, one of the results of the time-space duality that developed in Western culture, principally from the Renaissance on, was a separation within the arts. Music, which created symbols in time, and graphic art, which created symbols in space, became separate pursuits, and men gifted in one rarely pursued the other. Dance and ritual, which inherently combined them, fell in popularity. Only in drama did they remain united.

It is significant that of the four new media, the three most recent are dramatic media, particularly TV, which combines language, music, art, dance. They don't, however, exercise the same freedom with time that the stage dares practice. An intricate plot, employing flash backs, multiple time perspectives and overlays, intelligible on the stage, would mystify on the screen. The audience has no time to think back, to establish relations between early hints and subsequent discoveries. The picture passes before the eyes too quickly; there are no intervals in which to take stock of what has happened and make conjectures of what is going to happen. The observer is in a more passive state, less interested in subtleties. Both TV and film are nearer to narrative and depend much more upon the episodic. An intricate time construction can be done in film, but in fact rarely is. The soliloquies of *Richard III* belong on the stage; the film audience was unprepared for them. On stage Ophelia's death was described by three separate groups: one hears the announcement and watches the reactions simultaneously. On film the camera flatly shows her drowned where "a willow lies aslant a brook."

Media differences such as these mean that it's not simply a question of communicating a single idea in different ways but that a given idea or insight belongs primarily, though not exclusively, to one medium, and can be gained or communicated best through that medium.

Thus the book was ideally suited for discussing evolution

and progress. Both belonged, almost exclusively, to book culture. Like a book, the idea of progress was an abstracting, organizing principle for the interpretation and comprehension of the incredibly complicated record of human experience. The sequence of events was believed to have a direction, to follow a given course along an axis of time; it was held that civilization, like the reader's eye (in J. B. Bury's words), "has moved, is moving, and will move in a desirable direction. Knowledge will advance, and with that advance, reason and decency must increasingly prevail among men." Here we see the three main elements of book lineality: the line, the point moving along that line, and its movement toward a desirable goal.

The Western conception of a definite moment in the present, of the present as a definite moment or a definite point, so important in book-dominated languages, is absent, to my knowledge, in oral languages. Absent as well, in oral societies, are such animating and controlling ideas as Western individualism and three-dimensional perspective, both related to this conception of the definite moment, and both nourished, probably bred, by book culture.

Each medium selects its ideas. TV is a tiny box into which people are crowded and must live; film gives us the wide world. With its huge screen, film is perfectly suited for social drama, Civil War panoramas, the sea, land erosion, Cecil B. DeMille spectaculars. In contrast, the TV screen has room for two, at the most three, faces, comfortably. TV is closer to stage, yet different. Paddy Chayefsky writes:

The theatre audience is far away from the actual action of the drama. They cannot see the silent reactions of the players. They must be told in a loud voice what is going on. The plot movement from one scene to another must be marked, rather than gently shaded as is required in television. In television, however, you can dig into the most humble, ordinary relationships; the relationship of bourgeois children to their mother, of middle-class husband to his wife, of white-collar father to his secretary—in short, the relationships of the people. We relate to each other in an incredibly complicated manner. There is far more exciting drama in the reasons why a man gets married than in why he murders someone. The man who is unhappy in his job, the wife who thinks of a lover, the girl who wants to get into television, your father, your mother, sister, brothers, cousins, friends—all these are better subjects for drama than Iago. What makes a man ambitious? Why does a girl always try to steal her kid sister's boy friends? Why does your uncle attend his annual class reunion faithfully every year? Why do you always find it depressing to visit your father? These are the substances of good television drama; and the deeper you probe into and examine the twisted, semi-formed complexes of emotional entanglements, the more exciting your writing becomes.[1]

This is the primary reason, I believe, why Greek drama is more readily adapted to TV than to film. The boxed-in quality of live TV lends itself to static literary tragedy with greater ease than does the elastic, energetic, expandable movie. Guthrie's recent movie of *Oedipus* favored the panoramic shot rather than the selective eye. It consisted of a succession of tableaux, a series of elaborate, unnatural poses. The effect was of congested groups of people moving in tight formation as though they had trained for it by living for days together in a self-service elevator. With the lines, "I grieve for the City, and for myself and you . . . and walk through endless ways of thought," the inexorable tragedy moved to its horrible "come to realize" climax as though everyone were stepping on everyone else's feet.

The tight, necessary conventions of live TV were more sympathetic to Sophocles in the Aluminum Hour's *Antigone*. Restrictions of space are imposed on TV as on the Greek stage by the size and inflexibility of the studio. Squeezed by physical limitations, the producer was forced to expand the viewer's imagination with ingenious devices.

When T. S. Eliot adapted *Murder in the Cathedral* for film, he noted a difference in realism between cinema and stage:

Cinema, even where fantasy is introduced, is much more realistic than the stage. Especially in an historical picture, the setting, the costume, and the way of life represented have to be accurate. Even a minor anachronism is intolerable. On the stage

---

[1] *Television Plays*, New York, Simon and Schuster, 1955, pp. 176–78.

much more can be overlooked or forgiven; and indeed, an ex-
cessive care for accuracy of historical detail can become burden-
some and distracting. In watching a stage performance, the
member of the audience is in direct contact with the actor playing
a part. In looking at a film, we are much more passive; as audi-
ence, we contribute less. We are seized with the illusion that we
are observing an actual event, or at least a series of photographs
of the actual event; and nothing must be allowed to break this
illusion. Hence the precise attention to detail.[2]

If two men are on a stage in a theatre, the dramatist is
obliged to motivate their presence; he has to account for their
existing on the stage at all. Whereas if a camera is following a
figure down a street or is turned to any object whatever, there is
no need for a reason to be provided. Its grammar contains that
power of statement of motivation, no matter what it looks at.

In the theatre, the spectator sees the enacted scene as a whole
in space, always seeing the whole of the space. The stage may
present only one corner of a large hall, but that corner is always
totally visible all through the scene. And the spectator always
sees that scene from a fixed, unchanging distance and from an
angle of vision that doesn't change. Perspective may change from
scene to scene, but within one scene it remains constant. Distance
never varies.

But in film and TV, distance and angle constantly shift. The
same scene is shown in multiple perspective and focus. The
viewer sees it from here, there, then over here; finally he is drawn
inexorably into it, becomes part of it. He ceases to be a spectator. Balázs writes:

Although we sit in our seats, we do not see Romeo and Juliet
from there. We look up into Juliet's balcony with Romeo's eyes
and look down on Romeo with Juliet's. Our eye and with it our
consciousness is identified with the characters in the film, we
look at the world out of their eyes and have no angle of vision
of our own. We walk amid crowds, ride, fly or fall with the hero
and if one character looks into the other's eyes, he looks into our

---

[2] George Hoellering and T. S. Eliot, *Film of Murder in the Cathedral*, New
York, Harcourt, Brace & Co., 1952, p. vi; London, Faber & Faber, 1952.

eyes from the screen, for, our eyes are in the camera and become identical with the gaze of the characters. They see with our eyes. Herein lies the psychological act of identification. Nothing like this "identification" has ever occurred as the effect of any other system of art and it is here that the film manifests its absolute artistic novelty.

. . . Not only can we see, in the isolated "shots" of a scene, the very atoms of life and their innermost secrets revealed at close quarters, but we can do so without any of the intimate secrecy being lost, as always happens in the exposure of a stage performance or of a painting. The new theme which the new means of expression of film art revealed was not a hurricane at sea or the eruption of a volcano: it was perhaps a solitary tear slowly welling up in the corner of a human eye.

. . . Not to speak does not mean that one has nothing to say. Those who do not speak may be brimming over with emotions which can be expressed only in forms and pictures, in gesture and play of feature. The man of visual culture uses these not as substitutes for words, as a deaf-mute uses his fingers.[3]

The gestures of visual man are not intended to convey concepts that can be expressed in words, but inner experiences, non-rational emotions, which would still remain unexpressed when everything that can be told has been told. Such emotions lie in the deepest levels. They cannot be approached by words that are mere reflections of concepts, any more than musical experiences can be expressed in rational concepts. Facial expression is a human experience rendered immediately visible without the intermediary of word. It is Turgenev's "living truth of the human face."

Printing rendered illegible the faces of men. So much could be read from paper that the method of conveying meaning by facial expression fell into desuetude. The press grew to be the main bridge over which the more remote interhuman spiritual exchanges took place; the immediate, the personal, the inner, died. There was no longer need for the subtler means of expression provided by the body. The face became immobile; the inner

---

[3] Béla Balázs, *Theory of Film*, New York, Roy Publishers, 1953, pp. 48, 31, 40; London, Denis Dobson, 1952.

life, still. Wells that dry up are wells from which no water is dipped.

Just as radio helped bring back inflection in speech, so film and TV are aiding us in the recovery of gesture and facial awareness—a rich, colorful language, conveying moods and emotions, happenings and characters, even thoughts, none of which could be properly packaged in words. If film had remained silent for another decade, how much faster this change might have been!

Feeding the product of one medium through another medium creates a new product. When Hollywood buys a novel, it buys a title and the publicity associated with it: nothing more. Nor should it.

Each of the four versions of the *Caine Mutiny*—book, play, movie, TV—had a different hero: Willie Keith, the lawyer Greenwald, the United States Navy, and Captain Queeg, respectively. Media and audience biases were clear. Thus the book told, in lengthy detail, of the growth and making of Ensign William Keith, American man, while the movie camera with its colorful shots of ships and sea, unconsciously favored the Navy as hero, a bias supported by the fact that the Navy cooperated with the movie makers. Because of stage limitations, the play was confined, except for the last scene, to the courtroom, and favored the defense counsel as hero. The TV show, aimed at a mass audience, emphasized patriotism, authority, allegiance. More important, the cast was reduced to the principals and the plot to its principles; the real moral problem—the refusal of subordinates to assist an incompetent, unpopular superior—was clear, whereas in the book it was lost under detail, in the film under scenery. Finally, the New York play, with its audience slanted toward Expense Account patronage—Mr. Sampson, Western Sales Manager for the Cavity Drill Company—became a morality play with Willie Keith, innocent American youth, torn between two influences: Keefer, clever author but moral cripple, and Greenwald, equally brilliant but reliable, a businessman's intellectual. Greenwald saves Willie's soul.

The film *Moby Dick* was in many ways an improvement on the book, primarily because of its explicitness. For *Moby Dick* is one of those admittedly great classics, like *Robinson Crusoe* or Kafka's *Trial*, whose plot and situation, as distilled apart from the book by time and familiarity, are actually much more imposing than the written book itself. It's the drama of Ahab's defiance rather than Melville's uncharted leviathan meanderings that is the greatness of *Moby Dick*. On film, instead of laborious tacks through leagues of discursive interruptions, the most vivid descriptions of whales and whaling become part of the action. On film, the viewer was constantly aboard ship: each scene an instantaneous shot of whaling life, an effect achieved in the book only by illusion, by constant, detailed reference. From start to finish, all the action of the film served to develop what was most central to the theme—a man's magnificent and blasphemous pride in attempting to destroy the brutal, unreasoning force that maims him and turns man-made order into chaos. Unlike the book, the film gave a spare, hard, compelling dramatization, free of self-conscious symbolism.

Current confusion over the respective roles of the new media comes largely from a misconception of their function. They are art-forms, not substitutes for human contact. Insofar as they attempt to usurp speech and personal, living relations, they harm. This, of course, has long been one of the problems of book culture, at least during the time of its monopoly of Western middle-class thought. But this was never a legitimate function of books, nor of any other medium. Whenever a medium goes claim jumping, trying to work areas where it is ill-suited, conflicts occur with other media, or, more accurately, between the vested interests controlling each. But, when media simply exploit their own formats, they become complementary and cross-fertile.

Some people who have no one around talk to cats, and you can hear their voices in the next room, and they sound silly, because the cat won't answer, but that suffices to maintain the illusion that their world is made up of living people, while it is not. Mechanized mass media reverse this: now mechanical cats talk to humans. There's no genuine feedback.

This charge is often leveled by academicians at the new media, but it holds equally for print. The open-mouthed, glaze-eyed TV spectator is merely the successor of the passive, silent, lonely reader whose head moved back and forth like a shuttlecock.

When we read, another person thinks for us: we merely repeat his mental process. The greater part of the work of thought is done for us. This is why it relieves us to take up a book after being occupied by our own thoughts. In reading, the mind is only the playground for another's ideas. People who spend most of their lives in reading often lose the capacity for thinking, just as those who always ride forget how to walk. Some people read themselves stupid. Chaplin did a wonderful take-off of this in *City Lights*, when he stood up on a chair to eat the endless confetti that he mistook for spaghetti.

Eliot remarks: "It is often those writers whom we are lucky enough to know whose books we can ignore; and the better we know them personally, the less need we may feel to read what they write."

Frank O'Connor highlights a basic distinction between oral and written traditions: " 'By the hokies, there was a man in this place one time by name of Ned Sullivan, and he had a queer thing happen to him late one night and he coming up the Valley Road from Durlas.' This is how a folk story begins, or should begin. . . . Yet that is how no printed short story should begin, because such a story seems tame when you remove it from its warm nest by the cottage fire, from the sense of an audience with its interjections, and the feeling of terror at what may lurk in the darkness outside."

Face-to-face discourse is not as selective, abstract, nor explicit as any mechanical medium; it probably comes closer to communicating an unabridged situation than any of them, and, insofar as it exploits the give-take of dynamic relationship, it's clearly the most indispensably human one.

Of course, there can be personal involvement in the other media. When Richardson's *Pamela* was serialized in 1741, it aroused such interest that in one English town, upon receipt of the last installment, the church bell announced that virtue had been rewarded. Radio stations have reported receiving quantities of baby clothes and bassinets when, in a soap opera, a heroine had a baby. One of the commonest phrases used by devoted listeners to daytime serials is that they "visited with" Aunt Jenny or Big Sister. BBC and *News Chronicle* report cases of women viewers who kneel before TV sets to kiss male announcers good night.

Each medium, if its bias is properly exploited, reveals and communicates a unique aspect of reality, of truth. Each offers a different perspective, a way of seeing an otherwise hidden dimension of reality. It's not a question of one reality being true, the others distortions. One allows us to see from here, another from there, a third from still another perspective; taken together they give us a more complete whole, a greater truth. New essentials are brought to the fore, including those made invisible by the "blinders" of old languages.

This is why the preservation of book culture is as important as the development of TV. This is why new languages, instead of destroying old ones, serve as a stimulant to them. Only monopoly is destroyed. When actor-collector Edward G. Robinson was battling actor-collector Vincent Price on art on TV's *$64,000 Challenge*, he was asked how the quiz had affected his life; he answered petulantly, "Instead of looking at the pictures in my art books, I now have to read them." Print, along with all old languages, including speech, has profited enormously from the development of the new media. "The more the arts develop," writes E. M. Forster, "the more they depend on each other for definition. We will borrow from painting first and call it pattern. Later we will borrow from music and call it rhythm."

The appearance of a new medium often frees older media for creative effort. They no longer have to serve the interests of power and profit. Elia Kazan, discussing the American theatre, says:

Take 1900–1920. The theatre flourished all over the country. It had no competition. The box office boomed. The top original fare it had to offer was The Girl of the Golden West. *Its bow to culture was fusty productions of Shakespeare. . . . Came the moving pictures. The theatre had to be better or go under. It got better. It got so spectacularly better so fast that in 1920–1930 you wouldn't have recognized it. Perhaps it was an accident that Eugene O'Neill appeared at that moment—but it was no accident that in the moment of strange competition, the theatre had room for him. Because it was disrupted and hard pressed, it made room for his experiments, his unheard-of subjects, his passion, his power. There was room for him to grow to his full stature. And there was freedom for the talents that came after his.[4]*

---

[4] "Writers and Motion Pictures," *The Atlantic Monthly*, 199, 1957, p. 69.

Yet a new language is rarely welcomed by the old. The oral tradition distrusted writing, manuscript culture was contemptuous of printing, book culture hated the press, that "slag-heap of hellish passions," as one 19th-century scholar called it. A father, protesting to a Boston newspaper about crime and scandal, said he would rather see his children "in their graves while pure in innocence, than dwelling with pleasure upon these reports, which have grown so bold."

What really disturbed book-oriented people wasn't the sensationalism of the newspaper, but its nonlineal format, its nonlineal codifications of experience. The motto of conservative academicians became: *Hold that line!*

A new language lets us see with the fresh, sharp eyes of the child; it offers the pure joy of discovery. I was recently told a story about a Polish couple who, though long resident in Toronto, retained many of the customs of their homeland. Their son despaired of ever getting his father to buy a suit cut in style or getting his mother to take an interest in Canadian life. Then he bought them a TV set, and in a matter of months a major change took place. One evening the mother remarked that "Edith Piaf is the latest thing on Broadway," and the father appeared in "the kind of suit executives wear on TV." For years the father had passed this same suit in store windows and seen it both in advertisements and on living men, but not until he saw it on TV did it become meaningful. This same statement goes for all media: each offers a unique presentation of reality, which when new has a freshness and clarity that is extraordinarily powerful.

This is especially true of TV. We say, "We have a radio" but "We have television"—as if something had happened to us. It's no longer "The skin you love to touch" but "The Nylon that loves to touch you." We don't watch TV; it watches us: it guides us. Magazines and newspapers no longer convey "information" but offer ways of seeing things. They have abandoned realism as too easy: they substitute themselves for realism. *Life* is totally advertisements: its articles package and sell emotions and ideas just as its paid ads sell commodities.

Several years ago, a group of us at the University of Toronto undertook the following experiment: 136 students were divided, on the basis of their over-all academic standing of the previous year, into four equal groups who either (1) heard and saw a lecture delivered in a TV studio, (2) heard and saw this same lecture on a TV screen, (3) heard it over the radio, or (4) read it in manuscript. Thus there were, in the CBC studios, four controlled groups who simultaneously received a single lecture and then immediately wrote an identical examination to test both understanding and retention of content. Later the experiment was repeated, using three similar groups; this time the same lecture was (1) delivered in a classroom, (2) presented as a film (using the kinescope) in a small theatre, and (3) again read in print. The actual mechanics of the experiment were relatively simple, but the problem of writing the script for the lecture led to a consideration of the resources and limitations of the dramatic forms involved.

It immediately became apparent that no matter how the script was written and the show produced, it would be slanted in various ways for and against each of the media involved; no show could be produced that did not contain these biases, and the only real common denominator was the simultaneity of presentation. For each communication channel codifies reality differently and thus influences, to a surprising degree, the content of the message communicated. A medium is not simply an envelope that carries any letter; it is itself a major part of that message. We therefore decided not to exploit the full resources of any one medium, but to try to chart a middle-of-the-road course between all of them.

The lecture that was finally produced dealt with linguistic codifications of reality and metaphysical concepts underlying grammatical systems. It was chosen because it concerned a field in which few students could be expected to have prior knowledge; moreover, it offered opportunities for the use of gesture. The cameras moved throughout the lecture, and took close-ups where relevant. No other visual aids were used, nor were shots taken of the audience while the lecture was in progress. Instead, the cameras simply focused on the speaker for 27 minutes.

The first difference we found between a classroom and a TV lecture was the brevity of the latter. The classroom lecture, if not ideally, at least in practice, sets a slower pace. It's verbose, repetitive. It allows for greater elaboration and permits the lecturer to take up several *related* points. TV, however, is stripped right down; there's less time for qualifications or alternative interpretations and only time enough for *one* point. (Into 27 minutes we put the meat of a two-hour classroom lecture.) The ideal TV speaker states his point and then brings out different facets of it by a variety of illustrations. But the classroom lecturer is less subtle and, to the agony of the better students, repeats and repeats his identical points in the hope, perhaps, that ultimately no student will miss them, or perhaps simply because he is dull. Teachers have had captive audiences for so long that few are equipped to compete for attention via the new media.

The next major difference noted was the abstracting role of each medium, beginning with print. Edmund M. Morgan, Harvard Law Professor, writes:

One who forms his opinion from the reading of any record alone is prone to err, because the printed page fails to produce the impression or convey the idea which the spoken word produced or conveyed. The writer has read charges to the jury which he had previously heard delivered, and has been amazed to see an oral deliverance which indicated a strong bias appear on the printed page as an ideally impartial exposition. He has seen an appellate court solemnly declare the testimony of a witness to be especially clear and convincing which the trial judge had orally characterized as the most abject perjury.[5]

Selectivity of print and radio are perhaps obvious enough, but we are less conscious of it in TV, partly because we have already been conditioned to it by the shorthand of film. Balázs writes:

A man hurries to a railway station to take leave of his beloved. We see him on the platform. We cannot see the train, but the questing eyes of the man show us that his beloved is already seated in the train. We see only a close-up of the man's face, we see it twitch as if startled and then strips of light and shadow, light and shadow flit across it in quickening rhythm.

---

[5] G. Louis Joughin and Edmund M. Morgan, *The Legacy of Sacco and Vanzetti*, New York, Harcourt, Brace & Co., 1948, p. 34.

Then tears gather in the eyes and that ends the scene. We are expected to know what happened and today we do know, but when I first saw this film in Berlin, I did not at once understand the end of this scene. Soon, however, everyone knew what had happened: the train had started and it was the lamps in its compartments which had thrown their light on the man's face as they glided past ever faster and faster.[6]

As in a movie theatre, only the screen is illuminated, and, on it, only points of immediate relevance are portrayed; everything else is eliminated. This explicitness makes TV not only personal but forceful. That's why stage hands in a TV studio watch the show over floor monitors, rather than watch the actual performance before their eyes.

The script of the lecture, timed for radio, proved too long for TV. Visual aids and gestures on TV not only allow the elimination of certain words, but require a unique script. The ideal radio delivery stresses pitch and intonation to make up for the absence of the visual. That flat, broken speech in "sidewalk interviews" is the speech of a person untrained in radio delivery.

The results of the examination showed that TV had won, followed by lecture, film, radio, and finally print. Eight months later the test was readministered to the bulk of the students who had taken it the first time. Again it was found that there were significant differences between the groups exposed to different media, and these differences were the same as those on the first test, save for the studio group, an uncertain group because of the chaos of the lecture conditions, which had moved from last to second place. Finally, two years later, the experiment was repeated, with major modifications, using students at Ryerson Institute. Marshall McLuhan reports. . . .

In this repeat performance, pains were taken to allow each medium full play of its possibilities with reference to the subject, just as in the earlier experiment each medium was neutralized as much as possible. Only the mimeograph form remained the same in each experiment. Here we added a printed form in which an imaginative typographical layout was followed. The lecturer

---

[6] Béla Balázs, *op. cit.*, pp. 35-36.

used the blackboard and permitted discussion. Radio and TV employed dramatization, sound effects and graphics. In the examination, radio easily topped TV. Yet, as in the first experiment, both radio and TV manifested a decisive advantage over the lecture and written forms. As a conveyor both of ideas and information, TV was, in this second experiment, apparently enfeebled by the deployment of its dramatic resources, whereas radio benefited from such lavishness. "Technology is explicitness," writes Lyman Bryson. Are both radio and TV more explicit than writing or lecture? Would a greater explicitness, if inherent in these media, account for the ease with which they top other modes of performance?[7]

Announcement of the results of the first experiment evoked considerable interest. Advertising agencies circulated the results with the comment that here, at last, was scientific proof of the superiority of TV. This was unfortunate and missed the main point, for the results didn't indicate the superiority of one medium over others. They merely directed attention toward differences between them, differences so great as to be of kind rather than degree. Some CBC officials were furious, not because TV won, but because print lost. Scratch most of them and you find Student Christian-types who understand little of literature and contribute less, but, like publishers, have a vested interest in book culture. At heart they hate radio and TV, which they employ merely to disseminate the values of book culture. They feel they should dedicate themselves to *serious* culture. This is why they can't use radio and TV with conviction and they are afraid to use it comically, and so they end up with wishy-washy. They are like 16th-century scholars who saw the book revolution as simply a means of propagating old ideas and failed to realize it was a monumental change in sensibility, in thinking and feeling.

Official culture still strives to force the new languages to do the work of the old. But the horseless carriage didn't do the work of the horse; it abolished the horse and did what the horse could never do. Horses are fine. So are books.

---

[7] From a personal communication to the author.

Nobody yet knows the languages inherent in the new technological culture; we are all deaf-blind mutes in terms of the new situation. Our most impressive words and thoughts betray us by referring to the previously existent, not to the present.

The problem has been falsely seen as democracy *vs.* the mass media. But the mass media *are* democracy. The book itself was the first mechanical mass medium. What is really being asked, of course, is: can books' monopoly of knowledge survive the challenge of the new languages? The answer is: no. What should be asked is: what can print do better than any other medium and is that worth doing?

ALTERNATIVE SYSTEMS OF LEARNING

by GEORGE A. MILLER

IF we are to remain true to our democratic heritage, one of the most obvious implications of the predicted increase in population is that our already crowded educational system will have to be vastly expanded and overhauled. As knowledge increases and work becomes more technical, there will be a corresponding increase in the amount of information that will have to be imparted to a student. And as automation advances and new industries replace old, learning will not be regarded as ending with graduation from school, but will become a way of life for everyone. Put together the increased number of students, the increased knowledge to be communicated, and the increased

"Alternative Systems of Learning," by George A. Miller. Excerpted and reprinted from "Some Psychological Perspectives on the Year 2000" by permission from *Dædalus, Journal of the American Academy of Arts and Sciences*, Vol. 96, No. 3. Copyright © 1967 by the American Academy of Arts and Sciences.

duration of the educational experience, and then try to imagine what kind of educational system we will need by the year 2000. Can anything short of an educational revolution meet our needs?

I have followed recent innovations in educational practice with considerable interest. Some kind of change is obviously needed. Too often our children's most valuable return for their years in the classroom is a kind of shrewd skill in coping with a large, well-intentioned but often stultifying social institution. On the theory that any system that is not changed gets worse, there have been valiant attempts to revise curricula, to write better texts, and to provide more teaching aids, while at the same time making the best possible facilities available to every student. All of these excellent improvements and innovations are necessary, but are they sufficient?

I do not wish to sound critical of all that is being done, yet I feel that in their enthusiasm our educational revisionists sometimes forget a basic fact about the learning process. Most of the studies that have made a serious effort to evaluate the effectiveness of these new programs have shown that the method of packaging the information makes relatively little difference. Of course, if the information is wrong or irrelevant, a student cannot learn what is right or relevant; if, however, the same information is presented in alternative ways, the major factor determining how much a child learns is how much time he spends studying. Some learn faster than others, some learn more than others, but on the average, the generalization holds true. The problem, therefore, is how to motivate the students to study.

Obviously, we must see to it that the content of the teaching is clear, accurate, and up-to-date, that the teacher understands it, and that the student, whether he realizes it or not, really needs to know it. All of this is obviously conducive to a profitable educational experience. Yet it would be useless if students refused to study. Conversely, a student who is truly determined to learn something can learn it even under the most impoverished conditions.

I am not putting forth some radically new dogma. The fact that education is the reward for study is so banal that I am embarrassed to mention it, much less emphasize it. If it were not so important, I would prefer to leave it unsaid. But as every educator knows, the central problem of education is to make the students want it. Unfortunately, the problem is just as difficult as it is important. We know how to write better books and print them with three-color illustrations; we know how to shuffle the order of units within a curriculum; we know how to break up a unit into small steps and drill each step separately; we know how to use movies and field trips and special projects; but we do not know how to inject the urge to learn into a student's heart. So we do what we know how to do.

In defense of those who try to improve the packaging of the information that is presented to the student, I must agree that the finest motive of all for studying is love of knowledge for its own sake. Every subject matter has an intrinsic interest of its own, and a student who becomes intrigued with it on its own terms will certainly be the most gratifying to his teacher. My suspicion is that too often this experience is reserved for a fortunate few who are both highly intelligent and protected from more immediate personal distractions in their own lives. For most students study is a painful experience, and the social milieu of the public schools seldom encourages them to bear the pain until they learn to love it. Our schools, I fear, too often illustrate the irony of a self-fulfilling prophecy. A student is labeled as good or bad. First the teachers and then the student himself accept this classification. If he is mislabeled as good, he may become an "over-achiever," but if he is mislabeled bad, he accepts the judgment and fulfills the prophecy. How can we expect every student to acquire a detached love of learning under such conditions?

An essential ingredient in the motivational pattern of a good student is one that David McClelland and his colleagues call "need achievement." Need achievement manifests itself in a desire to do better, to compete against a standard. How our schools are to instill a desire for success in students who have not already acquired it at home is a difficult but important social question. Attempts have been made to teach people to think like achievers, to learn the opinions and behavior patterns that characterize the successful person. The first results have been encouraging; this kind of motivational training may prove both possible and practical. If it does, perhaps we can even reach some social consensus about its use, in which case psychologists would have contributed an important weapon to the educator's arsenal and helped to mobilize our human resources for the social good. But can parents who would refuse their children a relatively innocuous innovation like flouridation be persuaded to embrace such a deliberate public program of personality modification?

To my mind one of the most persuasive answers to this motivational question is that more initiative should be placed in the hands of the learner. If we want to motivate students to study harder, we should enlist their co-operation. This prescription would probably not be a universal panacea, but giving initiative to the student is important in adult education. Under existing conditions, however, it is not easy to give initiative to the student. In order to allow a learner to say more about what he studies, when he studies it, and how far he takes it, a teacher must adapt himself to the student's interests and abilities. When you recall that the teacher is usually outnumbered by thirty or forty to one in most schoolrooms, the impracticality of this solution becomes all too clear. Given realistic economic constraints on the expansion of our present educational system, I do not see how we could relinquish the initiative to students under that system. When it has been tried, as it often has in the beginning grades, the result has usually been to convert the class into a period of supervised recreation. We would have to change the system. I believe there are alternatives open to us that could achieve the desired result. If these alternatives do indeed prove to be better for motivating students to study, our schools may look very different by the year 2000.

The alternative systems I have in mind would exploit the modern, time-shared computer. Imagine a classroom partitioned into semi-isolated booths. In each booth are a pair of headphones, a typewriter keyboard, a screen similar to a television set's, and a photosensitive "light gun." All of these stations (and others in other classrooms) are in communication with a central computer. A student communicates with the computer by typing on the keyboard or by touching his light gun to designated spots on the screen; the computer communicates with a student by playing recorded speech through the student's earphones, or by writing or drawing pictures on the cathode ray tube. Each student can be working on a different lesson, or two on the same lesson can progress at different rates. A teacher walks from booth to booth, answers questions, sees that the stations are operating properly, and supervises requests for new materials.

A science-fiction fantasy? Not at all. Such systems are already operating. The one I have just described is operating in a public school in Palo Alto, California, as a pilot project under the direction of Patrick Suppes and Richard Atkinson of Stanford University. The children are learning about the same amount they would have learned under the regular system, but their attitude toward learning is entirely different. Learning is fun, they are more curious, and they enjoy studying from the computer. The cost—leaving out the cost of development—is only slightly more per student than before.

If the motivational advantages of this system persist when it is no longer a novelty, we can expect to see many more of these systems in the future. There are several reasons to think that a computer-based school makes sense. Students can go at their own pace. One who has trouble can get additional material; one who makes no mistakes can go on to more advanced material. Bright students are not bored while the teacher explains what they already know; dull students are not baffled by being left behind. There is no need for testing; students' records are maintained automatically. A teacher can teach and leave the threatening duty of evaluation to the machine. Within the broad limits set by what materials have been prepared for the computer, the student is free to study those things that are of most interest to him. And a computer treats all children alike, regardless of race, creed, or color.

For many people the computer is synonymous with mechanical depersonalization, and computerized instruction is frequently regarded as a way for the teacher to avoid his personal responsibility to his students. Fears have been expressed that the computer represents an assembly-line approach to the educational process that will increase alienation, identity crises, *anomie*, and so forth. Such attitudes seem overly emotional. The evidence points in the opposite direction. The computer gives the child a measure of individual attention that he could receive in no other way, short of a private tutor. To the extent that initiative can be left in the hands of the learner, rather than given to the machine,

I believe these devices can help to solve an important educational problem.

Needless to say, stations do not have to be located in class-rooms. They could be in libraries, or factories, or even private houses; all that is required is a telephone line to the computer. It should not be too difficult to make such facilities available for adult education. If economic considerations make it necessary, classroom stations in the public schools could be used for adult education in the evenings. It seems likely that businessmen will develop their own computer-based teaching systems; some of the most enthusiastic proponents of programmed self-instruction are businessmen who have used it to retrain their own personnel.

The shared use of a central computer by many stations at remote locations can be adapted to other purposes than public education. For example, it promises to be one of the more useful tools for enabling teams of experts to collaborate efficiently. I believe that the first time I heard the phrase, "on-line intellectual community with shared data base," it was intended as a summary of the various possibilities that Project INTREX (an M.I.T. adventure in library science headed by Carl Overhage) was con-sidering during its planning conference in the summer of 1965. In fact, a visionary description of the possibilities inherent in making a "data base" (for example, a library or some part of it) accessible "on-line" (direct communication to a computer from a remote location via telephone line) to an "intellectual community" (a group of scholars or scientists working on a com-mon problem) had already been written in 1965 by J.C.R. Licklider in his *Libraries of the Future*.

A number of organizations are presently working toward the introduction of computers into libraries, or vice versa. Not only can a computer provide a wide range of clerical services to its users, but a library of shared references will be available to them, their own data or other materials can be stored there, and the materials of other users can be made available on request—and all of this is accessible by simple requests initiated and fulfilled at the keyboard of a remote teletypewriter. Scholars in widely scattered locations will be able to work closely together without leaving their houses, and they will have the advantage of clerical, stenographic, library, telegraph, and publication services via the system. Something suggestive of such a computer system is already taking shape on a few college campuses; regional, national, or even international networks would be possible if they seemed desirable.

With just a little foresight in the development of these systems, they could turn out to be one of the greatest educational innovations since the invention of printing. If a student were provided with a console of his own, he could, at little or no cost to the intellectual community, have access to the most advanced thinking in his field of interest; a student in small or isolated colleges could be given the same access as the student at a great university. Moreover, the system would be responsive to his requests, so it would satisfy the requirements that initiative remain in the hands of the student.

VII

Defense and Diplomacy

Our policies are failing and our influence in the world is shrinking. Our enemies treat us with a rough contempt; and among us there is a sense of futility, of vain effort, and of problems—once seemingly so simple—that now elude the very categories of thought and political discourse by which we seek solutions.

—EDMUND STILLMAN and WILLIAM PFAFF,
The New Politics (1960)

THE PREVENTION OF WORLD
WAR III

by KENNETH E. BOULDING

WHEN we talk about preventing something
we imply two things. We imply, first, that there is a dynamic
system which is now proceeding that, if allowed to proceed
unchanged, will result in an event which is regarded as undesirable and which, therefore, we want to prevent. We imply
also that it is possible to change the dynamic system in question
and replace it by another dynamic system in which the unwanted
event does not occur. Thus, suppose we find ourselves driving
toward a railroad crossing and suddenly we see the red lights
flashing and a train approaching. Our dynamic system at the
moment consists simply of velocity and direction. We are proceeding, say at 50 miles per hour, toward the crossing. The distant
early warning system of our eyes informs us the crossing is
dangerous. The knowledge which we have of our existing dynamic
system informs us that if it continues we will arrive at the
crossing at the precise moment when the train is there. The
combination of a distant information system coupled with the
simple dynamics of automobiles enables us, however, to prevent
the disaster. We do this by putting on the brakes long before we
get to the crossing. This in effect changes the dynamic system
under which we have been operating. It introduces a new variable
into it, indeed a new dimension, deceleration. Because of this,
we are able to prevent the disaster, as we are able to avoid
simultaneous occupancy of the crossing by ourselves and the
train.

We must be careful, of course, in applying the analogy of a

"The Prevention of World War III," by Kenneth E. Boulding. Reprinted by
permission of the author and *The Virginia Quarterly Review.* Copyright ©
1962, *The Virginia Quarterly Review.*

simple psycho-mechanical system like a man driving a car to the enormous complexities and uncertainties of the international system. However, the international system is still a system, even though it has important random elements in it. Because it is not entirely random, it has elements of predictability. One of the greatest difficulties lies precisely in the stochastic nature of the system. We are driving a car, as it were, that may or may not respond to brakes according to whether dice held by the driver indicate "respond" or "fail." The situation is made all the more difficult by the fact that we face here a stochastic system with a very small universe, that is, a very small number of cases. Stochastic systems with a large number of cases can be treated by the theory of probability. We have a pretty fair idea, for instance, how many people are going to die in automobile accidents next year, although we do not know exactly who they are.

The problem of reducing the total number of automobile accidents is a very different kind of problem from the one that faces the driver of the preceding paragraph. Nevertheless, even with our present knowledge it would not be difficult to design an automobile and a road system which would kill, let us say, 20,000 people a year instead of 40,000. What we would be doing here would be to reduce the probability of disaster on the part of a single individual. It is by no means impossible to think of the international system in a rather similar way, and to talk about the things we can do to reduce the probability of disaster. What we mean by this is that if we had a very large number of planets roughly identical with our own we could postulate changes in the system which would reduce the number of cases in which disaster occurred. This would be the analogue of treating road deaths as a public health problem and seeking to reduce their probability. As far as we know, however, we do not have a large number of planets like ours and for our purposes at least there is only one. Hence, reducing the probability of disaster does us very little good if the disaster actually occurs. The problem of stochastic systems with a small number of cases has received insufficient attention in the theoretical literature. It is precisely this kind of system, however, with which we have to deal in international affairs.

I believe the present international system to be one which has a significant probability built into it of irretrievable disaster for the human race. The longer the number of years we contemplate such a system operating, the larger this probability becomes. I do not know whether in any one year it is 1 per cent, 10 per cent, or even 50 per cent. I feel pretty sure, however, that it is of this order of magnitude, not, shall we say, of the order of magnitude of .01 per cent. The problem of system change, therefore, is urgent and desperate, and we are all in terrible danger. This is largely because of a quantitative change in the parameters of the international system under which we now live. This is still essentially the system of unilateral national defense in spite of the development of the United Nations and certain international organizations. Unilateral national defense is workable only if each nation can be stronger than its potential enemies in its home territory. This is possible under two circumstances. The first is that the nations must be far enough away from each other, and the extent to which their power declines as they operate further away from their own home bases must be sufficiently great. Then each nation can be stronger than the other *at home* with on-the-spot forces because of the fact that in a nation's home territory the enemy operates at a certain disadvantage. There is a second condition, however, which is that each nation must be able to dominate an area around its home base equal in depth to the range of the deadly missile. Because of quantitative changes in these conditions even in the last few years the system of unilateral national defense has become infeasible on a world scale. No nation is now far enough away from potential enemies to be sure that it can dominate even its own territory. Furthermore, the range of the deadly missile is rapidly reaching 12,500 miles, which means that the second condition cannot possibly be fulfilled. The condition which unilateral national defense attempts to establish, therefore, which I call *unconditional viability*, is now no longer possible.

The urgent and desperate nature of the present situation is created by the universality of the disaster with which we are threatened. The system of unilateral national defense has never given permanent security. The rise and fall of nations and empires is a testament to this fact. Indeed, looking with a large historical eye, one may say that unconditional viability has never existed except perhaps for brief periods and the best that unilateral national defense could do for any society was to postpone disaster. The situation of the individual society, that is, is rather analogous to that of the individual, whose life, on this earth at any rate, must also end in irretrievable disaster, that is, in death. Where we have a large number of individuals, however, death for the individual is not death for the race. In fact death for the individual is necessary if the race is to survive. Where the number of individuals becomes smaller and smaller, however, there comes to be a critical point where death for the individual is also death for the race and the irretrievable disaster which the individual suffers is likewise irretrievable disaster for the species. The unilaterally defended national state now seems to me to have got to this stage in its development. It is no longer appropriate as a form of organization for the kind of technical society in which we live. Its death throes, however, may destroy the whole human race. The age of civilization out of which we are passing was characterized by a large number of nation-states or independent political organizations practicing unilateral national defense. Because of the large number of these organizations there were always some being born and always some ready to rise into the places of those which suffered disaster. With the number of effectively independent nation-states now reduced to two or perhaps at most three, the possibilities of irretrievable disaster become much greater.

The problem which we face, therefore, is how to effect a system change in the international order, or perhaps we should say the world political order, sufficient to lower the probability of disaster to a tolerable level. The critical problem here might be described as that of "system perception." To revert again to the analogy of the car and the railroad crossing, if the driver of the car does not see that he is approaching the crossing, if the warning lights are not working, and if he cannot see the train approaching, he will naturally not take any steps to avert the disaster. The world problem here is perhaps psychological rather than mechanical. There is a fairly widespread sense abroad of impending doom. The doom, however, is so large that we do not really believe it and we go about our daily actions as if it did not exist. This is the mechanism, as Jerome Frank has pointed out, known to the psychologists as "denial." Up to a point this is actually healthy. We all know that we are going to die sometime and we may die tomorrow; but we act pretty much as if we are going to live forever. We do not spend much time in taking tearful farewells and in writing our last wills and testaments. We plan ahead for months and even for years, in spite of the fact that these plans may never come to fruition. This perfectly legitimate response to uncertainty becomes pathological when it prevents us from taking steps which would postpone disaster or make it less likely. The man who is afraid that he has a cancer but who will not go to a doctor because he might find out that he has one is a good example. Where the prospect of disaster, therefore, is so vague or so uncertain that it merely results in pathological denial, it is necessary to bring the actor to a more realistic appraisal of the system within which he is acting.

If the problem of "denial" is to be overcome, it is necessary to do more than merely scare people with horrendous pictures of the possible future. Indeed, the more horrendous the picture which is drawn, the more it is likely to result in denial and pathological inactivity. The future which faced our driver at the railroad crossing was also horrendous, but instead of denying this and continuing on his way he presumably applied the brakes, that is, initiated a system change. The problem in the international system is that we seem to have no brakes. That is, it is hard for people to visualize the nature of the system change which is necessary for survival. This, then, is one of the major tasks today of the political scientist, the philosopher, the journalist, and the prophet: to give the people an image of changes in the international system which seem small enough to be feasible yet large enough to be successful. It is not useful to picture Utopias which seem utterly unattainable—this perhaps is the main difficulty with the World Federationists—even though the function of Utopias in providing a constant driving force in social dynamics should not be underestimated. The present situation, however, calls not for Utopia, but for political solutions. Indeed, one of our great difficulties today is that we have too many Utopias. We need to think, therefore, in terms of a world social contract: that is, a minimum bargain between the contending parties which will give the world a sufficient system change to relieve it from the intolerable burden which it now bears. This social contract does not even have to be explicit or contractual. It can begin by being tacit; indeed, one can argue that a world social contract already exists in a tacit embryo form. We can visualize perhaps the following five stages of development.

I. The stage of tacit contract. In systems which have an inherent instability, such as duopoly in the relations of firms, or a bipolar system of mutual deterrence in the relations of states, it is often possible to maintain a quasi-stable position for a long time through tacit contract: that is, through mutually consistent unilateral behavior on the part of each party. A quasi-stable position is like that of an egg on a golf tee—it is stable for small disturbances but not for large. For considerable periods of time, however, the disturbances may be small enough so that Humpty-Dumpty does not fall. Comes a slightly larger disturbance, however, and all the King's horses and men cannot put him together again. The international system under the Eisenhower administration exhibited this kind of quasi-stability. An important element in that stability was a tacit agreement between the United States and the Soviet Union to do nothing effective about civil defense. We agreed, in effect, that our civilian populations should be mutually exchanged as hostages, for we each had the power to destroy large numbers—at least half—of each other's civilians. This meant that the chance of deliberate nuclear war was very small, though the chance of accidental war was appreciable; indeed, the missiles almost went off on at least two occasions. A natural accident, such as a large meteor, or an electronic breakdown, or a social accident, such as a mad pilot, or a political accident, such as an unwise commitment to an irresponsible third party, could under these circumstances easily set off a mutual exchange of nuclear weapons, so that the system could not be regarded as more than a temporary expedient.

Another example of tacit contract was the mutual suspension of nuclear tests, recently broken by the Soviet Union. Here the fear, perhaps, of world opinion, and the fear also of the technical consequences of an uncontrolled race for technical development of weapons, created a temporary tacit agreement. We have had similar tacit agreements in regard to spheres of influence and intervention in third-party quarrels. The United States did not interfere in Hungary, nor the Soviet Union in Egypt during the Suez crisis. The Russians allowed themselves to be thrown out of the Congo, and are not threatening to be more than a nuisance in Cuba. The conflicts in Korea and Vietnam were temporarily settled by latitudinal partitions. The Arab-Israeli conflict does not become an arena of the cold war. All these represent systems of mutuality of conduct which might be classified as tacit agreement.

II. The fate of the tacit agreement on nuclear testing, and what looks like the impending fate of the tacit agreement on civil defense, is a testimony to the inherent instability of the tacit agreement in the long run. It is something like the gentleman's agreement in economic competition, which suffers from the defect that not all people are gentlemen. The danger is that in the absence of organization between contending parties their only means of communication is by a "threat system." A threat system, which is characteristic of unilateral national defense, is based on the proposition, "If you do something bad to me I will do something bad to you," by contrast with an exchange system, which is based on "If you do something good to me I will do something good to you." Both systems tend to lead to consummation, but whereas the consummation of exchange is an increase of "goods" the consummation of threats is an increase of "bads." War is mainly the result of the depreciation in the credibility of threats in the absence of their consummation; and hence a threat system has a basic instability built into it, which tacit contract may postpone but cannot ultimately avoid. The great problem, therefore, is how to get rid of threat systems. This, I suspect, happens historically mainly by their being overlaid with other systems of relationship—trade, communication, organization—until they fall so much to the bottom of the pile that they are no longer significant.

The essential instability of threat systems and the weakness of tacit agreements, therefore, make it highly desirable to pass into the second stage of formalized agreement, and the building of what might be called "peace-defending" organizational structures. The first of these obviously is an arms control organization designed at first perhaps only to limit the present arms race but capable of the ultimate hope of policing genuine disarmament.

We could begin, perhaps, with an organization for the prevention of accidental war. This will be a joint organization of the major armed forces of the world. Once this has been accomplished, a major system change is under way. It is the organizational disunity of the armed forces of the world which constitutes the real threat to humanity. If they were united they might threaten us with a great many disagreeable consequences but they would not threaten us with extinction. An arms control organization, therefore, would be the beginning of a very powerful social change. It would constitute the formal recognition of the fact that unilateral national defense is no longer possible. Once this initial break is made, system change may be expected to take place quite rapidly. It may be that we shall have to look forward to a substantial separation of the armed forces organization from the states which they are supposed to defend, and which they can no longer defend. Just as we solved the problem of religious wars by the separation of church and state, so we may be able to solve the problem of nuclear war by the separation of the armed forces from the state. The plain fact is that today the threat which the armed forces of the world present to their own civilian populations is much greater than any conflict among the nations. Arms control will be the beginning of the recognition of this social fact.

III. Arms control must move fairly rapidly into disarmament; otherwise it will be unstable. The organization of the world armed forces will be a loose and unstable one at first, and it will always threaten to break up. It may be, of course, that the major pressure towards disarmament will come from the economic side. Once the threat of war is removed by arms control and by organizational unity of the world armed forces, the economic burden of maintaining these monstrous establishments will seem intolerable, especially in view of the fact that it is the arms burden (equal to the total income of the poorest half of the human race!) which perhaps prevents the world from really tackling the problem of economic development and which condemns hundreds of millions of people and their descendants to live in misery. One looks forward, therefore, to the third stage of rapid and total disarmament, under the arms control organization. There are many difficult problems involved in this which have not been worked out and on which research desperately needs to be done. One research program is on the way at the moment on the broad problems of the economics of disarmament, conducted by Professor Emile Benoit of Columbia University. The United Nations is about to inaugurate a similar study. However, the organizational and social-psychological problems involved are very great and quite unprecedented. Growth is always much easier than decline and the problems of adjustment involved in a rapid decline in the world's armed forces still have to be faced. These problems, however, are difficult rather than insoluble.

IV. Even universal total disarmament, however, is not enough, for this too is likely to be unstable even though disarmament itself will reduce many of the sources of conflict, especially those which arise out of strategic considerations. It will not eliminate all conflicts by any means. In a world as divided as this, ideologically and economically, we may expect serious conflicts continually to arise. These conflicts will constantly present the temptation to the losing side to resort to violence and to redevelop organized armed forces. If disarmament is to be stable, therefore, there must be a system of conflict control. Conflict control is one of the essential functions of government. It is not, however, the only function. In thinking of world government, this is probably where we ought to begin. In the early stages it is more important to establish conflict control than to establish justice or to solve all social problems. Conflict control as a function of government has been inadequately studied and identified. This is perhaps because the study of conflict systems themselves is still in its infancy. However, this is a rapidly developing body of social science and one hopes that it may be possible in the not-too-distant future to develop a substantial body of knowledge on the identification and control of conflict systems. The problem, of course, is the identification of conflict processes in early stages before they become pathological. There are very difficult problems here in the definition of the pathology of conflict, as this, of course, goes very deep into our value systems. Conflict which is regarded as pathological by one person may not be so regarded by another. If, however, we regard violence as generally a sign of pathological conflict, we may be able to identify the processes of social dynamics which lead toward it, and we may therefore be able to interpose counterweights which will correct these processes. We may revert once more to the analogy of the car at the crossing. We need to develop both perception of dangers ahead and also organizations which can act as brakes. These processes have been fairly well worked out in industrial relations, where a whole profession of mediators and conciliators and personnel experts has come to being. There is no reason why these principles should not be applied in other fields of social life and especially to the conflict of states.

V. The last stage, of course, is true world government, capable not only of controlling conflict but of expressing and developing the common concerns and aims of mankind. At the moment this seems to be a long way off. Fortunately, the prevention of war does not depend, I think, on the establishment of full world government. If the stages of development which I have outlined can be pursued rapidly enough, war may be postponed for longer and longer periods until the postponement becomes indefinite by the establishment of a true world government. We must therefore find halfway houses and quarterway houses which are moderately habitable. We must not allow Utopian longings to deprive us of political bargains. The actual negotiation of the world social contract is going to be a long and arduous business. We need to put many more resources into this than we are now doing. Nevertheless, there is something here which can be done. There is a road which leads somewhere. If we are to break out of the apathy, irrationality, and despair which beset us, we must gain a vision of that road of escape and make at least one step along it. This is the great significance of the growing movement for peace research. Just as we no longer accept depressions as "acts of God," wholly unpredictable and uncontrollable, so we need no longer accept mass violence as unpredictable and uncontrollable. The fact that we cannot yet predict or control it should stir us to a great intellectual effort in this direction, for this way lies hope. The only unforgivable sin in the present crisis of mankind is despair.

NUCLEAR PROLIFERATION AND
RULES OF RETALIATION

by HERMAN KAHN

Nearly a decade has passed since any nation has announced an explicit decision to acquire nuclear weapons. Nuclear proliferation has been slow, at least by comparison with many of the pessimistic estimates made in the past, and some analysts expect that its pace will remain as slow in the next decade. Others take a very different view. They point out that the nuclear warheads and carriers are becoming—at least from the technological and economic points of view—ever more widely available, and they argue that, for this reason alone, rapid proliferation is much more likely in the next decade or two than in the past. India and Pakistan, Israel and Egypt, Brazil and Argentina, Sweden, Switzerland, Japan or West Germany, might not have to duplicate the efforts of France or China to acquire comparable nuclear capabilities. More important, it has become increasingly clear that quite rudimentary nuclear capabilities might satisfy the political, psychological and even strategic objectives of numerous potential "Nth" countries; it is not always necessary to overtake the superpowers. In short, as far as narrow military, technical and economic obstacles are concerned, proliferation in the coming decade or two might be unprecedentedly rapid. But focusing on military, technical, and economic issues alone is too narrow a view—precisely because these are not as constraining

Reprinted by permission of The Yale Law Journal Company and Fred B. Rothman & Company from *The Yale Law Journal*, Vol. 76, pp. 77-91.

This discussion is adapted from a Hudson Institute report prepared in collaboration with Carl Dibble. The ideas contained herein were first presented in a paper delivered to the Third International Arms Control Symposium, April 1966, and published in *Arms Control for the Sixties* (Princeton, N.J.: Van Nostrand, 1967), James E. Dougherty and John E. Lehman, Jr., eds.

as many thought. It would appear therefore that the political issues should be upgraded from important to dominant. Political analyses of such issues are, of course, inherently uncertain, at least in the medium and long run. Therefore, we will not be able to forecast reliably the future pace of nuclear proliferation. Yet two decades of slow proliferation do raise the hope that future proliferation may likewise be slow—perhaps even slower.

We should note that certain attitudes on nuclear issues are now widespread which were almost unheard of ten years ago, at least in general discussion. Policies aimed at dealing with nuclear proliferation should take some account of these. For example, ten years ago the strategic posture of the U.S. rested in large part on an ability and determination to initiate the use of nuclear weapons to thwart aggression. While this nuclear threat remains important in many respects, prevailing attitudes toward "first use" of nuclear weapons have changed considerably. The U.S. will probably adopt a virtual "no-first-use" policy—perhaps without making a deliberate decision to do so, and perhaps without even calculating all its results. Or again, while it was once believed that "escalation" would be more or less automatic and catastrophic, in the course of a mere five years we have come to believe that escalation might be deliberately controlled and perhaps even stopped or reversed. The notion of a U.S.-Soviet "spasm war," in which all weapons were fired immediately for maximum destructiveness, has ceased to guide military planning in the U.S. (and, it seems likely, in the Soviet Union, France, and elsewhere —despite much rhetoric to the contrary). A more or less implicit sense of appositeness about the use of nuclear threats and attacks has developed. All of this may eventually force some extensive alterations in deterrent strategy, arms-control thinking, and foreign policy in general; and, in turn, all these changes will affect the incentives of various nations to acquire nuclear weapons.

Even very extensive proliferation does not *necessarily* make worldwide holocaust inevitable—or even particularly likely. This is true even if twenty to thirty independent states have nuclear weapons of various kinds with various systems of command and control. Imagine, for example, that Che Guevara had two nuclear missiles available to him at some date in the near future. He has said that if this situation came about, he would be unable to restrain himself from launching the missiles at New York City and Washington. In fact, he would probably be considerably less likely to make such a statement, let alone carry it out, if he actually controlled two missiles. But imagine, hypothetically, that he had no sense of responsibility for the country within which he was operating at the time, and that nothing else restrained him from launching the missiles. The United States would probably retaliate in some dramatic and decisive fashion, and other small countries with nuclear systems would be induced as a result to take a second look at their arrangements for controlling nuclear weapons. Although these events would entail immense suffering and destruction, human life would go on. The general pattern of international relations might even continue much as before, and the United States would recuperate rapidly from the damage that the two missiles had inflicted.

Even widespread proliferation might not increase the likelihood of a catastrophic U.S.-Soviet thermonuclear war very much, if at all. Doubtless the probability of some nuclear use would increase, but even this might be very limited. In the first place, the kind of incident imagined above is not likely to happen more than once, if ever. And if proliferation continues, the attitudes about "first use," the risks of unsafe techniques, disproportionate response, etc., which now inhibit the United States and the United Kingdom might inhibit all or most of the other nuclear states as well.[1] All nations with large forces and most nations with small nuclear forces might acquire some capability for measured, controlled and deliberate response. Just as "our military and civilian leaders are unanimous," according to a recent Presidential address,[2] "in their conviction that our armed might is and always must be so controlled as to permit measured response in whatever crises may confront us," so the leaders of other nations would be likely to discover a similar need for controlled capabilities and flexible strategies. An international system in which there had been widespread proliferation might thus be much less accident-

---

[1] A fairly wide range of nuclear uses and the possible aftereffects of the situations are considered by *Edmund O. Stillman, Predicting the International Consequences of the Introduction of Nuclear Weapons* (Hudson Institute Pub. No. HI-621-RR, Jan. 26, 1966).

[2] *The New York Times*, Jan. 11, 1965, p. 16.

prone and aggression-prone than many people have estimated in the past. While we cannot, of course, make definite or reliable forecasts on these inherently uncertain matters, we can say that there are reasons to believe that although proliferation increases many dangers, it alleviates others. In any case one cannot prove that it would necessarily increase the probability of a very serious catastrophe for the U.S. or for mankind.

The argument can even be made that nuclear weapons make possible a "fair" solution to the problem of national defense, since one country does not have to buy its security at the expense of its neighbor's; in the past, by contrast, even if a country had obtained security by only a moderate superiority, it could usually hope to use that moderate superiority to overwhelm its opponent without suffering catastrophic losses. Any country with a properly designed nuclear deterrent system can hope (so the argument goes) to be strong enough for deterrence and yet not strong enough to execute a disarming first strike against another nuclear power. Thus one country's strength need not necessarily mean its neighbor's weakness—deterrence, unlike superiority, can be both effective and symmetric. Thus one might conclude with Pierre Gallois, that "the further we advance in the ballistic-nuclear age, the more possible it becomes to outlaw violence, even if the aggressor nation is stronger and more richly supplied with combat means than the nation it threatens."[3]

Yet despite all these arguments, we cannot be confident either that the future pace of proliferation will be slow or that its consequences would not be very serious.[4] In fact, analysts, scholars, policy makers, and men in the street agree not only that it is crucial to decrease the likelihood of nuclear use by those who possess nuclear weapons but also that the spread of those weapons to other countries is itself a source of danger. While all of these people may be wrong, I share their judgment at least in its less apocalyptic form. I will assume in this paper that the reader shares my concern about the danger of future proliferation and wants to improve even the current situation—perhaps by trying

---

[3] Pierre Gallois, *The Balance of Terror: Strategy for the Nuclear Age* (Boston: Houghton Mifflin and Co., 1961), p. 113.

[4] See Kahn, *On Escalation: Metaphors and Scenarios*, pp. 97–101 (Praeger, 1965), for a discussion of the pros and cons of nuclear proliferation.

to exploit some of the seemingly "desirable" characteristics of the nuclear trends mentioned above, since there may be much wisdom in some of the developments that have occurred or are now occurring.

While there is a wide consensus on the need to inhibit further nuclear spread or use, there are surprisingly few long-term policy ideas on how to do this. A reasonably complete list might go as follows:

1. Attempt, at least temporarily, to prolong the current situation, hoping meanwhile for desirable marginal or far-reaching changes.
2. If the status quo must change, attempt to make it evolve so slowly that much time will be bought and then hope that this time will allow other developments to occur (these other developments are rarely specified).
3. De-emphasize or ignore all long-range problems and deal with each issue as it comes up in a pragmatic and *ad hoc* fashion.
4. Accept the fact that proliferation will occur and try to live with this "inevitable" large-scale diffusion of nuclear weapons—again in an *ad hoc* or pragmatic fashion.
5. Work for universal and comprehensive arms-control systems or world government.

It may well be that this list covers the total range of practical policies and that one need not look for anything else; but this seems most doubtful. I have occasionally argued[5] that serious changes in the international system seem most likely to be made as a result of an intense crisis or a small or large nuclear war. I have also argued that it should be a major objective of negotiations to lay the groundwork for the constructive exploitation of such crises, or of small or large wars. It seems most unlikely that the world will be sufficiently motivated to work out a safer international system as a result of peaceful negotiations around a conference table. But national plans and international negotiations may lay a basis for action in the conditions of changed power relationships and nuclear attitudes which might be the immediate aftermath of some violent world experience or dramatic crisis.

I still believe in the value of such preparations. But some *ad*

---

[5] See, *e.g.*, Kahn, *Thinking About the Unthinkable*, pp. 153–58 (Horizon, 1962).

hoc and pragmatic but important *peaceful* changes could be made in the *current* institutional and international environment. These changes could prove large enough to make important differences and yet remain small enough to be achievable.

I will begin by proposing a set of criteria that any long-range "anti-nuclear" policy should try to meet. A description and discussion of such criteria is in itself an important part of the proposed investigation[6]—possibly more important than a debate on the specific proposals. They could, for example, help clear the air for proposals quite different from the ones suggested but which are—again—either more practical or more far-reaching than many which are currently discussed; in any case they attempt to focus attention on the main issues and long-range nuclear issues in general.

Fifteen Criteria for a Long-Range Anti-Nuclear Policy[7]

The fifteen criteria listed below are, of course, by no means holy writ, nor are they the only ones that could be listed, but they are at least specific examples of what a policy for the nuclear age should accomplish.

1. It should make nuclear weapons be and seem to be practically almost unusable—either politically or physically.
2. In particular, it should be likely to prevent nuclear intimidation.
3. It should decrease the prestige associated with owning nuclear weapons.
4. It should not require Italy, Japan, India, West Germany, or France to accept an *invidiously* inferior status or an *unnecessarily* precarious security position.
5. Yet if nuclear weapons are used, it should limit the damage that is done (it should not rely on deterrence working perfectly).
6. Thus, it should be competent to withstand crises, small and even large conventional wars, and some breaches and violations.
7. It should limit proliferation.

---

[6] For a discussion of these criteria see Herman Kahn and Carl Dibble, "Criteria for Long-Range Nuclear Control Policies," 55 *California Law Review* 473 (1967).

[7] The term "anti-nuclear" is used deliberately, in recognition that some readers would find it a suitable description of the ideas advanced. The term does make a crude sort of point. And there seems no other acceptable term: something like "nuclear defunctionalization" might be a little more precise, but it seems to be objectionable on stylistic grounds.

8. It should not be aimed at perpetuating U.S. status, power, and obligations, though it should be conservative in "using" U.S. prestige, morale, and influence.

9. It should not have been foreclosed or embarrassed by prior commitments of the U.S.

10. It should be responsive to national interests, sentiments, and doctrines, and should be negotiable.

11. It should be thoroughly planned so as to be able to become an object of "sudden diplomacy."

12. It should be presented as a political ("above the melee" of normal diplomatic in-fighting and posturing).

13. It should improve current international standards, but should not require thoroughgoing reform.

14. It should be potentially permanent (not necessarily a transitional arrangement) and yet flexible enough to constitute a hedge against events and opportunities in both negotiation and operation.

15. While not designed as a transitional arrangement, it should allow for major or basic developments and changes.

The most telling objection to this list may be not that it is idiosyncratic but that it is too stringent and therefore impractical. Perhaps no policy can meet all of these criteria satisfactorily, but I believe it important to go as far as one can toward meeting them; and the policy I am about to propose attempts to do so. And even if these criteria are idiosyncratic or impractical, the list is intended to be rounded, non-partisan, provocative (though not unnecessarily so) and of help to skeptics as well as to believers.

One Basic Proposal

Can nuclear weapons be made so limited in their usefulness that, by and large, they will have relatively little effect on the conduct of international affairs, even in relatively intense crises; moreover can this be done in a manner that improves U.S. security and the international order? An affirmative answer to this question would be a good beginning to meeting the suggested criteria for an anti-nuclear policy. The issue, therefore, is not simply whether nuclear weapons will spread, or increase in number. Rather we should be more concerned with the actual and perceived potential usefulness of these weapons, the prestige attached to their possession, their attributes of legitimacy, danger or terror, the felt necessity of various nations in the world to acquire them, and the special role they play in various national policies and postures in normal and crisis situations.

As a first approach imagine a world system in which each nation agrees and expects that nuclear weapons cannot be used legitimately except, possibly, for strict and proportionate retaliation. Each nuclear nation would have adopted a no-first-use policy and a *credible* policy of responding in commensurate kind and degree if nuclear weapons were used against it. Non-nuclear nations could have made arrangements to have such proportionate retaliation carried out by others. If these expectations seemed reliable and credible, nations could not credibly threaten to use nuclear weapons.

An objective, which could either supplement and complement such a system or be independent of it, would be to restrict legitimate possession (or further acquisition) of nuclear weapons to international organizations—nuclear defense alliances in Western Europe, East Europe, Asia, Latin America, North America, the North Atlantic, or even supra-regional nuclear defense organizations.

A third objective might be to establish nuclear-free zones, particularly in those areas of the world which do not currently seem likely to be the scene of direct nuclear confrontations, *e.g.*, Latin America, Africa, the Middle East, parts of Asia, possibly the rim of Europe outside the Western European Union.

All of these objectives are combined in the following long-term "anti-nuclear" policy:

1. A return to the law of (nuclear) *lex talionis*, which would be defined not only by the rule of *at least* an eye for an eye but also (at least between equals) by the further rule of *at most* an eye for an eye; or, to put it in current jargon, no escalation including *no-first-use*.[8]

---

[8] One might modify this rule to distinguish between *interior* escalation (first use of nuclear weapons on *one's own* sovereign territory) which does not justify any nuclear reprisal, and *exterior* escalation (first use of nuclear weapons on an *opponent's* territory) which does justify reprisal against the homeland. While there are grave objections to trying to make interior escalation legitimate (it would make possession of nuclear weapons more useful and therefore more attractive) it may be necessary to accept some such compromise to satisfy some European opinion.

2. A European nuclear retaliatory force whose sole purpose is to enforce the *lex talionis* in Europe. This might take the form of a European Strategic Defense Community based upon Western European Union, or it might take some other form. It might not be a Community, or it might be a Community which did not include the United Kingdom, or France, or West Germany.

3. An Asian Nuclear Defense Organization which would enforce the *lex talionis* in Asia. Probably this could not or should not take the form of an independent Strategic Defense Community, at least initially. Whatever form it did take, the nuclear defense organization might initially be based upon the United States, Japan, Australia, New Zealand, the Philippines, India, Pakistan, and perhaps Great Britain. It could also exclude some of these states, at least initially, and it would probably be—to some great degree—under the effective and perhaps legal control of the United States or perhaps Japan, India and/or Australia.

4. Nuclear-free zones in Latin America, Africa, Eastern Europe, the Middle East, and elsewhere, developed (with modification) from current proposals.

5. A more or less explicit (and perhaps interim) United States (and Soviet Union?) "talionic" guarantee to various non-nuclear areas, which could vary for different areas, and which could be established in terms of likely, minimum, or maximum responses to nuclear provocations as appropriate to each area. The nature of the guarantee might explicitly include provision for change over time.

6. For the denuclearized zones, a long-term program might simultaneously be developed for a non-aligned multilateral nuclear defense organization to play the same role for denuclearized zones as the European and Asian nuclear forces play for their own areas, thus possibly eventually replacing United States (and Soviet Union?) talionic guarantees.

7. Finally, a universal agency could be developed to replace, supplement, complement or absorb the various regional and national forces.

These arrangements probably seem Utopian. But if completely successful, they would limit nuclear weapons to the U.S., the Soviet Union, one international European organization, one international Asian organization, China, and possibly certain other international organizations. The credibility of the talionic response to a nuclear provocation—and therefore the deterrence of provocation—should be high. Not only should nuclear intimidation be difficult but with time even the mere thought of it might be eliminated from crises as well as day-to-day international relations. Yet, if deterrence failed and weapons were used, the result would not inevitably be Armageddon but (assuming expectations are fulfilled) whatever destruction was entailed in the tit-for-tat response. Then conceivably, there would be a return to some previous or *ad hoc* status quo. The system could conceivably withstand several failures of deterrence and many other intense crises. Except for participation in the Asian nuclear force, this system would immediately reduce U.S. obligations; eventually it would reduce them very sharply. While the United States would be relegated to a status of first among equals, in the long run this would probably be beneficial.

The *lex talionis* principle amounts to a return to the nineteenth-century law of reprisal or the practice of primitive communities —particularly ones in which there are no reliable means for maintaining order. By itself, it is therefore not an obviously Utopian notion. It would also seem to provide a clear improvement over a situation in which "spasm" or other all-out war occurs after the nuclear threshold has been crossed. Its damage-limiting potentialities might be exceedingly valuable, especially if alternative means to limit damage prove to be unavailable or unreliable.

In such a tit-for-tat situation (as in most current peace-keeping situations), one does not usually ask who is right. The objective is to bring the violence to a conclusion—"to stop the fighting as soon as possible"—and to create precedents that prevent recurrence. It should be obvious that it would be very difficult to bring violence between equals to a conclusion as long as there is clearly an open-ended account in which one side has done much more damage than the other. Therefore, there almost has to be some sort of "equitable," proportionate retaliation before peace can be restored. This is of course exactly the technique adopted by primitive tribes and for much the same reason—they wish to restrain violence, but they have no police and judicial system with which to do it. Of course, tit-for-tat occasionally results in long-continued blood feuds—in other words, it may generate further violence. But more often than not it brings equilibrium. It is only because, as a system, it is more likely to support and restore peace than not that it has been so popular in primitive communities. It may still be far better in supplementing the usual system than anything else that is actually available to the international system today.

In this regard it is worth noting that most intelligent laymen in the U.S. now readily understand such points as the following:[9] (1) if a small number of nuclear weapons are exploded in a country like the U.S., the President is more likely to ask questions than to press every button; (2) after his questions are answered and he understands the situation, he is still unlikely to lose all control of himself and launch a suicidal "spasm" response; rather he is likely to ask what is in the national interest of the United States, even if—and perhaps especially because—the situation is agonizing and emotion-filled; (3) the national interest may require a deliberate, measured, controlled and selective response; (4) such a response could occur as a tit-for-tat or other reciprocal retaliation; (5) as a result, millions of people could be killed and yet the war could come to a close with most of the weapons on every side remaining unfired.

Many analysts see the relatively rigid tit-for-tat procedure as a retrogression from modern strategic thinking; it seems to buck the current trend of emphasizing complete flexibility, control, *ad hoc* calculation and a certain amount of deliberate uncertainty about the response. My proposal does tend toward fixed response, indeed making it almost deterministic, but in a fashion which is quite different from the old massive retaliation doctrine. Rather than prescribing a simple spasm response I am arguing for a response which is never larger than the situation requires.

Thus, surprisingly enough, *lex talionis* arrangements would be basically consistent with current U.S. policy and with emerging political-strategic doctrine. They would extend, make explicit, and seek to institutionalize more generally the profound disposition toward proportionate response now widely held among American officials. Furthermore, this disposition, which certainly exists in other countries as well, is quite likely to affect the contingency policy of other nuclear powers, whether they realize it ahead of

---

[9] See Kahn, *op. cit. supra* note 4, at 185–86 & n. It is interesting to note that much current fiction as well as scholarly analysis has used proportionate response as being the only plausible response in situations in which the only other apparent alternatives are holocaust or an effectively passive acceptance of an extreme provocation.

time or not. In other words, these proposals are not "Utopian" in the sense of being based on a far-fetched principle; their Utopian character, if any, lies in requiring an unlikely degree of success in institutionalizing already well-known, sound, and comparatively desirable principles.

Of course, nuclear powers—particularly small ones—argue that a total spasm response is all that they can afford, and any capability for responding in corresponding degree and kind would dangerously decrease the value of their nuclear arsenal as a deterrent. Yet eventually they will almost surely have to propose plans for the contingency in which deterrence fails. Under their present "spasm" doctrine, they are now faced with the unacceptable choice between surrender and nightmarish calamity. Certainly at the "moment of truth" even small nuclear powers are likely to search desperately for alternatives to surrender or holocaust—and they might feel they need advance contingency plans and even declaratory policies that reflect the realistic situation, in order to limit the maximum damage that might occur and to enhance the credibility of their deterrent.

None of the above is certain, of course. But once concrete situations are envisaged, and sequences of events and calculations are spelled out, it is far from probable that a spasm response to nuclear attack will seem preferable. Rather what has now become layman's common sense might suggest basic principles and clearly reasonable assumptions on which to base long-range policy. The nuclear control arrangements envisaged do not presuppose that all nuclear powers will necessarily act calculatingly, and in a measured and controlled manner. But deliberate, measured and controlled behavior can be made more certain by cultivating the disposition to act that way on a world-wide scale (rather than only in the U.S.) and by institutionalizing the principles that seem to be implied in that disposition.

Any proposal that tries to do this will, of course, have to meet many particular objections and difficulties.

Some Basic Assumptions and Concepts

There are certain objections which could reasonably be made on the level of principle, or basic assumption, before going into any discussion of detailed feasibility. For example, the idea of "an eye for an eye" might be manifestly unjust when it actually means "a city for a city," and when the city attacked in retaliation is inhabited by persons with no special responsibility for the initial nuclear attack. Serious ethical and political questions are raised, which depend in part upon empirical, analytical and technical considerations, such as what response is proportionate or whether a talionic doctrine would be more unjust or unstable than alternative doctrines. The injustice and other defects of inflexible tit-for-tat must be compared with the possible infeasibility, risk, or even immorality of counterforce, massive city attacks, and other more or less flexible, ambiguous, or unpredictable doctrines as well as the possible consequences of not retaliating at all or not retaliating in a manner that deters further attack. None of these questions can be answered simply or dogmatically. In any case some allowance might be made for responsible authorities to avoid at least the most rigid kind of "city-for-city" retaliation.

The proposed European nuclear retaliatory force would differ in important ways from the multilateral force that was proposed by the U.S. and from the British proposal for an Atlantic nuclear force. I envisage a truly independent nuclear deterrent for Europe, which, while possessing a credible tit-for-tat response, would not permit any member-nation to launch a spasm retaliatory response. A European nuclear defense organization designed in this way would probably represent an increase, rather than a decrease, in the kinds of independence that European nations most desire. Moreover, distinguishing between talionic and escalatory responses lets us solve the problems of the "trigger" (who can launch nuclear weapons) and the safety catch (who can forbid launching). One over-simplified but illustrative possibility would be for everyone to have his finger on the trigger for talionic responses and his finger on the safety-catch for escalation responses, *i.e.*, any nation could authorize a proper tit-for-tat retaliation or forbid excessive escalation. More complex and practical arrangements are discussed in the forthcoming report.

One assumption underlying this proposal is that Western Europe is a "pluralistic security community"—that within the Western European subsystem war is almost literally "unthinkable" and the threat of physical coercion plays almost no role in relations among the nations within the community (though other kinds of threats are occasionally made). Thus no provisions are necessary for the protection of Western European nations from each other (though, in fact, the force could be adapted to such a purpose, if necessary; but this is not envisioned as an important purpose of the force). It is also assumed that Western Europe needs independent power mainly because it does not want to continue to be a protectorate of the United States, and not because it seeks to advance any aggressive designs against Communist or other nations.

The Asian countries do not constitute a pluralistic security community and, at least without the United States, there is not the same primarily bipolar (though also polycentric) international alignment as exists between Western and Eastern (including Soviet) Europe. Therefore an Asian nuclear defense organization would have to be different, perhaps more tentative and flexible, and probably with greater U.S. involvement. There might be a special role for Japan and India. Japan in particular seems likely to develop into the dominant non-Communist power in Asia (and it may become more powerful than China).

As time passes, an Asian force would have to develop according to the special requirements of the Asian area. It might ultimately become a true collective security force whose purpose would be to furnish security against aggression by its own members as well as by other nations. It is premature to try to specify details, though it may be noted that in contrast to the European situation, the two major non-Communist Asian nations, Japan and India, are not unlikely in the future to desire to fulfill national nuclear aspirations within the framework of a regional force, and this expectation is one of the bases (though not an essential one) on which the proposal is built.

Finally, it should be pointed out that while the proposal may seem to have many bizarre aspects, most of the bizarreness derives from coping with an unprecedented situation in which there has not been as much thought about long-range policies and prospects as there might have been. Thus the discussion in this paper will have achieved one important objective if it simply takes the edge off the bizarreness, *i.e.*, if it makes it easier to discuss the problem and to weigh various alternative policies on their merits, rather than on relatively thoughtless (though often deeply held) emotional reactions.

There is, of course, some reason for a quick emotional rejection of such proposals, since to consider them could create problems. Thus they could arouse ambitions for the acquisition of nuclear weapons in nations which are currently more or less satisfied with the status quo (in particular it may increase West German and Japanese nuclear ambitions). These proposals, if accepted, would bring many nations closer to nuclear weapons than they are today. Even the possibility that they may be realized in some form or other can create problems. For example, the so-called "MLF clause" (*i.e.*, the U.S. insistence that any anti-proliferation treaty allow for the creation of a multi-national force which absorbs one of the current nuclear forces) seems to be a major block in the negotiation of the current non-proliferation treaty. The possibility of an Asian nuclear force might create similar or greater difficulties. (But the analogy is not completely relevant. The major objection to the MLF clause comes from the Soviet Union, which is clearly worried about West Germany. Furthermore, West Germany's nuclear ambitions, if any, do not have the approval or support of any of its allies on the Continent. In this respect Japan seems to be in a much different position both vis-à-vis the Soviet Union and its own allies.)

Several important issues remain to be considered. For example, what would happen if the various multilateral or other nuclear forces were dissolved? Or if a nuclear organization allowed too much authority to decision makers who might feel substantially more independent of the "political authorities" than would representatives of a nation-state? There are also many possible Soviet reactions to the proposals, and I have not considered any of the pressures or problems that they might create if the proposal were seriously advanced. And nations in non-nuclear regions might object to their status once they see the real possibility of regional (or even national) deterrents working. Eventually they in turn may wish to have a regional deterrent of their own, or they might seek security in some other international organization. The crea-tion of a European Strategic Defense Community would probably increase pressures toward such a solution. And, as already men-tioned, my proposal might increase desire for national acquisition of nuclear status in Italy and West Germany. All of the above points and objections must be conceded, and others as well. Nevertheless it seems clear that there is insufficient thought in the government and in scholarly communities about the possibilities or implications of:

1. The use of *lex talionis* as a guiding principle.
2. The distinction between interior and exterior escalation or between talionic responses and escalation. (Neither of these distinctions seems to have been considered in relation to the MLF, yet they might make all the difference as to its role and to the "trigger" and "safety-catch" problems.)
3. The need for modifying U.S. guarantees if (or as) the Soviet Union acquires a reliable and large second-strike capability.
4. Coming to grips with a situation of increasing multipolarity in which the United States and the Soviet Union will not dominate international relations anywhere near as much as they still do, and in which guarantees which have any hint of "protectorate" about them will be less acceptable.
5. The need to divorce current nuclear arrangements from the political legacy of World War II. The victors must recognize that they cannot keep the nuclear club an exclusive victor's club.
6. The possibility of various *ad hoc* regional or other special institutions and practices that lie between the usual meliorative and comprehensive proposals, particularly suggestions that may exploit or deal with concepts suggested above.
7. The fifteen general criteria for a long-range anti-nuclear policy, listed above.

TOMORROW'S AGENDA

by ZBIGNIEW BRZEZINSKI

Each generation, it is often said, fights the wars of the preceding generation without knowing it. During the nineteenth century men died believing in the cause of royalty or republicanism. In reality, much of their sacrifice was rendered on the altar of the new nationalism. During the twentieth century men fought on behalf of nationalism. Yet the wars they fought were also engendered by dislocations in world markets and by social revolution stimulated by the coming of the industrial age.

Today, many Americans—and certainly most Communists—tend to see international conflict primarily in terms of the cold-war struggle between democracy and Communism. Inadvertently, some Americans thus accept, and project on the international scene, the basic Marxist-Leninist assumption that the decisive conflict of our age concerns the internal character of property relationships and the political organization of society, viewed in terms of the initial impact of the industrial revolution.

Yet these are no longer the basic issues facing mankind. The fundamental dilemmas to which we must respond are quite different and they cannot be analyzed properly in terms of the widely-accepted dichotomy of Western democracy versus totalitarian Communism. In the second half of the twentieth century the developed nations, given new scientific and social developments, will face a real threat to the continued existence of man as a spontaneous, instinctive, rather autonomous and even somewhat mysterious being; the less developed countries, because of overpopulation, economic backwardness and potential political disorder, will be challenged by a fundamental crisis of survival

"Tomorrow's Agenda," by Zbigniew Brzezinski. Reprinted by special permission from *Foreign Affairs* (July, 1966). Copyright © 1966, by the Council on Foreign Relations, Inc., New York.

of organized society. Responding to these twin challenges will require a basic reordering of our perspectives.

II

This is not to say that the cold war no longer exists, or that the United States should opt out of it. That conflict continues and it still dominates international affairs, largely because the Communist states, although now in different ways, still subscribe to the apocalyptic belief that they are riding the crest of the future and that the world is destined to become Communist. In China this belief is proclaimed with ringing militancy, though it is not matched by action. The Soviet Union has muted its verbal militancy but still abets and encourages Communist efforts to gain political control over other societies. The Communist powers remain militant because of the vested interest of their bureaucratic élites in the dogmatic commitment to a utopian and universalist ideology derived from the nineteenth-century notion that the industrial revolution would follow a uniform global pattern.

The cold war thus continues, but it is no longer a "real" conflict in the sense that the issues involved are no longer historically relevant. The West has long since abandoned whatever hopes it had of "rolling back" Communism—and those hopes were neither very widespread nor ever translated into a systematic and persistent policy. Today, the predominant Western attitude is that Communism will gradually moderate itself, eventually approximating social democracy. That hope is often mixed with a strong dose of wishful thinking; even relatively minor changes in the Soviet Union, such as the Liberman reforms, are hailed as a turn by the Kremlin toward capitalism. Chinese Communism is seen as a more retarded phenomenon, but by and large the predominant expectation seems to be that after Mao's death China will follow the Soviet evolutionary path.

Accordingly, the Western posture toward Communism is not one of crusading militancy. The West does not expect to dismantle the existing social-political organization of the Communist states, but rather relies primarily on the erosive effects of time and the pressures for change within the Communist states themselves. It therefore does not pose a direct threat to the survival of Communism. Of course, the very existence of thriving Western societies challenges Communist ideology, and specific conflicts of interest between particular Western and Eastern powers can be represented by Communist ideologues as involving an inveterate desire to destroy Communism altogether. But this ideological attitude is more revealing about the persistence of certain Communist myths than about the realities of international politics.

Even more important to the argument that the East-West conflict no longer touches on the "real" issues of the second half of the twentieth century is the growing evidence that Communism itself has exhausted its revolutionary potential and that its further major expansion is unlikely. Communism clearly will not take over any advanced Western society. The Communist parties there are decaying and desperately seeking social anchorage. Some, like the Italian, see salvation in opening an "ecumenical" dialogue with the Catholics; some, like the French, seek a common front with the Socialists. In almost all cases, the process involves profound revision along social-democratic lines and an erosion of the revolutionary Leninist tradition. Nowhere in the developed world is there any evidence that a Communist party with a program modeled on the Soviet experience would stand the slightest chance of making an effective popular and electoral appeal. It could only do so by "out-social-democratizing" the Social Democrats.

Moreover, on the level of the direct confrontation, the Soviet Union learned most painfully in October 1962 that it is still hopelessly outclassed by the United States as a military power. This asymmetry is not likely to be altered in the near future. The expectation of economically surpassing the United States by 1970, so boldly proclaimed just a few years ago by the Soviet leadership, has now given way to recognition of the fact that for a long time to come the Soviet Union will remain a second-class economic power, with major shortages in food and consumer production. Rising nationality tensions in the Soviet Union—which may soon assume major proportions—are likely to limit further the Soviet capacity for playing a very assertive role in the world.

In the Third World, the evidence is not so clear-cut, but recent developments there also suggest that the cold war is losing its external and internal relevance. The days of posturing and the grandiloquent, non-aligned internationalism of Sukarno, Nkrumah and others are giving way to inward-oriented, non-aligned nationalism, concerned primarily with internal economic development. The new élites, particularly the younger generation of engineers, professionals, doctors, are preoccupied with tackling the social-economic problems of their countries and extremely suspicious of solutions which imply some ideological short-cut to social well-being. They advocate programs specifically designed for their own needs, and capital investment—not ideology—is what really interests them. The fate of Communists in Ghana, Indonesia, Algeria and Egypt shows how utopianism is giving way to pragmatic nationalism.

This is not to say that the Third World has passed its crisis point—far from it, as will be argued below. But its future is not likely to be defined in terms of cold-war issues as we have known them during the last twenty years, and particularly not in terms of the Communist conception of the historical progression of mankind toward a Communist form of society.

III

The new issues that constitute the underlying reality of international politics today stem from a fundamental revolution in the more advanced countries of man's relationship to society (both social and political) and from a basic reordering of the international system into states that are developed and underdeveloped, increasingly affluent and impoverished, overwhelmingly powerful and relatively impotent. The first poses a challenge to the individual being; the second, to the survival of organized society. It would be disastrous if in the nuclear age statesmen responded to these twin challenges in terms of old conflicts that are no longer relevant.

The social revolution already in progress in the more developed states—above all in America—is likely to be shaped by the widespread adoption of automation and cybernation for social and economic purposes, and by the application of specialized sciences such as biochemistry and molecular biology to the genetic and personal development of man. Man's environment and man himself will more and more be subject to purposive control and manipulation. The consequence will be a fundamental transformation of our society.

Our concepts of work and leisure will in all probability undergo a basic reversal. Within a mere few decades leisure may become a burden while creative work will be a privilege increasingly restricted to the gifted few. The relationship between employment and way of life will then have to be revised. The concepts of retirement and of unemployment will have to be readjusted to the new realities of an increasingly automated economy. This will bring about basic changes in the social functions performed by trade unions—which may object to further reductions in the work-week—and by governmental welfare arrangements. The clearly defined relationship between earning capacity and consumption will also be blurred, with perhaps a need to establish arbitrary standards to assure a minimum level of consumption.

In some ways even more far-reaching will be the changes affecting the individual himself. How will we preserve the integrity and freedom of man as an individual? As a physical being he will become more malleable, given the trends in medical sciences. As a personality, he will become increasingly subject to external manipulation, capable eventually of altering his behavior, his intelligence, his psychological state, his sexual life—in effect, himself. As man approaches the stage where he can "program" himself as he now programs his computer, he may find himself increasingly denatured. The simultaneous weakening of religious belief may create both stress and emptiness. In some respects the alienated anti-Viet Nam war demonstrators are a portent of things to come. Their attitude as well as their personal behavior is a manifestation of a psychological crisis inherent in modern society. Viet Nam provides an outlet for basic cravings and fears, and if that issue did not exist, some other one would provide an excuse for the expression of personal and political alienation.

Cumulatively, these social and individual changes—many of which will make for a better life—may present a potent challenge to the relevancy and effective operation of our democratic processes. Our institutions are based on the belief that man can and should govern himself. Yet the problems that are likely to dominate our lives in the decades to come may creep upon us without attracting sufficient advance notice and may not fit into the established modes of our political dialogue. The issues that should increasingly agitate the citizen will have little in common with variants of welfare democracy or dictatorial Communism. Rather, the concerned citizen will have to take a stand on such questions as the form, organization and degree of permissible social control in providing for mass leisure; the character of education for a society in which a great many will not need their education for employment because much of the labor will be taken over by machines; the scope of social welfare in conditions which increasingly assume relative well-being for all; the psychological consequences of seemingly purposeless lives, with the consequent possibility of widespread individual and social malaise; the source of ultimate decision concerning the sex, personality and even the intelligence of one's own offspring; the integration on a national and even international basis of weather and climate controls.

These issues, to be sure, will still involve and perhaps even give new urgency to the old dilemmas of large versus small-scale social organization, of central versus local government, or of a proper balance between social responsibility and individual autonomy. The point, however, is that the discussion of them will require an entirely new frame of reference and perhaps even major changes in the political structure of our society. Neither the discussion nor the possible reforms—if they are to have meaning—can have much in common with the traditional concepts that still shape our domestic and external perspectives.

The problem is different, but no less urgent, with respect to the Third World. Present trends suggest that the next several decades may see a widening gap between the developed societies and the underdeveloped ones, not only in their ways of life but perhaps even in their perceptions of the meaning of life itself. If it is true that the developed societies—America first of all, but Europe and Russia in its wake—are about to undergo a major societal change, the chances are that the profound differences between them and the Third World will be further accentuated.

At the same time, the limited capacity of the new nations to deal with their problems of unemployment, overpopulation and even starvation may create conditions of chaos and contribute to a state of international anarchy. The widening gap between the two cultures and the growing frustration and hatred among the have-nots for the haves could also contribute to a mixture of racial populism, nationalism and international anarchism—the projection abroad of a nihilistic mood like that of the anarchists of some decades ago.

It could be argued that this threat to international stability will be minimized by the continuing revolution in weaponry that is contributing to the gap between the few powerful nations and the others, and certainly between the industrially advanced nations and the underdeveloped ones. A RAND Corporation study ("Report on a Long-Range Forecasting Study" by T. J. Gordon and O. Helmer, September, 1964) itemizes likely weapons developments in the next few decades. They range from biochemical devices, orbiting weapons systems, directed-energy weapons and terminal air-launched anti-missile defenses to the mass-hypnotic influencing of enemy forces and the use of domesticated dolphins for anti-submarine reconnaissance! Allowing for a certain amount of military-science fictionalizing, the basic pattern is none the less one of increasing disproportion of power among nation-states.

However, instability in the Third World can easily affect relations among the developed nations, reviving expectations rooted in otherwise fading ideological assumptions. Moreover, the asymmetry of power does not preclude nuclear proliferation among the weak, and perhaps the eventual use of nuclear weapons in their own conflicts. Finally, instability and hatred for the rich among the poor, and the irresistible temptation to the rich to engage in tactical manipulation of these conditions, will further impede any effort to come to grips with the basic problems of the Third World, thus perpetuating and aggravating the imbalance.

The governing ideologies of the principal developed states simply do not provide adequate guidelines for meeting these challenges. Unlike the past, when social change was slow enough to permit concomitant adjustments in man's outlook, today's pace of change is so fast that contemporary ideologies can hardly adapt to—even less anticipate—the problems of tomorrow. We are thus witnessing the spectacle of several major ideologies struggling to encompass the implications of situations for which their systems of thought have made little or no allowance. Ideology is becoming a conservative and not a revolutionary force. The end of ideology may not yet be at hand, but the relevance of several ideologies seems to be ending.

Soviet Communism, for one, has become a sterile and conservative dogma. The Party is a brake on social progress and its response to many social dilemmas, such as alienation or anti-semitism or delinquency, has been to pretend that they do not exist. The Catholic Church, having taken the historic step toward ecumenism in respect to religious doctrine, has yet to face the reality of overpopulation. Pragmatic American liberalism is finding it difficult to combine the responsibility inherent in America's global power with the role of precursor of global social revolution. As a result, it faces the danger of polarization, with conservatives emphasizing the global power and liberal-progressives emphasizing social responsibility, each side minimizing, possibly even negating, the other's objectives. Nationalism, in spite of the infusion into it of new social content, encourages license and excess by the élites of the new states and, in Western Europe, frustrates the more creative efforts to overcome the bitter legacies of national conflict. Moreover, the old ideologies (and the conflicts associated with them) are unresponsive to the fact that similar internal and external problems impose themselves on such otherwise ideologically different societies as the United States and the Soviet Union, or on India and China.

IV

The absence of an ideological tradition has often made America respond to contemporary challenges in an extremely short-range and excessively pragmatic fashion; we have over-concentrated on means and techniques at the expense of long-range perspectives. Yet paradoxically we have also tended to become wedded to particular formulas and concepts once they were formulated and crystallized.

Still, America has proved more adaptable than many other nations to changed conditions and novel circumstances. Thus we have accepted our inherent responsibility as the world's pre-eminent power, as well as the onerous task of turning international relations to the "real" issues facing mankind.

America cannot, as some would wish, ignore the cold war or abandon the obligations it has undertaken. A sudden, peremptory restructuring of the international balance of power would be destabilizing and dangerous. However, it is imperative that the cold war be seen primarily as a means of refuting the dogmatic ideological concepts of the Communists while gradually creating conditions such that some Communist nations—particularly the Soviet Union—begin to perceive the advantages of increased global coöperation among the more developed states.

A community of the developed nations must eventually come into being if they are to respond effectively to the crisis that the Third World now faces and will face with increasing gravity. Continued divisions among the developed states—particularly those derived from outmoded ideological concepts—will negate the efforts of individual states to aid the Third World, while in Europe itself they will contribute to a resurgence of nationalism.

That the Communist states are not immune to the process of change and to intelligent Western initiatives is attested to by the evolution of Jugoslav thinking and behavior. Less than twenty years ago, the Jugoslavs talked not unlike the Chinese of today, and it should be remembered that one of the reasons for the Stalin-Tito break was the Jugoslavs' pressure on the Soviets to adopt a more militant posture toward the West. Today, the Jugoslavs are leading all Communist states in economic reform, in the openness of their society, in ideological moderation. Recently they joined GATT and their membership in EFTA—eventually perhaps the Common Market—is a probability. While still committed to the notion of "socialism," their views on international politics are moderate and they have had a significant impact on Soviet thinking. In 1958, the Soviet leadership condemned the newly adopted revisionist Jugoslav program. By 1966 the Kremlin was liberally plagiarizing from it.

Similar trends are developing elsewhere in the Communist world. To be sure, they are opposed by entrenched bureaucrats, but in the long run the reactionaries seem to be fighting a losing battle. Social forces are against them and the conservative élites are everywhere on the defensive. It is doubtful that they can reverse—though they certainly can delay—the trend toward a more open and humanistic and less ideological society. The resistance of those régimes dominated by entrenched conservative bureaucracies would be further weakened if the West did more to discredit the cold war as a self-serving doctrine of the Communist rulers. President Kennedy's American University speech had some effect in that regard.

An even more complicated task is the one posed by domestic

change in the developed nations. Here, too, America is the pioneer, history's guinea pig. Our democratic process traditionally has involved a response to crises. Many of our governmental agencies—for example, the urban and welfare departments—developed because social needs belatedly made themselves obvious to all. Increasingly, the emphasis should be on anticipating needs and thus on the development of institutions capable of dealing with rapid social change and mitigating its consequences. This may require major reorientation in the average citizen's perception of the world around him. Finally, it would be desirable to stimulate a broad public discussion on the role and character of the individual in the scientific age about to set upon us and perhaps even to subsume us. In doing so, new and more relevant issues will come to the fore, replacing the repetitive cant of outmoded ideological conflict.

Our success or failure in adapting our democratic institutions to these new conditions, while safeguarding the individual personality, may in large measure determine the role this country will be playing in the world by the end of this century.

A NEW FOREIGN POLICY FOR THE UNITED STATES: BASIC ISSUES

by HANS J. MORGENTHAU

To characterize American foreign policy in one sentence, one could say that it has lived during the last decade or so on the intellectual capital which was accumulated in the

"A New Foreign Policy for the United States: Basic Issues," by Hans J. Morgenthau, is reprinted with permission from the January 1967 issue of the *Bulletin of the Atomic Scientists*. Copyright 1967 by the Educational Foundation for Nuclear Science.

famous fifteen weeks of the spring of 1947, when the policy of containment, the Truman Doctrine, and the Marshall Plan fashioned a new American foreign policy, and that this capital has now been nearly exhausted. This exhaustion is the result of the drastic transformation of the issues which the policies of 1947 met with outstanding success. These policies have become obsolete, and the United States has been unable to devise new policies capable of dealing successfully with the issues of a different age. What is needed for 1967 is, therefore, a task of renovation similar to that of 1947. We must free ourselves from the burden of obsolescent policies which have become mechanical routines and embark upon a radical rethinking of the issues and of the policies adequate to them.

Five basic issues await reconsideration. We must come to terms with our allies, with the communist world, with the uncommitted third of the world, with nuclear power, and with ourselves.

A Time of Nuclear Monopoly

The Atlantic Alliance was predicated upon the nuclear monopoly of the United States. Thus the origin of its crisis dates back to the fall of 1949. That is to say, the crisis of the Atlantic Alliance virtually coincides with its birth. When the Soviet Union exploded its first nuclear device in September 1949, it also undermined one of the foundation stones of the Atlantic Alliance and made it inevitable that sooner or later a new basis would have to be found for that Alliance.

When it was established, the Atlantic Alliance was for the nations of West Europe not a matter of choice but a question of life and death. It was the political, military, and economic precondition for their survival as independent national entities. One of these pre-conditions was the protective umbrella which the nuclear monopoly of the United States provided for the nations of West Europe. Thus the transformation of that monopoly into a bipolar relationship of mutual deterrence was bound to change the character of the Atlantic Alliance. In consequence of the newly acquired ability of the Soviet Union to do to the United States what the United States has been able to do to the Soviet Union since the end of World War II—that is, to destroy it as a going concern—the Atlantic Alliance is for the nations of West

Europe no longer an unmixed blessing. Mr. Khrushchev used to remind the nations of West Europe from time to time of this radical change in their relations with the United States. It is from this change that de Gaulle has tried to draw the political conclusions.

The issue de Gaulle has raised, phrased in its most elemental terms, is this: Who shall die for whom under what conditions? In the pre-nuclear age, de Gaulle argues, a nation could be expected to support an ally at the risk of war even though its vital interests were not affected: it risked, at worst, defeat in war with the attendant loss of territory and the loss of a tolerable fraction of its material and human resources. What could be expected in the pre-nuclear age because it was bearable, de Gaulle continues to argue, can no longer be expected in the nuclear age because it is no longer bearable. A nation whose vital interests are not at stake can no longer be expected to come to the aid of an ally if, by doing so, it risks its very existence. The reliability of alliances is thereby put into doubt. Here lies, according to de Gaulle, the crisis of the Atlantic Alliance.

De Gaulle has brought that crisis into the open through two courses of action: the development of a national nuclear capability; and the pursuit of national policies regardless of the interests of his allies. The professed aim of these courses of action has been the restoration of French independence and freedom of action on the international scene. In truth, however, de Gaulle's foreign policy is predicated upon the commitment of the American nuclear deterrent to the defense of France, a commitment to which even de Gaulle still attaches a considerable measure of credibility. The French nuclear capability serves the purpose of making that commitment operative. In other words, France enjoys her independence and freedom of action only by dint of the American commitment, and her nuclear capability, far from being an independent deterrent against a major nuclear power, can at best serve as a trigger to bring American nuclear power into action.

The crisis of the Atlantic Alliance will not be solved by the reiteration of slogans about "interdependence" and "partnership," for these slogans beg the question which the crisis of the Atlantic Alliance poses. Nor will it be solved by the manipulation of military technology, such as the multilateral seaborne force

(MLF). Three major political solutions appear to be logically possible.

It is possible to pretend that the crisis of the Atlantic Alliance really does not exist and that its appearances have been created by the contrariness of de Gaulle. This is the solution of business as usual, of the continuation of institutional arrangements and procedural routines, whose vitality has not survived the drastic change in the foundations of the Alliance referred to above. This course is most easy to follow in the short run, and it is indeed the course we have been following since we shelved the MLF. But in the long run such inaction can only serve to strengthen the disintegrating forces, of which France has thus far been the main exponent but is not likely to remain so for long.

It must be taken as axiomatic that the health of the Atlantic Alliance cannot be restored through attempts at preserving an unviable status quo but only through reformative action. This action will either go forward toward a much more intimate co-operation among members of the Alliance and a much closer coordination of their foreign policies, or else it will move backward to a narrower and more specific definition of the *casus foederis* than exists at present.

The present malaise within the Atlantic Alliance arises from the fact that the major allies pursue divergent policies throughout the world and there is hardly an important issue upon which all major allies see eye to eye. It is this divergence of policies rather than the actual and threatening proliferation of nuclear weapons that has undermined the Alliance. For if there existed among the members of the Atlantic Alliance such a community of interests that the policies of Ally A would automatically be supported by Ally B, and vice versa, the problem would not exist. The objectives on behalf of which A might want to threaten nuclear war would then be identical with those of B, and vice versa. In that case, the issue which de Gaulle has raised and other members of the Alliance are likely to raise in the future would have lost its substance.

While from a rational point of view this alternative appears to be the most attractive, it is not likely to be realized in the foreseeable future. The impetus toward supranational integration, which probably could have been transformed into fruitful political action during the first decade following World War II, has been replaced by a nationalism which puts in jeopardy even the existing traditional alliances. The United States can mitigate these nationalistic tendencies through its own foreign policies and thereby try to mitigate those tendencies in other nations as well. Yet as long as these tendencies persist, the United States must adapt its alliance commitments to them. We must narrow the gap between our comprehensive legal commitments and the limited sphere within which our interests and policies coincide with those of our allies. This is particularly imperative in view of actual and threatening nuclear proliferation. Because proliferation could involve the major nuclear powers in a nuclear war against their will the strictest legal and political safeguards are required. Otherwise we shall run the risk of a catastrophe not of our making and on behalf of interests not our own.

Communisms

It has become a triviality to say that communism has lost its monolithic character and has taken on the qualities of polycentrism. It is also obvious to draw from this statement the conclusion that this transformation of communism opens up new opportunities for the foreign policy of the United States. Yet it tells much about the power of outworn ideas that, while the truth of these two propositions is generally recognized in theory, we act as though communism were still a monolithic force uniformly threatening the interests of the United States. Our interventions in Vietnam and the Dominican Republic are cases in point. We intervened in both countries in order to "stop communism," taking it for granted that we knew *a priori*, without examining the concrete circumstances, what kind of communist threat we were facing.

Such an attitude of instinctive opposition was indeed in order 20 or even 10 years ago when any inroads communism made anywhere were tantamount to an expansion of Soviet power hostile to the United States. This attitude has become today not only intellectually untenable but also politically useless and even counter-productive. For it is again belaboring the obvious—and that this is so indicates the defects of our foreign policy—to say that we are today in the presence of a variety of communisms whose hostility to our interests depends upon the national interests of the individual communist governments and parties, and upon their relations to the two great communist powers: the Soviet Union and China. The degree of their hostility on the political and military plane—in contrast to the moral and ideological one—cannot be assumed, but must be determined in each instance through the empirical examination of the facts. Furthermore, the degree of hostility to be found in a particular case is not immutable but is susceptible to changes induced by our and other nations' policies. What is required of us, then, is a dual task: first, a subtle and admittedly risky examination of each communist government and movement in terms of the national interests it pursues and of its relations with other communist governments and movements; and second, the fashioning of policies which are not only appropriate to the kind of communism encountered but which also seek to minimize the hostility of that communism to the interests of the United States.

These standards must guide us in our relations not only with existing communist governments and parties but also with revolutionary movements exposed to communist influence. At this point the problem of our relations with communism overlaps with that of our relations with the uncommitted third of the world. For large parts of Asia, Africa, and Latin America are objectively in a pre-revolutionary stage, and it is likely to be only a matter of time until actual revolution will break out in one or the other of these countries. The revolutionary movements which will then come to the fore are bound to have, to a greater or lesser degree, a communist component; that is, they risk being taken over by communism. As a matter of principle, what should our attitude toward these movements be?

Nothing is simpler, both in terms of intellectual effort and practical execution, than to trace all revolutions to a common conspiratorial source, to equate all revolutionary movements with communism, and to oppose them with undiscriminating fervor as uniformly hostile to the interests of the United States. The United States would then be forced to oppose revolution throughout the world because of the ever-present threat of a communist takeover and would transform itself, in spite of better insight and intentions, into an antirevolutionary power per se. Yet such a policy is bound to fail. It might succeed if it had to deal with nothing more than isolated revolutionary movements which could be smothered by force of arms. But it cannot succeed since it is faced with revolutionary situations all over the world; for even the militarily most powerful nation does not have sufficient usable resources to deal simultaneously with a number of acute revolutions. Such a policy of wholesale opposition to revolution is bound to fail not only with regard to the individual revolutions to which it is applied but also in terms of its own indiscriminate anticommunism. For the very logic which makes us appear as the prime antirevolutionary power surrenders to communism the sponsorship of revolution everywhere. Thus the anticommunist crusade achieves what it aims to prevent: the exploitation of the revolutions of the age by communism.

The alternative to such a simple antirevolutionary and anticommunist policy would be risky and could not command anything approaching unanimous support on the part of an unprepared domestic public opinion. It would make the highest demands on the technical skill, the moral stamina, and the political wisdom of our government. But it is the only one that promises at least a measure of success.

Such an alternative policy would have to start from the assumption that the choice before us is not between the status quo and revolution, nor even between communist and noncommunist revolution, but between a revolution hostile to the interests of the United States and a revolution which is not hostile to these interests. In practice, far from opposing revolutions per se, it would compete with the main instigators of communist revolution —the Soviet Union, China, and Cuba—for the sponsorship of revolution. This sponsorship would serve two alternative aims: first, to protect the revolution from a communist takeover; and second, if we should fail in this, to prevent such a communist revolution from turning against the interests of the United States. Such a policy, substituting the yardstick of American national interest for that of communism, obviously constitutes a complete reversal of the positions we have taken in recent years and of which our policies in Vietnam and the Dominican Republic are the current prime examples. It also requires a radical change in the conception we have developed of our role in the world and of the purposes our foreign policy is supposed to serve.

What Is Possible

This conception was developed in the immediate postwar period and most strikingly formulated in the Truman Doctrine of 1947, committing the United States to opposition to communist aggression and subversion throughout the world. This unlimited global commitment was in practice narrowed down to the military containment of the Soviet Union, of which the Atlantic Alliance has been the instrument, and to the economic restoration of West Europe through the Marshall Plan.

The tasks with which the United States is faced today in its relations with other nations are more varied and infinitely more complex than those it discharged successfully in the immediate postwar period. The military containment of the Soviet Union, while still fundamental to everything else, has become by virtue of its success a matter of routine to be almost taken for granted. To this task have been added the multifarious problems arising from our relations to communism throughout the world and to the uncommitted nations. Yet the intellectual instrumentalities which we have brought to bear upon these new problems are still the ones we used so successsfully in the late forties: the Truman Doctrine and the Marshall Plan. In the process, the Truman Doctrine has been transformed from an ideology of military containment into a general principle of global policy, and the Marshall Plan has been transformed from a technique of economic recovery limited to West Europe to the global principle of foreign aid. In consequence, the United States has taken upon itself global responsibilities which it cannot discharge with a chance of success and which, if it were to try to discharge, would entail its ruin.

As I pointed out in 1951 (*In Defense of the National Interest*, New York: Alfred A. Knopf, Inc.): "As a guide to political action, it [the Truman Doctrine] is the victim . . . of two congenital political weaknesses: the inability to distinguish between what is desirable and what is possible, and the inability to distinguish between what is desirable and what is essential." The new globalism, which seeks to put the principle of the Truman Doctrine into practice by identifying revolution with communism and trying to stop communism everywhere, neglects these distinctions which are fundamental to a sound foreign policy. For while it would be desirable to contain communism within its present limits through the efforts of the United States, it is essential that only that type of communism hostile to the interests of the United States be so contained. Thus I have always regarded it as essential to the interests of the United States that the transformation of Cuba into a center of communist subversion in the Western Hemisphere and a military and political outpost of the Soviet Union be prevented. Similarly, I find the containment of communism in Vietnam to be desirable but not essential from the point of view of the interests of the United States, especially since this communism is likely to be an independent national communism after the model of Yugoslavia.

This latter position is contested by those who quote General Giap, the commander of the North Vietnamese army, to the effect that the war in Vietnam is a test case for all "wars of national liberation" and that the outcome of the war in Vietnam will determine the outcome of all such wars. If this statement were correct, it would indeed follow that the containment of communism in Vietnam is essential in view of American interests since without it communism would triumph throughout much of the uncommitted world. However, if one subjects General Giap's statement to empirical analysis one realizes that it is devoid of merit. There is no such thing as a typical "war of national liberation" whose uniform pattern can be detected throughout the world, and which could be causally connected with all the other wars of this kind. The war in Vietnam is *sui generis*, and no situation remotely similar to it exists, or is likely to exist, anywhere else in the world. In consequence, what happens or does not happen there can have no direct bearing upon what is going to happen elsewhere. Win or lose in Vietnam, there may still be a "war of national liberation" in, say, Indonesia or Venezuela or Algeria, which may be won or lost according to what may happen in those particular countries, but certainly not according to what is going to happen in Vietnam.

We are here in the presence of the kind of primitive dogmatism, arguing by abstract analogy, which one thought was a peculiar weakness of the communist mode of thought. However, this approach, incapable of discriminating among divergent historic situations, is appropriate to a globalism which, as we have seen, is by its very nature averse to making such discriminating judgments.

Even if we were to disregard the distinction between what is essential and what is desirable, we would still be up against the distinction between what is desirable and what is possible. We can stipulate it as desirable and we may even deem it essential, in view of the interest of the United States in world peace and order, that the United States should bring a modicum of order and stability to the underdeveloped nations through the instrumentality of foreign aid. Yet after long and disappointing experiences, we must have realized by now how narrow the limits are within which we can influence the development of foreign nations. More particularly, we must have realized the extent to which the development of other nations depends upon indigenous rational and moral qualities not susceptible to deliberate foreign influence.

Similarly, if we were to stipulate the containment of all kinds of communism as desirable or even essential, we would find, as has been indicated already, that the demands such a stipulation would make upon American military power by far exceed its capabilities. We are capable of dealing simultaneously with one Vietnam and one Dominican Republic. But with how many Vietnams and Dominican Republics could we deal at the same time without straining our military resources to such a point that we would either be compelled to distinguish between what is essential and desirable, and what is possible—or having to resort to nuclear war as the extreme remedy, which in its way is as lacking in discrimination as is the globalist conception of foreign policy?

In any event, such a commitment of all our military resources to the global containment of communism would deprive other U.S. interests of the necessary military support. Concentrating upon one aim incapable of achievement, we would incapacitate ourselves to pursue other aims in our relations with other nations. It is significant that General Gallois, one of the main proponents of an independent French foreign policy, in the August 1965 *Réalités* commends the United States for its intervention in Vietnam and the Dominican Republic on the ground that the commitment of large American resources to these theaters will make it possible for France to play a greater role in world affairs.

Nuclear Diplomacy

Nuclear power presents itself to the United States under two different headings: the management of nuclear power; and the influence which the availability of nuclear power has had upon the conduct of foreign and military policy.

Concerning the manipulation of nuclear power, we must come to terms with two interconnected problems: the abatement of the nuclear arms race and the prevention of nuclear proliferation. As long as the present nuclear powers continue to compete for the accumulation of nuclear weapons and delivery systems as instruments of their national policies, there appears to be no possibility of preventing other nations from following suit. Nuclear proliferation is a mere spatial expansion of the nuclear arms race. The former can be prevented only by stopping the latter.

The cessation of the nuclear arms race is required by two rational considerations. First, the unlimited accumulation of nuclear weapons, in contrast to conventional ones, is irrational, once a nation has acquired the capability, as have the United States and the Soviet Union, to destroy their prospective enemies many times over. Second, the use of nuclear weapons as instruments of national policy, in a manner likely to call forth retaliation in kind, is irrational by virtue of their indiscriminate destructiveness. What the nuclear powers have already been doing pragmatically, that is, refraining from the use of nuclear weapons, they ought now to do consistently and as a matter of principle: eliminate the use of nuclear weapons as instruments of national policy; assign to them exclusively the function of a deterrent, to be used only in suicidal desperation.

From this principle, four consequences follow for the conduct of foreign and military policy. (1) Since nuclear threats are inherently lacking in credibility, they ought to be eliminated from diplomatic practice. (2) For similar reasons, the use of nuclear weapons, except for the purpose of deterrence, ought to be eliminated from military planning. (3) Since nuclear weapons are thus irrelevant for the normal exercise of national power, foreign and military policy ought to concentrate upon the development and use of the nonnuclear instruments of national power. (4) Among these instruments, long-range communication, delivery, and transportation systems have radically altered the importance of the control of territory for national power. Foreign and military policy must take these changes into account.

The Question for 1967

Looking back on the development of American foreign policy during the last two decades, one realizes how the great innovations of 1947—containment, the Truman Doctrine, the Marshall Plan—have changed their functions under the impact of new conditions. The first postwar decade was marked by two factors: the unchallengeable supremacy of the United States, on the one hand; the limitation of its military commitments to Europe and their hesitant extension to Asia, on the other. The second postwar decade, especially in its last years, received its political character from the decline of the relative power of the United States, coincident with a global extension of its military commitments. The Truman Doctrine and the Marshall Plan, originally limited in their practical application to Europe, are now transformed into global commitments. These commitments have outpaced the power available to support them. It is a counsel of prudence to bring power and commitment again into harmony.

This requires, first of all, the restoration of selectivity in our commitment to national objectives in view of their essentiality and the possibility of attaining them. Among the objectives thus selected, a hierarchical order must then be established, again in view of these two standards. Both the process of selection and that of hierarchical ordering require a restatement of national purposes. What is it the United States seeks to accomplish in the world, and in what order of priority? This question was answered in 1947, and the answer was translated into viable policies. The same question must be answered again today.

UNCERTAIN ROAD TO THE 21ST CENTURY

by HERMAN KAHN

THERE are many reasons for believing that the world of tomorrow, 10 or 20 years from now, will be much different from the one we know today. For example, there is the possibility of arms control which could make the world substantially safer. On the other hand, there may be dangerous nuclear proliferation, a breakdown of current security arrangements, or widespread revolutionary unrest in the so-called Third World. More hopefully, the current détente might not only continue but it might develop into some kind of entente—an "agreement" or new unity—between East and West Europe, or between the United States and the Soviet Union, or all four groups. At the same time, China might develop rapidly and rise to true great power status. Non-Communist governments in South or Southeast Asia might collapse. There might also be a breakdown of the current political system in India because of economic or communal strains. Or there could be a European Political Community or even a United States of Europe. In any case, there will almost inevitably be a continuation of the Sino-Soviet split, further

"Uncertain Road to the 21st Century," by Herman Kahn. Reprinted by permission from *THINK* Magazine, published by IBM. Copyright 1967 by International Business Machines Corporation. The chart on page 341 and the remainder of the paragraph from the sentence beginning "The chart . . ." on page 342 is reprinted with permission of The Macmillan Company from *The Year 2000: A Framework for Speculation on the Next Thirty-Three Years* by Herman Kahn and Anthony J. Wiener. Copyright © 1967 by The Hudson Institute, Inc.

I would like to acknowledge a debt to members of the Hudson Institute staff for their collaboration in portions of the project on which this article is based, and especially to Edmund O. Stillman and Anthony J. Wiener. Topics in this article are explained in more detail in *The Year 2000*. H.K.

reemergence of Europe as an independent force and a further erosion of the Cold War and the bipolar international system.

While not all of the above are as likely as many observers have urged, I would argue that the range of serious possibilities is larger than the examples suggest. Other possibilities include: a China which is stagnating or even in a state of collapse; new and probably assertive roles for West Germany and Japan. Widespread racist or quasi-religious wars or other "irrational" violence in the recently decolonized areas; a "neo-isolationist" withdrawal of the United States and/or the Soviet Union from their intense participation in world affairs; and the emergence of what could be called a post-industrial culture in the currently developed nations. All of these are likely enough *to be* seriously considered.

First let's consider some other significant aspects of the present world which *are* taken for granted. Perhaps the most important is the growing belief by many in the United States, Europe and Japan that we are entering a period of relative stability, at least as far as wars threatening the homelands of the developed nations are concerned. The United States, of course, is currently engaged in a rather large war in Southeast Asia, but despite this it is much more difficult today to write a *plausible* scenario for escalation to an all-out war than it was 10 years ago.

In part, this is because of such important political changes as the revival in Europe and Japan of societies that are independent and vigorous (but not so much so that they create threats on their own). Large changes have also occurred in East Europe and in the Soviet Union which seem to diminish the Sino-Soviet threat. There has also been a better understanding on both sides of the Iron Curtain of the motives and objectives of the opponent. There is the relative lack of success of Communism in penetrating Africa and Latin America and even South and Southeast Asia; this political strength of the underdeveloped areas against Communism is often combined with a relative military weakness for offensive actions, which also, by and large, promote stability. Finally, there have also been a number of technical developments and changes in strategic forces and doctrine which seem to have reduced sharply the possibility of both premeditated and accidental war.

Another stabilizing factor is the relatively small pressures toward territorial expansion in North and South America, in Europe, and by Japan and Russia in Asia. To a startling degree, these "old nations" seem more or less satisfied with their current boundaries. (The German situation is not so stable, however, since reunification with possible border adjustments might be peacefully or violently accomplished. We should also admit the possibility of Chinese territorial aggression, of frontier changes in parts of Africa and Asia, and of turmoil generally in the so-called "new nations.")

One of the main reasons for the new attitude toward territorial expansion is that internal economic development now appears to be the most efficient road to wealth and perhaps power. The postwar experiences of Japan, West Germany and other European countries indicate that colonies are now economic liabilities and sources of political and military weakness rather than strength. Doubtless the pendulum of fashion has overshot, but this new attitude has important effects.

An even more important factor is the likelihood of many "pluralistic security communities" on the model of U.S.-Canadian relations in which war (or even the threat of violence) is unthinkable. The term "pluralistic security community" expresses more than just a willingness to accept or live with current situations: it indicates a willingness to live with a much *deteriorated* situation, as well as a determination not to let situations deteriorate too far. Because of this, a pluralistic security community is an important step forward to peaceful political unification. Important, too, is the often neglected fact that trade no longer follows the flag. Thus West Germany, which hardly possesses a Navy, is the second largest trading nation in the world today.

Of course, even if the stability continues, military capabilities will remain important in international politics. However, as far as the "old nations" are concerned, the uses of such powers are likely to be more sophisticated and subtle than in the 18th, 19th and early 20th centuries. In practice, most of the old and many of the new powers will have secure frontiers and access to world markets without much explicit need to enforce these rights.

This international context of seemingly great stability is most important in the consideration of the pressures on and roles of Japan and West Germany. Economically they are likely to be the third and fourth largest world powers and yet may be in very different positions in the international hierarchy in terms of po-

"SURPRISE-FREE" PROJECTIONS
FOR THE TEN MAJOR COUNTRIES

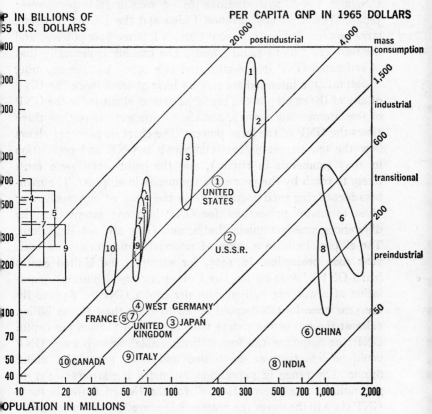

GNP IN BILLIONS OF
1965 U.S. DOLLARS

PER CAPITA GNP IN 1965 DOLLARS

POPULATION IN MILLIONS

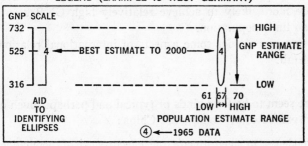

LEGEND (EXAMPLE IS WEST GERMANY)

GNP SCALE

732

525 — 4 ←— BEST ESTIMATE TO 2000 —→ 4

316

AID
TO
IDENTIFYING
ELLIPSES

HIGH

GNP ESTIMATE
RANGE

LOW

61 67 70
LOW ↔ HIGH
POPULATION ESTIMATE RANGE

④ ←— 1965 DATA

litical influence and military capability. What will this hierarchy look like? Most probably there will be 10 "major" powers. The U.S. and USSR will continue to be considered superpowers; Japan, West Germany, France, China and the United Kingdom large powers; India, Italy, and Canada intermediate powers; and the next 120 nations small powers. The ranking is generally that of estimated GNP in the mid- and late 1970s, but the grouping is natural: the intermediate powers have at least twice the GNP of any of the small powers, the large powers about twice the GNP of the intermediate powers, and the superpowers more than three times the GNP of the large powers. The chart on page 341 shows how the ten largest nations compared in GNP and population in 1965 (numerals in circles), and the points they seem most likely to reach by the year 2000 (numerals in ellipses). The numbers identifying each country are in the order of our medium or "best estimate" projections for GNP in 2000; except that the differences among Canada, India, and Italy are not significant. The ellipses indicate a range of reasonable uncertainty for each year 2000 projection. In 1965, for example, the United States had a GNP of $692 billion (by United Nations definition), population of about 195 million, and per capita GNP of $3,560. By the year 2000 its GNP could be up to more than $4,500 billion (almost the top of the chart) with more than $12,000 per capita GNP; or assuming the lowest "reasonable" growth rate, GNP could be less than $1,400 billion and GNP per capita under $5,000. The range in population estimates is narrower—291 to 361 million. Our "best estimate" for the United States is for a GNP close to the top of the "reasonable range" and for a relatively moderate population growth—$3,200 billion and 318 million people. The ellipses for India and China slope backward because they are more likely to achieve relatively high GNP growth if they can limit population.

Let us now consider some aspects of international relations in more detail.

II

There seem to be four kinds of typical and perhaps much exaggerated estimates of Communist China:

1. a tendency to overestimate the effectiveness of population—in effect, to multiply anything that happens in China by 750 million,

as if the 600 million or so peasants (as distinguished from the 150 million or so urbanized Chinese) constitute an overwhelming economic, military, moral or political force.

2. a tendency to credit the Chinese with a nearly magical ability to galvanize immediate revolutions not only in nearby regions but at great distances.

3. a tendency to assume perfect discipline in China (750 million "blue ants") and an inevitable and very successful industrial development in the next 35 years.

4. a tendency to size up Chinese leadership as wildly irrational and unlikely to be deterred even by credible and painful material or military threats. (It seems a fair statement that on Mondays, Wednesdays and Fridays the Chinese attempt to persuade us that they are crazy, and seven days a week the Soviets try to confirm this impression.)

Perhaps one source of these exaggerations is that many in the United States and Europe are looking for a new enemy to take the psychological and political role in internal politics formerly played by the Soviet Union. Yet almost all *expert* opinion in the U.S. seems agreed that China is today and may remain for the next decade or two rather weak in its ability to use offensive force (though its defensive capability may be large). Its large population is as likely to be a weakness as a strength. Its economic prospects are at best uncertain and perhaps poor. Its leaders, while rather inward-looking, chauvinistic and subject to biases, still seem to make and follow reasonable risk calculations. While they are likely to be as aggressive as practical and willing to run some risks, they are not likely to be wildly reckless. Indeed, in terms of their own values and goals, the Chinese leaders are probably less likely to be irrational on issues involving the risk of war than are many other leaders even in today's relatively conservative world. In addition, the specter of Chinese mass armies fighting in India or Southeast Asia is unrealistic. It ignores the logistic constraints. Even within China, the population is no true gauge of the size of the armies Peking could recruit and equip. Available surpluses—in money, food and productive capacity— are small. Further, the Chinese Communists have and will continue to have internal problems of morale, discipline, authority, etc. The picture of a monolithic ant heap completely responsive to the desires of Mao is clearly wrong. It is also important to note that Marshal Lin Piao's recent doctrinal statement on world revolution has been widely misunderstood. One is, of course, impressed by the very angry tone. However, what exactly was said is very weak. Lin Piao says, in effect, "We Chinese will help movements of national liberation, but not very much; you cannot depend on us but must do it on your own; if you don't, revolution will not work; outside help cannot be the decisive thing." Given that this was written in the context of the Vietnamese war, one could scarcely imagine a more restrained declaration coming from China.

Outlook for Red China

As time passes, the above points will become more widely understood and the Chinese will lose much of their present international charisma. Thus if they do better than many experts expect and average a growth rate of say 5 percent a year in GNP and about 2 percent a year in population, they will become substantially richer by the end of the century. This would give them a GNP of about $400 billion but a per capita yearly income of only about $250. This performance, while in many ways an extraordinary achievement, would not be very impressive compared to many surrounding countries, let alone the United States and the Soviet Union. (Other Asian countries such as Taiwan, South Korea, Thailand, the Philippines and Malaysia are likely to grow much more rapidly in per capita income and, as discussed later, most important of all, Japan seems likely to grow much more rapidly in total GNP.) In addition, the Chinese are likely to be technologically and economically even farther behind Japan than they are now. Thus, even if they continue their militant rhetoric, their influence will wane—in part because their extravagant claims and expectations are so obviously frustrated, and in part because Japan will overshadow them.

III

The Soviet Union is almost 50 years old. To some degree the system has evolved into an authoritarian rather than a totalitarian society, one that is in many ways successful, but also in many ways disillusioned. (To the great shock of traditional Marxists there is a good deal of intense discussion in both the Soviet Union and East Europe of the problem of alienation between man and job and man and society—a problem that was supposed to be solved with the abolition of capitalism.) Though the party stays in absolute control, it allows modest dissent. This is done to reward or stimulate people, to act as a safety valve and corrective, and to reduce criticism from Western and Soviet intellectuals, whose views have increasingly significant impact upon Soviet publics. Eventually this relaxation may lead to other important political concessions, including legal tolerance of some degree of political opposition. The Soviets still believe in world revolution and support subversion in many places in the world, but with lessened intensity, confidence and enthusiasm. There is a continuing erosion of the police-state and increasing "socialist legality." There is also an increasing embourgeoisement of the government, the managers and the masses. Nevertheless, the so-called "convergence phenomenon," the apparent and much publicized increasing similarities between Russia and the West, is likely to stop well short of parliamentary democracy.

The Chinese are likely to continue to compete with the Soviets for leadership of international Communism, emphasizing such current criticisms as the Soviet Union is:

1. capitulationist and revisionist (fearful of risking a confrontation with the U.S. and increasingly adopting capitalist practices),
2. counterrevolutionary (rich and no longer in sympathy with the poor),
3. not Afro-Asian (a predominantly white nation and therefore not to be trusted by the non-white peoples).

All of the charges sting—in part because they contain elements of truth. Yet the Soviets continue to build bridges with Europe and the United States. It is unlikely, however, that this bridge-building, *contrary to surprisingly widespread expectations*, will soon get to the stage of firm alliance. Nevertheless, communism as a world movement (now to be written with a small *c*) is likely to lose even more of its traditional discipline and direction.

IV

Germany is likely to remain divided—with East Germany likely to become a more legitimate and viable country with every year that passes. Eventually the Ulbricht regime will be replaced and the new regime may manage to acquire enough legitimacy and prestige so that it no longer needs Soviet bayonets. It could do this in part by making judicious internal concessions and in part by appealing to an increasing East German nationalism. Thus if the new regime successfully opposes the Soviets on a series of minor issues, its prestige will increase enormously.

While the East Germans and the Soviets will doubtless continue to pressure the United States and West Germany over various aspects of the Berlin question, all four countries are likely to be careful not to probe so deeply as to unbalance the situation, and to avoid incidents which could escalate into a serious confrontation.

In the meantime, the postwar political passivity of Bonn will increasingly be replaced by active and assertive policies. Germans who were young during World War II (by 1975 this is anyone under 50), will increasingly refuse to accept for themselves (or the German nation) any stigma. In East Germany nationalism may go even farther; indeed, East German national assertions are now a familiar, if carefully used, theme. Thus one can find in East Germany many articles and books which point out that, "of course West Germany is rich; it had the Marshall Plan, other U.S. support and a capitalist system—furthermore its riches have been corrupting." They then point out that East Germay has also been successful—*and under Communism*. (They seem to take a wry satisfaction and considerable pride, as do many West Germans, in the ability of Germans to do so well even without foreign help and in a non-capitalist society.) This growing success may well have an unexpectedly great appeal to young people and others in West Germany. In any case, by the mid-70s the East Germans should have a well-developed position of being true Germans—austere, purposeful and disciplined—thus espousing a sort of charismatic "Prussian Socialism."

In the rest of Europe there is probably more distrust of a revived West Germany than fear of Soviet aggression. Most Europeans feel that Soviet aggression is perhaps permanently deterred. In addition they tend to accept the "new" Soviet Union as a more or less responsible power. As a result, the West Germans feel increasingly isolated and are unwilling to believe that they can satisfy their aspirations in the current NATO framework. Of course the West Germans, partly as a result of their wartime and postwar experiences with the Soviets, partly because their country remains divided, and partly because they are on the firing line, are more preoccupied with the Soviet threat. As a result, United States and West German policies may remain in relatively close harmony: Washington and Bonn are the two capitals of the Western alliance which take the Soviet military threat most seriously (but, nonetheless, not very seriously). On the other hand, it has become clear that the previous identity of interest between Washington and Bonn is now more illusory than real. Washington's current interests in avoiding nuclear war with the Soviets, and in articulating the increasing number of issues on which Soviet and American interests coincide, are moving West German aspirations to a lower priority. Thus Bonn's major official interest, to regain the "Soviet zone," conflicts with Washington and West Europe's willingness to accept a détente based on the status quo. While Bonn will doubtless go along with the détente, and perhaps gain much commercially in doing so, it may also become increasingly resentful and restless. This is clearly true of much of German youth who increasingly ask their elders, "What is being done about reunification?" (According to recent polls, 80 percent of the young West Germans think of this as the major issue facing West Germany today.) Ignoring the almost miraculous postwar recovery of West Germany, the younger generation often argues that the postwar policies are almost bankrupt since they do not seem to have brought reunification closer.

Meanwhile, as Moscow's hold slackens in the "satellites," East Germany may also become more independent. But there is a serious potential for trouble in both Germanys—through more or less popular revolt, competition or even collaboration. It is also possible that the situation will evolve peacefully or stabilize itself on the basis of a mutual but acceptable frustration.

V

Japan in 1966 was still the invisible nation of Asia. Like West Germany, the other major loser of World War II, Japan was characterized by great economic strength and political passivity.

It is, however, a bigger country in population, has probably already surpassed West Germany in industrial production, is growing much more rapidly and, most important of all, is not held down by apprehensive allies and an overwhelming reunification problem. Thus Japan is likely to emerge in the 1970s as the true colossus of Asia—a further check on Chinese ambitions.

Partly because the Japanese are possibly the most achievement-oriented society in history, and partly because of their intense desire for prestige, their growth rates may well continue to be high, around 8 percent, for the rest of the century. At this rate they would double their GNP about every 8 or 9 years. Yet if there were a serious sustained depression, it would probably disrupt the current political balance, making much more likely a sharp swing either to the right or to the left, or to some extremist group, such as the Soka Gakkai's Komeito, which falls outside these categories. However, things seem likely to go reasonably smoothly, and while there may be some anti-foreign and pro-traditional reaction against excessive "Americanization," this is likely to be limited in effect.

VI

Some of the force of the Afro-Asian "revolution" has been spent and the future direction of this movement is now less clear. The revolution encompassed some elements that are exceedingly old—xenophobia, racial hatred, cultural exclusivism—and some elements that are new and even hyper-modern (for example, the "beat" quality of such Third World leaders as Castro and Lumumba). Among the newer elements are nationalism and Marxist ideology, both learned from Europe, though often in garbled form. But the ideological content of political movements in Afro-Asia is frequently exaggerated. While almost all Afro-Asian states describe themselves as "socialist" they are far removed from the political and economic system of the USSR or even Communist China. Their invocation of "socialism" is more a talismanic claim on modernity than an ideological commitment.

Of course, the mere fact that these movements called themselves socialist or Communist means that they often feel some identity with the Soviet Union or China, or both, and that they expect and often get aid from these countries. It is even possible that if they are in any way successful with their Afro-Asian socialism, they will attempt to deepen and continue this identity. But my prediction would be that Afro-Asian socialism will overwhelm the Marxist origins of these movements and any relationship to Chinese or Soviet Communism.

VII

Since the middle of the 19th century, Latin America has been chronically anti-Yankee. This antipathy, stemming from both rational and irrational causes, was much strengthened by U.S. political and military intervention. The "irrational" causes were many, but a crucial one, which will presumably continue, is the simple necessity for Latins to distinguish themselves as a culture from the predominantly Protestant, commercial, aggressive North American civilization which might otherwise engulf them.

There are, however, some important new trends. Brazilians, Mexicans and Colombians, at least, seem now to have a kind of national self-confidence that makes them psychologically less dependent on the U.S.—either positively or negatively. This confidence is primarily based on their recent success in industrializing their countries but also on, respectively: (1) creating a new kind of society, (2) making a successful social revolution and (3) an ability to handle the North Americans. Thus, many Latin Americans—particularly the growing urbanized commercial, technical and professional classes—no longer feel quite so overwhelmed or dominated by the colossus of the North. Further, the Christian Democrats (and other Democrats and Democratic-Leftists) are now leading a campaign for a new kind of relationship between the United States and Latin America involving more mutual respect and empathy.

Unlike much of Afro-Asia, where many of the problems seem overwhelming, most Latin American economic development problems seem either soluble or bearable. For one thing, the ratio of people to resources in Latin America is far more favorable. In contrast to Africa and much of Asia, Latin America is now capitalistic and technological, predominantly European in culture, and does not now suffer as much from the social disruptions of economic modernization.

However, the political conditions inhibiting parliamentary government and orderly development are still evident. Relatively violent and "illegal" changes of government are likely to persist; under Latin American conditions complex and subtle political systems—perhaps on the current Mexican model—may be more successful in maintaining a reasonable degree of order, liberty and development than parliamentary democracy.

In any case, with some luck or skill most of Latin America ought, by the end of the century, to achieve living standards comparable to or greater than Italy today (and with the same problem of unevenness, so that in the Latin American context the urban-rural problem replaces the Italian north-south disparities).

VIII

In the first decade after World War II the five principal victors either actually tested a nuclear device and then procured nuclear weapons or officially initiated programs with the intention of carrying them through to the test and procurement stage (for this purpose we will consider Peking rather than Taiwan a victor of World War II). But, rather startlingly, in the next decade no country officially initiated a nuclear weapons program, though many initiated "peaceful" nuclear energy programs which give them an option on a military program. It is still possible that in the absence of immediate objective military pressures, this precedent will be continued and even strengthened and further proliferation prevented. But there are other possibilities.

If one examines the candidates for status as Nuclear Power No. 6, the most obvious ones are Israel, India, West Germany and Japan. The first two have, in effect, created a basis or option for such a program. The last two are now doing so. However, it seems unlikely that either Israel or India will procure nuclear weapons, if only because the United States seems to have indicated that if they do, U.S. support will either be withdrawn or sharply cut, and they might be facing potential enemies alone. In the absence of new developments West Germany, of course, is firmly precluded by political constraints arising out of the war (and some ambiguous treaty obligations) from going ahead on its own.

That leaves Japan. Most Japanese and observers of the Japanese do not think that Japan will become the sixth nuclear power. Informal polls taken at Japanese universities, and by the author, however, indicate that many Japanese expect Japan to be No. 8 to go nuclear, after India and West Germany. However, I would argue that it will soon become clear to the Japanese that India and West Germany will not be Nos. 6 and 7. At the same time, the Japanese will almost certainly be increasingly assertive and self-confident in their own economic strength, desirous of increased prestige and independence, and concerned about their long-run security. Many Japanese will then argue that the easiest and most efficient route to these goals is to acquire nuclear weapons.

If Japan does try to be Nuclear Power No. 6, it seems quite plausible that West Germany will wish to follow suit. Credible military and political arguments could then openly be made for Germany's acquiring nuclear weapons. It is important to realize that once the "victors' monopoly" has been broken by one of the defeated powers of World War II, the other defeated powers will feel much less constrained by "war guilt." Bluntly, many in the West would be willing to tell the West Germans that they cannot revise the territorial results of World War II without going to war; but a few would be willing to say, "Until you win a war you are politically second-class."

Assuming, then, that in four or five years Germany follows Japan; then the Italians will probably follow. If the Germans have sufficient political status to acquire nuclear weapons, they, too, out of self-respect, must also have them. One could also conjecture, then, that such countries as Sweden, Switzerland, Australia and India would soon no longer feel they are rocking the boat by achieving nuclear status. If this proliferation in fact occurred in the '70s and the '80s, then in the '90s, any one of 50 countries or so might have access to such weapons.

While this prospect is very frightening, it does not necessarily mean an inevitable cataclysmic nuclear war. Nor does it necessarily increase the likelihood of a nuclear war between the United States and the Soviet Union. Indeed, nuclear war between two relatively undeveloped nations or one developed and one undeveloped nation would be much more likely—and it does not by any means follow logically, or practically, that such a conflict would develop into a general holocaust. And even here, if proliferation continues, the attitudes about "first use," the risks of unsafe techniques, disproportionate response, etc., which now inhibit the United States and the Soviet Union, might inhibit the other nuclear states as well.

Despite such arguments, one cannot be confident that future effects would not be cataclysmic. In fact, there is a surprising consensus among analysts, scholars, policy makers and men in the street in this respect. While they may be wrong, I share their judgment, at least in its less apocalyptic form, that proliferation is bad, and have discussed elsewhere ways to hinder it and deal with it if it occurs.

IX

By the end of the century there will be about six billion people on earth, and about 20 percent of these should be living at a standard substantially better than the current American one. This achievement could result in the transition of these affluent societies to a new post-industrial culture, a transition which may be as dramatic and important as the 17th-century transition to an industrial culture. That is, if our assumptions about stability and economic growth rates (which range for most countries from 2 to 10 percent) hold, we should be entering a sort of new Augustan age. Conditions in the superdeveloped countries might by the year 2000 be as different from those in Europe in the early and mid-20th centuries as conditions in the early Roman Empire differed from those of the previous ancient world. We are all too familiar with lurid clichés about the decline of the Roman Empire, but for better than nine-tenths of the time, the first 200 years of the Roman Empire enjoyed almost unparalleled peace and prosperity. It should be noted that it also started as an "age of anxiety" and apprehension. It is often argued—and plausibly— that the "moral fiber" of the Romans degenerated during this period probably because of the lack of challenge, possibly because of other events or environmental factors. While the questions of cause and effect are complicated and inconclusive, there are some parallels between Roman times and ours.

Thus, it is interesting to note that when Augustus came to power the free citizens of Rome had 76 holidays a year. When Nero died, not quite a century later, they had 176 holidays a year. Similarly, in our own case, if productivity per hour goes up by 3 or 4 percent a year (or by a factor of three or four by the year 2000), as is expected by most experts, it is likely that not all of this increased productivity will be used to produce more. Paradoxically, increased productivity could also cause a general de-emphasis of private industry, which could come to occupy a relatively small portion of society's efforts and attentions. Thus Daniel Bell has suggested that the private firm will no longer be as important a source of innovation and prestige in this post-industrial culture, but that this role will increasingly be played by government, the professions, the not-for-profit educational and research institutions, foundations and other non-business organizations.

It would not be appropriate in an article on international relations to spend too much time on the domestic aspects of the post-industrial culture in the 20 percent or so of the world that may achieve this state. It is sufficient to mention that while there are exciting prospects for a humanistic and creative culture, there may be serious problems of motivation, and of the use of leisure or even the possibility of a disastrous overreaction against work and achievement-oriented values. Projected to a national level, this overreaction could undercut the advancement of the national interest. Thus, some of these superdeveloped societies may have difficulty, in the long run, in international competition. But it seems more likely that, in spite of various internal strains and corrosive tendencies, enough citizens will continue—like the Roman stoics—to carry out the responsibilities of power.

A different aspect of this parallel which emphasizes international issues may also be worth mentioning. Here America plays the part of Rome, Europe of Greece, and the Soviet Union (or China) of Parthia, or Persia. There are indeed important similarities between the Greeks and the Europeans on the one hand, and the Romans and the Americans on the other. Greece eagerly seized the opportunity for World Empire, but failed. The Romans—more or less against their will—were forced three times to intervene in the Greek world to prevent its domination by a single power. The first two times they withdrew after accomplishing this mission. The third time they stayed. Indeed, under the necessity (seemingly sincere) of protecting weak powers the Romans found it necessary to take over and administer about half of the area which had previously been conquered by the Greeks, leaving the other half to the Parthians, with whom they had an uneasy coexistence.

One problem of this post-industrial society which has no real counterpart in classical times—except possibly with some aspects of the free distribution of food to Roman citizens—might be an immense worldwide welfare program. Such a program would run the danger of being carried out with excessive bureaucratic harshness or with an unwise permissiveness that leads to an unintended worsening of the problems it is attempting to alleviate.

We have seen both these problems in current U.S. welfare programs and in our foreign aid programs. An important and not atypical example is the food-for-India program. The U.S. currently supplies half the wheat consumed in India (this takes about one-fourth the U.S. production). While the Indians have increased their food production by 50 percent in the last 15 years, most experts believe that with relatively minor changes in programs and government attitudes—particularly towards such things as fertilizer—food production could have been increased even faster. Furthermore, if the government had been willing to initiate harsh and therefore very unpopular measures (such as raising the price of food), production would have gone up even faster and India could have had food surpluses. But for various reasons even the mild and obvious measures were (and are) politically unpopular, especially since many Indians have come to think of the stream of food from the United States as a vested right and therefore feel under no pressure to initiate such measures (and resent any direct pressure by the U.S. to do so).

The situation could get worse. For example, assume that in the year 2000 a minimum diet will cost roughly $100 (1965 dollars) a year (current food costs are less than $40 a year in India). Then if there are roughly three billion people in the underdeveloped world, $100 billion a year could furnish one-third of their food requirements. This would be about 2 or 3 percent of the expected U.S. GNP in the year 2000, and about one percent of the GNP of the developed portion of the world. Furthermore, there do not seem to be any serious bottlenecks or technical problems in converting these monetary calculations into actual production, provided that one makes reasonable preparations.

Assume now that the food-poor countries do not manage to increase their food production or reduce their population growth so as to maintain (or achieve) a balance and that this will be reasonably apparent in advance. Then, since it will be technologically and economically feasible for the developed nations to step in and prevent famine, many will feel there is a moral or political obligation for the affluent not only to do so, but to be prepared in advance to do so, since otherwise there may not be time to increase production drastically if there is a crop failure. One can agree with this and still be concerned that meeting this obligation, if done imprudently, could worsen the very problem it is trying to solve.

Thus we envision for the last third of the 20th century a condition in which such once vital questions as access to markets, frontier defense, and many other national security or economic issues are no longer dominating or immediate, at least for most of the industrialized nations of the world, in contrast to the new nations. Further, most nations—even the newer ones—will not feel under great pressure (or inducement) to expand aggressively and to grab available territories *now*—not even to prevent some other nation's grabbing them first or to balance previous grabs by even older nations. But within this framework, which is basically stable for the older nations, many important problems will arise or gestate—some of which could have disastrous consequences in the foreseeable, though even more long-range future.

The above picture is, of course, superficial and incomplete; it may also seem both too good and too bad to be true. Most thoughtful readers are also likely to feel that in addition to the many problems implicitly and explicitly set forth there will be some surprises even in the short run—some new trends or intense crises will arise well before the end of the 20th century and upset the delicate balance of forces. Many of the new nations will clearly be in turmoil, economic disparities and population pressures will increase, military technology will proliferate and increase in destructiveness, and there will be many occasions that will create at least some risks of war. Thus, to our crisis-prone expectations the predictions for the old nations may seem implausibly evolutionary and crisis-free.

We can invent many scenarios in which we get into trouble—in fact, too many to discuss. We must also concede that any lengthy period without serious challenge does indeed tend to create its own particular tensions that can degenerate into or create disruptive forces. Yet my feeling is that for the rest of the century, while surprises will surely occur as far as the old nations are concerned, these disruptive forces are likely to prove containable. While I scarcely like to be on record as arguing that the old nations—aside from their economic progress and the direct consequences of such progress—will change less in the final third of the 20th century than they did in either of the preceding thirds, I believe this is quite possible; thus the old nations may enjoy several decades of relatively stable and evolutionary change —much as the early Roman Empire did. This of course assumes continued care, vigilance and reasonably prudent policies by these nations. One obvious way in which this "forecast" could turn out badly would be as a self-defeating prophecy, in which too much confidence led to complacency and carelessness. And this is surely one of the risks, but one which is more likely to be avoided by objective, careful and candid, even if uncertain analyses, than by warnings made for political or morale purposes.

Clearly our most important task is to understand current trends and policy alternatives well enough to avoid disasters, to preserve stability, and to make reasonable progress in the next few decades. But this is not sufficient: we must use this "breather," if we are lucky enough to have one, to lay a foundation for dealing with the immensely destructive forces that remain latent and may yet erupt. Difficult as it is to make useful estimates and to plan appropriate policies for such a task, there is a further contingency that should not be neglected: several decades of stability and economic growth could create unprecedented opportunities for improving the quality of life. It is not too soon to analyze economic, political and social aspects of the projected situation, so that we will not be caught unprepared for policy decisions that would enable us to exploit these opportunities for wise and constructive purposes.

VIII

Redesigning Society

Designing is a complex and intricate task. It is the integration of technological, social and economic requirements, biological necessities, and the psychophysical effects of materials, shape, color, volume and space: thinking in relationships. Ultimately, all problems of design merge into one great problem: "design for life."
—LASZLO MOHOLY-NAGY,
Vision in Motion (1947)

PRIME DESIGN

by R. BUCKMINSTER FULLER

ENERGETIC-SYNERGETIC geometry discloses Nature's own system of coordination. Possessing this knowledge and taking the design initiative, man can enjoy Nature's exquisite economy and effectiveness.

We are reminded that at the everyday level of reality men do not build houses with materials; they organize visible-module structures comprised of sub-visible module structures. The principles governing structure operate independently of man-tunable spectrum range. Associative chemistry is structure.

For all time man has subconsciously coordinated himself with universal evolution. He does not consciously push each of his millions of hairs out through his scalp at man-preferred rates or selected patterns and colors.

Man now enters the phase of meager yet conscious participation in the anticipatory design undertakings of Nature. This conscious participation itself is changing from an awkward, arbitrary, trial and error ignorance to an intuitively conceived, yet rigorously serviced, disciplined elegance.

Man has been flying blindly into his future on scientific instruments and formulas. The great news on the artist-scientist-intellectual frontier is that as the fog-and-black shadow of ignorance and misconception recedes, there looms a sublimely comprehensible conceptual patterning, which characterizes all the mathematical principles heretofore only formulatively employed by the scientist, yet intuitively pursued by the artist as potentially modelable. Experimental science has validated the artist's intuitions but not his disciplines.

"Prime Design," from *Ideas and Integrities*, by R. Buckminster Fuller. © 1963 by Richard Buckminster Fuller. Published by Prentice-Hall, Inc., Englewood Cliffs, New Jersey.

The frontiers of physical experimentation have found no basic "building blocks" structuring nature. There are no thing-particles. Only pattern transactions in pure principle have been discovered. Man has therefore been forced to abandon the misconception of a "smallest fundamental particle," upon which the age of materialism was axiomatically predicated.

Where do we go from here? We are dealing with a complex integrity of complementary patterning transformations. Realization is objective integrity. Science, in its disciplined preoccupation with myriad subjective differentiations, serviced by an inbreeding specialization, has unwittingly eluded comprehensive social responsibility for objective potentials or the consequences of its findings and acts.

Engineering and architecture, though objective and integrative, have no economic initiative. These men design professionally only when employed by a patron. The patron becomes the prime designer. The patron initiates that which is to be detailed within the patron-conceived limits of undertaking and responsibility.

Ivory towerism in the scientist and professional-securityism in the architect-engineer have left social initiative to political man, who in turn has passed the buck to the military. The hired military serviceman has done his best within his limits as prime design initiator. His design authority is limited, however, to the augmentation of his tools. His tools—weaponry; their physical objective—killingry, the negative of livingry.

The historic pattern of weaponry is epitomized in the TV Western. The bad man draws first; the good man starts late but finishes first. The bad man is finished. Now comes the surprise. The range has been so increased, and the dueling has become so sophisticated, that both sides can get their effective shots in, and nobody wins.

Today's warhead travels at fifteen thousand miles per hour. With five thousand miles to go, it takes twenty minutes to reach its target. Man's eyes, augmented by radar, penetrate around the world at a velocity of six hundred million miles per hour. As he spots the warhead's takeoff in his direction, he has more than nineteen minutes in which to get his own warhead under way. There is ample time for each side to obliterate the other. Both "good" and "bad" man lose. Even the world political leaders realize that the pursuit of weaponry has reached absurdity.

When Sputnik was launched, it made the airplane obsolete as the number one weapon. In the half century of the airplane's weapon supremacy, two and one-half trillion capital dollars invested by the world nations, converted the highest scientific and technical capabilities of man into the historically most advanced phase of integrated, generalized, mass production tooled industry.

No private individuals, nor the massed credit potential of any group of private individuals, could have underwritten so astronomical an acceleration in the comprehensive industrial technology as was underwritten by the negative mandate articulated by the military. So vast was the production facility thus developed that in this short fifty-year span, all that had been technically scarce, and therefore on highest priority, became plentitudinous.

All the future jet plane production requirements for the swiftly developing world transport system, and all the future military rocket production, together can utilize less than ten per cent of the industrial mass-production facility created to implement the airplane as the premier weapon. Much excess capacity is generalized.

History's amalgam of total experience, its derived knowledge and wisdom as altogether converted to highest industrial mass productability and omni-distribution, has boiled over. Wealth, as the organized physical ability to deal successfully with forward evolutionary events, has attained almost infinite magnitude.

The "organized physical ability" means entire automation of world industry. This eventuality was always inherent in the intellectual pacing of industry. Its complete attainment is suddenly imminent. Marx's worker, the automaton, the muscle and reflex machine, is replaced by automation. Man, losing all significance as physical producer, becomes utterly essential to the industrial equation only as the regenerative consumer. The industrial wealth potential of automated production capability may only be realized by an anticipatorily designed, systematically established and credit-accounted matching consumer capacity. The efficiency of the industrial equation is directly proportional to the numbers consuming.

The political economy, winning and holding the largest proportion of the world's consumer population, can operate at the highest efficiency, at the lowest cost, while attaining the fastest rate of realized wealth augmentation.

The world's political leadership will now undertake the exploitation of the abundance of the "bestest" to win for its respective political camps the heretofore unserviced world customers of the industrial equation. But they will discover also that total world resources invested at the performance per pound level of presently designed livingry will serve only forty per cent of the world's population.

To serve one hundred per cent will involve a world design revolution, not just design of end-products, but of the comprehensive industrial network equations including world-around livingry-service systems, at regenerative occupancy rentals, mutably installed in anticipatory facilitation of total world enjoyment of individually respected total man. This comprehensive design will include not only the network means of production, distribution, maintenance, search, research and continual improvement of service, but also the continual, methodical withdrawal of progressively obsolete facilities tonnage, its reprocessing and recirculation at ever higher performance ratios per pounds of physical resource investment—together with design of the economic implementation of greater numbers of consumers to match the increasing tooled-up production capabilities, and together with designed consumer traffic patterning controls permitting higher frequencies and velocities of electively enjoyed services devoid of individual interference incidents and restraints.

Such designing has brilliant prototype precedent in the telephone system's anticipatorily successful and inherently regenerative physical network instrumentation evolution. The contact instruments of the world-around livingry services must be anticipatorily networked and its consumer-contact instruments and facilities must be installed at consumer request (not sold) for a nominal service fee. The network services utilized by the consumer through his contact equipment will be billed only "after the month" and after the provision of the accruing regenerative advantage realizations by the consumer, whereby the wealth may be established to refund the services in the accounting system designed into the comprehensive undertaking. The prime design must also provide for the orderly transfer of the world consumer population from the obsoleting worker payrolls to the world educational system's advanced search, research and vital regeneration functioning. Einstein's norm of constantly transforming evolutionary patterning must designedly replace Newton's now invalidated static norm.

Prime designing augments wealth. Wealth permits increased freedom of personal time investment. Prime design may multiply the alternate physical facilities for desirable anatomical, mental and cultural development. Desirable time investment alternatives inherently decrease over-all baby-making time. That explains "the rich getting richer and the poor getting children." Prime designing commands the fundamental solution of the over-population threat. As with all fundamental problems of man on earth fundamental solutions are not to be had by political reforms of either the peacetime prohibitory law enforcement variety, or of the never convincing wartime annihilation variety. Fundamental solutions are not for sale. Mass subscriptions to support professional do-gooders are futile.

Fortunately population explosion is only the momentary social hysteria's cocktail conversation game. Real population crisis is fundamentally remote. There is room enough indoors in New York City for the whole 1963 world's population to enter, with room enough inside for all hands to dance the twist in average nightclub proximity. There is ample room in the New York streets for one half of the world's population to amble about in, leaving enough room inside buildings for the other half to lie down and sleep. This would be a good moment to call for all scientists, engineers, tool makers, machine fitters, mechanics and aircraft pilots present, all of whom amount to less than one per cent of humanity, and to send them out from New York City all around the world to get total automation of world production and services going. After this the world's population could start enjoying the whole earth as students, archeologists, playwriters, players, poets, artists, dancers, skin divers, tourists, etc. There would be no further muscle and animal reflex jobs to be done and no need to earn a living, for the living would be generated as effortlessly as apples grow on trees. If you want to go to work you just tell yourself to go to work, you can shovel beach sand from here to there with the beach-playing children, or you can go to work in the library and find out, if you can, how this miracle came about and how to keep it going. You will have plenty of work to do.

The comprehensive prime design scientist-artist-poet will have to do a great deal of work to comprehend his task and to discover the most efficient and effective order of priority of his progressive sets of anticipatory escalator undertakings.

Only the free-wheeling artist-explorer, non-academic, scientist-philosopher, mechanic, economist-poet who has never waited for patron-starting and accrediting of his coordinate capabilities holds the prime initiative today. If man is to continue as a successful pattern-complex function in universal evolution, it will be because the next decades will have witnessed the artist-scientist's spontaneous seizure of the prime design responsibility and his successful conversion of the total capability of tool-augmented man from killingry to advanced livingry—adequate for all humanity.

THE DESIGNERS AND THE POLITICIANS

by R. BUCKMINSTER FULLER

THERE is a new idea aloft in our era, one in which we do not think of our great world dilemmas in terms of politics. For years we have been telling the politicians to solve our problems, and yet the crises continually multiply and accelerate in both magnitude and speed of recurrence.

As automation eliminates physical drudgery, we will spend more time in the future in intellectual activity. The great industry of tomorrow will be the university, and everyone will be going to school. World society is going to concentrate on regenerating its capabilities and its wisdom of their employment.

"The Designers and the Politicians," from *Ideas and Integrities* by R. Buckminster Fuller. © 1963 by Richard Buckminster Fuller. Published by Prentice-Hall, Inc., Englewood Cliffs, New Jersey.

When we talk about wealth today, we are not talking about money or gold. We went off the gold standard between world wars. There are still some gold exchange laws and international trade in which gold is involved, but they are ways of balancing books and not fundamental. After World War I, Germany discovered it would not, if it paid all its reparations, have the wealth necessary to rise again, so the agreement was simply abrogated by the establishment of a new government. The Germans had the blast furnaces, the iron, the coal and the know-how to make steel, so they began to make steel. They began to demonstrate what we really mean by wealth, which is to organize physical capability and to organize energy. Energy flows around the universe and is then shunted and canaled into valvability upon the ends of the levers which we make out of the physical energies interactive in patterns which we call "matter."

Industrial wealth consists of three main constituents: energy, as matter which is energy as gravitation and the radiant energies. The radiant energies are focusable, and therefore canalizable, and we can get them valved out onto the ends of the levers. We then take the radiation energy we call power and apply it to the convergent energy we call matter, organized as machinery.

Physicists like Einstein and Max Planck saw that energy left one's system only by joining another system. They discovered, by experimentation, that no energy could be created and no energy could be lost. The physicists thus developed the concept, called the law of conservation of energy, that energy could neither be created nor lost. That's a finite package of energy, the finite physical universe, which is the Einsteinian world.

If no energy can be created and no energy lost, and we put together energy as matter and energy as radiation to make machinery run by power other than our backs and muscles, then the constituent of what we call wealth is actually indestructible. When I was brought up, we used to have the idea that wealth was something that was continually running downhill and wearing out. But the revival of the German economy without money taught us something new.

There is a third constituent of wealth, which is *intellectual*. Every time I make an experiment, taking some radiant energy and applying it to reforming metals and making a better piece of machinery, I have learned more. This constituent of wealth is therefore inherently and regeneratively self-augmenting. Even if a physical part wears out, the intellectual constituent improves. This concept of wealth is changing our whole system of life.

Conservation will no longer mean withholding from use, but insistence upon widest, practical, active usefulness. The physicist's law of Conservation of Energy means that the physical universe cannot wear out or run down or become exhausted by use. The law of Conversation of Intellect tells us that human use of intellect always improves human capability. The new scientific era conservative is inherently committed to multiplying reinvestment of capability which is complex and provides the only experimental test of synergy. The conservative realizes that the more that wealth is usefully reemployed, for more people, the more wealth is amplified. Socialism was one of yesterday's ways of dealing with inadequate wealth. Socialism is now as obsolete as the stone hammer. So also is undeveloped static property, or gold capitalism. Gold coins wear out; land erodes. That is why capitalism is obsolete. Industry and biology are metabolic; they grow.

Up to and including World War I, there had been great masters of the earth, masters of commerce (you could call them pirates) who had built powerful ships and gone out and taken the other fellow; and they were running the world. They looked at the world as a great, comprehensive undertaking, where enormous wealth could be earned, and they planned a hundred years ahead.

With World War I the old masters went out of business because they were physically coordinated men who judged things in terms of their own eyes, ears, taste and touch. They didn't trust others. But with the new technology, ninety-nine per cent of what was going on was utterly invisible, which is why we have scientists to deal with the invisible world. When the old masters went out, they were not coordinated in the invisible world, but in a sensorial world. Also, their gold was utterly inadequate for the magnitude of the new industrial productivity.

The world did not know of the departure of the old masters until the crash of 1929. The depth of the depression was 1932, when we completed the isolation of the ninety-second chemical element. Chemistry's pantry shelves were now full.

We were ready for a great new venture. If we only had known what we were doing—we were dealing in invisibles—we would have realized that our society was not in a mess at all. The economic disaster was simply a disaster in terms of the economics and accounting of the old masters, who had become obsolete.

When the old masters went, some of the citizens found that their economies were in great trouble. This led to the assumption of power by dictators because people didn't know what to do about their problems. It was the beginning of a society where people thought the politicians could solve the problems of the world, but the politicians have truly no idea of what to do about them.

In the hierarchy of events that reshape the face of the world as far as man's participation goes, man, ecologically, has been sweeping out larger and larger areas. Ecology, as I have explained, is the science of the various patterns of life, the different species of life, the flora and the fauna. There is a unique ecological pattern for each kind of life. Man is the only living species which has altered its ecological patterning in the history of life on earth. He has progressed from a local sweep-out of perhaps a twenty-four-mile radius in the early ages of man, or perhaps a walk to the visible horizon and back to his home.

Until World War I an American man walked an average of thirteen hundred miles per year, and rode three hundred and fifty miles by some other vehicular means. As we came out of World War I, Americans were sweeping out an average of sixteen hundred miles a year by mechanical means and still walking thirteen hundred; but for the first time man had become primarily a riding device instead of a walking device. Instead of sitting in a static chair, he sat in an automobile chair.

In 1941 we were averaging six thousand, five hundred miles a year, despite the fact that the housewife was covering ten thousand miles, the salesman thirty thousand and the airline hostess one hundred thousand (invalids and so forth brought down the average). At the present time our sweep-out averages twelve thousand miles a year.

So man has, from the beginning, been participating in larger and larger patterns on the earth. This is the hierarchy of events. With the right kind of training the individual thinker as a scientist leads science and gives it new steps forward. Science paces technology, but it is hard for science to convince technology. Technology paces industry, but there is a long lag in the process. Industry paces economics. It changes the tools, a great ecological change. And in that manner we come finally to everyday life.

The politician is someone who deals in man's problems of adjustment. To ask a politician to lead us is to ask the tail of a dog to lead the dog.

While I was speaking at Harvard recently, a number of Harvard students went to Washington in company with students from many other universities. They saw their congressmen and pleaded with them to abandon war and nuclear bombs. They said their congressmen were wonderful and let the students talk a lot. But the representatives said, "Don't make us more miserable, we're already dealing in trouble, and you want us to be a little more negative about trouble."

Just being negative doesn't do any good. I tell students to stop using their feet and start using their heads. Our tails and our feet can't lead us. This realization is beginning to move students, and we will hear a great deal more about it. We will soon have to design the over-all industrial network for making the world work for all humanity.

In 1835 Thomas Malthus, a well-to-do man with some influence and access to government data, was able to see certain figures being collected by English economic representatives all over the world. It was the first time any one man was faced with the facts about population and production. And what Malthus saw was startling. It was apparent that people around the world were multiplying more rapidly than they could produce and support themselves.

A generation later Charles Darwin developed his concept of the interpatterning of all biological species and his theory of the evolution of the species, and its corollary, the survival of the fittest.

Up to this time in history, men had believed that their fate rested on the whim of God or gods. Armed with the information that there would not be enough production to go around, and that mankind was being subjected to a survival of the fittest, certain statesmen conceived the idea of national defense a century ago. When the old masters were gone, the politicians, finding potential in their economies, decided it was their mandate not to let their economies run down. So they tossed the problem to their military colleagues, ordering them to invest total scientific and technical capability in defense. This was the beginning of the great arms race.

It is important to realize that there are people in this world other than politicians trying to do something. I would guess that one hundred years from now, historians will note that in the period of 1927 to 1967, man was so preoccupied and so relatively illiterate that he thought it all right to leave the problems of the world to the politicians. This idea will look preposterous in the perspective of history.

We are shooting to get to the moon. What soldiers want is to get the first commanding platform in space. That's what the militarists are after. To be able to send a man to the moon, you first have to be able to give him his own private little earth, and he's been living on an enormous earth with great energy-exchanging patterns he knows very little about. He knows a little about the air he breathes or the gas plants give off. He doesn't know why men's temperatures are ninety-eight and six tenths degrees Fahrenheit when in good health. He doesn't really know about his extraordinary energy balance.

Our processes are so secret that nobody really knows anything about plumbing. Everything fundamental about our sewage system was invented in India by 2500 B.C. No one has made significant improvements since that time. No architect ever looks back of the purple tiles, no scientist ever studies plumbing. We never hire scientists to look at our homes. Scientists, however, work with weaponry, and its by-products go back into our homes, but it is completely inadvertent. What would happen if the scientists helped us to use everything he and we've learned to make the world a success for man?

This is what is going to happen with our explorations into space, because we can no longer be wasteful. We will have extraordinary energy cycles developed in our behalf by the scientists. We're going to have to give our spaceman enough food—he needs a ton a year, and he'll have to process that. We are going to have to find out how to use that valuable chemistry we have been turning over to Nature's landscape to process for us. While we look the other way the spaceman won't be able to get rid of it. If he spits there is no gravity to take it way. It stays right there in front of him in space. We are not going to send the spaceman out into space to find out what to do with his chemistry to make him survive. If our scientists on earth haven't figured it all out very satisfactorily in every respect, psychologically and esthetically, as well as chemically, before we send that spaceboy "out," he'll never come back "in" again—alive.

For the first time in history we are employing scientists to work on a little house. It hasn't been thought of, architecturally, as a house, but it's the most important house that's ever been worked on. In America we are spending three billion dollars a year and in Russia they are spending six billion dollars a year on this autonomous dwelling device—for man.

The little black box that will take care of our sanitation will be more effective than anything that's been used before. Men will control their environment and be very healthy. I believe that the telephone company will start expanding those little country telephone booths into replicas of space houses. Out of the prototype for the space age will come the scientific knowledge for the actual production of this autonomous dwelling device.

In a few years you may be able to walk into a telephone company booth one morning and ask them to put up a dwelling device on a certain mountain that afternoon. When you're through with it, you will call the company, and ask them to remove it. The company will have your environment control waiting for you wherever you want it at low cost for dream high standards.

There is a new dedication on the part of the young in this world. Students are corresponding with each other all over the globe. This young world is about to take over, to help us design ourselves to make man a success on earth. If this is successfully done, the Malthusian and Darwinian frustrations will be completely irrelevant. There will be enough to go around, and the politicians will have no mandate to build weapons. To get rid of weapons we must design our way to positive effectiveness, and not just be negative about politicians and what they are doing.

THE NATURE OF SYSTEMS ENGINEERING

by SIMON RAMO

Systems engineering—the invention, the design, and the integration of the whole ensemble—is actually an old and ever-present part of practical engineering. Any device, no matter how simple, represents to some extent a systems engineering kind of problem. This applies to a chair as well as to a transcontinental railroad, to a hand tool as well as to an intercontinental ballistic missile. There is always the need to break down the over-all problem into its component parts and to specify the requirements of each of those parts. There is always the problem of relating the parts to the whole, and the whole to the outside world that will be the user and that will expect a useful result. Why, then, is this subject particularly timely?

There is now a tremendous interest in systems engineering that did not exist a few decades ago. The systems with which we are now concerned are more complex and more difficult to engineer, and we are rapidly taking large steps in technology. Much more than in the past, a typical new system depends on immediate application of the newest discoveries of basic science. Furthermore, the relationships between the engineering considerations and the economic, military, governmental, and even sociologic considerations have become increasingly important. In these times, in which technology is altering our world so rapidly and in which government and industry must continually adjust to these changes, it is quite natural that systems engineering has become a topic of widespread interest in many circles that previously had little or no concern with it.

Excerpted from "Parts and Wholes in Systems Engineering," by Simon Ramo. Reprinted with permission from *Parts and Wholes* (The Free Press, 1963), edited by Daniel Lerner.

Right at the present, it is true, the major projects in systems engineering—that is, in the size and importance of new complexes of men and machines—are largely in the military field and related to our national survival. But it is equally true that an increasing percentage of our everyday peacetime pursuits are requiring major systems engineering. The system operations of our growing, more highly technical civilization, be they production, communications, transportation, or tax collection, are every day becoming more complex, faster paced, and geographically more widespread. In turn, this results in new interactions and interconnections among people and machines and in new over-all relationships of technology to nontechnical problems. These aspects more and more characterize modern systems engineering in its efforts to optimize the application of science and technology to create a more secure world and a more orderly one that can provide for the needs of the earth's populations.

My general plan here will be to describe the nature of systems engineering and some of the special techniques and tools required for carrying it out successfully, to comment on the teaching of systems engineering, and finally to engage in some speculations about the future.

Systems engineering becomes more interesting and its problems newer and more important to us as the scope of the system grows. In discussing the general nature of systems engineering, we shall therefore most often have in mind the larger and more complex systems. Because of the breadth and complexity of our subject, we shall not find it convenient to make a complete, detailed analysis of it. Rather, we shall be able only to touch upon some of its highlights and possibilities, and to attempt in this way to convey a general feeling for the subject.

We might start out by raising the most basic question of all: should the new system be created in the first place? For many people, the full impact of the need for going into such a question takes some time to register. The question has two broad aspects: the technical and the nontechnical.

The average systems situation is one in which the engineer is asked to meet largely technical requirements, although, of course, he is generally aware of the economic constraints on the system.

Often at the start, it is known that the so-called requirements are only an ideal goal and that they cannot be met with any system that is technically feasible in the immediate future. Therefore, new and more practical requirements have to be established as the work goes along. Systems engineering in modern technology requires an unusual degree of matching the requirements and the end objectives with the state of the technical art.

Let us take, for example, an intercontinental ballistic missile. Even if the over-all objective of the systems engineer were simply to design a system that does a good job of delivering a nuclear warhead several thousand miles away—and this is too simple a description of the over-all problem—it is clear that the propulsion, guidance, structure, and re-entry problems are all wrapped up together in an exceedingly complicated relationship. If we can develop guidance systems having greater accuracy, we can achieve the necessary effect at the terminal end with less weight of warhead. Carrying a smaller warhead makes easier its protection from the tremendous heats of re-entry into the atmosphere from space. If the re-entry can be faster, if we can develop designs or materials to accept the greater heat, then there is less wind dispersion of a random type, which eases the guidance accuracy requirement. The size of the warhead (including its protection) is also related to the propulsion system because the smaller the warhead, the smaller the propulsion system that is needed to push it up to the necessary speed to travel thousands of miles. But proper control of the propulsion system is harder to achieve if high accuracy is insisted upon. It is clear that the question of technical feasibility can be difficult to answer and that a certain number of calculated risks may have to be taken along the way.

Feasibility of a major systems engineering project is not a matter of technical feasibility alone. We need to ask simultaneously whether arrangements to do the job can in fact be made. The financing of the project, the interactions with associated or displaced equipment and organizations, and the use of large quantities of technical and physical resources can all be of such consequence that the mere arrangement-making problem becomes an important parameter in the over-all systems engineering task. As an example, we know that technically we can send freight around the world by air-breathing guided missiles. But even assuming that the potential profits are attractive, can suitable financing be obtained? Will such vehicles be permitted to use existing airports or will special fields have to be built for their exclusive use? What about the hazards of collision with other aircraft? And can the new vehicles be tied in with existing systems of air traffic control? The list of such questions on a major project may be numbered in the dozens.

From all of these comments, it is evident that the practice of modern systems engineering needs to start with trying to find out what the over-all problem really is, in both its technical and non-technical aspects, and that it could end by eliminating the problem as one that deserves no solution, or is impossible to solve within today's technical art or within our arrangement-making capabilities.

At this point we can make the observation that modern systems engineering is characterized in part by the existence in the problem of a large number of parameters, both technical and non-technical. Even if we limit our discussion to the technical parameters, when the number that must be considered in any problem becomes sufficiently large, it begins to be difficult to be quantitative and precise. This results in a tendency to carry out the engineering of large, complex systems in a loose manner or, at best, with purely qualitative methodology, rather than with scientific and quantitative techniques. In such instances, systems engineering becomes a matter of "opinion" or "belief," as with politics or religion. In practice, what often happens is that some of the parameters are chosen arbitrarily. Of course, the moment this is done, there is the risk that accidents and bias will control, for sometimes the parameters that have been chosen arbitrarily will turn out in the end not to be the most important.

Obviously, the systems engineering team needs to include experts in all of the fields touched by the over-all system, technical and nontechnical. But since the technical part of the team is almost always much the larger part, let us examine it a bit further.

As indicated earlier, one of the frequent characteristics of modern systems engineering is that we are setting out to do things that are radical advances over the past, and in the process we have to make use of the very latest in scientific knowledge. This alone would require that the technical team include scientists who understand the newest scientific discoveries, but there is also another aspect involving scientists. In most respects, trying to understand the workings of a complex engineering system in a quantitative sense is basically not very different from the attempt by a good research scientist to understand any complex segment of nature that he is studying. We must try to write the system's laws of behavior. We must devise experiments, sometimes of a unique nature, that will test our hypotheses. The kinds of individuals capable of analyzing and predicting the actions of a complex multiparameter system are very much the same as those who seek to improve our understanding of the basic laws of nature.

But while it is true that modern systems engineering rests on a broad scientific foundation, it is also true that it is equally dependent upon known engineering techniques and upon existing components and subsystems. The practical engineer is needed not only because he has the necessary store of information on these subjects but also because he has the practical touch to make the system work as planned. This is especially important in systems containing large numbers of components with complex interconnections. Here, lack of acquaintance with the esoteric art of debugging, and with problems of reliability in what might otherwise be considered as staid old components, can prevent the success of the project so that it never gets a chance to demonstrate the progress that could have resulted from the application of new scientific discoveries.

This discussion of the members of the systems engineering team reminds us that in the modern systems approach, most systems include men a well as machines. We cannot isolate these two parts of the system and deal with them independently and separately as though the other part did not exist. We must, in other words, think of the human beings in the system as major subsystems or components. As best we can, we must introduce their characteristics into the over-all system synthesis and analysis.

From the beginning, the human assignments must be specified, and estimated as to cost, performance, stability, and time for de- velopment. Hopefully, this is done just as clearly as we list the inanimate portions of the system and subject them to analysis. We are on weaker ground here, of course, and are less confident that we can extrapolate as we do from the relatively simpler laws of physics. On the other hand, we have had a lot of experience with human beings on which we can draw. In some situations, for example, we can unhesitatingly reject a proposed systems design because it asks too much of the human beings in the system. (By contrast, in other situations, we may find it more difficult to accept or reject a system on the basis of doubts about some simple electronic component, such as a transitor.)

We have had long experience with the extension and replace- ment of man's muscles by the machine. Here, it is a matter of good engineering to select those functions that can be better per- formed by a machine: the application of large forces, operation at high speeds, movements of precise magnitudes, operation in un- favorable environments, and the like. Ideally, we do not have a man dig a ditch; we have him steer a machine that does the digging. Man is capable of subtle motions and the application of complex combinations of forces. He should be reserved for such situations.

Something similar is indicated in the extension and replacement of man's sense and his brain. No computer or thinking machine in existence or imagined as being practical has a total capacity that is more than a tiny fraction of man's brain. It would be absurd, then, to even consider replacing man by a completely automatic system in most situations in which he uses his brain or his senses. But, again, man's remarkable system is being misused if he is given easy assignments to do—too easy for the tremendous powers of his brain and sensing system—or if the total quantity of opera- tions is beyond the man or is tedious to an extreme. To illustrate, consider a constant decision-making operation in which there is at the most a need for deciding between two or three possibilities, easily identified, but coming at a rate of thousands per second. This is simultaneously a job too simple for the human system and yet, in sheer quantity of simple actions per unit of time, well beyond human ability to operate at all.

The degree to which a system is to be made automatic, the

specialized education and training required for the human operators, and the extent to which the human eyes, ears, and brain will be used as participants in the system are all considerations that play a major part in modern systems engineering. The procedure is to some extent straightforward. We must visualize what actions need to be performed in the system; we must ask throughout whether they are best performed by a one-hundred-and-fifty-pound man or by some other total weight of automatic apparatus. We must compare the abilities, the investment, the maintenance, and the reliability of these alternates.

THE POLITICS OF POWER AND
THE POLITICS OF GROWTH

by KARL W. DEUTSCH

In discussing autonomy and memory, we discussed some aspects of political aspirations. Any autonomous system of memories and self-steering decisions is apt to have its own set of internal probabilities in terms of which it will not merely behave at any one moment but also project or propose its behavior for the future. As P. W. Bridgman once put it in my hearing, "The future is a program"; that is, the future may be viewed as a set of probabilities implied by the present distribution of resources and environmental factors. In this sense every autonomous system tends to act out the future implicit in the distributions of its memories and in the configurations of its communication channels; and insofar as its behavior leads it to ac-

"The Politics of Power and the Politics of Growth," reprinted with permission of The Macmillan Company from *The Nerves of Government* by Karl W. Deutsch. © The Free Press of Glencoe, a Division of The Macmillan Company 1963.

quire new memories and to change some of its internal communication patterns by learning, it will remake itself and its future to a limited extent at every such step. If the system has consciousness, if it monitors its own behavior, and derives and remembers images of itself that it applies to its own actions, then it may well also derive and use images projecting its behavior into the future. It will thus use goal images and entertain explicitly formulated aspirations.

When do such political aspirations harden into political will? The literature of political science is rich in references to political will, but far less rich in attempts to analyze the meaning of the term. From the viewpoint of communication, *will* may be taken to consist in the putting into operation of data proposed from the past of a decision-making system in such a manner as to override most or all of the information currently received from its environment. In its extreme form, will in politics functions somewhat like the deadline in a newspaper or the departure of a train. It assesses the relevance of events and messages in terms of time: information received before the moment of decision may be treated as relevant, but later messages are not. Will in this sense implies the operational priority of predecision data over postdecision data. Emotionally, it may mean to individuals and groups the acting out of their own preferences, personality characteristics, and culture patterns, unburdened by the task of having to reassess or revise them in terms of ever new data from the present.

Since will implies the ability to stick to a decision, it may thus appear as an escape from the psychological burden of further decision-making. In groups or governments where a decision may have been reached only after considerable difficulties, persisting, for example, in a foreign-policy decision and freezing the policies designed to execute it may have an important advantage—not having to reopen the original problem, and thus avoiding renewed domestic conflict. Similarly, in situations where decisions involve conflicts between different values, persistence may prove easier than revision.

In cases of major decisions, will may involve the commitment of major resources to decisions that must not be revised. In this sense, it may involve the suspension or abandonment of the learning process, and may imply the desire not to learn, or at least not to learn anything that may prove incompatible with what has been willed.

In the poetry and folklore of extreme political movements, this type of will has found its appropriate symbol in the image of the dead man who returns from his grave in order to act out some political aspiration or decision, single-minded and impervious to all distractions or blandishments of the world of the living. In such imagery, the dead hero serves as a symbol of escape, from all compromises and frustrations, and the frequency and appeal of the symbol of the irresistible army of the dead—the appeal, as it were, of the "death urge" in politics—may perhaps tend to increase with the amount of the fears and frustrations experienced in social and political life and in the ordinary political process.

The notion of a will that is not merely inflexible but actually irresistible implies the notion of power. By *power* we mean, in everyday language, the ability to get "our way" or to get "our" will. As we have seen, power implies the ability to act out with little or no modifications the behavior implicit in our memories and in the configurations of our personal preferences and values. Power thus means for persons and groups the ability to act "in character," whatever that character may be.

In this simple sense, power is a quantitative concept. It could be measured in each case, in principle, by the extent of modification of overt behavior accepted by a person, a group, or a decision system in response to its environment (and perhaps particularly in response to the behavior of other autonomous systems) compared to the extent of modification imposed on the environment. In this sense, power corresponds to the notion of hardness among minerals, or of a peck order among chickens. In all these situations power is epitomized in the answers to the questions: Which process can impose the greater modification on the other? And which process imposes greater modifications upon all others?

If "will" implied the desire not to learn, "power" may imply the ability not to have to do so. In this simple sense, both will and power may form aspects of the pathology of social learning, and the ceaseless warnings of moralists, philosophers, and theologians against both will and power may be understood in this context. By pathological learning in the case of an individual or an organization we may understand a learning process, and a corresponding change in inner structure, that will reduce rather than increase the future learning capacity of the person or organization. Will and power may easily lead to such self-destructive learning, for they may imply the overvaluation of the past against the present and future, the overvaluation of the experiences acquired in a limited environment against the vastness of the universe around us; and the overvaluation of present expectations against all possibilities of surprise, discovery, and change.

If carried to extremes, the simple forms of will and power may destroy the decision systems in which they become dominant. However, power may be quantitatively measured in a less primitive way. In an extended sense, we might define *power* (or "strength," if another word is wanted) as the ability to act out a particular preference in behavior, or to reach a particular goal, *with the least loss of ability to choose a different behavior*, or to seek a different goal. Power in this extended sense is thus related not merely to the absence of imposed modification of behavior but also to economy of commitment, and to the capacity for alternative commitments in the future.

If we bear in mind the simple and extended meaning of power in politics, we may be able to study not merely the pathology of power; we may also be able to think of will and power as elements in the politics of growth.

It is often said that it is the task of politics to promote the "public interest" or the "common good" of a nation or of a larger society over and above all special or lesser interests. If we admit that there can be such a common good and that social life is not exhausted by group conflicts, we must ask what this good is. Despite wide differences in cultures and values, we may assume provisionally that one of the most widely accepted values is the *survival* of the family, community, people, or nation. In terms of their probability of survival, we may divide all political systems or organizations into four categories:

1. *Self-destroying systems*, which are apt to break down eventually even in relatively favorable environments.
2. *Nonviable systems*, which are unlikely to survive under the range of difficulties found in most environments (though they need not be likely to be self-destructive).

3. *Viable systems*, which are likely to preserve their original probability of survival over a limited range of environmental conditions; and

4. *Self-developing or self-enhancing systems*, which are able to increase their probability of survival and their ranges of possible action over an increasing variety of environments.

While social organizations are radically different from organisms, the last three of these categories happen to parallel somewhat the medical notion of "health," and to parallel closely the biologist's concept of "evolutionary progress." This latter concept is also based on the notion of probable long-run survival and on the probability that in the long run most environments may change very considerably, so that only self-changing and self-enhancing systems and organizations are apt to survive eventually, thanks to their ability to cope with many different environments and to increase their relative independence from any one of them.

Neither the biologist nor the social scientist need deny that there may arise on occasion some nonviable organisms or some nonviable or self-destructive organizations. All they need say is that such highly self-destructive organizations will tend in fact not to survive, even though they may function as a dangerous environment for those organizations and individuals committed in some way to the values of life and survival. In the legislative control of the behavior of individuals, we similarly draw up laws on the assumption that most persons value life, and desire the survival of individuals and communities dear to them; and we treat suicide and attempts at suicide as exceptions that, though real, are not likely to change the basic rules of the game for the survivors.

The consequence of these notions, from Emile Durkheim's notion of social health to Julian Huxley's concept of evolutionary progress, is the recognition of growth, of adaptability, and of learning capacity as essential for the survival of societies and cultures. What are the dimensions of this growth, and what can politics contribute to it?

As the first dimension of growth of a political system, we may count the growth of *manpower* and population included in it, as well as gains in their physical and mental health. In the second place, we may count *economic growth*. Without trying to summarize the literature on economic growth, we may merely note that this would include particularly the amounts of disposable factors of production, such as capital goods, land, and labor, as well as the growth of skills and technical knowledge. A further condition would be that the rate of growth of the second category, economic resources, should exceed in the long run the rate of the growth of population. The meeting of these conditions requires the maintenance of rates of savings and of investment in capital-goods industries, which without government aid have been attained only in a few countries, and only for limited periods, and which often may require political decisions.

In the third place, we may list the criteria of growth that bear on the availability of material and human resources for recommitment to new uses. Particularly we may list here the development of *operational reserves* in the system that may be committed to the pursuit of new goals or to the meeting of new stresses or new challenges from the environment.

The fourth group of criteria of growth refers to the growth of autonomy, or *self-determination*. This implies, on the one hand, a growth in the resources and functions that bear on social cohesion, that is, the growth, range, speed, and effectiveness of internal communications, both among individuals and among institutions or parts of the society or the political system. On the other hand, it implies growth in the steering performance of the system, in the effectiveness of its use of data recalled from memory, and of information received from outside. It will require, therefore, a growth in the facilities of memory and recall, and thus of institutions of learning, record-keeping, and the like; a growth in the variety and effectiveness of channels for the intake of new ranges of information from the outside world; an improvement in goal-seeking operations, through increases in the gain and lead, and through the cutting down of lag by reducing the delays due to either slowness of communication or to inertia or inner resistance in response.

A possible fifth criterion is implied in the fourth. A growing organization, and hence also a growing state or government, must be able to change its own patterns of communication and organization, so as to overcome the results of the "scale effect." It must resist the trend toward increasing self-preoccupation and eventual self-immolation from its environment; and it must reorganize or transform itself often enough to overcome the growing threats of internal communication overload and the jamming up of message traffic. One of the most effective responses to these threats—highlighted by such writings on politics and administration as "Parkinson's Law"—consists in *strategic simplifications*.

Often in history, growth in organization and progress in technique appear to imply just such a simplification of some crucial link or coupling in the chain of interlocking and self-sustaining processes by which the organization is kept going. Thus the maintenance of an ever-growing written tradition is facilitated by the invention of increasingly simple alphabets and increasingly simple methods of writing and, eventually, printing. The many tasks of modern languages are facilitated by the sloughing off of many of the ancient inflections and the replacement of their semantic functions by means of word position and context. Other examples of this process of strategic simplification are the replacement of trolley tracks by rubber tires; of telegraph wires by radio; and many other processes of this kind, ranging all the way to the increasingly simple symbol structures of the central theories of physics from the cumbrous models of Ptolemy and Copernicus to the simpler and more general formulations of Newton and Einstein.

Cases of this sort are cited by A. J. Toynbee, but the interpretation proposed here is somewhat different from his. In none of the cases of simplification which he cites do we find a simplification—or a reduction in the number of elements—for any of the systems cited *as a whole*, be they systems of transportation, communication, or theoretical physics. On the contrary, each system as a whole is becoming more complex; what is becoming simpler are particular links in it, which are crucial or strategic. Thus a modern radio station is a far more complicated piece of electric equipment than the original wire telegraph of Samuel Morse; but its ability to transmit signals without telegraph wires permitted man to put its increased complex of resources to other and more fruitful uses. With this qualification, however, there seems to be a good deal of evidence supporting Toynbee's surmise that some such strategic or crucial simplifications may well be essential for any extended process of growth.

An important special case of such strategic simplifications might perhaps be seen in the replacement of gross operations or experiments with major physical resources by much simpler and quicker operations or experiments by means of symbols. An increasing shift from operations with gross resources toward a growing proportion of operations by means of symbols is thus another possible criterion of growth; and most of the cases of what Mr. Toynbee has called "etherealization" as an important aspect of growth could be brought perhaps under this heading.

All these elements of growth, taken together, may go far to meet one of the tests for growth once proposed by Simon Kuznets: the ability of an organization, an economy, or a state to approach the goals it happens to have chosen. In this sense, growth as the ability to approach previously chosen goals is closely related to the increase in the will and power characteristics of the system. The more rigorously the system is able to exclude all outside resistance in its way, the more likely it may be to reach the particular goal chosen. In this sense, will and power represent the ability to harden and deepen the temporary commitment of attention and resources, and are essential instruments of short-run steering performance, autonomy, and growth.

The sixth group of criteria deals with long-run growth. These include increases in *goal-changing* ability, in the range of different ends the society, culture, or political system is able to choose and to pursue. Here we find learning capacity, not merely in terms of limited operational reserves but also in terms of the capacity for deep rearrangements of inner structure, and thus for the development of radically new functions. Here we list the growth in the possibility of producing genuine *novelty*, of applying some of the resulting new combinations of information to the guidance of behavior as *initiative*, and of producing eventually new patterns in the physical or social environment in processes of *creativity*.

Thus far, all criteria derived from our growth model have applied primarily to the decision system as a whole. However, an essential characteristic of any human organization, in contrast to an anthill, is the interplay between the dimensions of growth of the organization and the growth of the individuals and of the more or less autonomous subgroups that compose it. In this sense, the growth of human organizations is always the growth of several levels of autonomous systems, and the autonomous growth and enhanced self-determination of individuals is one of its touchstones. To a lesser but still very real degree, this may apply to the growth of lesser autonomous organizations within the system. The growth of the whole decision system may thus also be "measured" in terms of progress in articulation and multiple autonomy, and thus as progress in what some psychologists have called "integrative behavior." Gains in the capacity for integrative behavior—which does not destroy the autonomy of the units integrated—may in turn be related to the ability of a society or state to deal with other societies or states without suicide or mutual destruction. A combined growth in power and in the awareness of limits; in depth of memory and in openness to new ranges of information; in social, intellectual, and emotional resourcefulness and creativity; and in the capacity for *integrative behavior*; these, taken together, may well be most conducive to survival in international politics.

If we accept provisionally this sketch of the criteria of growth, politics can contribute much to fulfill them. Within the general field of social innovation and social learning, politics can function as the sphere of decision. If we define the core area of politics as the area of enforceable decisions or, more accurately, of all decisions backed by some combination of a significant probability of voluntary compliance with a significant probability of enforcement, then politics becomes the method par excellence for securing preferential treatment for messages and commands and for the reallocation of human or material resources. Politics thus appears as a major instrument for either retarding or accelerating social learning and innovation, and it has been used in both functions in the past. Politics has been used to increase the rigidity of already semipetrified social systems, and it has been used to accelerate ongoing processes of change.

Examples of the conservative function of politics can be found in many cultures. Perhaps it has been a peculiarity of Western politics to have developed a range of significant techniques for accelerating innovation. Perhaps three of the most important of these techniques are majority rule, the protection of minorities, and the institutionalization of dissent.

Autonomous organizations may be prone to overvalue internal or parochial information, as well as familiar data from the past, as against data and information derived from new or wider ranges of experience. Resistance to change and innovation may thus be one of the "occupational risks" of autonomous organizations. Political patterns requiring unanimity—as does much of Oriental village politics—may tend to slow down the rate of change to a very low level. Majority rule in the western manner permits, on the contrary, a change to be carried out much earlier and thus much faster. At the same time, Western traditions for the protection of minorities may prevent majority-imposed rates of change from disrupting the integrity and dignity of dissenting individuals or groups, or of breaking the bonds and communication channels of social cohesion. Finally, the institutionalization of dissent, and the provision of acceptable channels and modes for the expression of criticism and self-criticism, of counterproposals and of new suggestions, protect not merely the majority of yesterday but also provide potential growing points for the majorities of tomorrow. Taken together, majority rule, minority protection, and institutionalized dissent, reinforced by highly conscious, analytical, critical and combinatorial modes of thought, provide Western societies and political systems with an unusually wide range of resources and instrumentalities for rapid social learning and innovation. Even though other cultures may not copy these institutions in their Western shape, they will have to provide by some means for the functions of wide exploration and rapid recommitment these Western institutions have performed.

Politics, like all techniques of making and implementing decisions, is not an end in itself. Indeed, we have a range of generous visions, from early Christianity to H. G. Wells, envisaging a state of social development where all social compulsion, and with it all politics, will become obsolete. Whatever one may think of these hopes, politics in the world of today is an essential instrument of social learning. It will be more likely to function as an instrument of survival and growth, rather than destruction, if it is guided by cognitive insights. All studies of politics, and all techniques and models suggested as instruments of political analysis, have this purpose: that men should be more able to act in politics with their eyes open.

This perspective is no less relevant to those among us who see politics chiefly as a contest rather than as a process of awakening. Competition in world politics in the second half of the twentieth century resembles less a tug-of-war than a race; less a hundred yard dash than a marathon; less a marathon than a slalom; and less a slalom than a combined course in survival, and persuasion, as well as in learning and discovery. In this contest, too, government and politics will long remain indispensable instruments for accelerated social learning, by which mankind in its various subdivisions, still organized in states, can adapt more quickly to the dangerous but hopeful tasks of growing up.

NOTES ON DECENTRALIZATION

by PAUL GOODMAN

I. What Is Meant by Decentralization and What Is Not Meant

Decentralizing is increasing the number of centers of decision making and the number of initiators of policy; increasing the awareness by individuals of the whole function in which they are involved; and establishing as much face-to-face association with decision makers as possible. People are directly engaged in the function.

Conversely, centralization is organization with top-down decision making (on the basis of "upward communication"), departmentalization of the function, chain of command or bureaucracy, and maximum standardization of performance and procedure. People are personnel of the organization that performs the function.

"Notes on Decentralization," by Paul Goodman. Reprinted by permission from *Dissent*. Copyright © 1965, Dissent Publishing Association.

Decentralization is not lack of order or organization but a different kind of co-ordination. Western science from 1500 to 1900 was entirely decentrally co-ordinated. In its high early period the free enterprise system of joint-stock companies was decentrally co-ordinated. The American political system of limited powers and checks and balances is decentralist in principle.

Many functions must be centralized by their nature: where there are no natural limits, or the function extends over the whole system, or the logistics is more important than the particulars —e.g., epidemic control, setting of standards, certain kinds of production and distribution, unification and scheduling of transportation. Also, in situations where force must be collected and directed to an emergency. At present we ought to centralize further in some functions: e.g., we ought to have modular standards and standard parts in building and in machinery; "natural monopolies" like telephone-telegraph or railroads; and, internationally, where vast capital is required, like the moon shot.

At present there is a strong trend to spontaneous decentral political action—in the direct-action movements, and also some trend in cultural fields, like off-Broadway or Summerhill. But to decentralize, to delegate autonomy to many centers, can also be a political decision of a central power, usually compelled by the fact that the centralization is not working. For example, the New York City Board of Education is experimenting with decentralizing.

In the present period decentralized centers need not be narrow, isolated, or "provincial." We exist in a post-urban, post-mass communication, post-centralist period. The decentralist kibbutzim might, by some, be considered as fanatical but scarcely provincial.

The fact of great populations does not prevent decentralization. Decentralizing is primarily a question of sociological organization rather than geographical dispersal, though that is sometimes involved. In a big city the organization of arrondissements with neighborhood city halls can importantly decentralize. A big university should be run by its many faculties.

Decentralizing is largely an empirical question and requires research and experiment (which it is not getting). The maxim of decentralization is to decentralize where, how much, and how it is expedient. For example, a gang or collective contract is used in important assembly-line manufacture in Coventry, whereby the

gang determines its own working schedule, persons, and operations. In what industries in the U.S. is this feasible? How should
it be tailored?

II. Present Excessive Centralization

In some aspects of social organization there is historically a
discernible cyclical swing between excessive centralization and excessive decentralization. Within the nation states at present there
is, in most major functions, excessive centralization or centralism
on wrong principles (just as internationally there is decentralization on wrong principles). Our emphasis ought to begin to be the
other way.

Our present overdeveloped centralism goes back to a bureaucratic style perfected in the eighteenth century for taxation and
policing; a military style developed with the emergence of the
nation states for logistics and to wage war; an economic style
dominated by abstract money-profits rather than specific uses
and work processes; and—to a lesser degree—a style of industry
determined by large concentrations of machinery around steam
prime-movers, cash cropping, and enclosures.

These have produced overcapitalized and often inappropriate
technology, an inflexible and insecure tightly interlocking economy, ignorant mass consumption with a complicated standard of
living of inferior quality, the development of sprawling urban
areas rather than towns and cities, brain-washing mass communications, mass democracy without real content, and mass
education that is both wasteful and regimenting.

With these there is a prevalent superstition that no other
method of organization could be more efficient or is even possible,
and that in all functions the reasonable mode of operation is by
"rationalization" (subdivision, standardization, cash accounting).
Because of the superstition and the inflexible organization, these
beliefs are self-proving. No other kind of operation or administration is paid attention or subsidized; no research is done into
possibilities of decentralizing. Breakdowns in the centralizing
system are handled not by examining the system but by patchwork or imposing new levels of control according to the same
administrative style. Meantime the hidden costs involved in
centralization are omitted from the cash accounting.

This superstition confounds the real confusion accompanying

unique conditions of modern life, new technology, urbanization, and one world. For instance, automation, a centralized mode of production, is applied both where it is appropriate and where it is inappropriate, but little attempt is made to analyze these differences. And in automatic production itself, although there is a necessary concentration of capital in the equipment, it does not follow that programing should be under central control of the same corporation.

My bias is that automation should be applied to the maximum in the production of hardware and perhaps subsistence goods, in clerical work, etc.; but automation, computing, and standardizing methods in general, should be severely restricted in all human services, education, restaurants, social-work, hospitals; e.g., there should be a standard high-grade TV machine made by the millions and at minimum price—even though this would lose certain excellences of highest quality, styling, workmanship —but the larger part of programing should be decentralized and for specific audiences.

In all forecasts of the fairly immediate future, it is said that employment in commodity production will be sharply diminished. But for useful leisure, the development of community culture, human services, and education, the rationalizing and cash-accounting style is inappropriate, whereas the decentralist style is enriching.

The grave threat in modern urbanization is *anomie*, the rootlessness and helplessness of individuals, the loss of citizenry. When it tries at all to cope with this, centralized administration tries to encourage "participation," but participation is empty unless it involves the possibility of initiating and deciding—that is decentralized administration. It is interesting to contrast the dull formality of a PTA meeting at which nothing important can be decided with the liveliness of the public meeting of a local school board to which important authority has been delegated.

"Association" and "participation" are not mere interpersonal relations; they are sharing in objective enterprise.

III. Prevalent or Inevitable Defects of Centralization

However competent, the few at the top who decide in large centralized enterprises are not enough minds to do an adequate job. Top managers—and independent professionals—are the most overworked members of society.

In "upward communication" of information, at each level there is processing and abstraction from the concrete; and with each abstraction there is the accumulation of mere approximation and of actual misfitting. Much is left out altogether.

To cope with the multifarious details and persons of large enterprises, recourse is had to standardization. This leads to inevitable misfitting and loss of peculiar appropriateness and quality. It is rare that the standard procedure is the best in any particular case.

The subordinates, meanwhile, necessarily become stupider, since they cannot learn by initiation and responsibility. In a departmental system, much of each man's capacity is unused. Each man knows only part of the process and so cannot really understand what he is doing. There is increased reliance on extrinsic motivations of salary, security, and perquisites, because subordinates cannot take satisfaction in completing the function. Finally, activity becomes timeserving and status-maintaining, regardless of the function.

In established organizations those who rise to the top also tend to be chosen by systematic rather than functional criteria. They are safe men. The image of performance is more important than the actuality. Since those who could criticize—colleagues, consumers, electorate—become stupider, the top men also become stupider.

The inflexible departments do not always dovetail; communication breaks down since few men have a sense of the whole. The resulting difficulties are solved by adding higher levels of control, more administrators.

Finally, the systems tend to run for their own sake. Since so much capital and so many persons are tightly interlocked in them, they cannot afford to risk any change; and any novelty or experiment involves dislocations and is "not worth the trouble." A system running for its own sake loses touch with its ostensible function and becomes isolated from the environment; its chief function is to protect, reward, and incestuously recruit its own personnel; its chief business is paper work, public relations, and the maintenance of a routine production.

Unfortunately, when such systems are very large, they pre-empt the social means and space for carrying on their functions at all. There is no way to be effective outside the system and no way in the system, so people with inventive ideas and initiative become discouraged and either drop out or resign themselves to token performance. Worst of all, in many functions of society, simple direct action becomes quite impossible, even though it is commonsense and would meet with general approval. Eagerness and earnestness are stymied by licenses, merely formal standards, due process, confronting stuffed shirts, and the need for amounts of capital entirely disproportionate to the enterprise.

By and large our country at present is constituted of a rather small number of great commercial baronies, organized as described, which are private powers; these are checked by the great public power of governments; and there are also great entrenched organizations like the Pentagon, the FBI, the major universities and school systems, the labor unions, and a few others.

The baronies compete semimonopolistically, fix prices, and generally maintain the structure; and their relations with the labor unions are analogous. When Private Power confronts Public Power, e.g., in the regulatory agencies, the result is often a stalemate, so that there is no social motion. Often, however, there are alliances, as in the military-industrial, scientific agencies-universities, Urban Renewal-real estate promoters, etc., and these alliances lead to further aggrandizement of the same overgrown organizations and the products are not distinguished by ingenuity, beauty, thrift, or precise utility.

A major area of abuse by interlocking is the pre-emption of Research and Development money in all fields by giant corporations. But recent reports of the Senate Anti-Trust Committee show that most invention *and innovation* come from individuals and small companies, and at far less cost. The big corporations use public subsidy for R and D mainly for what amounts to packaging for the consumer.

Despite the good intentions of many individuals in the system, this vast machinery of social power is almost powerless in most simple practical matters. Everyone in society, from lowly citizens to topmost leaders, shares the sneaking suspicion that "Nothing Can Be Done."

IV. Examples of Overgrown Systems

A. New York School System: A Classical Bureaucracy

(Let me say that I have affection for the earnestness of the N.Y.C. school system, its attentiveness to the children as the main object, its sincere egalitarianism, its concern for all types and conditions; its dreamy desire to experiment. But its structure is a disaster.)

The structure has been aggrandized from an ancient plan with little change. E.g., in 1900, 6 per cent of seventeen-year-olds graduated from high school; now more than 60 per cent. The system now serves 1,000,000 children, there are 750 schools rather rigidly controlled by one headquarters; the annual budget exceeds $700 millions—excluding capital improvements.

The following are expected, and actual, situations: to remove rats from a school, the principal cannot call an exterminator but must appeal to headquarters and go, in principle, to the Board of Estimate. To remove a door catch ("city property") requires years of appeal.

An architect is told that he is not allowed to consult the teachers of a school he is to replace; he must simply adapt standard plans that are a generation out of date and were not good to begin with. Because of specific pedagogic conditions, a principal asks for soundproofing, but no money can be allotted for that, although there is provision for much less urgent needs. A very old-fashioned type of door hardware is specified, which is kept in production, for reasons of nepotism, only for the N.Y. school system.

Despite this bureaucratic pedantry, there are public scandals because janitors have been taking home $50,000 a year, or a roof costs $750,000 to fix, and still leaks. On the other hand, there are scandals because of trivialities: a high school student has done carpentry on a boat for a school official.

When local school boards (with rather unspecified powers) were re-established in 1962, at the end of a year of operation it was said that their main achievement so far was to make it possible for the field superintendents to communicate with headquarters (through the free wheeling of the local boards), something which had not occurred in two generations. For instance, a rubber stamp from the superintendent in charge of building was required to make alterations to a wall to install a valuable new press given to the School of Printing; all this would cost the city nothing, yet the rubber stamp was delayed for nearly two years, with a mountain of correspondence, till a local board complained loudly and got the stamp.

In recruiting teachers for such a vast system, processing takes nearly a year. Naturally many of the bright new graduates go elsewhere, to the suburban communities. (Yet the civil service type of procedure is necessary to avoid nepotism and political pressure.) Entirely irrelevant qualifications, and the tie-in with the graduate schools that license teachers, keep many fine teachers out. It takes many years to change an outmoded rule; for instance, the rule that a teacher must have no trace of a foreign accent, that made sense during the height of the immigration three generations ago, was a disaster when some districts had 35 per cent Puerto Rican children who could not speak English, yet one could not recruit bilingual teachers; the rule has only recently been modified.

The administrators, superintendents, and secretaries, principals, assistants, clerks, guidance, attendance officers, etc., proliferate; yet the fundamental educational fact, the number of children per teacher, cannot be altered because of the expense; but the large classes do positive damage to both children and teachers, so that the whole system perhaps does more harm than good. Correspondingly, each school is too large. Where intelligent principals ask for 400, there are schools of 1800 and the official limit has finally been reduced to 1200. The requirements of educational community are necessarily sacrificed to administrative convenience and ignorant public pressure.

Timidity, administrative unwieldiness, the need for standardization put insuperable obstacles in the path of experiment. When an experiment—e.g., the tailor-made Higher Horizons—succeeds on a small scale, it is diluted by being standardized.

(A considerable useful leeway *is* given to the principals—in both staffing and methods—so that the schools differ a good deal depending on the principal; but the teachers and staff meeting have far too little leeway.)

Finally, this vast system is made increasingly inflexible by its interlocking with the other aggrandizing systems of society, to form one nationwide educational monolith. E.g., the textbook manufacturers, the graduate schools of education, the National Science Foundation, the proliferating national testing services, the corporations, the church, the Pentagon.

B. Monolithic Mass Communications: A Constitutional Danger

The interlocking systems of mass communications with a few decision makers at the top of each system produces inevitable brain washing and makes democracy impossible.

Some kinds of news and events do warrant standard national researching and broadcast. Only great news services and networks can perform such services. Therefore we need a mixed system.

Fewer than 60 towns have competing newspapers (in 1900 there were 600). These are served by, now, only three international news services. With the best will in the world, these few persons cannot know what is all the real news. Three big broadcasting networks get most of their news from the same source.

The standard of living (how to be decent) and what is correct and tolerable in expression and entertainment is determined by these networks, the movies, and a few national magazines; but the sustaining advertisers are the same and the ownership elaborately interlocks.

This system requires creating a pervasive mass audience and attitude. Anything that might offend a large segment (a few hundred thousand) must be excluded; the vast capitalization demands a vast audience to pay for itself. There is thus an inevitable restriction to the sensational and the bland. (The "storm of angry letters" that the sponsors fear may finally be as few as twenty.)

Since there must be limited broadcasting channels, if the networks control most of them there is an implicit censorship. And this becomes explicit when tapes are wiped out and certain speakers are officially or unofficially blacklisted. The FCC has proved powerless to compel reasonable coverage of everything worth while. The licenses once given are apparently in perpetuity.

The networks, once established, can wield enormous political pressure. (In one case of being threatened, a network was promptly able to produce 10,000 telegrams sent by children.) The equal-time provision has been abrogated for national elections—the networks are trying to extend the revocation to state elections.

If they also control most of the local stations, this makes it impossible for new political thought to enter into discourse.

The expensive network time makes for minute and second scheduling, and thus a format that prevents freedom of thought or art. Also the discouragement of using especially TV to cover actualities—since these might always prove either boring or untoward.

In publishing of books, there is similar concentration of capitalization (huge presses and teams of salesmen and promotion), and this increasingly determines the content and format of books, in order to make it possible to set such big capital in motion. And there is interlocking with magazines for serialization, with book clubs, with Hollywood.

The flood of publication, broadcasting, and journalism in the style, format, and acceptable content of the mass media, decided by the few who rise to the top in such vast semimonopolies, finally swamps independent and dissenting thought and style and constitutes a virtual censorship in depth. Overexposed to one fairly homogeneous kind of interpretation, and underexposed to any rival interpretation (and in some localities and on the TV medium not so exposed at all), people begin to take the interpretation of the interlocking mass media for the reality; that is, they are brain-washed. This is a constitutional crisis for democracy.

C. Cars and Roads: Hypertrophy of a System Beyond Function

During the twenties automobiles began to be sold for style and status rather than more serious function and convenience; this removed natural limitations on the proliferation of such formidable and expensive objects. Meantime, the middle-class suburbanites pressured the building of parkways. There is now a car for every 2.7 Americans, considerably more than one to a family.

The cars exist as the crucial element in a vast complex—of fuel, servicing, and highways—that entirely transforms the environment. Highways are built at a cost varying from $500,000 to $3 million a mile. After armaments, highway construction is the big item in federal budgets, and it looms immensely in state budgets.

By 1970 the cost, with accrued interest, of roads for a single car trip five miles to the center of Washington will come to two

and a half dollars (per car trip) each way. Fifty per cent of central
Los Angeles has been given over to the roadways.

General Motors alone employs 600,000 people; its annual turnover is $14 billion. The automotive complex (including oil and
roads) has become indispensable to keep the economy going, so
that a falling off of car sales can precipitate a serious recession.
"What is good for General Motors is good for the country."

Three or four car manufacturers control the market, competing
semimonopolistically with fixed prices and improvements spooned
out slowly. Progress in design has been determined entirely by
profits; the increase in power has been largely for sales and is
unfunctional for most situations. Even safety features are neglected. (Forty thousand are killed annually in automobile accidents.) Only the competition of European small cars made, for
a time, a radical change. No effort has been made, e.g., to develop
an efficient small slower-moving electric for urban use (taxis).
Also, expensive as they are, cars are built not to last, and the
companies push for laws to exempt them from supplying parts
for longer than five years.

Because of direct and indirect subsidy, cars and trucks have
pushed other kinds of transportation out of the picture, especially
for commuting. There is little effort to achieve a balanced transit
pattern, using all means for the general convenience. In most large
cities traffic congestion and parking are almost intolerably inconvenient; the fleets of cars on the suburban parkways make
no economic or psychological sense.

The cars and highways have imposed an entirely new and disruptive community plan. The tremendous suburbanization has
become their creature. Villages and city neighborhoods are disrupted by highway shopping centers. Families are dispersed and
the lives of children depend on automobility. Centralized plants,
including central schools, claim per-product efficiency, but the
hidden costs of the highways and transportation are not counted.

Of course most of this imposition of a new pattern would have
been impossible if there had not been advantages and conveniences
in the cars; but by hypertrophy the system has itself become
the dominant cause. The highway planning now occurs independently and determines the location of communities and the
manner of life in them.

In the mess we are in, however, the only conceivable remedy

is public centralized regulation and planning. The automotive complex must now be treated as a "natural monopoly" and regulated.

D. Supermarkets: Logistic Planning That Proves to Be Inefficient

The effect of the hyperorganization of food production, processing, distant transportation, and supermarket retailing has been that the farmer's share of the take has persistently diminished (e.g., 44 per cent in 1953, 38 per cent in 1963), whereas the profits of the chains themselves have *not* risen, and food prices to the consumer have risen slightly. This is an application of Borsodi's Law: as the cost of production per unit diminishes because of centralized operation, the cost of processing and distribution increases disproportionately. This law is relevant especially for bulky and perishable commodities like foodstuffs, and where the fixed capital investment *can* be relatively low in proportion to the product (as in natural farming).

At present, one out of every two dollars spent for food goes to one hundred corporate or (not Rochdale) co-operative chains. Seventy per cent of all food sales is through the central systems. The ten largest chains sell 30 per cent of all food.

In this system both farmers and retailers fall under the control and decision making of the chains. Farmers contract long beforehand, regardless of weather or the ability to take advantage of sudden opportunities. The emphasis is entirely on large-scale cash cropping. Farmers' markets in the towns and cities are closed. Inevitably, marginal farms must discontinue, and this is an important cause of the present excessive urbanization. (Farm families now make up less than 7 per cent of the population.)

It is clear that in many thousands of cases people would choose the farm way of life if there were any possibilities of getting any cash at all; e.g., in some states a small rise in the farmer's price for milk results in many marginal farms resuming operation. But at present farm subsidies overwhelmingly favor the big operators.

With the concentration of growing in huge plantations in Texas, Florida, California, etc., breeding and hybridization are determined in terms of canning, ability to preserve and ship, and appearance for mass sale, rather than freshness, flavor, or nutrition. Very little is naturally nurtured or naturally ripened. There is excessive use of pesticides.

In the retailing there is a profound change in consumer habits. Packaging assumes great importance, no matter what is in the packages. Consumers pay several cents more for a brand-name product (e.g., Clorox, although a locally bottled bleach is identical in every respect). Independent grocers are forced out, adding to the anonymity and *anomie* of urban neighborhoods.

Nevertheless, despite these disruptive changes in the way of life of farm and city, brought on by rationalization of food production and distribution, there is little increase of actual efficiency. And there is a tremendous social and economic cost in forced urbanization and rural depopulation.

V. Costs in Service Enterprises with Different Organization and Motivation

Consider a range of services where staff and overhead are the chief costs. With extrinsic motivation and organization not growing from the function, the cost may rise by a factor of 3, 5, or 10, or more. E.g., the following somewhat comparable enterprises:

On Broadway a modest play (without music) requires upward of $100,000 to rehearse and mount, and $20,000 a week to run. The standard estimate for an off-Broadway production, e.g., as at the Living Theater (now defunct except in Europe), is $20,000 to mount and $2000 a week to run. Professionally, these productions will be comparable in every way—we are not here considering the aesthetic or community value. Contrast with both these types an ad hoc production by artists, e.g., a play in the loft of the Judson Church: this might cost $50 to $500 to mount and nothing at all to run, since the script, acting, staging, and space are all gratis.

In TV, NBC sponsored time costs $143,000 an hour for 220 stations, $650 per outlet for the network, or $2000 for one station. This does not include the cost of the program: a very modest half-hour program costs $10,000 to produce. Now compare two non-profit (educational TV) stations: WNDT in New York costs $650 an hour to run, not much cheaper than commercial television (but this figure includes the cost of programing). On the other hand, KQED in San Francisco runs for $225 an hour. The difference is that the top salary at WNDT is $45,000, the staff about 150, etc., whereas at KQED the top salary is $15,000, the staff about 50, etc. Professionally the two stations are equivalent, but KQED is much more daring and lively. (Characteristically, the staff turnover at KQED is almost nil—we are obviously relying on artistic and technical motivation—whereas WNDT is a way station for persons moving toward higher salaries elsewhere.)

In radio, WMCA charges $700 an hour for air time, excluding the cost of the program. But WBAI, a listener-supported station of comparable power, costs $38 an hour to run, including programing (provided gratis by artists, academics, or the politically minded). WBAI is one of the three stations of the Pacifica Federation, which exchange tapes but are entirely independent.

A good non-residential private school in New York, class size 20, costs about $850 per pupil per year, not counting plant and some endowment. An elementary pupil in the New York Public School system costs $750, also excluding capital costs for plant and replacement; the class size is officially 29, but in fact most classes are 32–35. Thus public and private costs are similar. By contrast, a Summerhill school in Stony Point costing $500 per child, provides, for 50 children, three full-time paid instructors and the equivalent of about five more voluntary teachers from among parents who are artists or professionals and teach part time. (The public system, by and large, discourages the entry of unlicensed teachers into the classroom.)

College tuition at Columbia or Cornell is $1700, which is estimated to be a little more than 50 per cent of the actual cost per student for "education and educational administration." The markup over actual classroom costs is 400 per cent. (At smaller liberal arts colleges, e.g., Wesleyan in Connecticut, the markup is 300 per cent.) Especially in the freshman and sophomore classes, the professors lecture to very large classes and the smaller groups are taught by ill-paid section men. In the small colleges proposed in *The Community of Scholars*, the tuition is estimated at $650, with ten professors for 150 students.

The Peace Corps is a model of efficient and dedicated bureaucracy. Yet it costs more than $12,000 to select, train, and maintain a volunteer for one year ($9000 for the volunteer, $3000 for central administration, liaison with host countries, etc.). The Friends Service VISA program, which is comparable in essential respects, provides the same service for $3500 a volunteer. For another comparison, Operation Crossroads, prorated for the same period, costs $5000. Important causes of expense in the Peace Corps are the very rigid selection to protect the image abroad (only one of eight original applicants is finally sent), training in the setting of an American university, and propaganda and promotion. The Friends spend nothing at all on administration (the program is taken care of as an extra duty by their regular offices), prefer to train in the field where conditions are known, and their candidates have a service philosophy to begin with.

Official urban renewal planned for the West Village in New York City was to cost $30 million (including a $7 million subsidy), to provide net 300 units after demolition and relocation. A counterplan proposed by a neighborhood group would cost $8.5 million, without subsidy for net 475 units, without neighborhood disruption and relocation. The savings in this case come from tailoring to the actual needs by real architects rather than bureaucrats and promoters. The neighborhood plan comes to $18,000 a unit. Incidentally, in a similar neighborhood, with the unpaid labor of friends, I remodeled a commercial loft to a comparable standard for $500, and the rental at ordinary market value and amortization came to considerably less. That is: the professional neighborhood housing is cheaper than official housing, but artists' lofts are cheaper still.

There is no mystery about what swells costs in commercial, official, and Establishment enterprises, where the organization, motivation, and procedure are not designed directly to fulfill the function. It is profits, patents, and rents; semimonopolistic fixed prices; need for union protection of workmen hired for somebody else's enterprise, union scales and featherbedding; salaries determined by considerations of status because the personnel is not intrinsically motivated to the task; expense accounts; proliferation of administrators, paper work, business machines; the waste of skill by departmentalizing task roles and standardizing procedure inflexibly; high cost of contingencies because of tight scheduling; public relations and promotion to shore up the image.

On the other hand, when enterprises are run autonomously by

professionals and artists intrinsically committed to the task, people make do on means and procedure; they become inventive by making decisions flexibly as opportunity presents; they keep an eye on the essence rather than the convention; they put in as many hours as are necessary without watching the clock; they use all available skills wherever available; they eschew status and sometimes live on a subsistence wage; and administration and overhead are tailored to what is indispensable for the concrete function.

VI. Typology of Enterprises in Terms of Engagement

A. *Enterprises Extrinsically Motivated as Part of the Organized System:*

1. Commercial enterprises, run for profit as well as status, etc.
   (E.g., NBC or the Broadway theater)
2. Official or Establishment non-profit enterprises
   (E.g., Columbia University, WNDT)

B. *Enterprises Determined by the Function or Concrete Task:*

3. Professional
   (E.g., KQED, Friends Service, West Village Neighborhood)
4. Artistic or community
   (E.g., Judson Players, WBAI, the Barker School, artists' lofts)

Profit-motivated enterprises may or may not be more efficient than Establishment non-profit enterprises. Since performance in the non-profit field is largely symbolic, there is no attempt to cut costs. But the cutting of costs in profit enterprises is largely offset by the grasping, padding, and status seeking of the personnel. An extremely extravagant model is the *combination* of centralized commercial and official, as in cost-plus contracts. This is the opposite of the TVA idea, where the official was to serve as a yardstick.

Intrinsic professional performance necessarily costs more than artistic and community performance (which really costs nothing beyond materials and subsistence) because the persons are members of a licensed or peer-group guild; they are institutions, and this is usually necessary for continuous operation over a range of occasions. Artistic performances, on the contrary, are ad hoc. (For a continuously productive artist, each work is ad hoc.)

Add to these four types two other extreme types of production and service. On the one hand there are family, amateur, and folk enterprises, which do not enter the cash nexus at all but are very important for the economic and social well-being. For instance, one nation might have a per capita "income" several times more than another, and yet the actual standard of living be very little different, since the "poorer" nation is more skilled and self-reliant.

On the other hand, there are the great background enterprises that fill universal needs, necessary for a modern society to function: municipal services, natural monopolies, literacy, subsistence, etc. It is probably most convenient and efficient to run all of these by free appropriation. The standards and motives of personnel should be strictly professional. (This is Marx's "administration" that is supposed to supersede the "withering away of the state," but in my opinion he extends the range of these functions too far and would make the whole society lifeless. These functions are best regarded as merely supportive and background.)

VII. Idea of a Mixed System

The above six types of enterprise are, in one form or another, operative in any modern society. But the proportions are, of course, very various—so the United States, Russia, Sweden, Nigeria, etc., have different real constitutions.

The idea of a mixed system is a proportioning among types of enterprise so that they in fact influence one another pluralistically and if necessary can check one another.

A mixed system would try to keep the proportion of the types roughly within limits of maximum cost efficiency. (I doubt that the American proportion is at all within these limits. E.g., it takes $30,000 in new investment to re-employ one workman.) This might involve *lowering* the GNP: e.g., co-operative enterprises often avoid cash transactions; a quality standard of living is less cultured and often costs less; skilled and engaged people do more directly for themselves and one another, e.g., repairs; a better rural-urban ratio, say 20 percent instead of 7 per cent, would be more efficient as well as more socially and culturally satisfactory.

A mixed system would allow various types of motivation and

organization to do what they can do most appropriately and cheaply.

A mixed system would reopen opportunities for people to choose the way of working and living that most suits them, and would thus re-create the possibility of engagement.

HUMAN POTENTIALITIES

by RICHARD E. FARSON

At the risk of sounding naïve, I am going to describe an optimistic view of our future. Unquestionably, it seems difficult at the moment to make hopeful predictions about life twenty years from now. Many present trends, if continued, seem to point to an Orwellian world, depersonalized and dehumanized by the technological Juggernaut. On a worldwide scale, we face the prospect of irreversible pollution and destruction of our natural environment; mass starvation in the southern hemisphere as the industrialized northern half grows richer; the possibility of nuclear catastrophe. The entire globe is in a tumult of violent conflict and upheaval as people everywhere demand a share in the benefits of technology. Even in America, the freest, richest nation in history, there are scenes reminiscent of the French revolution in city after city as police and militia battle deeply angry citizens—not only the poor and segregated, but on occasion, middle-class protesters as well. All this makes the pessimists among us seem merely hard-headed, down-to-earth realists.

"Human Potentialities," by Richard E. Farson. Reprinted from *Glamour*; copyright © 1966 by The Conde Nast Publications Inc.

This paper was prepared from a presentation to the International Design Conference of Aspen, Colorado, June 26, 1966. An adaptation appeared in the January, 1967, issue of *Glamour* under the title, "The World of 1984." The contributions of Toni Volcani in the preparation of this paper are gratefully acknowledged.

Nevertheless, I think there are grounds for optimism in the very phenomena that seem most disquieting—in the ghetto riots, the rebellion of youth, the "crisis in values" . . . for it looks as though we are entering upon an age of protest. And in the West, it seems to me, this protest reflects a radically new attitude toward life—a radically new view of man himself.

People are never satisfied. Once their needs are met at the survival level, they move on to needs of a higher order. They begin to need freedom, democracy, education. And while it is true that these needs are interrelated with the demands of technology in a positive feedback system, I think they are evidence, on a deeper level, of a revolutionary change in our feelings and beliefs about the purpose of life and about the human potential.

The infants of 1967 will be the high school graduates of 1984. And though the world has changed enormously since the Second World War, I don't think we can smoothly extrapolate those changes to the world of 1984; about all we can be certain of is that life will be vastly different from life today. Every change follows more quickly on the heels of the previous change; if we plot the curve of innovation we can see that it rises more and more sharply and that the plateaus are fewer and fewer. In the past, however, man has always been able to make a change and coast a while, rest on the new plateau, and catch his breath until what seemed alarmingly radical became acceptable and then traditional. In the future, *change will be a way of life*. It is hard to imagine what that will mean, but we can be sure of this: not only will life be very different, but concepts, values, patterns of living, the way people feel about themselves will be quite different from anything we can easily imagine today. Human nature is *not* immutable and a world in which change is a way of life will give rise to new human needs.

Marshall McLuhan has said that, "Technological changes recast the entire character of the individual and compel him to rediscover himself in depth instead of in detachment and objectivity." I agree that this is already taking place, and that the age of protest springs not only from man's attempt to rediscover himself, but from a radically new view of the human potential. And in the future, people will demand above all the right to fulfill their potentialities. This, not material possessions as such, will be seen as the means to the good life.

We have had a limited view of what people can do and be. We have assumed that only the sensitive and gifted few can create or appreciate beauty; that only the mystic is capable of transcendental experience; that only certain kinds of cognitive activity constitute "intelligence" which is possessed in high degree by only a few. I think man is beginning to take himself much more seriously. As we begin to believe that we are all playing with a full deck, we will change the rules of the game. And as each of us comes to believe that he is *potent*, he will demand the right to develop and fulfill his potential. Simply by virtue of his humanness, he will demand the right to experiences that have in the past been considered luxuries to be enjoyed by the few. For the high school seniors of 1984, the good life will be focused on *experiencing their humanness*; their values, I think, will be experiential, rather than utilitarian, and the purpose of life will not be to use themselves for ulterior goals, but to experience themselves, not to use others, but to experience others, not to use their environment, but to experience it in the fullness of its possibilities for richness and beauty. So I want to talk about the realistic, practical demands I think people will be making to help them attain this.

People will be demanding a new Bill of Rights—not a replacement of our constitutional Bill of Rights guaranteeing civil liberties, but a Bill of Rights guaranteeing *human* liberty. But since the satisfaction of one set of needs gives rise to a new set, my suggested Bill of Rights can only be an interim measure, based upon needs we can now foresee.

My first item in the new Bill of Rights is the Right to Leisure. That is a safe one to start with because we already have leisure. But by today's definition, leisure means time-off-from-work. I am talking about a society in which leisure will not mean time off, but the *right not to work* and still be considered a worthy human being. Work, today, means labor-for-pay. Many authorities believe that this kind of labor will be done by a relatively small percentage of the population, so that the chances for many of us to have jobs in the traditional sense—to "bring home the bacon" —will be limited. This poses a serious problem. How are we going to feel worthy, achieve self-esteem and the esteem of others, without feeling useful?

I think that in the world of post-technical man our whole idea of the usefulness of things and of people will be quite changed. For the past two hundred years or so, we have been thoroughly imbued with the notion that the way to achieve self-respect is to work hard, deny the present for the sake of the future, be of service to others. We require that objects and processes be useful, functional—"Does it *work*?" We even defend beauty, pleasure, leisure as being useful: "Good design is good economics." "Recreation and leisure enable people to work more productively." "Good interpersonal relations are important for smooth organizational functioning." Curiously, though, we don't ask "Does it work?" of the things that we value most. We never ask that of a sunset, of a symphony, of a love affair. We believe these experiences are in some way enriching, of value in and of themselves. It is my guess that we will ask this utilitarian question less and less often, for I think we are discarding the value system, derived from the Protestant ethic, in which work is an end in itself.

In the future we will see a fusion of work and play. Play will be our work, as it is for children. Work will be our play; we will demand the right to occupy ourselves with deeply fulfilling activities that we can cry about and laugh about and be engrossed in for many, many hours at a stretch; and so we will demand that our homes, buildings, and cities be designed not just for efficiency, but for leisure, for delight, for romance, for play.

Second in my new Bill of Rights is the Right to Beauty. I think this, too, is a safe one to predict because people are already beginning to rebel against ugliness in their surroundings; they are proposing legislation to remove billboards, establish green belts, hide junkyards, renovate and beautify our cities. "Beauty," "culture," and "life" will not be compartmentalized as they are today. As human energy is replaced by cybernetic slaves, as culture, leisure, work, and play are fused, people will increasingly turn to experiences that refresh the spirit and expand the senses. We are discovering that beauty is a human need; ugliness will be regarded, literally, as a crime against life.

The next right will surely be the Right to Health. Logically, perhaps, that should come first, but though at present the idea that medical care should be guaranteed to all is controversial, in 1984 the right to health will surely seem as fundamental and as essential to society as the right to an education. We will redefine "health," however, to mean not merely the *absence* of illness, but the *opposite* of illness—a positive condition of well-being, with peak moments of vigor, strength, coordination, ease. I can't help wondering what methods, what experiences, what chemical agents will we use to bring about or enhance these peak moments and open the way to new realms of sensory experience?

The same will be true for mental health. We will no longer be talking about the mere absence of symptoms; we will talk about emotional *wellness*, a positive state of well-being in which our emotions are integrated with our behavior, giving us a feeling of potency, of euphoria. We will increasingly be concerned with the normal problems of normal people, the problems of everyday life—loneliness, superficiality, frustration, fear, guilt, anxiety, despair. And we will deal with these problems not only in clinics, but in the basic institutions of our society—in schools, churches, in homes, in industries, in the neighborhood. This job can't be left to psychologists. We will learn how to make use of the therapeutic resources that exist in all human beings. People are very good for each other. They can be enormously helpful if we can arrange circumstances in which they can really reach each other. How are these circumstances to be designed? Perhaps intensive small-group experiences—"group therapy"—increasingly used today in all sorts of settings, will become as normal and everyday a form of human interaction as the cocktail party, the discussion group, or the social club.

The fourth right is the Right to Intimacy. In this busy, urbanized, crowded society, our complicated relations with so many people seem inevitably to lead to appalling superficiality, and physical proximity has, paradoxically, brought emotional distance. Millions of Americans have never had, and never will have, in their entire lives one moment of intimacy with another human being, even with those who are closest to them—one moment in which they could be honestly, authentically, genuinely themselves. People need to get acquainted with their own feelings, and they need to be able to share those feelings. But in our society, we are actually embarrassed about intimacy; we have the notion that it should occur only in the privacy of the family circle; the trouble is that shared-feeling kind of intimacy seldom takes place even there. I think that we will intentionally search for authentic, intimate relationships and, at the same time, be relatively satisfied with relationships that may be only fleeting or transient. For intimacy need not, as we seem to think, be the outgrowth of time. We need intimate relationships, whether of long or short duration, to remind us of our membership in the human race, to give us a sense of community, to help us be less afraid of one another, to permit us to laugh and cry with one another. We need new designs for living which will encourage unforced emotional intimacy. This will be one of the ways we will meet our need to experience ourselves and others more fully.

Fifth on my tentative list is the Right to Truth. Some sociologists distinguish between two styles of behavior in relations, "presenting" and "sharing." You can "present" yourself to another person, try to insure that you make a favorable impression on him, or you can "share" yourself with him by letting him in on what it is like to be you at that particular moment. Almost all our relationships—at work, at school, at parties, even at home —are of the "presenting" kind. Sharing of oneself is much more common among the younger generation—which has been called the "Honest Generation." Teenagers and college students seem much less likely to censor what they say; they seem to want more of the truth from themselves and from others, more honest relationships, and they reject what they call "adult hypocrisy."

When I think of how much we censor our thoughts before speaking, I am reminded of a little experiment which a friend of mine conducts. He asks the people he interviews to wear earphones that feed them "white noise"—something like radio static combined with the sound of a jet plane getting ready to take off. The noise is activated by the subject's voice, but he can't hear himself talking. In this situation, where the interviewer can both talk to the subject and hear what he says, but the subject can only hear the interviewer, some interesting phenomena turn up. One of them is that people lose some of their ability to control and censor their speech. For example, a man asked, "How do you and your wife get along?" might reply, "We get along just fine," and then add very quietly, "That's a lot of crap." When the taped recording is played back to him, he doesn't remember making the second statement.

Our demands for the right to truth are more and more evident, I think as we move toward a more open society. We seem less willing to go along with the deceptions and secrets we have tolerated for so many years. We are demanding truth in product claims, in packaging, in advertising. As science and technology give us more and more control over heredity, and over the thoughts and behavior of others, we are becoming alarmed about wire-tapping, psychological testing, computerized dossiers, psychologically coerced confessions, and the like. I believe we must deal with our new power by reducing deception and secrecy. In the long run, for example, I doubt that people will permit information about themselves to be collected and stored in data banks or in thick personnel folders to which they have no access. Furthermore, I doubt that people will submit to psychological tests of any kind unless they are sure that such tests are designed to benefit them. People will resist giving personal information to anyone; they will refuse to subject themselves to unclear procedures as they become more aware of the controls that can be exercised over them. I believe there will soon be sweeping legislation that will radically change our practices of record-keeping, testing, experimentation, investigation, and communication—and I believe these changes will not be in the direction of Orwellian cradle-to-the-grave surveillance, as some writers have suggested, but rather in the opposite direction. Moreover, as the communication network becomes larger and more finely meshed, it will be harder, not easier, to conceal or distort the "facts behind the news," and thus manipulate or control opinion.

Right number six on my tentative list is the Right to Study. I was going to call this the Right to Education, but that's not what I'm talking about, for "education" is presently designed to prepare people to earn a living, enter a profession, serve the needs of technology and industry, and we have the right to that sort of education pinned down. I am talking about the right to lifelong study and learning, to the enriching experience of *learning* as an end in itself. The quest for knowledge and understanding is uniquely human, but we often act as though people must be driven to it by competition for grades, by discipline or fear of failure, by all sorts of pressures. In the future, learning will be an integral part of creative living; we will be studying and learning throughout our lives because it is as enjoyable as becoming a good skier or improving one's backhand.

Leading educationists have broadened their concept of education so that they now talk about it in terms of experiences that develop the total person. So the concept of "learning" will be broadened to include the affective, emotional, interpersonal dimensions as well as the cognitive, intellectual aspects of development. We are beginning to realize that learning must encompass all these dimensions if people are to live fully human lives in a world of machines, to cope with unceasing change and enjoy it, to meet the human and social problems of such a world. So we will be educating for awareness, for honesty, intimacy, and interpersonal competence—and people will continue to develop these skills, too, throughout their lives.

The seventh right is the Right to Travel. Soon travel will be so inexpensive, so delightful, and so rapid, the exotic places of this world so accessible, that people will insist on the right to travel. I can foresee the possibility that union contracts written in the coming decades will demand as a fringe benefit the right to travel at company expense. An inevitable consequence of large-scale travel is that we shall develop a new kind of citizen, a citizen of the world. He will return from his travels changed in many ways. Take the Peace Corps volunteer for example. One of the major benefits of the Peace Corps is the new attitude it instills in its members, for quite apart from what they are able to contribute to the countries in which they work, it is clear that their experiences have tremendous impact on them. Probably the most important changes accomplished by the Peace Corps are within the volunteers themselves, and certainly they are returning to the United States as knowledgeable citizens of the world.

The eighth right is the Right to Sexual Fulfillment. We are still plagued by ignorance and guilt and fear, but I think and hope that we are the last generation to settle for so much less than full enjoyment of our sexuality. Sexual pleasure will be as legitimate as the pleasures of eating or drinking or listening to music, and we will be freed to derive erotic enjoyment from all sorts of experiences. We might as well face it, the sexual revolution is already well under way. We might as well relax and enjoy it, but I think it will bring about some unexpected changes, particularly in our ideas of sexual roles, and role differentiation. When sex is no longer simply a means to an end—procreation, or economic security for women and ego-security for men—we will be able to deploy and enjoy the whole range of our sensory and emotional potential. For the generation that comes of age in 1984, sexual fulfillment and erotic experience will not only be a delightful and taken-for-granted aspect of life, as it has been in many cultures other than our own, but I think it will be more than that. We will explore the possibilities of sex to find new ways of experiencing ourselves, new ways of expanding our physical, mental, and emotional potentials, and new ways of relating to others.

Ninth in my new Bill of Rights is the Right to Peace. Of the apocalyptic Four Horsemen, War has usurped the place of Pestilence and Famine as the most devastating threat to mankind. I think we can hope for international peace of a sort by 1984, in which the current unstable "balance of terror" has been replaced with a more stable form. But I am not envisioning a world of brotherly love and tranquillity, either. In the age of protest, revolutionary ferment will probably increase in the underdeveloped half of the world. But already in the widespread support for the UN, in the increasing number of peace-oriented groups and peace demonstrations, in the use of non-violent techniques to achieve Civil Rights legislation, in the "hippie" phenomena, people in the Western nations are voicing their demand for the right to peace. Our growing understanding of social processes is being applied to problems of international conflict, and all over the world behavioral scientists are studying and developing new non-violent techniques for conflict resolution—devising, for example, research models of the world community by which the outcomes of various strategies can be tested in a simulated "world."

The great majority of mankind has always desired peace; today I think that fewer and fewer of us see violence as the only or ultimate solution to conflict. Indeed, we are rediscovering what children know: that in many situations we can achieve our "ends" by transforming them into "means." Negroes who want to desegregate a lunch counter do not picket—they simply sit down at the lunch counter; college students are showing that the way to achieve a relevant education is to create their own free universities.

Finally, I think we will demand the Right to Be Unique, to be different, to be autonomous. Today the pressures toward conformity are enormous and they will become even greater as the inevitable consequence of living and working in groups. The War on Poverty has been called the war of the middle class against the lower class. If the middle class wins, a homogenized society will be the result—and I think we will be very sorry. For example, we look at Skid Row as the embodiment of failure and misery, but some sociologists who recently studied Skid Row society report that they really liked it. Apparently something *truly* exists in Skid Row culture that we *say* exists in middle-class culture: people do care about one another on Skid Row; they go the distance with each other; they help each other; they truly regard themselves as their brothers' keepers. One sociologist said, "You know, if I didn't have a family I think I'd live there."

We will delight in diversity, we will value and accentuate variation. We will want to preserve the customs, practices, ethnic differences among us; we will delight in whatever is idiosyncratic, unique, evidence of the strange and wonderful inventiveness of man as he invents himself. We will preserve these differences in depth, not just as traditional pageants that we revive once a year. As we redesign our cities, we will have to decide not only what to change, but what to preserve. I don't mean only historical landmarks, but other places—charming, quaint, romantic, sentimental, highly valued and highly functional places. What smelly delicatessens, what smoky taverns, what dim and dusty old-book shops, what meeting places for old people do we want to keep?

But the right to be unique poses some fundamental questions today. How can we enable people who are trapped in ghettos to improve their lives and enjoy full citizenship and, at the same time, help them retain for the benefit of all of us the richness of their culture? It may be that celebrating these ethnic differences rather than pretending to ignore them will do more to achieve full citizenship, full humanity for all of us. Young Negroes are turning away from "white" values, discovering in the history of black Africa a source of pride and dignity; wearing their hair "natural," they are proclaiming their autonomy, and that to be different is *good*. They are demanding the right to full citizenship without being required to assimilate, and they are right, I think, for how can we realize the multiformity of the human potential if we set up boundaries for its expression?

It's not easy to talk about the human potential because there is probably no limit to it. The human potential is not only what it *is* at any given moment, but it is also determined by what we *believe* it is; what we think it is or want it to be has a lot to do with what we find it to be. We simply do not know much about the conditions that evoke high-order behavior. We do know that environment is an important determinant of human potential, that environment can expand or stultify cognitive functioning, sensory-acuity, emotional response and awareness. And as a matter of fact, probably the best way to predict a person's behavior is to study the *situation*, not the person's life history. For example, people don't smoke in church. It doesn't make any difference what their life histories are, nobody smokes in church.

As people demand the right to fulfill their potential, their rights to beauty, leisure, intimacy, honesty, autonomy, the environments and situations must be designed to meet these needs. But the most difficult, the most frustrating fact of life is this: the more progress we make, the more we must make. The more needs we satisfy, the more needs we develop. Improvements bring higher expectations and demands for more improvements. We have seen this in the civil rights movement. We keep thinking, "Okay. Now we've provided the Negroes with legislation for equal educational benefits, equal chance at the polls, equal job opportunities. That's been a difficult struggle for all of us. Why don't they appreciate these improvements, rest a minute, and let us catch our breath? Then we'll do something more. Can't we just coast for a little while first?" But of course we can't. On the contrary, as a result of our successes we must step up the pace even more. The closer people come to their goals, the more anxious and impatient they become, so the business of trying to make life better is endless and frustrating.

When people feel their potentialities are not being realized, they grumble or rebel. But these grumbles and rebellions are to be valued because they reflect high-order motivation—what Abraham Maslow calls "meta grumbles." Actually, of course, we would not hear such grumbles were it not for the fact that man's future and the quality of life are for the first time within our control. I think we can have the better life that humanity is demanding if we can understand that the real barrier to a better world is our own resistance to change. William Carlos Williams writes, "The mind is the cause of our distresses, but of it we can build anew . . . A new world is only a new mind."

A SELECTED READING LIST

Since *Beyond Left and Right* is designed to open, rather than close, the concerned mind to the radical thoughts presented in its pages, this selective bibliography points to more elaborate discussions of the issues and ideas raised here. The various items are classified under headings that correspond to the divisions of the book; but a single heading sometimes subsumes two categories. This bibliography does not pretend to be either complete or definitive. It arose as a list of books and essays which, to varying degrees, informed my own thinking; and were this a larger book, I would look to them for further material. I hope that a perusal of these works would show, contrary to fashionable belief, that the most profound social thinking of our time still manages to slip into print.

I. MAN AND HIS FUTURE

Altizer, Thomas J. J., and Hamilton, William. *Radical Theology and the Death of God*. Indianapolis: Bobbs-Merrill, 1966.

Beckwith, Burnham Putnam. *The Next 500 Years*. New York: Exposition, 1967.

Boulding, Kenneth E. *The Meaning of the Twentieth Century*. New York: Harper & Row, 1962.

———. *The Image*. Ann Arbor: University of Michigan, 1956.

———. "The Concept of World Interest," in Bert Hoselitz, ed., *Economics and the Idea of Mankind*. New York: Columbia University, 1965.

Brown, Norman O. *Life Against Death*. Middletown, Conn.: Wesleyan University, 1959.

———. *Love's Body*. New York: Random House, 1966.

Casserley, J. V. Langmead. *In the Service of Man*. Chicago: Regnery, 1967.

Cox, Harvey. *The Secular City*. New York: Macmillan, 1965.

Fuller, R. Buckminster. *Ideas and Integrities*. Englewood Cliffs, N.J.: Prentice-Hall, 1963.

———. *Nine Chains to the Moon*. Carbondale: Southern Illinois, 1963.

———. *No More Secondhand God*. Carbondale: Southern Illinois, 1963.

Kubler, George. *The Shape of Time*. New Haven: Yale University, 1962.

Kuhn, Thomas S. *The Structure of Scientific Revolutions*. Chicago, Ill.: University of Chicago, 1962.

La Barre, Weston. *The Human Animal*. Chicago, Ill.: University of Chicago, 1954.

Manuel, Frank E., ed. *Utopias and Utopian Thought*. Boston: Beacon, 1967.

Marcuse, Herbert. *Eros and Civilization*. Boston: Beacon, 1955.

———. *One-Dimensional Man*. Boston: Beacon, 1964.

McClelland, David C. *The Achieving Society*. Princeton: Van Nostrand, 1961.

McHale, John. "2000," *Architectural Design* (February, 1967).

Morison, Elting. *Man, Machines and Modern Times*. Cambridge, Mass.: Massachusetts Institute of Technology, 1966.

Platt, John Rader. *The Step to Man*. New York: Wiley, 1966.

Pope John XXIII. "*Pacem in Terris* [Peace on Earth]."

Reiser, Oliver L. *Cosmic Humanism*. Boston: Schenkman, 1966.

———. *The Integration of Human Knowledge*. Boston: Porter Sargent, 1958.

Teilhard de Chardin, Pierre. *The Phenomenon of Man*. New York: Harper & Row, 1959.

———. *The Future of Man*. New York: Harper & Row, 1965.

Thomas, William L., Jr., ed. *Man's Role in Changing the Face of the Earth*. Chicago, Ill.: University of Chicago, 1956.

Ubbelohde, A. R. *Man and Energy*. Baltimore: Penguin, 1963.

Wager, W. Warren. *The City of Man*. Boston: Houghton Mifflin, 1961.

Wall Street Journal. *Here Comes Tomorrow*. Princeton, N.J.: Dow Jones Books, 1967.

Whyte, Lancelot Law. *The Next Development in Man*. New York: Mentor, 1950.

Williams, Raymond. *The Long Revolution*. New York: Columbia University, 1961.

II. TECHNOLOGY AND SOCIETY

Aron, Raymond, et al. *World Technology and Human Destiny*. Ann Arbor: University of Michigan, 1963.

Ashby, W. Ross. *An Introduction to Cybernetics*. New York: Wiley, 1956.

Bargit, Leon. *The Age of Automation*. New York: Signet, 1965.

Bell, Daniel. "Notes on the Post-Industrial Society," *The Public Interest*, 6, 7 (Winter, Spring, 1967).

————, ed. *Toward the Year 2000: Work in Progress*. Boston: Houghton Mifflin, 1968.

Brown, Harrison, et al. *The Next Hundred Years*. New York: Viking, 1957.

Calder, Nigel, ed. *The World in 1984*. Two vols. Baltimore: Penguin, 1965.

Carr, Donald E. *The Breath of Life*. New York: Norton, 1965.

Clarke, Arthur C. *The Challenge of the Space Ship*. New York: Harper & Row, 1959.

————. *Profiles of the Future*. New York: Bantam, 1967.

————. *Voices from the Sky*. New York: Harper & Row, 1966.

Cole, Dandridge M. *Beyond Tomorrow*. Amherst, Wis.: Amherst Press, 1965.

————. *Social and Political Implications of the Ultimate Human Society*. Philadelphia: General Electric/Space and Missile Vehicle Dept., 1961.

————, and Cox, Donald W. *Islands in Space*. Philadelphia: Chilton, 1964.

————, and Levitt, I. M. *Exploring the Secrets of Space*. Englewood Cliffs, N.J.: Prentice-Hall, 1963.

Dechert, Charles R., ed. *The Social Impact of Cybernetics*. Notre Dame, Ind.: University of Notre Dame, 1966.

Deutsch, Karl W. *The Nerves of Government*. New York: The Free Press, 1963.

————. *Nationalism and Social Communication*. Rev. Edit. Cambridge, Mass.: Massachusetts Institute of Technology, 1963.

Diebold, John. *Automation*. Princeton, N.J.: Van Nostrand, 1952.

————. *Beyond Automation*. New York: McGraw-Hill, 1964.

Drucker, Peter F. *Landmarks of Tomorrow*. New York: Harper & Row, 1965.

————. *The Next Twenty Years*. New York: Harper & Row, 1957.

Dunlop, John, ed. *Automation and Technological Change*. Englewood Cliffs, N.J.: Prentice-Hall, 1962.

Elsner, Henry, Jr. *The Technocrats*. Syracuse: Syracuse University, 1967.

Ferry, W. H., et al. *The Triple Revolution*. New York: Liberation, 1964.

Frye, William, ed. *Impact of Space Exploration on Society*. Tarzana, Calif.: American Astronautical Society, 1966.

Fuller, R. Buckminster, and McHale, John. *World Design Decade*,

1965–1975. Documents I–VI. Carbondale: World Resources Inventory, Southern Illinois University, 1963–67.

Gabor, Dennis. *Inventing the Future*. New York. Alfred Knopf, 1964.

Gordon, Theodore J. *The Future*. New York: St. Martin's, 1965.

Gould, Jay M. *The Technical Elite*. New York: Augustus M. Kelley, 1966.

Greenberger, Martin, ed. *Computers and the World of the Future*. Cambridge, Mass.: Massachusetts Institute of Technology, 1962.

Heinlein, Robert A. "Pandora's Box," *The Worlds of Robert A. Heinlein*. New York: Ace, 1966.

Helmer, Olaf. *Social Technology*. New York: Basic, 1966.

Hilton, Alice Mary, ed. *The Evolving Society*. New York: Institute for Cybercultural Research, 1966.

Hoffer, Eric. *The Ordeal of Change*. New York: Harper & Row, 1963.

Innis, Harold. *The Bias of Communication*. Toronto: University of Toronto, 1964.

Kahn, Herman, and Weiner, Anthony J. *The Year 2000: A Framework for Speculation*. New York: Macmillan, 1967.

Kavanau, Lawrence L., ed. *Practical Space Applications*. Sun Valley, Calif.: American Astronautical Society, 1967.

MacBride, Robert O. *The Automated State*. Philadelphia: Chilton, 1967.

MacGowan, Roger A., and Ordway, Frederick I., III. *Intelligence in the Universe*. Englewood Cliffs, N.J.: Prentice-Hall, 1966.

McLuhan, Marshall. *The Gutenberg Galaxy*. Toronto: University of Toronto, 1962.

———. *Understanding Media*. New York: McGraw-Hill, 1964.

———, and Carpenter, Edmund S., eds. *Explorations in Communication*. Boston: Beacon, 1960.

———, and Fiore, Quentin. *The Medium Is the Massage*. New York: Bantam, 1967.

Mesthene, Emmanuel G., ed. *Technology and Social Change*. Indianapolis: Bobbs-Merrill, 1967.

Michael, Donald A. *Cybernation: The Silent Conquest*. Santa Barbara, Calif.: Center for the Study of Democratic Institutions, 1962.

Morse, Dean, and Warner, Aaron W., eds. *Technological Innovation and Society*. New York: Columbia University, 1966.

Nader, Ralph. *Unsafe at Any Speed*. New York: Grossman, 1965.

Ong, Walter J., S.J. *In the Human Grain*. New York: Macmillan, 1967.

Phillipson, Morris, ed. *Automation: Its Implications for the Future*. New York: Vintage, 1962.

Piel, Gerard. *Science in the Cause of Man*. New York: Vintage, 1964.

Pierce, John R. *Science, Art and Communication*. New York: Potter, 1968.

————. *Symbols, Signals and Noise*. New York: Harper & Row, 1961.

Prehoda, Robert W. *Designing the Future*. Philadelphia: Chilton, 1967.

Rabinowitch, Eugene. *The Dawn of a New Age*. Chicago, Ill.: University of Chicago, 1963.

Scientific American, ed. *Information*. San Francisco: W. H. Freeman, 1966.

Shanks, Michael. *The Innovators*. Harmondsworth, England: Penguin, 1967.

Shannon, Claude, and Weaver, Warren. *The Mathematical Theory of Communication*. Urbana: University of Illinois, 1949.

Silberman, Charles. *The Myths of Automation*. New York: Harper & Row, 1966.

Simon, Herbert A. *The Shape of Automation*. New York: Harper & Row, 1965.

Skinner, B. F. *Science and Human Behavior*. New York: Macmillan, 1953.

Stover, Carl F., ed. *The Technological Order*. Detroit: Wayne State University, 1963.

Sullivan, Walter. *We Are Not Alone*. Rev. edit. New York: McGraw-Hill, 1966.

Theobald, Robert. *Free Men and Free Markets*. Garden City, N.Y.: Doubleday Anchor, 1963.

————, ed. *The Guaranteed Income*. Garden City, N.Y.: Doubleday, 1966.

Von Braun, Wernher. *Space Frontier*. New York: Holt, Rinehart & Winston, 1967.

Von Neumann, John. *The Computer and the Brain*. New Haven: Yale University, 1958.

————. "Can We Survive Technology?" *Fortune* (June, 1955).

Weiner, Norbert. *Cybernetics*. Cambridge, Mass.: Massachusetts Institute of Technology, 1961.

————. *God & Golem, Inc*. Cambridge, Mass.: Massachusetts Institute of Technology, 1964.

————. *The Human Use of Human Beings*. New York: Avon, 1967.

III. ENTERPRISE AND REMUNERATION

Bazelon, David T. *The Paper Economy*. New York: Vintage, 1965.

Beer, Stafford. *Decision and Control*. New York: Wiley, 1966.

Cage, John. *A Year from Monday*. Middletown, Conn.: Wesleyan University, 1967.

Downs, Anthony. *Inside Bureaucracy*. Boston: Little, Brown, 1967.

Drucker, Peter F. *The Concept of the Corporation*. Expanded edit. New York: Mentor, 1964.

————. *The New Society*. Expanded edit. New York: Harper Torchbook, 1962.

————. *The Practice of Management*. New York: Harper & Row, 1953.

Forrester, Jay. *Industrial Dynamics*. Cambridge, Mass.: Massachusetts Institute of Technology, 1961.

————. "A New Corporate Design," *Industrial Management Review*, VII, 1, (Fall, 1965).

Galbraith, John Kenneth. *The Affluent Society*. Boston: Houghton Mifflin, 1958.

————. *The New Industrial State*. Boston: Houghton Mifflin, 1967.

Gordon, William J. J. *Synectics*. New York: Harper & Row, 1961.

Keynes, John Maynard. "Economic Possibilities for our Grandchildren," *Essays in Persuasion*. New York: Norton, 1963.

Moore, Wilbert E. *The Conduct of the Corporation*. New York: Random House, 1962.

Muller-Thym, Bernard J. "Cultural and Social Changes," in Hoke S. Simpson, ed., *The Changing American Population*. New York: Institute of Life Insurance, 1962.

Schon, Donald A. *Invention and the Evolution of Ideas*. New York: Barnes & Noble, 1967.

————. *Technology and Change*. New York: Delacorte, 1967.

Simon, Herbert A. *The New Science of Management Decision*. New York: Harper & Row, 1960.

Stern, Philip M. *The Great Treasury Raid*. New York: Random House, 1963.

IV. ARCHITECTURE AND CITY PLANNING

(A) Architecture

Abrams, Charles. *Man's Struggle for Shelter in an Urbanizing World*. Cambridge, Mass.: Massachusetts Institute of Technology, 1964.

Doxiadis, Constantinos A. *Architecture in Transition*. New York: Oxford University, 1963.

Hall, Edward T. "Quality in Architecture: An Anthropological View," *Journal of the A.I.A.* (July, 1963).

Heyer, Paul, ed. *Architects on Architecture*. New York: Walker, 1966.

Marks, Robert W. *The Dymaxion World of Buckminster Fuller*. Carbondale: Southern Illinois University, 1966.

McHale, John R. *R. Buckminster Fuller*. New York: Braziller, 1962.

(B) City Planning

Abrams, Charles. *The City Is the Frontier*. New York: Harper & Row, 1965.

Appleyard, Donald; Lynch, Kevin, and Meyer, John R. *The View from the Road*. Cambridge, Mass.: Massachusetts Institute of Technology, 1964.

Chermayeff, Serge, and Alexander, Christopher. *Community and Privacy*. Garden City, N.Y.: Doubleday Anchor, 1963.

Doxiadis, Constantinos A. *Ekistics: An Introduction to the Science of Human Settlements*. London: Hutchinson, 1967.

————. *Urban Renewal and the Future of the American City*. Chicago: Public Administration Service, 1966.

Duhl, Leonard, ed. *The Urban Condition*. New York: Basic, 1963.

Ewald, William R., Jr., ed. *Environment for Man*. Bloomington: Indiana University, 1967.

Goodman, Paul and Percival. *Communitas*. Rev. edit. New York: Vintage, 1960.

Gruen, Victor. *The Heart of Our Cities*. New York: Simon & Schuster, 1964.

Gutkind, Erwin A. *The Twilight of Cities*. New York: Free Press, 1962.

Hall, Edward T. *The Hidden Dimension*. Garden City, N.Y.: Doubleday, 1966.

Jacobs, Jane. *The Life and Death of the Great American Cities*. New York: Vintage, 1961.

Lynch, Kevin. *The Image of the City*. Cambridge, Mass.: Massachusetts Institute of Technology, 1960.

Moholy-Nagy, Sybil. "The Four Environments of Man," *Landscape* (Winter, 1966–67).

Spilhaus, Athelstan. "The Experimental City," *Daedalus* (Fall, 1967).

Vernon, Raymond. *Metropolis 1985*. Garden City, N.Y.: Doubleday Anchor, 1960.

Xanakis, Iannis. "The Cosmic City," *Art and Literature*, 10 (1966).

V. PEOPLE AND RESOURCES

(A) Man and His Environment

Arbib, Michael A. *Brains, Machines, and Mathematics*. New York: McGraw-Hill, 1964.

Bernal, J. D. *World Without War*. London: Routledge, 1958.

Brown, Harrison. *The Challenge of Man's Future*. New York: Viking, 1954.

Calder, Nigel. *Eden Was No Garden*. New York: Holt, Rinehart & Winston, 1967.

Carson, Rachel. *Silent Spring*. Boston: Houghton Mifflin, 1962.

Gaffney, Mason, et al., "The Polluted Air," *Bulletin of the Atomic Scientists*, XXI, 6 (June, 1965).

Jarrett, Henry, ed. *Environmental Quality in a Growing Economy*. Baltimore: Johns Hopkins, 1966.

Jones, Jack. "Depth Conservationism: A Post-Marxist Ideology?" *Centennial Review*, X, 3 (Summer, 1966).

Landsberg, Hans, et al. *Resources in America's Future*. Baltimore: Johns Hopkins University, 1963.

Maddox, John. *Revolution in Biology*. New York: Macmillan, 1964.

Mattson, Howard W. "Food for the World," *International Science and Technology*, 48 (Dec., 1965).

McCulloch, Warren S. *Embodiments of Mind*. Cambridge, Mass.: Massachusetts Institute of Technology, 1965.

Miller, George A. *The Psychology of Communication*. New York: Basic, 1967.

————, Galanter, Eugene, and Pribram, Karl H. *Plans and the Structure of Behavior*. New York: Holt, Rinehart & Winston, 1960.

Muller, Hermann J. "The Gene Material as the Initiator and the Organizing Basis of Life," *The American Naturalist*, C, 915 (Sept.-Oct., 1966).

————. "Should We Weaken or Strengthen Our Genetic Heritage?" in Sol Tax and Charles Callender, eds., *Evolution of Man*. Chicago, Ill.: University of Chicago, 1960.

Petersen, William. *The Politics of Population*. Garden City, N.Y.: Doubleday, 1964.

Rostand, Jean. *Can Man Be Modified?* New York: Basic, 1959.

Senders, John W. "Human Performance," *International Science and Technology*, 55 (July, 1966).

Smith, Audrey U. *Biological Effects of Freezing and Supercooling*. Baltimore: Williams and Wilkins, 1961.

Sonneborn, T. M., ed. *Control of Human Heredity and Evolution*. New York: Macmillan, 1965.

Udall, Stewart L. *The Quiet Crisis*. New York: Holt, Rinehart & Winston, 1965.

Weyl, Nathaniel. *The Creative Elite in America*. Washington: Public Affairs, 1966.

Whyte, Lynn, Jr. "The Historical Roots of Our Ecological Crisis," *Science* (March, 1967).

Wolstenholme, G., ed. *Man and His Future.* Boston: Little, Brown, 1962.

Wooldridge, Dean E. *The Machinery of the Brain.* New York: McGraw-Hill, 1963.

Young, T. Z. *Doubt and Certainty in Science.* New York: Oxford University, 1960.

(B) Harbingers of a New Life

Cohen, Mitchell, and Hale, Dennis, eds. *The New Student Left.* Rev. edit. Boston: Beacon, 1967.

Fiedler, Leslie A. *Waiting for the End.* New York: Stein and Day, 1964.

Friedenberg, Edgar Z. *Coming of Age in America.* New York: Random House, 1965.

———. *The Dignity of Youth and Other Atavisms.* Boston: Beacon, 1965.

———. *The Vanishing Adolescent.* Boston: Beacon, 1959.

Ginsberg, Allen. "The Great Marijuana Hoax," *Atlantic Monthly* (November, 1966).

Goodman, Paul. *Growing Up Absurd.* New York: Random House, 1960.

Jacobs, Paul, and Landau, Saul, eds. *The New Radicals.* New York: Vintage, 1966.

Kostelanetz, Richard. *The Theatre of Mixed Means.* New York: Dial, 1968.

———, ed. *The Young American Writers.* New York: Funk & Wagnalls, 1967.

Leary, Timothy. "Predition," *S. Calif. Oracle* (October, 1967).

Michael, Donald N. *The Next Generation.* New York: Vintage, 1965.

Miller, Michael V., and Gilmore, Susan, eds. *Revolution at Berkeley.* New York: Dial, 1965.

Simmons, J. L., and Winograd, Barry. *It's Happening.* Santa Barbara, Calif.: Marc-Laird, 1966.

Solomon, David, ed. *LSD: The Conscious-Expanding Drug.* New York: Putnam, 1964.

VI. EDUCATION

Bell, Daniel. *The Reforming of General Education.* New York: Columbia University, 1966.

Bloom, Benjamin S. *Stability and Change in Human Characteristics*. New York: Wiley, 1964.

Brown, B. Frank. *The Non-Graded High School*. Englewood Cliffs, N.J.: Prentice-Hall, 1963.

Bruner, Jerome S. *The Process of Education*. New York: Vintage, 1960.

————. *Toward a Theory of Instruction*. Cambridge, Mass.: Harvard University, 1966.

deGrazia, Alfred, and Sohn, David A., eds. *Programs, Teachers and Machines*. New York: Bantam, 1964.

Fuller, R. Buckminster. *Education Automation*. Carbondale: Southern Illinois, 1962.

Goodlad, John I. *The Changing School Curriculum*. New York: Fund for Advancement of Education, 1966.

————, and Anderson, Robert H. *The Non-Graded Elementary School*. Rev. Edit. New York: Harcourt, Brace & World, 1963.

Goodman, Paul. *The Community of Scholars*. New York: Random House, 1962.

————. *Compulsory Mis-Education*. New York: Horizon, 1964.

Gross, Ronald, and Murphy, Judith, eds. *The Revolution in the Schools*. New York: Harcourt, Brace & World, 1964.

Kimball, Solon T., and McClellan, James E. *Education and the New America*. New York: Random House, 1962.

Licklider, J. C. R. *Libraries for the Future*. Cambridge, Mass.: Massachusetts Institute of Technology, 1965.

————. "Televistas: Looking Ahead Through Side Windows," *Public Television*. New York: Bantam, 1967.

Murphy, Judith, and Gross, Ronald. *Learning by Television*. New York: Fund for the Advancement of Education, 1966.

Ramo, Simon. "A New Technique of Education," *Engineering and Science Monthly*, XXI (October, 1957).

Read, Herbert. *Education Through Art*. Rev. Edit. London: Faber and Faber, 1958.

Schramm, Wilbur, et al. *Four Case Studies of Programmed Instruction*. New York: Fund for the Advancement of Education, 1964.

VII. DEFENSE AND DIPLOMACY

Aron, Raymond. *On War*. Garden City, N.Y.: Doubleday Anchor, 1958.

————. *The Great Debate: Theories of Nuclear Strategy*. Garden City, N.Y.: Doubleday, 1965.

————. *Peace and War*. Garden City, N.Y.: Doubleday, 1966.

Boulding, Kenneth E. *Conflict and Defense*. New York: Harper & Row, 1962.

Brennan, Donald G., ed. *Arms Control, Disarmament, and National Security*. New York: Braziller, 1961.

Brodie, Bernard. *Escalation and the Nuclear Option*. Princeton, N.Y.: Princeton University, 1966.

————. *Strategy in the Missile Age*. Princeton, N.J.: Princeton University, 1959.

Brzezinski, Zbigniew. *Alternative to Partition*. New York: McGraw-Hill, 1965.

————. *America in the Technetronic Age*. New York: Columbia University/School of International Affairs, 1967.

Bull, Hedley. *The Control of the Arms Race*. New York: Praeger, 1965.

Clark, Grenville, and Sohn, Louis B. *World Peace Through World Law*. Rev. edit. Cambridge, Mass.: Harvard University, 1966.

Deutsch, Karl W. "Toward an Inventory of Basic Trends and Patterns in Comparative and International Politics," *American Political Science Review* (March, 1960).

Dougherty, James E., and Lehman, J. F., Jr., eds. *Arms Control for the Late Sixties*. Princeton, N.J.: Van Nostrand, 1967.

Draper, Theodore. *Abuse of Power*. New York: Viking, 1967.

Falk, Richard A., and Mendlovitz, Saul H., eds. *The Strategy of World Order*. Four vols. New York: World Law Fund, 1966.

Fisher, Roger, ed. *International Conflict and Behavioral Science*. New York: Basic, 1964.

Fulbright, J. William. *The Arrogance of Power*. New York: Vintage, 1966.

Gallois, Pierre. *The Balance of Terror*. Boston: Houghton Mifflin, 1961.

Grodzins, Morton, and Rabinowitch, Eugene, eds. *The Atomic Age*. New York: Basic, 1963.

Haas, Ernst. *Beyond the Nation State*. Stanford, Calif.: Stanford University, 1961.

Halperin, Morton. *Limited War in the Nuclear Age*. New York: Wiley, 1963.

Hollins, Elizabeth Jay, ed. *Peace Is Possible*. New York: Grossman, 1966.

Kahn, Herman. *The Nature and Feasibility of War and Deterrence*. Santa Monica: The RAND Corp., 1960.

————. *On Escalation*. New York: Praeger, 1965.

————. *On Thermonuclear War*. Princeton, N.J.: Princeton University, 1960.

————. *Thinking About the Unthinkable*. New York: Horizon, 1962.

Kaplan, Morton A. *System and Process in International Politics*. New York: Wiley, 1957.

————, ed. *The Revolution in World Politics*. New York: Wiley, 1962.

Knorr, Klaus E., and Verba, Sidney, eds. *The International System*. Princeton, N.J.: Princeton University, 1961.

Niebuhr, Reinhold. "The Social Myths in the 'Cold War,' " *Journal of International Affairs*, XXI, 1 (1967).

Osgood, Charles E. *An Alternative to War or Surrender*. Urbana: University of Illinois, 1962.

Schelling, Thomas C. *Arms and Influence*. New Haven: Yale University, 1966.

————. *The Strategy of Conflict*. Cambridge, Mass.: Harvard University, 1960.

————, and Halperin, Morton. *Strategy and Arms Control*. New York: Twentieth Century Fund, 1961.

Stillman, Edmund, and Pfaff, William. *The New Politics*. New York: Coward-McCann, 1961.

————. *The Politics of Hysteria*. New York: Harper & Row, 1964.

————. *Power and Impotence*. New York: Vintage, 1967.

Steel, Ronald. *The End of Alliance*. New York: Viking, 1964.

————. *Pax Americana*. New York: Viking, 1967.

Also see *Bulletin of the Atomic Scientists*, 1945 to the present.

VIII. REDESIGNING SOCIETY

(A) New Knowledge and Political Process

Bertalanffy, Ludwig von. *Problems of Life*. New York: Harper Torchbook, 1960.

Buckley, Walter. *Sociology and Modern Systems Theory*. Englewood Cliffs, N.J.: Prentice-Hall, 1966.

Dechert, Charles. "A Pluralistic World Order," *Proceedings of the American Catholic Philosophical Association* (1963).

Deutsch, Karl W. *The Nerves of Government*. New York: Free Press, 1963.

Duckworth, W. Eric. *A Guide to Operational Research*. New York: Barnes & Noble, 1965.

Easton, David, ed. *Varieties of Political Theory*. Englewood Cliffs, N.J.: Prentice-Hall, 1966.

Lerner, Daniel, ed. *Parts and Wholes*. New York: Free Press, 1963.

Milsum, John, ed. *Positive Feedback*. Oxford: Pergamon, 1967.

(B) Parameters of Planning

Bell, Daniel. "Twelve Modes of Prediction," in Julius Gould, ed., *Penguin Survey of the Social Sciences 1965*. Baltimore: Penguin, 1965.

Fuller, R. Buckminster. "Comprehensive Designing," *Trans/formation*, 1 (1950).

Goodman, Paul. *People or Personnel*. New York: Random House, 1965.

———. *Utopian Essays and Practical Proposals*. New York: Random House, 1962.

Mills, C. Wright. *The Sociological Imagination*. New York: Oxford, 1959.

Moholy-Nagy, Laszlo. "A Proposal," *Vision in Motion*. Chicago, Ill.: Paul Theobald, 1947.

CONTRIBUTORS

DANIEL BELL, born in New York City in 1919, is currently Professor of Sociology at Columbia University. Previously an editor of both *Fortune* and *The New Leader*, he served as a member of the National Commission on Technology, Automation and Economic Progress and as chairman of the American Academy of Arts and Sciences' Commission on the Year 2000. The author of *Work and Its Discontents* (1956), *The End of Ideology* (1960) and *The Reforming of General Education* (1966), he is now completing *The Post-Industrial Society*.

KENNETH E. BOULDING is Professor of Economics and co-director of the Center for Research in Conflict Resolution at the University of Michigan. Born in Liverpool, England, in 1910 and educated at Oxford, he emigrated to the United States in 1937. He has contributed essays to many magazines and written a dozen books, including *The Organizational Revolution* (1952), *The Image* (1956), *Conflict and Defense: A General Theory* (1962), *The Meaning of the Twentieth Century* (1964), and *The Impact of the Social Sciences* (1966).

ZBIGNIEW BRZEZINSKI was born in Warsaw, Poland, in 1928 and came to the United States in 1938. Educated at McGill (B.A., 1949) and Harvard (Ph.D., 1953), he has taught at Harvard and Columbia Universities. The director of the Research Institute in Communist Affairs at Columbia, he was recently on leave as a member of the Policy Planning Council of the Department of State. Among his several books are *The Soviet Bloc: Unity and Conflict* (1961), *Ideology and Power in Soviet Politics* (1962), *Political Power: U.S.A./U.S.S.R.* (co-authored, 1964), and *Alternative to Partition* (1965).

EDMUND CARPENTER was born in Rochester, New York, in 1922, and took his Ph.D. in anthropology from the University of Pennsylvania. He has made prize-winning films, conducted research in such far-off fields as the Arctic, Siberia, Borneo, and Outer Mongolia, and taught at the University of Toronto and San Fernando Valley State College. The author of *Time-Space Concepts of the*

Aivilik (1958), *Eskimo* (1959), and *Anerca* (1960), he co-edited *Explorations in Communication* (1960) with Marshall McLuhan. Recently he has been collaborating with McLuhan at Fordham University.

KARL W. DEUTSCH, born in Prague, Czechoslovakia, in 1912, received his doctorate in law and political science from Charles University (Prague) in 1938. Emigrating to the United States before World War II, he earned a Ph.D. at Harvard, where he is now Professor of Political Science. Among his many books are *Nationalism and Social Communication* (1953: revised, 1964), *The Nerves of Government* (1963), and *Arms Control and the Atlantic Alliance* (1967).

CONSTANTINOS A. DOXIADIS was born in Stenimachos, Greece, in 1913. He studied engineering and architecture in Athens and Berlin. He has served as chief town-planning officer of the Greater Athens area, taught architecture, town planning and "ekistics" at Greek universities, and founded Doxiadis Associates, which undertakes planning and architectural projects through its offices around the world. He has published several books in German, Greek and English, including *Architecture in Transition* (1963) and *Ekistics: An Introduction to the Science of Human Settlements* (1967).

JOHN P. EBERHARD is director of the Institute for Applied Technology at the National Bureau of Standards. He was born in Chicago in 1927 and trained in architectural design at the University of Illinois (B.S., 1952) and in industrial management at M.I.T. (M.B.A., 1959). He previously served as president of Creative Buildings, Inc., designers and manufacturers of prefabricated structures, and director of research for the Sheraton Corporation of America.

RICHARD E. FARSON, born in 1926 in Chicago, Illinois, studied at Occidental College and the University of Chicago, where he received his Ph.D. in psychology in 1955. In 1959 he founded the Western Behavioral Sciences Institute of La Jolla, California, which he now directs.

R. BUCKMINSTER FULLER was born in 1895 in Milford, Massachusetts. He attended Harvard and the U.S. Naval Academy, designed a radically original automobile in the 1930's, invented both a new system of mapping and the geodesic principle of building construction, and has lectured around the world. He is now Professor of Comprehensive Anticipatory Design Science at Southern Illinois University and director of the World Resources Inventory. He has written a long poem, *Unfinished Epic of Industrialization* (1963), and four major books: *No More Second-Hand God* (1962), *Education Automation* (1962), *Ideas and Integrities* (1963), and *Nine Chains to the Moon* (1938; reprinted, 1963).

LESLIE A. FIEDLER, born in Newark, New Jersey, in 1917, is Professor of English at State University of New York at Buffalo. He has contributed critical essays to many magazines, collecting some of them into *An End to Innocence* (1955) and *No! in Thunder* (1960); written two major studies of cultural history, *Love and Death in the American Novel* (1960) and *Waiting for the End* (1964); and published two novels, two collections of shorter fiction, and many poems.

PAUL GOODMAN, born in New York City in 1911, took his B.A. at City College (New York) and his Ph.D. at the University of Chicago and has since been a peripatetic teacher-lecturer-agitator. He has published over a score of books, covering nearly as many subjects. Among them are *Growing Up Absurd* (1960), a novel, *The Empire City* (1959), *The Community of Scholars* (1962), *Compulsory Mis-Education* (1964), *Three Plays* (1965), and *Like a Conquered Provence* (1967). With his architect brother Percival, he co-authored *Communitas* (1948; revised, 1960).

EDWARD T. HALL, Professor of Anthropology and Organization Theory at Northwestern University, was born in Webster Groves, Missouri, in 1914. He has taught at several universities, conducted field research all over the world, directed between 1950 and 1955 the Point Four Training Program for the Department of State's Foreign Service Institute, and written two books, *The Silent Language* (1959) and *The Hidden Dimension* (1966).

HERMAN KAHN, director of the Hudson Institute of Harmon, New York, was born in Bayonne, New Jersey, in 1922 and educated at U.C.L.A. and California Institute of Technology. From 1948 to 1961 he was a senior physicist at the RAND Corporation. Kahn has published essays in dozens of magazines and written four controversial books: *On Thermonuclear War* (1960), *Thinking about the Unthinkable* (1962), *On Escalation* (1965), and, with Anthony J. Wiener, *The Year 2000* (1967).

JOSHUA LEDERBERG, born in Montclair, New Jersey, in 1925, received his B.A. from Columbia in 1944 and his Ph.D. in biology from Yale in 1947. He has taught at the University of Wisconsin and Stanford, where he is Professor of Genetics and director of the J. P. Kennedy Jr. Laboratories for Molecular Medicine. In 1958, Dr. Lederberg received the Nobel Prize in physiology and medicine for his research into the genetics of bacteria. He writes a weekly newspaper column syndicated by *The Washington Post*.

MARSHALL McLUHAN, born in Edmonton, Alberta, in 1911, received his B.A. and M.A. from the University of Manitoba and his Ph.D. in English literature from Cambridge. Professor of English at St. Michael's College, University of Toronto, he has edited the magazine *Explorations* (1953–59) and published scores of essays on literature and culture in addition to four books: *The Mechanical Bride* (1951), *The Gutenberg Galaxy* (1962), *Understanding Media* (1964), and, with Quentin Fiore, *The Medium Is the Massage* (1967). For 1967–68, he holds an Albert Schweitzer Chair in the Humanities at New York's Fordham University.

ARCHIBALD T. McPHERSON retired recently as associate director of the National Bureau of Standards, after a long career as a research scientist and administrator. He is devoting most of his time to writing and lecturing on food problems. He was born in 1895 in Marceline, Missouri.

GEORGE A. MILLER, born in 1920 in Charleston, West Virginia, earned his Ph.D. at Harvard University in 1946. Currently Professor of Psychology and co-director of Harvard's Center for Cognitive Studies, he has co-authored *Plans and the Structure of Behavior* (1960) and has written *Language and Communication* (1951), *Psychology: The Science of Mental Life* (1962) and *The Psychology of Communication* (1967).

HANS J. MORGENTHAU, born in Coburg, Germany, in 1904, practiced and later taught law in Germany. He emigrated in 1937 to the United States. Since 1943 he has taught political science at the University of Chicago, where he is Albert A. Michelson Distinguished Service Professor. A prolific contributor of essays to many magazines, he has written *Politics Among Nations* (1948), *In Defense of the National Interest* (1951), *The Purpose of American Politics* (1960) and *Politics in the Twentieth Century* (1962).

BERNARD J. MULLER-THYM, born in Kansas City, Missouri, in 1909, is a management consultant in private practice in New York. He earned his A.B. from Rockhurst College and his Ph.D. in philosophy from the University of Toronto. During the thirties, he taught medieval studies at the University of St. Louis. In recent years, he has been Visiting Professor of Industrial Management at M.I.T. He is writing a book on *The Shape of Work*.

GAYLORD NELSON, born in 1916 in Clear Lake, Wisconsin, graduated from the University of Wisconsin Law School in 1942 and has since practiced law in Madison, Wisconsin. He served from 1948 to 1958 in the Wisconsin State Senate and from 1958 to 1962 as governor of his home state. Since 1963, he has been a member of the United States Senate.

GARDNER C. QUARTON, born in 1918 in Boston, Massachusetts, is program director of the Neurosciences Research Program of the Massachusetts Institute of Technology. A psychiatrist by training, he is affiliated with the Massachusetts General Hospital and Harvard Medical School.

SIMON RAMO, born in Salt Lake City, Utah, in 1913, earned his B.S. at the University of Utah in 1933 and his Ph.D. from California Institute of Technology in 1936. Previously on the research staffs of General Electric and Hughes Aircraft, he currently serves as vice-chairman of TRW, Inc., formerly Thompson-Ramo-Wooldridge, and a director of Bunker-Ramo, Inc. He has published many technical papers, general essays and two books, *Introduction to Microwaves* (1945) and, with John R. Whinnery, *Fields and Waves in Modern Radio* (1953) as well as co-edited, with Eugene M. Grabbe and Dean E. Wooldridge, *Handbook of Automation, Computation and Control* (1959).

OLIVER L. REISER, born in 1895 in Columbus, Ohio, is Professor Emeritus at the University of Pittsburgh, where he taught philosophy for over forty years. He has published over a dozen major books, including *The Alchemy of Light and Color* (1935), *Philosophy and the Concepts of Modern Science* (1935), *The Promise of Scientific*

Humanism (1940), *The World Sensorium* (1946), *The Integration of Human Knowledge* (1958), and *Cosmic Humanism* (1965). He is currently finishing a study of *Magnetic Moments in Human History.*

MOSHE SAFDIE was born in Haifa, Israel, in 1938 and came to Canada in 1954. He studied architecture at McGill University and designed Habitat '67 for the 1967 exposition in Montreal, where he now lives, and belongs to an architectual firm.

ROBERT THEOBALD was born in India in 1929. Since 1957 he has been studying the effects of abundance on the American socio-economy. He has published *The Rich and the Poor* (1960), *The Challenge of Abundance* (1961), and *Free Men and Free Markets* (1963), as well as edited two anthologies, *The Guaranteed Income* (1966) and *Social Policies for America in the 70's* (1968).

ANTHONY J. WIENER was born in 1930 in Newark, New Jersey. He took his A.B. and LL.B. at Harvard and has served as instructor in political science at the Massachusetts Institute of Technology, consultant for Arthur D. Little, Inc., research fellow of the Society for the Investigation of Human Ecology, and research associate of the U.S. Joint Commission on Mental Illness and Health. He has been since 1961 a member of the Hudson Institute, where he now serves as Chairman of the Research Management Council. He is co-author, with Herman Kahn, of *The Year 2000* (1967).

A Note About the Author

Richard Kostelanetz lives and works on the top floor of a small house in the East Village of New York, the city where, in 1940, he was born. There he has produced a study of the new dramatic forms entitled *The Theatre of Mixed Means* and several anthologies, including *The New American Arts, On Contemporary Literature,* and *The Young American Writers.* His articles and criticism have appeared in many periodicals, ranging from *Commonweal, Partisan Review,* and *Salmagundi* to *Esquire, Look,* and *The New York Times Magazine.*

He received his A.B. from Brown and his M.A. degree in history from Columbia. He studied at the University of London on a Fulbright grant. Mr. Kostelanetz has aslo held a Pulitzer Fellowship in Critical Writing and a fellowship from the John Simon Guggenheim Memorial Foundation.